Edward Armstrong, Martin A. S. Hume

Spain

Its Greatness and Decay. Second Edition

Edward Armstrong, Martin A. S. Hume

Spain

Its Greatness and Decay. Second Edition

ISBN/EAN: 9783337236502

Printed in Europe, USA, Canada, Australia, Japan

Cover: Foto ©ninafisch / pixelio.de

More available books at **www.hansebooks.com**

SPAIN

ITS

GREATNESS AND DECAY

(1479—1788)

BY

MARTIN A. S. HUME
EDITOR OF THE CALENDARS OF SPANISH STATE PAPERS,
AUTHOR OF "THE YEAR AFTER THE ARMADA," "PHILIP II," &C.

WITH

AN INTRODUCTION

BY

EDWARD ARMSTRONG
FELLOW OF QUEEN'S COLLEGE, OXFORD,
AUTHOR OF "ELIZABETH FARNESE," &C.

SECOND EDITION, REVISED AND CORRECTED.

CAMBRIDGE
AT THE UNIVERSITY PRESS
1899

[*All Rights reserved*]

GENERAL PREFACE.

The aim of this series is to sketch the history of Modern Europe, with that of its chief colonies and conquests, from about the end of the fifteenth century down to the present time. In one or two cases the story will commence at an earlier date: in the case of the colonies it will usually begin later. The histories of the different countries will be described, as a general rule, separately, for it is believed that, except in epochs like that of the French Revolution and Napoleon I, the connection of events will thus be better understood and the continuity of historical development more clearly displayed.

The series is intended for the use of all persons anxious to understand the nature of existing political conditions. "The roots of the present lie deep in the past," and the real significance of contemporary events cannot be grasped unless the historical causes which have led to them are known. The plan adopted makes it possible to treat the history of the last four centuries in considerable detail, and to embody the most important results of modern research. It is hoped therefore that the series will be useful not only to beginners but to students who have already acquired some general knowledge of European History. For those who wish to carry their studies further, the bibliography appended to each volume will act as a guide to original sources of information and works more detailed and authoritative.

Considerable attention will be paid to political geography, and each volume will be furnished with such maps and plans as may be requisite for the illustration of the text.

G. W. PROTHERO.

First Edition 1898. Second Edition 1899.

PREFACE.

THE mere relation of the events of history adds but little to the stock of useful knowledge, unless it enables us to apply the experience of the past to the conduct of the present, and so to avoid for our own time some of the errors into which previous generations have fallen. This end can best be attained by regarding history not as a disjointed collection of facts, but as a harmonious concatenation of causes and effects. In the case of most national histories this is difficult, because the actions and the results which follow them are usually distant in point of time, obscured by side issues and complicated by intervening circumstances. It is otherwise with the history of Spain. There the ordinary observer may see the working of the process by which nations are ruined. He who runs may read the lessons that unsupported pride and unwarranted ambition are as disastrous to nations as to men, that riches gained without labour produce no extended or lasting prosperity, that the true basis of wealth is industrial production, that beneficent ends cannot be attained by means which disregard human sufferings or trample on human rights, and, above all, that the hereditary transmission of unrestrained power from father to son is certain to end in disaster, because sooner or later the power must descend to an individual too weak or too vicious to exercise it worthily.

The period dealt with in these pages covers the rise and decadence of Spain and the commencement of a fallacious resuscitation. The rise was unwarranted by the stage of development which the nation had reached, and the ruin was consequently complete. In the history of no other European country is the whole cycle of national potency and exhaustion presented in so small a space, or in so simple a form. The tale is one of almost unexampled and unrelieved misfortune, and yet each succeeding catastrophe, each recurring disgrace, each repeated sacrifice, can be traced almost with certainty to the unwise act or short-sighted policy from which it sprang.

To the modern student of political economy the financial and administrative systems successively adopted by Spanish ministers will appear grotesquely perverse and calculated to destroy the sources of wealth. Statesmen will note that the first and greatest disaster of Spain was the inheritance by her King of extended territories in Central Europe, which made her the great continental power with a prospect of universal dominion; and that trade, in her case, did not "follow the flag," notwithstanding the strenuous efforts to maintain a monopoly, because the home manufactures were crushed with intolerable burdens, while the workers were demoralised by constant wars, and by the false belief that coin was wealth, instead of a token of value. It will be observed that despotic personal government, with its consequent suffering and disaster, only became possible when the weakness of the people's representatives allowed the national purse-strings to be wrested from their grasp by force or bribery; and that the oppression of the people and the sacrifice of their welfare followed as a natural result from the emasculation of the national parliaments.

These are a few of the lessons which may be learnt from the history of Spain more easily than from that of any other nation; and for this reason, amongst others, it is to be deplored that so little attention has hitherto been devoted to its study by English readers. In order to render the application the more direct, the history of Spain related in the following pages has been separated, so far as appeared possible, from the tangled skein of European foreign politics, and the vicissitudes of the Spanish nation itself have been traced with as much detail as the limited space permitted. An attempt has been made to present the story with absolute impartiality, and to render it a trustworthy and readable relation of events.

MARTIN A. S. HUME.

LONDON, *September* 1898.

EDITORIAL NOTE.

The result of the Spanish-American conflict renders it necessary to say that the Introduction, containing a reference (p. 5) to Cuba and other islands as still forming part of the Spanish colonial Empire, was printed off before the recent war broke out.

G. W. P.

TABLE OF CONTENTS

INTRODUCTION.

		PAGE
§ I.	The Rule of Ferdinand and Isabella	1
§ II.	Philip I and the Regency of Ferdinand, 1504—1516. Charles I (V), 1516—1529	31
§ III.	Spain and Europe, 1529—1556	64

CHAPTER I.
Philip II, 1527—1551 101

CHAPTER II.
Philip II, 1551—1560 114

CHAPTER III.
Philip II, 1560—1568 . . . 133

CHAPTER IV.
Philip II, 1568—1581 . . 152

CHAPTER V.
Philip II, 1580—1598 . 171

CHAPTER VI.
Philip III, 1598—1621 197

CHAPTER VII.

	PAGE
PHILIP IV, 1621—1640	224

CHAPTER VIII.

PHILIP IV, 1638—1643 244

CHAPTER IX.

PHILIP IV, 1643—1665 266

CHAPTER X.

CHARLES II, 1665—1678 284

CHAPTER XI.

CHARLES II, 1675—1700 . . 295

CHAPTER XII.

PHILIP V, 1700—1714 . 318

CHAPTER XIII.

PHILIP V, 1714—1731 . . 346

CHAPTER XIV.

PHILIP V—FERDINAND VI, 1732—1759 370

CHAPTER XV.

CHARLES III, 1759—1788 392

BIBLIOGRAPHY OF SPANISH HISTORY, 1479—1788 412

INDEX . . 423

MAPS (at end). 1. Spain, 1527—1788.
2. The European possessions of the Spanish Monarchy.

INTRODUCTION.

SECTION I.

THE RULE OF FERDINAND AND ISABELLA.

The conquest of the weak and divided kingdom of Granada was, perhaps, no heroic feat: but, none the less, it was a momentous crisis in the history of Spain. Europe itself was startled by it; the loss of Constantinople seemed to find its compensation in the fall of Granada; the left wing of Islam had been beaten back upon its African reserves. For Spain the consequences were far-reaching. The task of centuries was complete; she must now seek another. A people which for generations had lived to fight, whose whole social and political organisation had developed out of war, could not lie down to sleep. The union of Castile and Aragon and the acquisition of Granada formed a power of first-rate importance; it was certain to exercise its young strength in fresh expansion.

It is true that to modern notions the union of Castile and Aragon was incomplete; the marriage of their sovereigns was their only tie. The two kingdoms stood back to back, with different characters and different interests; common service against the Moors had not obliterated mutual dislike. Yet the unity of the king and queen was so entire, and the personality of each so strong, that for purposes of external policy Castile and Aragon were already Spain. Portugal still preserved her independence, but it had for long seemed likely that Castile would unite with Portugal rather than with Aragon.

The little kingdom of Navarre also formed a breach in Iberian unity. It lay like a pair of saddle-bags across the western Pyrenees, tempting both France and Spain to bestride the ridge. A French house was, indeed, already in the saddle. Queen Blanche, Ferdinand's half-sister, had bequeathed Navarre to her divorced husband Henry IV of Castile, but he failed to hold it against her sister and successor Eleanor, who had married into the house of Foix. Eleanor's heir again had married Madeleine, sister of Louis XI, who acted as regent successively for her two children, Francis Phebus and Catherine. Isabella, with a view to the ultimate absorption of Navarre, had schemed to marry each of these children into her own family, but Madeleine had foiled her plans. At the date of the Conquest of Granada Navarre was ruled by Catherine and her husband, Jean, of the French house of Albret. It seemed unlikely, moreover, that the kingdom, differing in customs, language and ethnology, should gravitate towards Spain.

On the eastern flank of the Pyrenees lay another saddle-state. To the south was Catalonia, to the north its dependent counties, Roussillon and Cerdagne. These latter in the troubled times of John II had been mortgaged to Louis XI; after much sharp dealing and hard fighting they had remained to France. But as Spanish Navarre was Basque, so was Roussillon Catalan, alien to France, full of Catalan if not of Spanish feeling. It had revolted from Louis XI because he had suppressed the inalienable right of private war. Roussillon and Cerdagne, even after their final union to France under Louis XIV, remained Catalan in customs until the days of Arthur Young, who describes them as a Spanish country tempered by the blessings of French administration.

Spain's difficulty has always been that she has so many sides, so many possibilities, so many alternative policies.

There were causes enough in Navarre and Roussillon for dispute with France. Yet the northern frontier may almost be left out of consideration. At either end of the Pyrenees the country is difficult, incapable in early days of supporting considerable armies. The two nations might skirmish on this side or on that, but they could not close, they could not strike vital blows. If rivals they were to be, the fight must be fought elsewhere.

There remained then three sides to Spain. The Portuguese discoveries pointed to the Atlantic. Where Lisbon led, Cadiz and Seville, Ferrol and Corunna must some day follow. The voyage of Columbus was so nearly coincident with the conquest of Granada that they may be considered in connection. The discovery of America, even though its full bearings were not realised, from the first struck the imagination, turning men's minds westwards, tempting the pent-up energy of a people, whose blood was boiling, to adventure rather than to war, to the sea rather than to the land. Had Castile at this time been united with Portugal instead of Aragon, the world's history might or must have been very different.

There was yet another alternative. Long before the conquest of Granada Spanish and African adventurers had raided each other's shores. Spain until the present century has had to feel only too acutely that she has a southern seaboard. Her own Moors had not been exterminated; many had sought shelter with their African brethren and so added to their strength. Here chronic hostility was intensified by recurrent outbursts of fanaticism. Was it not then the obvious policy of Spain to follow up her conquest of Granada, to break the forces of Islam which were forming anew upon the opposite coast? With a huge Moorish population, imperfectly Christianised in the old kingdoms, and professedly Mussulman in Granada, could Spain risk the chances of a reaction, and that with the power of the Osmanli advancing by leaps and bounds in the eastern Mediterranean? Nor was this all. Sicily is by situation and tradition almost as much African as European. Her southernmost shores lie below the northernmost point of Africa. Thrusting herself athwart the Mediterranean, she must be either a basis of operations against the Turk and Moor, or the objective of their common attacks. No power that holds Sicily can afford to neglect Tunis. Further east again the kings of Aragon had long-dormant claims on Athens, and even on Salonica, claims that as a crusading power they might one day make good against the Turkish conquerors of Greece, or as a South Italian power against the commercial monopoly of Venice.

If the glance of Castile wavered, that of Aragon looked steadily eastward. The conquest of the Balearic isles had been but a stepping-stone to Sardinia. Early in the 15th century Alfonso had all but conquered Corsica, and had reduced Genoa to the last extremities. Pressure on the north of Italy had only been relieved by diversion to the south, where the warlike king on a dubious title won and held the kingdom of Naples. Although he left this to his bastard, and not to his brother John II of Aragon, the legitimate heir, yet there was now in southern Italy an Aragonese dynasty strengthened by the importation of Aragonese nobles and ecclesiastics. Moreover across the straits lay Sicily, Aragonese for more than two centuries. If therefore Isabella allowed her husband to direct her European policy it was certain that Spain would exercise her united strength upon the neighbouring peninsula.

As if these problems were not enough, within a few years of the conquest of Granada the Catholic kings must add another. The marriages of two princesses to the heirs of England and the Netherlands were destined to force Spain to play the leading part in the religious conflict of the future; she must pick up the glove as champion not only of Cross against Crescent, but of the Faith against the heretic.

The history of Spain is therefore the tragic result of an embarrassing wealth of alternative policies. It was impossible that a country with no common feeling or constitutional unity between its principal sections, containing an alien race fundamentally opposed in faith and customs, herself sparsely populated, her material resources undeveloped, should permanently succeed in all the tasks imposed upon her by nature or ambition. That she sank after a century and a half of greatness need excite no wonder. Marvellous rather was the tenacity which held its grip so long. Into the 18th century Spain retained her hold of a moiety of the Netherlands; only lately Spanish princes have lost the two Sicilies and Parma. Cuba and the Philippines still represent her Colonial Empire in the Western and Eastern Indies, while in the independent States of Southern and Central America handfuls of Spaniards still plunder at pleasure the masses of industrious emigrants from other European states. In Africa the Spanish flag still flies in somewhat fitful triumph over her first conquest, Melilla. Christendom, all deductions made, has reason to be grateful to the conquerors of Lepanto, to the missionaries of the Indies. Catholicism must place to Alba's credit the long-untainted orthodoxy of the Belgian provinces. It was not when Spain was at her height, but when her decline was already obvious, that a French writer in Richelieu's service stated that Spain surpassed all nations in the art of government. If by this phrase be meant, not the gift of administration, but the power to rule, it may pass muster.

It is difficult to apportion between Ferdinand and Isabella the glories of their reign. Spanish writers, being at once courteous and Castilian, exalt their queen at the expense of her Aragonese partner. Italian contemporaries speak only of Ferdinand. This is natural, for European policy was his especial field; whatever troubles occurred at home upon Isabella's death, his success abroad scarcely received a check. As here the husband led the wife, so did the little kingdom of Aragon lead the larger sister nation. From Ferdinand's reign dates the long conflict between the French and Spanish peoples. But this quarrel was not Castilian. The thoughts of Castile had been turned south and west, to Granada and Portugal; her relations with France had almost invariably been friendly. But Aragon had been opposed to France in Roussillon and in Navarre; it had contested with the French crown the possession of Genoa, with the French house of Anjou that of Sicily and Naples.

After the fall of Granada the Catholic kings were prepared to devote themselves to internal organisation. Any superfluous energy might well have been employed on African conquest or American discovery. At this moment their hands were forced by the ambition of their more powerful neighbour. The Granada of France was Brittany; the marriage of the young duchess with Charles VIII was the equivalent of the "last sigh" of the fallen Boabdil. Ferdinand had employed both arms and diplomacy to preserve the independence of Brittany, but in vain. The marriage took place in 1491, and the French king had thus a start of just a year. The long-deferred intervention in Italy was now possible. Charles VIII would enforce the claims, which the house of Anjou had bequeathed to the Crown, against the Aragonese occupants of Naples. Meanwhile Granada fell, and Charles realised that he must buy the abstention of the legitimate line of Aragon. By the treaty of Barcelona, Roussillon and Cerdagne were ceded on the Catholic kings' engagement that they would give no aid to the enemies of France, saving the Pope, that they would suffer no intermarriage with the houses of Hapsburg, England or Naples. Thus Aragon recovered her lost provinces, and Spain once more had a foothold on soil geographically French.

To Ferdinand, half a treaty, his own half, was always better than the whole. Before Charles VIII left France, and again when he marched out of Rome towards Naples, protests were presented by Ferdinand's envoys. No sooner was Naples taken than Ferdinand elaborated the league of Venice which cost the French king his conquests. Coincident with this was the double marriage of his children with the house of Hapsburg, and the marriage of his sister to the restored Aragonese king of Naples. Even before Charles VIII died, Ferdinand opened negotiations for a partition of the Neapolitan kingdom (1497). Early in the reign of Louis XII this actually took effect (1500). The spoilers soon quarrelled, for thieves are singularly sensitive as to their own proprietary rights. Gonsalvo's military skill and Ferdinand's diplomatic lack of scruple decided the contest in favour of Spain. Within eleven years Spain had won Granada, Roussillon and Naples.

Upon Isabella's death Ferdinand's administration in Castile was threatened by his son-in-law Philip, who was supported by his father the Emperor Maximilian. For protection Ferdinand turned to France; he married Germaine de Foix, the French king's niece; upon the child, who was only born to die, were settled the rights of the two crowns in Naples. This new friendship led naturally to the partition treaty of Cambray. In this Louis XII seemed to have the lion's share; to his Duchy of Milan were assigned the wealthy cities of Venetian Lombardy from the Adda to the Mincio; while to Ferdinand fell only the towns on the Apulian coast which Venice held in compensation of her expenses in the war of 1495—6. No sooner had Ferdinand obtained the cession of these towns than he formed a fresh combination against France. He won to his side the very Pope, the prime mover of the League of Cambray, and Venice the professed enemy. The result was the expulsion of the French from Lombardy. Meanwhile Ferdinand had utilised the difficulties of Louis XII to occupy the Spanish territories of his ally the king of Navarre. Thus he had closed the second gate through the Pyrenees. Navarre retained its separate Cortes, its legal customs, its financial independence. But, notwithstanding that its earlier relations had been with Aragon, Ferdinand cleverly incorporated it with the crown of Castile, thus pledging the more powerful kingdom to the maintenance of his conquest.

In Italy it was already clear that the Spaniards would not be content with Naples; they soon felt their way up both coasts of the peninsula. In 1505 Gonsalvo de Cordova assumed the protectorate of Pisa during her revolt against Florence; in 1512 at Ravenna the Spaniards barred the French advance southwards through Romagna. Two years later a Spanish army fired on Venice from the shores of her lagoon, and in retreating scattered the powerful Venetian forces near Vicenza. If the Swiss had the main share in expelling the French from Lombardy, and if the new native Duke, Maximilian Sforza, sat uneasily on Swiss pikes, yet a Spanish force lurked round Verona. When Francis I at Marignano (1515) beat these selfsame Swiss, this Spanish *corps* was watching the passage of the Po at Piacenza. The Swiss defeat was to none more profitable than to their Spanish ally. Henceforth Lombardy must be the battlefield between France and Spain.

Ferdinand relied less on arms than on diplomacy. Truly marvellous was his power of combination. He had already united Maximilian of Austria and Henry VII of England in defence of Breton autonomy, enabling Henry to enter the coalition by filching from France her traditional ally Scotland, for the marriage of James IV and Margaret Tudor set England temporarily free. Whenever the restless French king moved he found himself checked by Ferdinand's combinations. After the conquest of Naples Charles VIII was confronted by Ferdinand, Maximilian, the Pope, Venice and Milan (1495). The success of Louis XII in Venetian Lombardy was nullified by the coalition of Spain, England, the Swiss, the Papacy and Venice (1511). If France detached Venice from this Holy League, Ferdinand drew over Maximilian to his side. Making a peace with France in 1513, he threw Henry VIII and Maximilian against her at Guinegate, and hurled the Swiss on Dijon. The last act of his life was a coalition which should check Francis I in the full tide of victory after Marignano (1515).

In these combinations marriage was naturally the chief resource. The matches made by Ferdinand's children would be alone sufficient to prove the prominence of Spain in European politics. Great importance was, indeed, still given to Pan-Iberian projects. The eldest Infanta, Isabella, was married to John II of Portugal (1490), and on his death to his brother Emanuel (1495). When the Spanish Infante, Juan, died (1497) it seemed likely that Isabella's son, Miguel, would unite the crowns of Spain and Portugal. But in these Portuguese marriages passing-bells followed fast on wedding peals. Miguel scarcely survived the birth which proved his mother's death (1497), and for two more generations the union with Portugal was deferred.

Other marriages were purely diplomatic; they were intended to consolidate the anti-French coalitions. Thus the negotiations for the alliance of Prince Arthur and Catherine date from the days when Spain and England had common concern in the defence of Brittany (1486). Catherine was sent to England when Louis XII had increased his power by the occupation of Milan. Her marriage with her deceased husband's brother is contemporaneous with the conflict of France and Spain for Naples. So too the League of Venice against France had caused the double marriage of Maximilian's heir Philip with Ferdinand's second daughter, Juana, and of the Infante Juan with Philip's sister, Margaret. In these complicated matrimonial schemes Ferdinand overreached himself. He was no Maximilian, he had no dreams of universal dominion for his family, his range of vision was limited by the practical and the possible. Yet the successive deaths of Juan, Isabella and Miguel left Juana the heiress to the crowns of Spain; her child must inherit the possessions of Hapsburgs and Burgundians, and a claim, already quasi-hereditary, to the Empire.

Ferdinand was not only the most successful statesman of his age; he may claim to be founder of a school. This school is often regarded as Italian, but it is pre-eminently Spanish, and more particularly Aragonese. If Machiavelli wishes for a type of unscrupulous statesmanship he turns to Spain. His hero is Cæsar Borgia, a Valencian; his ideal of successful villainy is Ferdinand of Aragon. "There is a certain prince of the present time," he writes, "who never preaches aught but peace and good faith, and yet of both he is the greatest foe." Guicciardini again and again returns to the same theme, "I am convinced that above all other men he is a master of pretence." The tale is told of Ferdinand himself that when Louis XII complained that he had twice been deceived, the Aragonese exclaimed, "The drunkard! he lies. I have cheated him more than ten times." This precise quality Guicciardini in his first embassy attributed to the whole Spanish nation, "In profession and in externals they are most religious, but not in practice; they are men of infinite ceremonies, which they perform with much reverence of manner, with great humility of phrase, with honourable titles and kissings of hand; everyone is their lord; they are at everyone's command; but they are men to keep at arm's length, and to trust but little." In Ferdinand's school were trained the least scrupulous diplomatists of Charles' reign, such as Juan Manuel and Hugo de Moncada; Ferdinand hated the former because he was too like himself. Every student of the age of Philip II can lay his hand upon the later exponents of the great master's principles. The home of Machiavellism was not Italy but Spain.

For Ferdinand Africa was but a "jumping off" spot for Italy; for his minister Jiménez it was the chief object of external policy. At his own expense the Cardinal undertook the conquest of North Africa. Under his auspices Algiers was blockaded by the possession of Peñon; Oran, Bugia, even distant Tripoli, were won for Spain. Had he received his master's hearty support he might have realised Isabella's dream and conquered the great Moorish kingdom of Tlemcen.

The Spaniards might have gained a firm hold upon North Africa before the Turks appeared in the Western Mediterranean. As it was, Spanish garrisons, scantily supplied with food and even water from Spain or Sicily, clung desperately to their ports and the few yards of territory beyond the walls. A force is lost that always acts on the defensive. Not only Italy but America was diverting the attention of Crown and people from Africa. Before the death of Ferdinand permanent occupation did not extend beyond the islands, but explorers had ranged from Florida to the River Plate, and had claimed for Spain the shores of the Pacific. Already the *Cadres* of religious and governmental administration were established; already the Crown was in public interest infringing the charters of those who had borne the brunt of discovery and conquest.

There is little doubt that the extension of the dominions of the Crown under Ferdinand and Isabella added greatly to their intrinsic power within their territories. It placed them on a pedestal high above the strongest nobleman, or the wealthiest ecclesiastic; it gave distance and atmosphere to royalty. Yet this very extension would have been impossible or dangerous had not king and queen resolutely increased also the intension of their power. On the accession of Isabella the fortunes of the Castilian Crown were at their lowest. Royal revenues had been almost completely alienated, royal justice was corrupted or defied, there was no regular military force on which the Crown could count. The Crown had lost its character and prestige; of the two classes on which it might naturally rely, the clergy was secularised or demoralised, the towns divided or wasted by the factions of the nobles. Isabella's very succession was disputed by her niece, whose only disqualification was the doubtful legitimacy of her birth. The lack of proof gave a pretext to the rebellion of the nobles; the claimant was supported by the Crown of Portugal and favoured by that of France.

Yet Isabella had some advantages. The alienations of

revenue had been in great part recent; they were alike irregular and unpopular. There was in Castile a very high theory of royal justice; the power of the nobles in this respect was rather of usurpation than of right. The nobles had used their power for personal rather than for class interests; they were deeply divided; they did not constitute an oligarchy, but perpetuated anarchy. Anarchy, like despotism, when it becomes intolerable, produces its own cure. The Spaniards, with all their moral lapses, had genuine religious instincts; the purification of the Church would find public favour. The towns, if once the Crown could touch them, were both rich and militant.

Isabella and her husband grasped the situation. The interest of the monarchy and of the towns was order. Together by drastic measures they broke the power of the nobles. Isabella herself stamped out, for the moment, private war. She destroyed the unlicensed castles in Galicia, she summarily stopped the noble feuds which had devastated Andalusia. The organisation of the Hermandad acted in the same direction. Originally this had been a private association of towns, resembling the town leagues of Germany, and, like these, caused by the weakness of the executive. It had been directed against the brigands who infested the high-roads, against the noble enemies of the towns, sometimes against the Crown itself. It was now organised as a governmental institution. With great wisdom its popular and representative character was preserved; it had no connection with the regular judicial system; it was a measure of police, supplementing the criminal jurisdiction in country districts. The Hermandad dealt exclusively with crimes of violence committed in the country, or where the criminal took refuge in the country. The Supreme Junta consisted of delegates from each province. They, and not the Crown, appointed provincial officials to try cases of first instance and to collect contributions. Each village had one or more elected magistrates; every hundred hearths provided a horse archer. Thus the Crown was brought into contact with every village in the country.

This system was marvellously efficient. A criminal was hunted from parish to parish, fresh relays of archers taking up the hue and cry. The police had the fullest rights of search; they could ransack suspected castles and force the gates of towns. The criminal, once caught, was haled to the scene of his crime, and within three days punished. Lesser offenders escaped with mutilation, the greater were set against a wall or tree and shot to death. As times mended the Hermandad was found both oppressive and expensive. The Junta and superior offices were abolished in 1498; it survived only as an efficient police force, the members still electing the petty magistrates and police sergeants. Its methods had been too severe to be completely popular. There were petitions that the Hermandad should adopt the merciful methods of the Inquisition, and strangle its victims before it shot them. It is noticeable that the Hermandad, as the Inquisition, was extended from Castile to Aragon and there survived until the Cortes of 1510.

Not content with breaking the power of the nobles in the provinces the Crown diminished it in the Royal Council. The legal element, always present, was increased. This class was drawn from the lesser nobility and upper *bourgeoisie*. The gentry, driven off the roads, took service with the Crown or with the towns. This was the origin of Spanish bureaucracy, which, ultimately oppressive and deadening, was at first beneficial as encouraging a sense of order, and order was what Spain chiefly needed. At this time also the great Crown offices, monopolised by the nobility, lost much of their importance. The Grand Chancellorship was attached to the See of Toledo, the Grand Constable and Grand Admiral retained their dignity at the expense of their importance. The provincial governorships had often become hereditary, and this system, if unchecked, would crystallise into a new feudal formation. The Crown modified or abolished the system of heredity, or skilfully instituted new officials, who, nominally collateral or inferior, drew away the practical power from the titular magnates.

It was of consummate importance that the grandmasterships of the three military orders, Santiago, Alcántara and Calatrava, were, as they became vacant, conferred upon Ferdinand. The Crown revenues were thus very largely increased. The kings in each order gained the command of a small disciplined force, of a large number of vassals, of considerable territory and numerous fortresses, especially on the Castilian-Moorish frontier. The gentry were now attracted to Court service by the commanderies, the pensions, the benefices, the crosses of the Orders. The kings could reward their supporters without trenching on their own revenues. Above all the possession of the grandmasterships by the king kept them from the hands of the great nobles, who could easily make them dangerous. The king became the sole and only leader of the old chivalry of Spain, as of its modern military system[1].

This centripetal process was aided by the Moorish wars. The Crown gave employment to the nobles by enlisting their interest in the conquest of Granada, and to a less extent in that of Naples and Navarre. It was now the military centre of the nobility. The influence of the early Renaissance in Spain had similar effects. The Crown early became the intellectual centre; the new learning became a fashion, bringing the nobility nearer to the Crown, and adding lustre to the Court. Nobles flocked to the Universities, they even looked to University appointments as a career instead of arms.

The elaborate ceremonial of the later Spanish Court is ascribed to the Burgundian influence. But the tendency had already begun under the Catholic kings. Isabella loved to see herself surrounded by a numerous suite; while boasting

---

[1] The Grandmasterships were permanently annexed to the Crown by Pope Hadrian VI.

of her simplicity, she was notorious for the magnificence of her costumes. While the king increased in grandeur, the nobles were forbidden their usurped privilege of using the royal style, of quartering the royal arms; their long trains of mules and horses were strictly limited. In some of the above measures the nobles themselves voluntarily concurred; in the outburst of national enthusiasm they too were influenced by public opinion, and realised the necessity of strengthening the Crown. Thus, at the Cortes of Toledo in 1480, they consented to the resumption of royal estates, and some of the great nobles set the example in promoting the Hermandad.

The clergy in Spain were very influential and very rich, always zealously extending their property and jurisdiction. Ferdinand and Isabella did little to check the former, because a large proportion of the wealth found its way to the royal coffers. They strove, however, to control ecclesiastical jurisdiction, though not with complete success, and the struggle between the royal officials and the clergy long outlived them.

Peculiar privileges had from time to time been conferred by the Papacy on the Crown in the nomination to bishoprics in territories conquered from the Moors. These privileges Ferdinand and Isabella revived and extended, insisting on the sole right of nomination, protesting against the conferring of sees on foreigners, and the consequent non-residence. The conflict reached its climax under Sixtus IV in the case of the bishoprics of Cordoba and Cuenca; it ended in the victory of the Crown. This has often been called the Spanish Concordat, but the Papacy did not so formally recognise defeat. The Crown had already, by Papal aid, imposed financial burdens on the clergy, such as the "royal thirds," or strictly speaking two-ninths of the tithe, which became a permanent source of revenue. Fourths or tenths were granted by the Pope for special emergencies, and a large proportion of the tithes of Granada was vested in the Crown. This was a recognition of the crusading character of the Spanish kings, a principle which was hereafter to receive unlimited extension.

The rigorous reformation of the clergy was effected by Ferdinand and Isabella in complete independence of the Papacy, and at a time of great corruption in the Papal See. The Crown posed as a religious power, as the head of the Spanish Church, and this explains the attitude of Charles V and Philip II to the Church and the Catholic revival. The reform was not only one of discipline and morals, its object was also to purify doctrine, to stimulate theological learning, to produce a highly educated clergy, promoted not by birth but merit. Indirectly this increased the royal authority. The great sees were no longer the appanages of the magnates, while the Crown had more control over prelates of lesser social rank whose promotion depended upon itself. By its reforms the government also placed a check on the independence of the Religious Orders; on the other hand the Inquisition, which was in the hands of the friars, lowered the authority of the bishops; the numerous attacks made by the Inquisition upon bishops form one of its most peculiar features.

The Spanish Inquisition was introduced to meet peculiar circumstances not existing in other countries. It bears some analogy to the Hermandad. As the latter was independent of the normal system of justice, so the Inquisition lay outside the regular ecclesiastical jurisdiction. The Hermandad crushed the social anarchy in the country districts, which was due to special and temporary causes. The Inquisition in the great towns re-established doctrinal order which was threatened by the mixed character of the population. There had hitherto been no efficient Inquisition, and yet religion and nationality were alike in peril. Purity of blood and doctrine was being tainted, especially in the upper classes, by intermarriage with Jews. The contagion was spreading throughout society; Judaism was the peculiar heresy of Spain. To meet this the Spanish Inquisition was established. Its powers centred in the Dominican order, reinforced by a secular element of lawyers. Its original victims were not Jews, but nominal Christians falling from their faith. The institution must needs be strong, because the Jews and Judaisers were powerful, monopolising the medical, banking and tax-farming professions, and backed by a prosperous industrial population. The Judaisers were numerous in the municipal bodies, and were protected by nobles, many of whom were descended from Jewesses. So also some of the upper clergy were of Jewish descent, notably Talavera, Isabella's confessor and archbishop of Granada. Seville was the centre of the heresy, and here, therefore, was the original centre of the Inquisition.

Heresy, it was found, could not be checked as long as the Jews themselves went scatheless, and the revival of old restrictive laws did little to diminish their influence. Hence in 1492 the sphere of the Inquisition was extended to Jews, who were subjected to forced conversion or to exile. The movement and its motives may be compared to the recent measures of the Russian government, whose object also was to purge not only orthodoxy but nationality of an alien element.

The conquest of Granada widely extended the functions of the Inquisition. The Crown guaranteed religious liberty, and at first propagandism was solely persuasive. This method was too slow for Jiménez, who by vexatious regulations drove the people to revolt. The guarantees were then withdrawn, and forced conversion applied (1500). The Crown had a direct interest in its rapidity, for upon this depended the pecuniary favours of the Pope. Thus for more than one reason it was a joyful moment when Jiménez declared that not an unconverted Moor remained in the kingdom of Granada.

The Inquisition was not exclusively a royal constitution, for the Pope confirmed the Inquisitor General whom the Crown nominated, and claimed powers of regulation; more than once Popes interfered to mitigate the Inquisitor's severity. Yet being a purely Spanish institution it was practically worked by the Crown. It gave the king a complete hold over Jews and Moriscos, its financial profits were considerable, it was held *in terrorem* over the nobles whose Christian blood was seldom pure, it was always threatening to become a secular source of monarchical oppression.

The popularity of the Inquisition was not universal. In Cordoba there was open revolt headed by the chief nobleman of the town, supported by the municipality. This was so far successful that the Inquisitor General and his obnoxious agent were removed. In Aragon, Valencia and Catalonia resistance was more general. In Saragossa the Inquisitor was murdered before the altar; there was scarcely a noble house in Aragon which was not concerned in the conspiracy. The nobles dreaded the Inquisition, the Bishops and the lawyers were jealous of it; the lower classes usually applauded it, their blood was purer, their fortunes not so tempting, they regarded it as a scourge wherewith to chastise the nobles.

Ferdinand and Isabella relied mainly for support upon the Castilian towns. In their origin these towns had been military colonies in the territories conquered from the Moors. From the first the dominant element was the chivalry rather than the *bourgeoisie*, and industry was rather agricultural than commercial. The town and its lands were divided between the Crown, the religious bodies and various classes of inhabitants, but a large territory remained to the commune. This surplus was far greater than need required, and this explains the capacity of the towns to bear so long the burden of rising taxation. The original charter, *for* or *fuero*, regulated the relations of the commune to the Crown, and of the citizens to each other. The towns had been completely self-governing, having their own fortresses, electing their judges (*alcaldes*), police and municipal councils (*regidores*, in some towns named the Twenty-four). To the king belonged only certain royal pleas, and cases of appeal. The Crown lawyers, however, twisted the local *for* into conformity with an alleged royal *for* which professed to have higher authority. Royal pleas and cases of appeal, originally exceptional, became numerous.

In some towns the Crown appointed a *corregidor*, at first a concurrent authority with the *regidores*, who gradually became virtually the town governor. The disorders of the towns ultimately gave the Crown the control of the municipal councils. The office of *regidor* fell into the hands of the leading families, and every election led to faction fights. The Crown interfered, often substituting nomination for election, and making the offices lifehold. Then it began to sell these offices, and by a natural process they became practically, though not technically, hereditary. The number of *regidores* was increased for reasons purely pecuniary, and this laid an additional burden upon town finances. The great aim of every ambitious burgher was to gain a place in the governing bodies, which became close and selfish oligarchies. The non-official classes still, however, retained a voice, if not a vote, in the body termed *jurats*, who watched the proceedings of the Council in the inhabitants' interest, raising protests against unpopular measures.

The growth of monarchical influence at the expense of municipal independence was long previous to Ferdinand and Isabella, but they completed and regularised the system, one of their first measures being to place a *corregidor* in every town where the office did not already exist. This act was very unpopular, yet generally throughout Isabella's reign the Crown and the towns were so fully in harmony that it is difficult to determine their relative power. Notwithstanding the control which the Crown had gained, it continued throughout the 16th century to treat the towns with high consideration, making known to them individually every important national event, and receiving almost as foreign ambassadors the commissioners whom the towns sent to court.

Under Ferdinand and Isabella the prosperity of the towns greatly increased, partly from the re-establishment of order, partly from the fostering commercial policy which gave an impetus to manufacture. But there were elements of discord, firstly between the *corregidor* and the municipality; secondly between the legal and commercial factors, the former having a disproportionate preponderance; thirdly between the knightly and popular elements, the exempt and the tax-paying. In some towns the gentry almost monopolised the government, in others they were excluded from it. If there had been an absolute line of birth it might have been better, but the constant struggle to rise from one class to the other threw a growing burden of taxation on those who remained poor. Very dangerous was the influence of the great nobles in the cities where they had their palaces. They either unduly influenced the town government, or else provoked hostility, especially if they added to wealth and family influence the official position of *corregidor*. If there were two such families as at Cadiz, Seville or Zamora, the city was rent by their factions.

The Castilian towns were combined in the Cortes. There was no regular summons to nobles and clergy, though these two orders usually attended on great ceremonial occasions, for instance, for the recognition of the heir to the throne. The nobles also were summoned when financial sacrifices were expected, as in 1480 and in 1538. But the Cortes were essentially a taxing body, and while the nobles paid no direct taxation, that of the clergy depended on the Pope. Thus the Cortes were complete without either nobility or clergy, whose presence gave no additional validity.

The represented towns had formerly been numerous, but in Isabella's reign they were eighteen only, Granada being the last addition. Each town sent two proctors, but the methods of election varied. Sometimes members were drawn by lot from among the town councillors, sometimes one was elected from the *regidores*, the other from the *jurats*. Occasionally certain noble families had the right of nomination. In some towns the gentry (*hidalgos*), were elected by turn, in others by the vote of the Council or the body of *hidalgos*. The majority of the proctors were *regidores*, that is, the Cortes consisted mainly of members who had received their town offices from government. Theoretically the members were not delegates but representatives, having full power to act to the best of their judgement. Practically, however, they were bound by secret instructions and oaths.

The Cortes had an important voice in the succession to the throne, which in doubtful cases they determined. They received the oath from the new sovereign, they took the oath to the heir, they confirmed a sovereign's testament, and assented to a Council of Regency. Of more frequent importance were their financial functions. They were summoned to vote a subsidy or to negotiate for the commutation of the tax termed Alcabala. The Crown could raise no new form of tax without consent, and this was not always granted. But supply preceded redress and was not conditional thereon. Thus the Cortes had no legislative power proper. They regularly presented a long list of petitions which the Crown either granted or evaded. But the act of legislation was the king's and was by no means confined to the embodiment of these petitions in a statute. Nevertheless the Cortes were and remained a very real check upon the Crown, for future supply did in some measure depend on past redress, and the right of petition was freely and boldly used.

The regularity of the summons of Cortes depended less on the constitutional tendencies of a king than on his pecuniary necessities. Thus under Charles V and Philip II, absolute as they were, meetings were frequent. Ferdinand and Isabella disliked parliamentary government, while Jiménez had a horror of the Cortes; if people were once allowed to talk, he would say, they were certain to become unruly. Thus after the kingdom was restored to order, by measures taken in the Cortes of 1476 and 1480, there was, except perhaps in 1482, no other session until 1498. That they then became frequent (1499, 1501, 1502) was due partly to the expenses of a more enterprising policy, partly to deaths in the royal family.

We already find under Ferdinand and Isabella the multiplication of councils or departments which became the peculiarity of Spanish administration. Quite early in the reign the functions of the Royal Council were differentiated, although the so-called Councils of State, of Castile, and of Finance might still be regarded as merely sections. Originally the Royal Council of Castile had consisted of great nobles and ecclesiastics. Then as the towns grew powerful their representatives had been admitted, but these the Crown succeeded in ousting, replacing them by lawyers. The nobles still retained a right of session, with a deliberative but not a decisive voice. The lawyers acting in royal interests drew to themselves all the more important legal business of the country, to such an extent, indeed, that judicial business monopolised the time of the Council. They also set themselves to destroy one by one such legislative prerogatives as the Cortes had once possessed.

From this Council we find, under Ferdinand and Isabella, the Council of State or Secret Council definitely separated. This was in fact a Privy Council depending on the king's pleasure, changing its character with each successive monarch. There was no fixed body of rules or procedure; its members had no fixed place on ceremonial occasions. The king was its president, and apart from him it had no existence. Its functions were consultative, relating especially to foreign affairs, and to the interests of the several kingdoms held by the two Crowns. It was easily converted into a Council of War by the addition of the leading military authorities.

Very different was the Council of Castile or Royal Council. This was and remained the most important institution in Spain, having a fixed number of members, fixed rules of procedure, fixed hours of meeting, and very definite functions. The president, usually a learned ecclesiastic, was the first subject of the kingdom. This Council exercised control over every department of internal life; on the sovereign's death it assumed the government. Appointed by the Crown it became the chief engine of absolutism. It was strong with all the strength of the Crown, but not strong as against the Crown; it rarely, if ever, thwarted the power of the Crown, as did occasionally the Parliament of Paris, which in many respects it resembled.

Ferdinand and Isabella increased the professional element in the Council. It now consisted of nine lawyers, three nobles and one bishop. The monarchy used it to lower the power first of the nobles, and then of the Cortes. The Council had not only judicial but legislative functions; by a majority of two-thirds it enacted or repealed a law, the result of the deliberation being laid before the king for assent. By the signature of the king, of the president and of four councillors a petition of Cortes could be converted into a law.

In the king and the Council of Castile centred the judicial system of the country; the appointments made in the Council brought the monarchy in touch with every corner of the land. The king was practically, and not merely theoretically, the fount of justice. Ferdinand and Isabella sat in judgement every week, and this was regarded as part of the royal duty. No pains were spared to make justice adequate and pure. There were Chanceries or Audiences, that is, Courts of Appeal, at Valladolid for the country north of the Tagus, and at Granada for the south. Each of these had its civil and criminal section. Another judicial body accompanied the Court, while Seville and Galicia had their separate Audiences. In each Court there were paid advocates for the poor; excessive appeals were prevented by a pecuniary limitation, and by arrangements for fresh trial by an afforced bench in the local courts.

Between the great Courts, the rising power of the town *corregidores*, and the Hermandad, the provincial officers of justice withered away, the king in important cases preferring to send temporary commissions from the Court. A peculiar feature were the Inspectors, *pesquisidores* or *veedores*, who kept touch between the Court and the local magistracy, making rounds to enquire into abuses, to force the *corregidores* to do their duty, to prevent the encroachments of the magnates on the ecclesiastical courts, to inspect prisons, to examine the condition of fortresses, roads and bridges, and the collection of the taxes. The ideal of justice was in Castile extraordinarily high; a glance at the petitions presented at any session of Cortes will prove the importance attributed to it. Yet there were chronic evils in corruption and undue influence, not completely checked by the practice of annual appointment, and by rigorous examination at the close of office. The contrast between the ideal of honour and the practice of pecuniary corruption has always been a peculiar feature of Spain and her settlements.

If the Council of Finance was still closely connected with that of Castile, the Council of Aragon was necessarily distinct. As the king was usually absent from Aragon, which was only personally united to Castile, he was advised by Aragonese subjects, constantly in attendance on his person. This precedent probably decided the question whether, when administration became more complex, the Council should be divided into committees and so preserve its unity, or whether for each distinct department a separate Council should be created. Thus during the joint reign the Councils of the Inquisition, of the Military Orders, and temporarily that of the Hermandad, were created. These were followed under Ferdinand's regency by that of the Bull of Cruzada, which administered the proceeds of the Sale of Indulgences.

Little need here be said of the institutions of Aragon, because, interesting as they are, they affected but little the general course of Spanish history. The kingdoms of Aragon and Valencia and the principality of Catalonia were in extent less than a quarter of the kingdom of Castile. The three states themselves were only united by a personal tie; each had its separate Cortes, its distinct institutions. The power of the Crown was small; to the days of the Bourbons Aragon was described as a republic of which the king was only president. The Cortes of Catalonia and of Valencia were of the usual type, comprising the three estates. Those of Aragon, however, possessed the peculiarity that the great nobles formed a separate estate from the lesser gentry. These magnates could attend by proxy and in their estate unanimity was required. The powers of the Aragonese Cortes were very wide. Redress preceded supply, and supply was granted with extreme reluctance. Every law required the assent of each of the four estates. A standing committee of the four estates exercised considerable control over the executive, especially in the department of taxation.

The judicial system also possessed a peculiar feature in the office of the *Justicia*. His functions were to protect individual liberty and the *fueros* of the kingdom against the encroachments of the ordinary courts. By his *firma* he could protect the person and property of any who complained that a *fuero* was being violated. By the right named *manifestacion* he could remove to his own prison any who appealed to him until the case had been decided by the competent court. He thus stood between the people and the ordinary tribunals, and more particularly between the nobles and the Crown. This great official was appointed by the Crown, but could only be removed by the Cortes; in the time of Ferdinand the office was virtually hereditary in the house of Lanuza. There was a growing tendency to check the power of the *Justicia*, both on the part of the Crown and of the Cortes. The Cortes employed the agency of his two lieutenants, who were annually drawn by lot, while a parliamentary committee was each year appointed to receive complaints. Ferdinand, on his side, from 1493 imposed upon the *Justicia* a board of five legal assessors, whereas of old he was at liberty to choose his own.

The constitutional liberties of Aragon had their darker side. Individual liberty was often a high-sounding term for brigandage and vendetta. The nobles were all-powerful; to their wretched tenants were extended none of the guarantees so liberally granted to other orders. Between nobles and towns, between municipal governments and artisans, feeling ran high and hot. The Crown resented the insolent independence of its kingdom. "Aragon is not ours," Isabella would say, "we ought to conquer it."

The royal revenues in Castile were derived in the first place from its extensive domains, from mines and the monopoly of salt. There was, however, a prodigal habit of alienation. Lands had been lavished to win support, to raise ready money, to pamper favourites. An equally ruinous system was the practice of mortgage or *juros*, which was applied also to the taxes. The Crown raised a loan, and assigned the product of certain estates or taxes in payment of interest, often at the rate of ten per cent. In spite of her large resumptions, Isabella soon renewed this practice. The revenues of the grand-masterships added largely, as has been seen, to the royal revenue. The Indies also were a new source of wealth, but until Charles' reign the returns were of uncertain amount and probably not large. The royalty consisted of one-fifth of all precious metals, while there was an export and an import duty of one-eighth.

The most important of the taxes was the *alcabala*, originally an extraordinary tax, which later became part of the royal revenue. This tax was a duty of one-tenth of the value of everything sold, and it was usually farmed. Ferdinand and Isabella often accepted a commutation, which the town raised as it pleased and paid direct to the Crown: this proved a great economy to both parties. The import and export duties at the sea-ports amounted to one-eighth, and so also at the 'dry-ports' on the frontiers of Aragon and Portugal. Tolls were levied on the sheep and cattle moving from their commune, or from the winter pastures of Estremadura to the mountains. Finally, the *Servicio*, the subsidy demanded at each session of the Cortes, became more and more essential.

Ecclesiastical taxation formed an important element. The two-ninths of the tithes had been permanently granted. The Pope from time to time for special reasons conferred upon the Crown the *sussidio*, a tenth of ecclesiastical revenue. The Bull of Cruzada was a dispensation from the more extreme forms of Lenten abstinence, and was practically forced upon the people for a money payment. Originally granted for war against the Moors, it became an almost regular item of royal revenue. Under the head of ecclesiastical resources may also be mentioned the confiscations inflicted by the Inquisition, of which the Crown reaped the benefit. Revenue was almost wholly derived from Castile. Aragon and its dependencies contributed little. The Cortes were here so troublesome that Ferdinand rarely summoned them. The domains of the three kingdoms were deeply pledged, yet Catalonia was very prosperous. Sicily, and afterwards Naples, were heavily taxed, but the regular receipts and the subsidies granted by their Parliaments did little more than meet the local expenses of administration and defence.

Previous to the war of Granada the army had been purely mediæval, consisting of the military orders and their tenants, the feudal levies, and the militia of the towns, each body comprising cavalry and infantry. In this war the archers of the Hermandad appeared as a regular force, and Ferdinand kept increasing the gendarmerie, until the *corps* reached some 3000 men, of whom two-thirds were light horse. After the Italian wars, the enrolment of Stradiots from Albania, and of mounted harquebusiers, raised the cavalry to more than 4000 men. The light horse were admirable of their kind, but the "heavies" were never equal to the French, and the best troopers in Spanish service were, perhaps, the Walloon or Italian auxiliaries or mercenaries.

The feudal levies were, after the war of Granada, replaced by a militia proper. One man in twelve was drawn; the force received pay and was regularly reviewed; it was liable to service at home and abroad. This system, like that of the French franc-archers, was cheap but inefficient, and owing to the distant African and Italian wars it gave way to a regular mercenary force of professional soldiers, who were, however, disbanded at the close of war, and lived as best they could until there was fresh employment.

Gonsalvo de Cordoba was unquestionably the creator of the Spanish infantry in its more celebrated form. It was originally armed with sword, shield and javelin, but in the Italian wars, finding it unable to meet the Swiss in French service, he introduced the pike and harquebus. Henceforth each of ten companies contained 200 pikes, 200 swords and 100 harquebuses, while two more were exclusively armed with pikes. As was natural in mountain warfare, the unit was at first small, the company of 500 men. After passing through an intermediate stage, termed the *coronelia*, under Gonsalvo, it became in the reign of Charles the far-famed *tercio* consisting of three *coronelias* or twelve companies of 500. These legions of 6000 men were named after their original headquarters, Naples, Sicily, Lombardy, and Malaga.

The Moorish War had been mainly a war of sieges, and had really been decided, as the Anglo-French War (1415—53) in its later stages, by artillery. What the two brothers Bureau were to Charles VII, Francisco Ramirez was to the Spanish Crown. Ferdinand devoted great attention to this arm, but under himself and his successor the guns were chiefly made in Germany, and Germans also were the more experienced gunners. The ex-corsair Pedro Navarro, who originally learnt his trade in Florentine service, revolutionised the art of engineering, especially in the mining department. To him

Gonsalvo's success in South Italy was greatly due. After Pedro's capture at Ravenna, Ferdinand had refused to ransom him, and he passed into French service. Gonsalvo retired to his estates in something like disgrace; Antonio de Leyva was perhaps the best Spanish general that Ferdinand bequeathed to Charles.

The Spaniards were admirable military material. Sober and temperate, they were more easily provisioned than any European troops except the Turks. This was of especial consequence in the Neapolitan campaigns, where the French always suffered from wastefulness and excess. In physique the Spaniards were short but muscular and lissom. When the pike was introduced, the Venetian Quirini feared that in this solid formation they might lose the advantage of their activity. Drawn from mountainous districts, at seasons very hot and very cold, Spanish troops could stand climatic changes, and have always been celebrated for marching powers. Peculiarly uneducated, they had remarkable natural intelligence in soldiery, and hence made excellent marksmen, learning easily the art of cover and of reserving fire. Though the *esprit de corps* and sense of military honour were higher than in any other nation, yet the Spaniards had no false shame in declining action with superior forces; they seldom attacked except at an advantage. They distinguished themselves especially in the attack and defence of fortresses, and in retreats. Military discipline was easily learnt, but, as Ferdinand confessed, Spanish troops required a very strong hand. Serving as mercenaries they were mutinous if unpaid, but even in mutiny they preserved their military consistency under elected officers, and were therefore the more dangerous.

No reign, perhaps, can compare in volume and variety with that of the Catholic kings. From their untiring minister Jiménez to the ragged uplander who was shipped to Messina with one of Gonsalvo's drafts, or to the long-shore boatman who sailed with Columbus for Heaven knew where, every Spaniard seemed infected with his rulers' energy. Within these thirty years Spain laid her hand heavily on Italy and America, lightly, perhaps too lightly, upon Africa. Yet more marvellous than the energy was the discipline. A disorderly nobility, a dissipated priesthood bowed to a yoke that was at once political and spiritual. A standard of justice and of religion was set up, which might never be attained, but which for generations served as an ideal towards which national aspirations strove. The result was the more remarkable in that energy and discipline were the very qualities which seemed incompatible with the indolence and pride which trained Italian observers noted as the national characteristics. How long would pride submit to discipline, and energy overmaster indolence?

At all events the aims were set for posterity and the instruments lay ready to hand. With a disciplined infantry, a guileful diplomacy, a purified Church, Spain was fully equipped for the conquest of territory or the control of opinion. Impoverishment and exhaustion might have been foreseen, but it would have been difficult to predict whether this new pushing power had, in her army and her Inquisition, forged the tools of reaction or of reform.

SECTION II.

PHILIP I AND THE REGENCY OF FERDINAND, 1504—1516. CHARLES I (V), 1516—1529.

Isabella was well aware that the mental derangement of her daughter Juana rendered her unfit to reign. She therefore bequeathed to Ferdinand the regency of Castile, until her grandson, Charles, born in 1500, should be of age; the Cortes duly confirmed her will. The supremacy of the Crown had seemed complete, yet Castilian character was not profoundly altered. Strong abroad through his diplomacy, his alliances, his army, Ferdinand was weak at home. Castile resented the rule of an Aragonese. His second marriage was unpopular; it was believed that, if he had issue, he would separate Aragon from Castile, or subject Castile to a king with no Castilian blood. Juana's husband, Philip, was intriguing with the nobles; even Gonsalvo de Cordoba was suspected of infidelity. When Philip and Juana landed (1506), the magnates seized the opportunity of recovering their power; one by one they fell away from Ferdinand. The Aragonese king had not Isabella's sympathy with the towns, he had looked askance at their extensive privileges. Left defenceless he surrendered the regency and sailed to secure Naples.

Philip kept Juana in close confinement and ruled alone. Flemings or favourites filled every place of trust. Of the nobles some grovelled before the throne, others were in rebellion. In Andalusia the old faction fights blazed out anew. Philip recklessly alienated the royal revenues and slighted the Inquisition. His death (September, 1506) came as a relief. Juana's condition was aggravated by her hysterical grief, and Philip's party wished the Emperor Maximilian to assume the regency for his grandson. Public opinion, however, turned towards Ferdinand. The magnates who remained in arms were easily reduced; the military spirit was diverted to Africa, Navarre or Italy; Ferdinand working hand-in-hand with Jiménez had little trouble for the remainder of his regency.

Ferdinand's intentions as to his succession have been much debated. His favourite grandson was Charles' younger brother, Ferdinand, who had been educated as a Spaniard. Should this boy be king of Aragon? Should a kingdom be manufactured for him in Italy? Should he be, as regent, virtual ruler of Spain, while Charles directly administered the Netherland and German possessions of the Hapsburgs? It has been thought that the French victory at Marignano and the threatening attitude of the Castilian nobles induced Ferdinand to abandon any thought of partition. But all this is guesswork. On Ferdinand's death (1516) Charles succeeded, in nominal conjunction with his mother, to Castile and Aragon. Jiménez was left as regent until Charles' arrival. Again the nobles struggled for power, some by open revolt, others by making the Council of State an instrument of oligarchy. Once more Jiménez held them down. The story is told that they demanded to see his authority: "There," he answered, "is my authority," as he pointed to the park of artillery beneath the palace windows. Yet he failed to create an urban militia which should overawe the magnates, and they successfully intrigued against him at Charles' court. Jiménez protested against the growing foreign influence in Castile, against the withdrawal of revenue to Flanders, which prevented the due defence of land and sea; he unceremoniously thrust aside Adrian of Utrecht, Charles' tutor, who was sent as coadjutor in the regency. But Jiménez never swerved from loyalty. In defiance of public opinion he proclaimed Charles as king, and stifled the pretensions of young Ferdinand to an independent authority.

The reign of Charles opened under auspices of ill-omen. He seemed intentionally to alienate affection. Above all things Castilians craved for a resident king. Yet twenty months expired before Charles landed, under stress of weather, in the wilds of Asturias. For two months more he wandered about by-roads, entering no important town. It was alleged that he was reluctant to meet Jiménez; his heartless letter which ordered the Cardinal's retirement was coincident with the old statesman's death. Then at length (November 1517) Charles entered Valladolid, but in all this interval he had not learned Castilian. His minister Guillaume de Croy, lord of Chièvres, was practically absolute. He was believed already to have sacrificed Spain to secure French friendship for the Netherlands. Toledo, the primacy of Spain, was given to his boy nephew. Another Fleming, Sauvage, was Chancellor. Flemings monopolised all posts of profit, they swept Spain bare of her currency, they studiously insulted the Castilian nobles. Some exaggeration there may have been, but contemporary Italians confirm Spanish accounts of their vulgarity and greed. Adrian of Utrecht, himself a Netherlander, earnestly warned Charles against these abuses. The powerful city of Toledo was exasperated by the nomination of a foreigner to its see, and by the confiscation of the large fortune which Jiménez had bequeathed to local charities.

When Charles summoned his first Cortes to Valladolid the friction was unmistakeable. A deputy for Burgos, Dr Zumel, headed an outspoken opposition. Charles was not recognised as joint ruler with his mother until he had sworn to maintain Castilian privileges and to exclude foreigners from office. Then at length a subsidy was granted, but the towns reserved the right of collection and would concede no other until the expiry of the three annual instalments.

In Aragon opposition was yet more pronounced. Charles, it was argued, could not summon the Cortes until he was king, and king he could not be until he had taken the oath before the standing Committee. The oath taken, the Cortes raised the objection that they had already recognised Juana. Disputes were perhaps purposely prolonged because the municipality of Saragossa reaped a rich harvest from its monopoly of provisions, which ruined the Court and starved the poor. A popular rising against the nobles and the burghers turned the scales in Charles' favour. Yet the scanty subsidy, when granted, by no means met the expenses of obtaining it. That an epidemic carried off many of the foreigners was no great loss; the Chancellor Sauvage was succeeded by Gattinara, a clever indefatigable Piedmontese, who knew Spain well. From May 1518 to January 1519 Charles was occupied in this wrangle. For yet another year he was the sport of the mocking Catalans in their Cortes of Barcelona. Here he received the news of his election as Emperor in Maximilian's place. The delays had made it impossible to receive the recognition of Valencia. War with France was certain; to visit Valencia was to risk the alliance of England and the fidelity of Germany.

Meanwhile Castilian discontent had grown. Why, it was asked, had the great kingdom yielded so readily, when the pigmy states of Aragon and Catalonia held out so long? Charles had broken all his promises; he had sent Ferdinand out of Spain; he was rejecting a Portuguese for an English marriage; he was heaping offices upon Flemings; he had farmed the rising taxes to money-lenders; he was already demanding a fresh subsidy for objects which Spain disliked: instead of residing he was hurrying to England and Germany; he had summoned the Cortes to Santiago in Galicia beyond the border of Castile, an unprecedented departure from custom which entailed grave expenses on the towns. Discontent led to the unconstitutional action of Toledo, which substituted irregular deputies for the proctors duly drawn by lot; to the violent rising at Valladolid, which Charles escaped by minutes only; and to the organised opposition of the Cortes at Santiago. Charles, finding a subsidy refused, transferred the Cortes to Corunna, and here by intimidation and corruption manufactured a majority. Indignation culminated when Adrian was appointed regent; he had, indeed, protested that Castile was for Castilians, but he was no Spaniard and no statesman.

It had seemed antecedently probable that civil conflict in Spain would be between Crown and nobles. Events proved the contrary. The humiliation of the grandees had increased the pretensions of the towns. Hitherto the Third Estate had been in harmony with the Crown, but when differences arose the towns resolved to show that they had outgrown their leading-strings.

Before Charles left Corunna the revolt broke out, spreading speedily from Toledo to Segovia, Burgos and Zamora. It took the form of attacks on deputies who had voted the subsidy, on foreign merchants, and government officials. If the proscribed individuals escaped, their furniture, their very cocks and hens were thrown into a bonfire. The movement was not always democratic. Among the leaders was Pedro de Giron, an Andalusian magnate with a long record of faction and rebellion. More characteristic were Juan de Padilla and Pedro Laso, both noblemen actively engaged in the municipal affairs of Toledo. It is noticeable that in their first manifesto they denounced Charles' alleged breaches of noble privilege.

The greater nobles were generally neutral, though sometimes sympathising with the revolt; Adrian even informed Charles that the wires were pulled by the grandees. Leading municipal families, noble, legal or commercial, were often actively engaged. In the clothworking towns, however, the artisans were soon found in the forefront. At Madrid, Guadalajara and Siguenza the democracy overthrew the existing government and excluded nobles from office; at

Segovia the gentry were from the first in danger. Most radical of all the leaders was Antonio de Acuña, Bishop of Zamora, who enrolled the lower clergy and the friars.

The regent had few troops and no resources; his only allies were officials of evil reputation, the lost souls of absolutism. An attack upon Segovia united the moderates with the mob. The royalists, in attempting to seize the artillery parked at Medina del Campo, burnt the town. This was the *baptême de feu* of the revolution. Indignation spread revolt throughout New and Old Castile and thence to Jaen and Murcia. In Andalusia it was rather a recrudescence of local feuds than organised resistance to the government. Of this the real area lay between the Douro and the Tagus, the very heart of Castile. There was at first no profession of fighting against the Crown: the revolution was conducted in the names of Juana and Charles. A few, indeed, wished to make Juana's power actual, and Acuña vapoured of Italian republics and their liberty.

How far could towns with different traditions and separated by difficult country combine in revolution? The central provisional government, the Santa Junta, was organised at Avila (August 1520). This was the geographical centre of disturbance, as being on the border line of Old and New Castile. The regent and his Council were deposed; the Junta declared the supreme royal authority. Padilla surprised Tordesillas, where Juana lived, and broke up and imprisoned the royal Council. The news flashed through Spain that Juana was not mad and that she sympathised with the Junta. Had she signed a document Charles was lost. But, excited as she was at first, she soon relapsed into sullen neutrality; the entreaties and threats of the Junta could wring nothing from her obstinate reserve.

The rebellion was spoiled by meeting with no resistance. The Junta instead of destroying the few remnants of royal government memorialised the absent Emperor. The eighty-two clauses of the petition embody an epitome of past, present and future discontents. The dislike for foreigners was manifested in the demand for their exclusion from magistracies and benefices, from household or military service; in the protest against letters of naturalisation. For native manufactures the preemption of Spanish wool was claimed, and the extension to foreign goods of the stringent supervision over home-made cloth. The petitioners complained that Castile was ruined by the withdrawal of the precious metals; they denounced the export of cattle, sheep and pigs as having trebled the price of meat, candles and shoes; fearing the diversion of the American trade to Flanders, they would confine it to Castilians, and retain Seville as the sole authorised port. In relation to the Indies one unselfish touch is found; public opinion had been stirred by the preaching of Las Casas, and the Junta stigmatised the leasing of gangs of natives for forced labour in the mines as the virtual enslavement of a Christian people, for which the increased output of gold and silver was no excuse.

Ecclesiastical and judicial abuses form the *refrain* of each successive Cortes. The Junta too demanded that magistracies should not be granted to the nobles' nominees nor to youngsters fresh from the Universities: the courts should be periodically inspected, the conduct of outgoing magistrates strictly scrutinised: all municipal offices must be annual and elective, no *corregidor* should be appointed except on petition by a town. The sale of offices and the promise of reversions was pronounced a detestable system. Under equal condemnation fell the arbitrary transference of cases from local to royal courts, the payment of judges by fees and fines instead of salary, the promise of confiscated property before sentence, the plurality of offices.

The encroachments and expenses of the ecclesiastical courts were the subject of fierce attack. For the Cortes was claimed the decision whether the Bulls of Cruzada for the sale of Indulgences should be published; it was insisted that their

purchase must be purely voluntary, and not forced on the
people by itinerant friars who, to gain their small commission,
kept the congregation whole days in church, and refused
absolution to all who would not buy. Non-residence and its
attendant evils were ascribed to Roman influences, to the
practise of provisions, reservations and pensions on Spanish
sees; the only remedy was compulsory residence and the non-
payment of the stipend during absence. The petition did not
spare the more direct abuses of Charles' government. The
king's table, it protested, cost tenfold that of his predecessors;
the system of purveyance, grosser in Castile than in any other
Christian or pagan land, had spread from the royal suite to
judicial and financial officers, to police, to noblemen and
prelates. It was insisted that old arrears of the *Alcabala*
should be written off, that it should be collected by the towns
and commuted, in spite of the rise of prices, at the rate fixed
in Isabella's will.

So far the proposals were conservative in their general
drift, but this conservatism was but a stalking-horse for revolution. It was demanded that the constitution of the Cortes
should be radically changed; that in each represented town
the clergy, the gentry and the commons should respectively
elect a proctor, who should be bound by pledges to vote according to his constituency's will; that these delegates should
debate in private, and that death should be the penalty for
receiving a gratuity from the Crown, direct or indirect: every
three years the Cortes should meet, with or without summons,
while the notaries who attended should be their officials and
not the king's. The sessions of Santiago and Corunna were
pronounced unconstitutional, the subsidy and gratuities voided.

Less academic was the Junta's attitude towards the nobles,
whom the petition debarred from office in the revenue or
domain or royal fortresses: their towns and villages, previously
exempted, must be assessed, and lands, rents and services
illegally appropriated restored within six months; the Crown

should redeem the older assignations upon revenue and resume without compensation grants subsequent to 1504. The grant of letters of nobility by the Crown was denounced as being prejudicial to the remaining tax-payers. Charles himself was ordered to return, reside and marry, to revoke immediately Adrian's commission, to dismiss all officers who had offended the communes, to deprive of office for ever the members of the Councils of State and Castile. Henceforth during the king's absence or minority the regent must be a native, acceptable to the people, elected by Cortes and the Council of Castile.

The drafting of Utopian programmes is not statesmanship. The attitude of the Junta towards the nobles drove them for refuge to the Crown. Charles corrected his great mistake as the Communes committed theirs. He nominated as co-regents with Adrian the Constable and Admiral, the chief titular officials of Castile; he threw himself upon the loyalty of the nobles. Feigning a consciousness of strength he empowered the regents to summon Cortes, but to abate not a jot of the prerogative; towns, which refused to attend, should for ever forfeit their representation; the Junta must be immediately dissolved.

The fortunes of the Communes began to flag. Their power was after all confined to the two Castiles, with outposts in Galicia, Navarre and Murcia. Andalusia and Granada, as a whole, were loyal. At Santiago and Corunna their deputies had been outspoken, those of Cordoba had refused the subsidy. But in the king's absence they would join no unlawful association. Seville and Cordoba, realising that in noble factions lay the germ of civil war, requested the magnates to withdraw beyond their walls, and rigorously forbade any armed gatherings round the noble houses. At Cordoba a price was put on the head of a friar and a shoemaker, the agents of revolt among the masses. Finally at La Rambla these towns formed a loyal union of Andalusia, which offered to the king 6000 horse and 20000 foot if only he would return to Spain unaccompanied by foreign troops.

In the North the Communes suffered actual shrinkage. Opinion was long divided in Burgos, which lay on the extreme fringe of the area of rebellion, and was jealous of the influence of Toledo. It now seceded and admitted the Constable; Dr Zumel, the first leader of the constitutional opposition, became a loyalist. Hitherto there had been little fighting, because the Communes had no enemy to fight. Now each town was harassed by its traditional foe. Sometimes even within a city civil war swept down the street and up the very aisles of the Cathedral. Valladolid had become the insurgents' military centre, but their mistake in not early seizing Simancas, the only royalist town, with its strong castle on the Pisuerga, made communications difficult. The royalists although inferior in wealth and numbers were allowed to surprise Tordesillas; they thus recovered possession of the person of Juana and imprisoned the members of the Junta who were with her.

Not only was there shrinkage at the circumference of revolt, there was cleavage at its very centre. The first leader Padilla had been superseded by the Andalusian noble Pedro de Giron: the latter, when suspected of treason, sullenly withdrew to his estates. Then followed the contest for command between Padilla, the showy soldier, pushed into prominence by his brilliant wife, and Laso, the capable politician. The mob beat the moderates and elected Padilla; Laso and the Junta began to look towards compromise with the Crown.

Of all the rebel leaders the most radical, the most inflammatory was the Bishop of Zamora. Forming his lower clergy and the friars into regiments, feeding the war with the plunder of churches and monasteries, he had fanned the passions of the people by midnight services, by wild processions where the torchlight fell upon a medley of crucifix and pike. He had operated chiefly in the north-western districts, but hearing that the Prior of San Juan was threatening Toledo he marched southwards to its relief. At this moment the news arrived of the young Flemish archbishop's death. The mob hoisted the Bishop upon their shoulders, and seated him on the primate's throne. Even this "Second Luther," as he was termed at Rome, could not accept election so uncanonical. He strove to starve the chapter into electing him, but Castilian sobriety stood the canons in good stead. The Bishop's violence set all moderate and religious men against him; the clergy who had once preached war now began to plead for peace. The Prior, moreover, proved more competent in the field than did the Bishop.

The conflict had now settled down into a social war. The Communes had protested against the appropriation of royal lands by nobles; but they had themselves seized not only lands, but mines and saltworks, the proceeds of the *Alcabala*, and of the Bulls of Cruzada. Not content with this, they confiscated the possessions of the nobles in the towns, threatened their rural estates, harried their sheep. The revolutionary movement spread from the towns to the peasantry and seemed likely to become a Jacquerie. The last act of the Communes before the end was to enrol bands for the express purpose of pillaging the nobles' houses.

Meanwhile the magnates were themselves divided. The Constable insisted on rigorous repression, the Admiral on a generous compromise. Left by Charles without resources, many thought of making terms to save their lands and cattle. They were so jealous, wrote Adrian, that any noble would gladly lose an eye if it cost one to his rival. Yet they were more patient than their enemies. While the Constable collected troops, the Admiral detached the moderates; the revolutionary party had broken up before the final action of Villalar.

The popular hero Padilla showed little military competence. He did, indeed, storm the strong position of Torrelobaton, but he did not follow up this brilliant action. At length becoming aware of his isolation, he moved westwards to effect a junction with the forces of the western Communes. The nobles followed with their cavalry and light guns. In pouring rain the rebel foot pressed forward to gain the shelter of Villalar. The loyal cavalry felt their yielding flanks, and threw in a few shots from their guns. The heavier artillery of the Communes stuck in the mud, and the gunners deserted. Then the loyalist horse were on them; there was a wild rout; only five rebels really fought, only one of their opponents fell (April 1521). On the next day Padilla and two other leaders were executed. In the North there was no further resistance; Toledo made a gallant resistance under Padilla's widow, who stained her heroism by treasonable intrigue with France. Acuña aided her until he saw that the game was played out; then he fled, to be captured just as he reached the French frontier. The widow, more fortunate, escaped with her family to Portugal.

The war of classes had gone against the masses. When all was over Charles returned. He had scarcely raised a finger to suppress revolt, he had not lent a ducat or a man to the cause which was originally his. Perhaps he was not unwise; he had not been brought into direct conflict with his subjects; he had beaten one dangerous element by another. On his first visit Charles had brought his Flemish courtiers, on his second he was accompanied by some 4000 German foot, and a train of German artillery. The nobles after their victory had been scrupulously moderate; Charles was not cruel, but he was obstinate and knew no compassion. Scarcely 300 rebels were excluded from the amnesty, and few of these suffered in person. But the penalties dragged on. The nobles in vain implored their sovereign to forgive; even after the victory of Pavia the friar Antonio de Guevara must needs plead for pardon so long deferred.

A rising in Valencia preceded and outlasted that of the Communes. With the latter it had no original connection, it was rather social than constitutional, the result of long ill-feeling between the gentry, who dominated the Cortes and judicature, and the thriving middle and lower classes, especially in the capital. Early in 1519 Moorish corsairs had hovered off Valencia. Owing to the absence of the gentry during the plague, defence had devolved on the artisans, who thus gained a military organisation. This was followed by a political organisation of their several trade-guilds in a league, termed the *Germania*.

The Crown meanwhile was at cross purposes with the nobles and the Cortes, owing to Charles' refusal to visit Valencia to receive and take the oath on his accession (October, 1519). When Adrian appeared in January 1520, the Cortes absolutely declined to recognise a mere representative, and they were undoubtedly in the right. Even before this the government had coquetted with the *Germania*; it now definitely recognised its organisation, and Adrian formally reviewed the armed trades. From Corunna Charles ordered that one-third of the municipal magistrates should be plebeians, yet he left in Diego de Mendoza a viceroy acceptable to the nobles. The Crown trifled with the situation; wishing to embarrass the nobility it underrated the gravity of the movement.

The trades, half encouraged and half irritated, took the law into their own hands. They formed of sailors, artisans and peasants a Committee of Thirteen, which was intended to be permanent; it was agreed that at least one member should always represent the peasantry, one the velvet and two the woollen trade. An active propaganda throughout the kingdom produced corresponding committees in other towns. The lower classes, flying to arms, swept all before them, massacring defenceless nobles with their wives and children. The gentry concentrated for defence at Denia in the southernmost corner of the kingdom, while Valencia, Jativa and Alcira were the centres of revolution.

In this revolt the social line was absolutely distinct; no noble fought for the *Germania*, every town but Morella sent a contingent to the commons. The middle class early shrank back from the conflict and finally joined the nobles. The Thirteen of Valencia themselves were soon outpaced and lost control; the original leader died broken-hearted at the atrocities of the extremists. The clergy were divided, some preaching against excesses, others stimulating the infuriated mobs. The Moorish peasants on the lords' estates rose in defence of their masters, but were forced to baptism or exterminated by the commons. Nor were these always alternatives—"Plenty of souls for heaven and plenty of money for our pockets," was the cry, when 600 Moorish peasants were first baptized and then hewn to pieces. Revolution seemed likely to spread beyond Valencia; it just crossed the southern border of Aragon, while in Majorca the war of classes was internecine.

At length the nobles, reinforced from Murcia and Andalusia, took Valencia. But the insurgent leader, Vicente Peris entered by surprise, and a fierce street fight ensued. Five thousand noble troops stormed the rebels' quarter house by house, under a hail of tiles, crockery, furniture and boiling water. Peris was dragged from his home and killed. Valencia itself was subdued, but the revolution flickered up again in Jativa and Alcira under a picturesque impostor, who professed to be a son of the deceased Infante Juan. Charles was now in Spain and sent aid to the nobles, who forced the two towns to capitulate (September, 1525). Of the lower classes 14,000 were said to have fallen, and their condition permanently deteriorated; the noble victors were well-nigh ruined. The towns had capitulated under promise of amnesty, but Charles would have none of this. The punishment of individuals and corporations was entrusted to the dowager-queen Germaine, and the frivolous Frenchwoman used her authority with ferocity.

While Spaniards were flying at each other's throats their ruler was guiding Spain towards the long national conflict, which was only closed by the substitution of Bourbon for Hapsburg. Ever since the election of Charles to the Empire, war with his rival Francis I became a certainty. In such a war Spain had the most direct concern. If Charles held that the duchy of Burgundy had been filched from his patrimony, the Crown of Aragon had under false pretexts extorted the cession of Roussillon, and had driven the French from Naples, the Crown of Castile had robbed the French house of Albret of its Spanish territories. Spanish and French troops had contested the dominion of North Italy at Ravenna; Spaniards, but for their general's caution, would have fought shoulder to shoulder with Swiss against French on the field of Marignano.

From one grandfather, Maximilian, Charles had inherited hostility to France intermittent and sentimental, but that of the other, Ferdinand, had been practical and ceaseless. To the ruler of the Netherlands peace with France was essential. The government of Philip and that of Charles himself had stood aside in the previous wars, and had even shown strong French sympathies. The treaty of Noyon (1516), which was Charles' first act after his accession to the Spanish Crown, was denounced in Spain as sacrificing her interests to the commerce of the Netherlands with France. Twice during the later conflict between Charles and Francis, the Regent of the Netherlands made a separate truce for her provinces, which had no concern in the quarrel.

Personal rivalry was, perhaps, the immediate cause of war, but there were national causes of more depth and permanence. It was unjust to urge that the European negotiations which kept Charles from Spain were indifferent to her fortunes. The wars to come were Franco-Spanish wars for the dominion of Italy; they had been rendered inevitable by the Spanish occupation of Naples and the French occupation of Milan. Flemish gold and German blood were lavished to maintain for Spain the frontier of the Pyrenees, to win for Spain the passes of the Alps.

The combatants were not badly matched. To all appearance the Emperor's resources were the greater. Substantial aid from Germany was, however, discounted by the independence of the princes, and by troubles directly or indirectly springing from the Lutheran movement. The Netherlands had one enemy at their gate and another within their doors. Robert de la Marck from his principality of Bouillon was a constant menace to Luxemburg and Namur. The descendants of Charles the Bold paid dearly for his confiscation of Guelders. The dispossessed Duke not only found a welcome in his own state, but terrorised the provinces lying round the Zuyder Zee. He was, moreover, the French recruiting sergeant for German lanzknechts, and Francis drew as largely from this mercenary market as did Charles. The Swiss, the other great mercenary nation, were divided in the first campaign, but thereafter, according to custom, usually sold their aid to France.

In Italy the possession of Naples and Sicily balanced that of Milan. The population of the duchy had within four years learnt to hate the French and to long for the return of the titular duke, Francesco Sforza. On the other hand Charles' reign opened with actual revolt in Sicily, while his ambassador at Rome described the administration of Naples as deplorable. In Spain itself, after the suppression of the *Germania*, the stubborn resistance of the Valencian Moors to conversion employed a considerable royal force, while, of the two chronic factions which divided Navarre, one necessarily looked toward the house of Albret and found support in popular feeling.

A glance at the map would seem to show that Charles, especially after the conquest of Milan and Genoa, held France as between the extended finger and thumb, and could at will increase the pressure on her eastern and southern provinces. But the French king had the advantage of acting on interior lines. This was not only militarily, but financially important. The movement of the Imperial troops was ruinously expensive, costing, as Charles complained, at least one-third more than that of the French. Spain was protected by arid stretches of mountains from invasion, but the French kings had long assumed the right of passage through Savoyard territory, and could therefore easily make elbow-room by pushing into Lombardy.

The Spanish infantry had a magnificent reputation, but after all it had been beaten at Ravenna. The lustre of Marignano still shone on the French lances and field pieces; if the native infantry were decidedly inferior to that of Spain, the Swiss and German mercenaries balanced the German and Italian troops of Charles. The French generals, Francis I himself, La Trémouille, La Palisse, the Duke of Albany and Bayard would seem to outweigh the Spanish-Italian chiefs, Prospero Colonna, the Marquis of Pescara, Antonio de Leyva. It was no good sign that in Naples alone six generals contested the command-in-chief.

Both monarchs were from the first in desperate financial straits. Francis had been unable to utilize his victory of Marignano because the roads in France had been eaten bare, and the taxes for the ensuing year already spent. Charles had to borrow from Henry VIII his passage money to Spain; his ambassador at Rome, Juan Manuel, was crippled with debt incurred on his master's behalf, and plaintively wished that he had the wherewithal to buy his bread. Above all Charles throughout his whole dominions was hampered by Parliamentary control over subsidies, from which Francis I was free. France, Louis XI had said, was a fair meadow whose owner could mow it as often as he pleased.

With forces so equal much would depend upon alliances. In later days Francis looked mainly to the Lutheran princes and the Turk, but in the present French and Spanish diplomatists were courting the coyest of princes, the King of England, and the Pope. The Tudor king, inferior to either rival in military power, was sufficiently strong to hold the balance. He could ruin the trade of the Netherlands and make communication with Spain impossible. On the other hand the French coasts from Boulogne to Bayonne lay open to his fleets, and his territorial claims in France might be the pretext of war and the reward of victory. English revenues were more flourishing than those of France and Spain. No prince, it was said, was so rich in ready money as Henry VIII; he could finance Swiss or lanzknechts or Italian condottieri. The princess Mary was but a babe, but she was dandled before both courts, and was promised first to the Dauphin and then to the Emperor. Charles, indeed, was told by Cardinal Schomberg that Mary would never marry either, and laughed heartily when it was explained how in time of war the English used princesses as owls for luring birds.

Leo X occupied in Italy the position which Henry VIII held in Europe. The Spaniards in Naples and the French in Milan being evenly balanced, Leo, who also controlled Florence, could turn the scale. With Papal aid the Spaniards could march through friendly territory to the Milanese frontier, or the French to that of Naples. Leo X was better armed and wealthier than any previous Pope, he could subsidise the needy Emperor or the spendthrift King A Pope's price was usually the interest of his family. If English princesses were owls, the Papal *nipoti* were vultures gorged by the battles of the nations. Yet Leo's chief aim was, perhaps, a state sufficiently strong to awe either foreigner.

Charles had risked his hold on Spain for a personal interview with Henry VIII. His English visit at least secured friendly neutrality, and discounted the effects of the coming meeting of Henry and Francis at the Field of the Cloth of Gold. It really, moreover, decided the attitude of the Pope, though he pretended to be hard to win. Leo X already dreamed of the marriage of his baby grand-niece, Catherine de' Medici to a French prince, with Naples under his own administration as their appanage. More definite was the demand for the absorption of Ferrara in the Papal States, but the sacrifice of this faithful ally Francis I refused. Charles was more generous; he not only abandoned

Ferrara, but would detach Parma and Piacenza from Milan. Nor was this all—after his coronation at Aix Charles met the Diet at Worms, where his personal influence determined the condemnation of Luther (May, 1521). This spiritual support of the Papacy decided the political alliance of the Pope.

Hostilities had practically begun in March by attacks of Robert de la Marck and the Duke of Guelders on the Netherlands. Francis I, disavowing responsibility, retorted that Charles had encouraged Milanese exiles, had neither paid tribute for Naples, nor done homage for Flanders and Artois. When in May French troops in D'Albret's name overran Navarre, a declaration of war could not be postponed. The French had blundered in delaying until the *Communeros* had been beaten. The attack on Navarre made Charles' cause common to all Castile; even Toledo sent her contingent to fight the French.

The Pope, feeling that Charles was now committed, declared his alliance. The German princes, resenting the French king's insult to their elected Emperor, withdrew or modified their opposition to his authority. Immediately before war broke out De Chièvres died. In Spanish history he has left an evil name, but he was a good friend to his native Netherlands, and, while abandoning no essential interest, he had skilfully postponed war until Charles could fight at an advantage. In after years Charles spoke of De Chièvres with high respect, but henceforth no minister was his master. *Ce bon enfant l'Empereur*, as Leo X called him, entered on his first great war as an autocrat with a will and a policy of his own.

It cost four campaigns to expel the French from Lombardy, and to replace their partisans by the Imperialist faction at Genoa. Striking events were few. At the battle of Bicocca the Spaniards had their first marked success against the Swiss. The mountaineers, clamouring for pay, battle, or dismissal,

blundered to their doom; they were mown down by the
Spanish harquebusiers crouching in the cornfields before they
could push the pike home. Lautrec, the French general, was
no match for the cautious Italian veteran Prospero Colonna,
who may be said to have introduced the system of a war
of positions. Both Lautrec and his successor Bonnivet were
outgeneralled by the fiery Neapolitan nobleman Pescara,
adored by his soldiers, taking full advantage of the enterprise and intelligence of the Spanish foot. At the last
skirmish on the Sesia, Bayard received his fatal wound after
a quarter of a century of Italian fight.

The Imperialists had been aided by Milanese hatred for
the French; Italian friars had preached a crusade against the
oppressor. But the Emperor's hand was already heavy; he
used or abused alleged Imperial prerogatives, which passing
centuries had abandoned to the antiquary. His generals
enforced by military execution the requisitions assessed upon
the free states in proportion to their resources for the support
of the Spanish garrisons in Lombardy. Although Francesco
Sforza returned to Milan, his investiture with the Duchy was
delayed.

Venice had passed from the French to the Imperial
alliance, but Charles found difficulty in keeping the Papal
contingent with his colours. Leo X had just lived to see
Parma and Piacenza added to the Papal States. The Conclave
after his death was a national struggle between the French and
Spanish parties, which his cousin, the Cardinal Medici, decided
in Spain's favour. Unable as yet to secure his own promotion,
he won the tiara for Adrian of Utrecht (January, 1522). To
Charles it was a gain that the unpopular regent, the symbol of
Flemish domination, should be removed from Spain on so
flattering a pretext. But Adrian was not prepared to be the
Imperial tool. From the first he was at disaccord with Juan
Manuel; he would take no share in the alliance against France.
Partly Adrian was offended by the arbitrary measures of

Charles' officers in Lombardy, partly he had a heartfelt desire for peace. Only the misconduct of his own Cardinals of the French party drove him to the Emperor's side shortly before his death (September, 1523). The election of the Cardinal Medici as Clement VII in November seemed to make Charles' position at Rome secure; he had been the life and soul of the Spanish party in Leo X's court. The Duke of Sessa, the new ambassador, assured Charles that his power was now so great that he might convert stones into obedient sons. But Charles was, like others, destined to discover that his Popes were the most deceptive and disappointing of mankind.

From 1521 to 1524 there had been desultory fighting on the Flemish and Burgundian frontiers. Henry VIII, after half-hearted efforts at mediation, openly joined the Emperor (1523). English troops twice invaded Picardy, while English squadrons hovered off the Norman and Breton coasts, yet the revival of the old English-Spanish-Burgundian alliance was more interesting than important. Within France herself Charles found a strange ally in the greatest French nobleman, the Constable Bourbon (1523). Machiavelli had said that France was only vulnerable through her feudal nobles. Charles exaggerated the importance of Bourbon's defection; he promised him the hand of his sister Eleanor, the widowed Queen of Portugal, and gave other pledges which hampered him hereafter. The French crown had outgrown its great feudatories; moreover a rebel who runs away hurts no one but himself. Bourbon's desertion gave to Charles a brave trooper, a generous recruiter, an importunate suitor, a general conceited above his competence.

Imperial success in Lombardy had been marred by a mishap in Spain. The French, invading Navarre, turned suddenly on Fuenterrabia, the key of Guipuscoa, and occupied the strong position in force (September, 1521). Here there was brisk fighting by land and sea, but the professional Spanish soldier found service in the Pyrenees less profitable than in Italy. The French retained their foothold on Spanish soil

4—2

until 1524. The force which ultimately expelled them was of such poor quality that it had immediately afterwards to be disbanded. A similar cause had made an invasion of Guyenne, which Charles intended to lead in person, abortive and ridiculous (1523).

The campaign of 1524 in Italy had been fought almost literally to the last crown and the last loaf. The Spanish soldier had this advantage, that the loaf lasted him longer than it did the French. The Constable Bourbon had pawned his jewels, the Duke of Sessa his plate, to pay the troops. Charles was so exhausted that he longed for peace, while Francis was equally anxious for a truce. The failure of negotiations made fighting brisker. The allies determined not only to invade but to dismember France. Wolsey had but lately exclaimed that, if peace was ever to exist, the French must be exterminated. While the English were to attack Picardy and the Emperor Languedoc, Bourbon and Pescara were ordered to invade Provence and at all costs to take Marseilles.

The invasion of Provence alone really took effect. Had it succeeded the consequences to Spain would have been momentous. To Bourbon was promised a kingdom consisting of the two old Imperial fiefs, Dauphiné and Provence, and his own possessions in the Bourbonnais. This was no mere war-dream. Dauphiné had lost its independent existence little more than half a century; the incorporation of Provence with France counted but thirty years, and Charles somewhat relied upon its disaffection. An intermediate kingdom would have barred the access of France to Italy. Marseilles was the port which thwarted Spanish control of the western Mediterranean, threatening at once Genoa and Barcelona. From Marseilles had sailed the fleets which throughout the fourteenth and fifteenth centuries had contested Sicily and Naples with the lords of Aragon. Deprived of Marseilles France would virtually cease to be a Mediterranean power; the gulf of Lyons would become a Spanish-Italian lake. Bourbon, irreconcileable with the French Crown, wedded to the Emperor's sister, might in name have been an English feudatory, but in fact must have become the client of the Crown of Spain, until his dynasty was old enough to hold the scales. This very kingdom, with the substitution of Savoy for the Bourbonnais, the gifted Charles Emmanuel within the century well-nigh made a reality.

The bulk of Provence was easily occupied, but the invasion met with no co-operation from Emperor or English. Charles' insufficient forces broke against the walls of Marseilles, defended by the hatred of its inhabitants for Aragon, and by the skill of the Italian *condottiere* Renzo da Ceri. Bourbon and Pescara disagreed. The latter complained that Bourbon was always in a passion, as was also the English ambassador who held the purse,—"the captains were between two passions." There was no alternative but a terrible retreat. "Lost an army, somewhere in the mountains of Genoa," was the Roman witticism on the struggle of the Imperialists to regain Lombardy.

Francis I, who had gathered a large force upon the Spanish flank at Avignon, stormed over M. Genèvre. The French seemed irresistible; plague and famine opened the gates of Milan. The Imperialist generals skilfully confined defence to two strategic points. The occupation of Pavia would check an advance on Naples, while behind the Adda, guarded by Lodi, reinforcements could be gathered from Tyrol. Francis I must needs besiege one town or the other. He despatched a seemingly sufficient force to hold the Imperialists at Lodi, while in person he sat down before Pavia, which it would have been madness to leave untaken. Francis, however, made too sure of its capture, and weakened his forces by detaching the Duke of Albany to Naples and directing a division against Genoa.

The capture of Pavia would have opened communications with Rome and Florence, and the Medicean Pope, lord of both, inveterate Imperialist as he was believed to be, was changing sides. Clement VII made a secret treaty with France; he allowed the Duke of Albany to levy troops on Papal territory; he permitted or ordered his cousin Giovanni de' Medici to join Francis with his Black Bands, the choicest troops in Italy.

"I hear," wrote the Englishman Pace on October 29, 1524, "Francis is about to attack Pavia; if defeated his whole military reputation is lost, if victorious his object is gained; at Pavia therefore he ought to be resisted to the uttermost." Charles, as well as Francis, thought that French success was certain, though he was resolved that it should not be final. The campaign of the winter of 1524—5 is perhaps the greatest triumph of Spanish arms, though not more than a third of the Imperialist troops were Spaniards, and though a full meed of praise is due to the Frenchman Bourbon and the Suabian Frundsberg. Yet it was Leyva who kept his garrison of Pavia, mainly German, true, and inspired the inhabitants with his own devotion; it was Pescara, Spaniard by origin and sympathy, who brushed the French army of observation from the line of the Adda, and marched his trained forces and the German levies to the relief of Pavia. The troops were unpaid, unclothed, unfed; when an appeal was made to the Spaniards they abandoned their pay, and offered their cloaks, their very shirts to satisfy the Germans. The French were beaten before the great battle was fought. The Spaniards superior in discipline and ingenuity harassed their quarters with *camisades*, destroying the *morale* of all but their finest troops. Starvation at length forced the Imperialists to risk their all against an enemy superior in numbers and position. When they broke into the park of Mirabello, the headquarters of the French besieging force, the first triumphant rush of the French cavalry withered away under the sustained fire of the Spanish harquebusiers. At Ravenna the Spanish foot had proved their superiority to French and German infantry, but had succumbed to the highly-trained French horse. Pavia marked their triumph at once over Swiss pikes and French lances. Their fire was mainly responsible for the immortal victory.

The older generation of French generals, trained in the wars of three successive reigns, was annihilated at Pavia, and it was long before France replaced it. The king was a prisoner, but this in no way weakened the defensive capabilities of France. We need not here retell the thrice-told tale of the captivity of Francis I. Francis was forced to accept the treaty of Madrid from want of courage to bear captivity. An unscrupulous character never lacks for consolation. Francis flattered himself that he was no liar because he solemnly stated before a notary that he was lying. Charles V was forced to abate his more extreme pretensions by his absolute inability to pay his victorious army, and by the uprising of Italian sentiment against Spanish sway. England had proved herself an ally at once exacting, ineffective and untrustworthy; it was now certain that Wolsey was leading her into the enemies' camp.

Charles' Burgundian inheritance still probably held the first place in his affections. In 1524 he had formulated six alternative schemes for peace with France; in all the central idea was the interchange of the Duchies of Milan and Burgundy. In the treaty of Madrid he abandoned his claim to annex Languedoc to Aragon, but insisted on the cession of Burgundy and of French suzerainty over Flanders, Artois and Tournai. Spanish interests were not, indeed, neglected. Francis was pledged to withdraw support not only from the Duke of Guelders but from the house of Navarre. His abandonment of all Italian claims seemed to secure the supremacy of Spain in the peninsula. But Charles no longer demanded Dauphiné and Provence as an appanage for the Constable Bourbon, and his sister Eleanor was betrothed to the French king instead of to the rebel duke. France thus retained her point of contact with Italy.

Meanwhile the attitude of the Italian states had become

most threatening. Clement VII had been "as a dead man" on hearing of Charles' victory. His friendship was of sufficient importance to extort from the Emperor a favourable treaty, but from the other side appeals were made to his Italian patriotism, to his fears of a General Council, to his greed for territorial gain. Other Italian princes were harassed by contributions, their subjects ruined by the starving soldiery. There was in Italy a passionate desire to rid herself of the Spaniard, which would not now imply the reinstatement of the French. The transference of Francis I from an Italian to a Spanish prison caused an agony of alarm; Charles, it was believed, would make peace with Francis at the expense of Italy. This was no idle fear. The Emperor professed, indeed, to be 'a good Italian.' His Council was divided. One party headed by Lannoy, Viceroy of Naples, urged that peace with France was essential, and that Charles must find his compensation in Italy. The Piedmontese Gattinara, hitherto Charles' most influential adviser, pleaded loyally for Italy: there could be no peace until Francis was humbled to the dust: Burgundy would never be surrendered if Francis were suffered to go free: to effect the Emperor's high aims Italy should be made a partner and not a subject: above all the investiture of Milan should be granted to Francesco Sforza as a pledge of honourable intentions.

It became clear that Gattinara's influence was waning. Milan, Venice, and the Papal Counsellors, while negotiating for a European league formed a purely Italian alliance for Italian liberty—"Italia farà da se." The aim was to restore the system of the five chief states, as it existed before the disastrous cataclysm of 1494. A Sforza still ruled in Milan, a Medici in Florence; Venice and the Papacy seemed substantially unchanged. The military monarchy of Naples should provide the soldier who was to rally round him the manhood of Italy, the armed prince who should make Machiavelli's dream a waking reality. The Italianised line of

Aragon was, indeed, no more. Could it not be replaced by the one Neapolitan house which, as long as hope existed, had loyally stood by its late masters? D'Avalos, Marquis of Pescara, was a Spaniard by origin, but his family had been naturalised in Naples for nearly a century. If he were virtually Italian, his wife, Vittoria Colonna, the most distinguished woman of Italy, was a Roman of the Romans. Who was more fit then than Pescara to avenge on Charles the treason of Ferdinand to the unfortunate king Frederick?

Pescara more than any man had won Pavia for the Emperor, yet he had been deceived and pushed aside by Lannoy; he had ruined himself to keep the Emperor's armies in the field, and yet was denied the modest rewards that he had claimed. Moreover, the clever Milanese secretary, Pescara's intimate friend, thought that he might be tempted by the Crown of Naples; he would bring to the Italian league the military prestige which its generals lacked. His troops were after all mercenaries; Spaniards, Germans and Italians looked rather to the eloquent, liberal, courageous soldier, than to the Flemish Emperor, whom none knew and few respected. The great conflict, which might have been, between Spain and Italy, was decided once for all within Pescara's breast. Spanish traditions or military loyalty kept him true to Spain. He betrayed Morone's confidences, he decoyed the secretary himself, his troops simultaneously occupied Sforza's chief fortresses. The ingenious fabric of Italian liberty fell like a house of cards. Italy by herself, leaderless and divided, was powerless before Spain; she was only dangerous because she could still lean upon French lances and English money-bags.

This aid seemed to be forthcoming. The eternal treaty of friendship between Charles and Francis was immediately followed by the league of Cognac for the expulsion of Charles from Italy. The Italian opposition to Spanish supremacy in Italy was merged in a European opposition to the universal dominion which Charles's enemies believed him to covet, and to which his friends urged him to aspire. The Italian states, Venice, Milan, the Papacy and Florence, were hounded on by France to enter the lists against the Emperor. Henry VIII was named Protector of the Holy League, but although his diplomatic activity had been unceasing, he lent little or no practical assistance. He made it, however, a *sine qua non* that Milan should pass not to the French king, but to its native Duke. Nevertheless Italy was fighting for France rather than for herself.

The prospect before Charles in Italy was gloomy in spite of the collapse of the national conspiracy. Papal and Venetian troops were marching to the relief of the citadel of Milan, where Francesco Sforza still held out. Pescara was dead, Bourbon had not the same authority with the troops; these were scattered over Lombardy, alternately plundering and starving. In Milan itself there was a rising of despair against the Spaniards; in town and country assassination was daily thinning their numbers. Had the French crossed the Alps, or had the Italians possessed a resolute leader, the doom of the Imperial army was sealed. But the Duke of Urbino, who led the Venetian forces, was caution personified, and no friend of Clement VII and the Medici, who had once robbed him of his state. With their usual tenacity the Spaniards clung to the siege of Milan citadel, and forced Sforza to capitulate. The German *condottiere* Frundsberg had led his lanzknechts from Tyrol over Alpine tracks, hitherto untrodden by armed men. The Imperialists were now stronger and better led than any army which could oppose them. The Duke of Milan had already suffered for his desertion of the Imperial cause; the hour of reckoning was approaching for the Pope.

Charles had a long account to settle with Clement VII. It was hard to forgive the Pope's desertion of his cause during the critical months which preceded the battle of Pavia. Since

then Clement had wavered between reconciliation with the
Emperor and open alliance with France; exorbitant demands
had alternated with time-serving humiliations. The "willing
and not willing" brought ruin upon Italy and himself. Lannoy
and the Duke of Sessa, now Spanish ambassador at Rome,
had striven their utmost for accord. Hugo de Moncada, an
envoy extraordinary, an old officer of Caesar Borgia, violent
and unscrupulous, employed more drastic measures. Finding
his terms rejected he utilised the disaffected house of Colonna
to surprise the Vatican; Clement fleeing to the Castle of Sant'
Angelo had a foretaste of horrors to come (September, 1526).
Charles, indeed, on Moncada's own advice, disavowed the
outrage, and Clement took vengeance on his baronial enemies.
The storm was to break not from the South, but from the
North, not from Naples but from Milan.

In February 1527 Frundsberg's German levies, mainly
Lutherans, effected their junction with Bourbon's troops.
Mad with hunger and suffering, these 25,000 men staggered
through Italy towards Rome, dragging their generals with
them. Frundsberg was struck down by paralysis in attempting to quell a mutiny; Bourbon won the affection, if not
the obedience of his men, by showing that he too was a
ruined soldier of fortune with the rest. Lannoy made a
convention with Clement for the payment of the troops, but
neither realised the full danger. They could not believe that
an unfed mob, wholly unprovided with artillery, would dare to
attack Rome, and, if they did, Renzo da Ceri, who had held
Marseilles against the Imperialists, could easily beat them
off; the army of the League had followed Bourbon's troops
through Italy; a single check must mean the invaders' annihilation. This very certainty gave the Imperialists desperate
courage. Bourbon was shot as he scaled the walls, but after
an hour's fight Rome was at the mercy of the wild horde
(May 6, 1527). Clement barely escaped to Sant' Angelo;
in the space of three *credos* more he would have been

caught. Then followed the unutterable horrors of the sack of Rome. A month more, and Sant' Angelo capitulated; the Pope was now the Emperor's prisoner.

It was Charles' fate that all his apparent triumphs turned to gall and wormwood. He wrote to the Princes of Europe expressing his sorrow at the terrible occurrence; he would sooner, he said, be conquered than win such a victory. He ordered his court into mourning, he summarily suspended the rejoicings for the birth of his son Philip, he ordered the clergy to offer prayers for the Pope's liberty. But he took no step to effect this liberty, he resolved to derive full diplomatic advantage from Clement's captivity. Nevertheless his former difficulties were in no sense removed. Plunder does not serve for pay; the only powerful Imperial army was ruined by its excesses. Bourbon was dead and Lannoy was dead. Dead also was the experienced envoy, the Duke of Sessa. The Prince of Orange, the new general, could scarcely rally his troops to fight, while Moncada, now Viceroy of Naples, had none of the antecedents of a peacemaker. France and England had entered into a definite treaty to procure Clement's freedom. Henry VIII, wishing to divorce Catherine, the Emperor's aunt, needed the Pope's favour; this seemed to promise that his intervention would be serious. Lautrec's French troops poured into North Italy; Pavia and Alessandria fell; Andrea Doria recovered Genoa for the French faction.

This French invasion of Italy was not Charles' only difficulty. In Spain public feeling was outraged by the Pope's ill-treatment. The Duke of Alba and the Archbishop of Toledo had at once protested. It was on the remonstrance of the Grandees that Charles had stopped the festivities of the Court. Quinoñes, General of the Franciscans, had told the Emperor that he must release Clement if he did not wish to be dubbed the Lutherans' Captain. All Spaniards rejoiced at Bourbon's death. Spaniards in Italy, indeed, who knew the

Papacy at first-hand, regarded the sack of Rome as a divine visitation, they only hoped that God would find its authors worthy. Soria, envoy at Genoa, recommended the extinction of the temporal power, the source of all European wars. From Rome Bartolommeo Gattinara wrote that some sort of Papal government should exist, but entirely under Imperial control.

The small but influential party of intellect at Charles' Court, which took Erasmus as its guide, had long written and spoken against the Curia; the two brothers Alfonso and Juan Valdés in the Chancellor's service had far outstripped their religious leader in the freedom of their opinions. They now fought the Emperor's cause with pamphlet and despatch. But this very fact gave their enemies a handle. Dominicans and Franciscans had thundered against the Erasmian sect, had refused to be silenced by Emperor, Inquisitor General or Pope. They now drew public opinion over to their side. In the Cortes of 1527 the nobles used their class privilege to refuse a subsidy; the clergy declined on the express ground that the war was against the Pope.

Under pressure such as this the Imperial agents abated their pretensions. Clement surrendered the military keys of the Papal States and guaranteed the payment of the soldiery. Before the convention was executed he escaped to Orvieto, where, though sheltered by the army of the League, he professed neutrality. The French troops pushed on towards Naples; the handful of Imperial troops, evacuating Rome, had only just time to garrison the Southern capital. Moncada engaging the Genoese squadron in the bay was killed, and his ships sunk or taken (April, 1528). A Venetian fleet meanwhile was capturing the Emperor's Apulian ports. Spanish power was well-nigh swept from Italy.

For all this the Imperial troops clung desperately to their defences. Neglected, unpaid and mutinous as they were, the Spaniards, when it came to fighting, showed their quality. They could be temperate and sober when occasion needed, whereas the French could never resist the strong, rich Neapolitan wines so fatal to the weak stomachs of their nation. Naples was once more the grave of a French army which rotted in its trenches. Francis I by insane illiberality alienated the real ruler of Genoa, the naval *condottiere*, Andrea Doria. His fleet sailed for Naples, not now to attack but to relieve the Spaniards. Lautrec's luckless career was ended by the plague. The remnants of the French army making a forlorn retreat was forced by the Prince of Orange to capitulate at Aversa (August, 1528). The veteran refugee Pedro Navarro died a traitor's death in the castle of Castelnuovo, which he had once won for Ferdinand.

One more battle and the war was really over. In Lombardy the French sought to retrieve their Neapolitan disasters. But at Landriano the gouty old general Leyva surprised the dashing young Saint-Pol (April, 1529). Such was the exhaustion of both combatants that this final decisive battle was fought by 8,000 Spaniards against 12,000 French.

It was fortunate for Clement that he had so long wavered. The timid neutrality of the Medici at last turned to his advantage. An Anglo-French alliance might, indeed, have avenged his wrongs, have rid him of the spectre of a General Council, have given to the spiritual power its due independence from the authority of Cæsar. But Clement was first Medici and then Pope; even as Pope his temporal outweighed his spiritual interests. On the fall of Rome Florence had expelled the Medicean government. The Papal States were falling to pieces. The Duke of Urbino was in possession of Perugia, the Venetians, "stealing the cloaks of those that fought," had slipped into Ravenna and Cervia, a Malatesta returned to Rimini, the Duke of Ferrara held Modena and Reggio. All these were the allies of France; from France therefore the Pope could not expect restitution. This alone Charles, now virtually master of Italy, could grant, and that the Pope had remained neutral when French success seemed certain, made the Emperor his debtor.

Charles had little lust for world dominion; he was content with his success; his finances did not guarantee further triumphs; in Germany the existence of the Empire and of Catholicism was threatened alike by Turks and Lutherans; Spain was clamouring for peace. Thus it was that in the treaty of Barcelona Clement received generous terms: Charles engaged to restore the integrity of the Pope's dominions, he bound him to his interests by the marriage of his bastard daughter Margaret to Alessandro de' Medici, who was to become Duke of Florence (June, 1529). Henry VIII and Francis I had vainly warned Clement against peace. But Henry also found that war was ruining the Anglo-Flemish trade, while Margaret, Regent of the Netherlands, could extract no more subsidies. Thus a truce was made for England and the Netherlands, a truce which in the clever hands of Margaret and the Queen-mother, Louise of Savoy, expanded into a general peace. In the treaty of Cambray, the Ladies' Peace, the more humiliating concessions forced on Francis at Madrid were waived. Charles consented to release the French princes for a ransom, to leave his claim to Burgundy to legal process. But the French king withdrew his protection from Robert de la Marck and the Duke of Guelders; from Italy he was absolutely excluded (August 15, 1529).

SECTION III.

SPAIN AND EUROPE, 1529—1556.

CHARLES could at length leave Spain for Italy. He had long craved to be in the forefront of events. His advent, wrote Orange, would be worth 10,000 men. The Italians regarded it with terror; when Charles set foot on shore at Genoa they saw their country under the tyrant's heel. At Bologna Charles received the iron crown of Lombardy, and Clement placed on his head the Imperial coronet (February 1530). The Emperor's generosity was unexpected. The Duke of Ferrara was pardoned for his recent change of sides. Upon Francesco Sforza was conferred the Duchy which he had forfeited. His health was already shattered, but the Emperor gave to him his young niece Christine of Denmark; there could be faint hope that his line would be perpetuated. Venice made her peace, restoring Ravenna and Cervia to the Pope, and her recent Apulian conquests to the kingdom of Naples. Florence alone held out: the republican party would have no surrender to the Medici. Charles was pledged to his ally; in the battle of Gavignana, which decided the fate of the Republic, the Spanish harquebusiers once more turned the fortune of the day. For a second time the Medici returned to Florence under Spanish escort (August, 1530).

To outward appearance Charles had restored Italy to her previous condition before the battle of Marignano had wrested

Lombardy from a native prince. Yet all men felt that all was altered. The Pope was little more than the Emperor's chaplain, with the Papal territories for his stipend. The Dukes of Florence, Milan and Savoy, married to a daughter, a niece, a sister-in-law of Charles, were lesser stars in the family constellation; the Dukes of Mantua, Ferrara and Urbino moved in the Imperial orbit. Between Florentine and Papal territory a Spanish garrison nominally protected the Sienese republic against her exiles. Venice was intact and independent, but, once the strongest of the Italian states, she was relatively weak against a King of Naples who was also King of Spain.

Charles gained by his very liberality. By giving the County of Asti, the old possession of the house of Orleans, to the Duke of Savoy he bribed the porter of the Alps to close his gates against the French. Profitable above all was his generosity to Genoa. The town recovered her liberty and her territory; Doria was her truly national and patriotic Doge. But for all this Genoa was for more than two centuries Spain's water-gate to Italy. Through Genoa poured the Spanish levies which were henceforth to hold Lombardy, which tramped over Alpine passes to Franche Comté and the Netherlands, or opened communications with the allied Hapsburgs in Vorarlberg and Tyrol. Henceforth the Spanish Crown found in the Dorias its admirals; their squadron, the most seaworthy in Italian waters, was permanently hired to the Kings of Spain. If Spanish supremacy at sea was threatened by Turks and Barbaresques, it had at least established itself at the expense of France. Barcelona and Genoa, Naples and Palermo formed the quadrilateral of the Western Mediterranean. Genoa, moreover, was tied to Spain by golden chains; her bankers fattened on the extravagance of the Spanish Crown and people; her merchants monopolised the profitable trades in every port of Spain and Sicily. To the ruling capitalist class revolt from Spain meant ruin.

From the summer of 1530 to the close of 1532 Charles

was in Germany, vainly striving to check the rank growth of heresy. That he was at length forced to make concessions to the Lutheran princes in the compromise of Nuremberg was mainly due to the advance of the Turk upon Vienna. Charles put himself at the head of the Imperial army; but for the Sultan's retreat the Spanish foot would have tested its worth against the Janissaries in the Danube valley.

During these years important changes befell Charles's immediate circle. On June 5, 1530, died Gattinara, who since the death of Chièvres had exercised an important though not a controlling influence. This, however, had waned during Francis I's imprisonment, and Gattinara had been for a season almost in disgrace. Charles's chief ministers were henceforth Granvelle and Cobos, the former undertaking mainly the affairs of the Netherlands and Germany, the latter those of Spain and Italy. In December Charles lost his aunt, Margaret, Regent of the Netherlands, who had acted at once as his mother, and as instructress in the art of policy. She was replaced by his sister Mary, the widowed queen of Hungary, who proved herself as capable, as devoted, and yet more masculine. Charles's brother Ferdinand was in January 1531 elected King of the Romans. Charles thus in the most formal manner secured the succession for the collateral line; it was a definite proof that Spain had become the centre of his own interests and hopes. A free hand was left to Ferdinand and Mary in their respective spheres. The system may almost be described as a family federation, and may be compared with that of Napoleon in the height of his power.

In passing through Italy on his return to Spain Charles formed a defensive league with the Italian states. Yet his hold upon Italy was insecure. Clement was already veering round towards France. In Charles's interest, indeed, he excommunicated Henry VIII, but he married his cousin, Catherine de' Medici, to the French king's second son, and held a suspicious interview with Francis at Marseilles

(November 1533). Francis was intriguing both with Pope and Protestants. At his instance Philip of Hesse restored the exiled Duke Ulrich to Würtemberg; the rich principality was lost to the Catholic Hapsburgs and won for their Lutheran opponents (1534). Francis, confident in his new alliances, was demanding Milan, Genoa and Asti, when Clement VII died (September 1534). This was the Emperor's gain. The shiftiness of the Medicean Pope had been so incurable, his punishment so terrible, that the Papal-Imperial alliance could never be secure. Clement could never have forgiven Charles, and Charles could never have trusted Clement. The election of Cardinal Farnese as Paul III was hailed as an Imperial victory. Charles might hope for the security of the Spanish possessions in Italy, for willing aid against heresy in Germany, for zeal in the reform of the Catholic Church, for a generous percentage on the revenues of the Spanish clergy.

The years from 1533 to 1541 form perhaps the most essentially Spanish period of Charles's reign. In nothing was he more in harmony with his Spanish subjects than in the burning desire to check the advance of Mahommedan power in the western Mediterranean. This was no mere Quixotism. The very existence of Spain, Sicily and Naples seemed at stake. The enemies were no longer the unwieldy Moorish kingdoms, always liable to disruption from internal faction or the attack of less civilised African fanatics. The foe was now the pirate state of Algiers ruled by Barbarossa. This corsair and his elder brother, natives of Lesbos, were pirates from early youth. The elder brother, invited by the Arab ruler of Algiers to expel the Spaniards from Peñon, killed his host and usurped his state. Wiser than the Spaniards he attempted to create a territorial kingdom by the conquest of Tlemcen. He was, however, beaten and killed by the Moors and the Spanish garrison of Oran (1518).

The younger brother Kheir-ed-Din, nicknamed Barbarossa, reduced to the possession of Algiers, put himself under the suzerainty of the Porte, and became the first of the Turkish Beglierbegs of North Africa, carrying the Crescent to the Straits. Janissaries were sent to his aid; he could buy at will the fighting population of Anatolia. Algiers became the Alsatia for adventurers, refugees and renegades from the whole of Southern Europe. Barbarossa's chief reliance was on a corps of renegades, while he had a body-guard of Spaniards. His troops were recruited also from the captives chained to the galleys, many of whom abjured their faith to gain wealth and freedom in the corsair's service. To these were added the most adventurous of the Moors expelled or voluntarily migrating from southern Spain, full of traditional hatred of the Spaniards, and accustomed to their methods of warfare. Thus the Spaniards had to fight, not with swarms of undisciplined Moors, but with troops of as good material as their own, and as highly trained. The corsair ships were in point of construction the finest in Europe, and their captains among the best seamen. Barbarossa also and several of his successors became admirals of the Turkish fleet, which was thus added to the squadrons of North Africa.

The government of Charles fully realised the danger of this union of Barbarossa and the Turks. The African experiences of the reign had not been fortunate. Hugo de Moncada's attack on Algiers had ended in capitulation, massacre and headlong flight (1519). The capture of Rhodes by the Turks in 1522 might seem, indeed, of not unmixed disadvantage to Spain, for Charles had settled the expelled Hospitallers at Tripoli and Malta, thus drawing a bolt between the western and eastern Mediterranean. But the Algerian corsair was fully a match for the Hospitallers and the Spaniards. He created a territorial kingdom, taking Bona and Constantine, and then annihilated the Spanish garrison at Peñon (1529). In 1533 he utilised the distracted condition of Tunis to drive the feeble king, Muley Hassan, from the throne, and spread his sway far into the interior.

The occupation of Tunis was a direct threat to Sicily and Naples; it was then the key of the western Mediterranean, while it brought the ruler of Algiers into easy communication with the Porte. Thousands of captives were yearly carried off from Spain and Italy; Morisco emigrants were conveyed by Barbarossa from Granada and Valencia to settlements in North Africa. The Spanish sea-board was becoming a wilderness, while that of Africa was growing in wealth and population.

Charles's determination to take Tunis created wild excitement. Nobles and artisans, friars and even women crowded to Barcelona to join the fleet. It was a genuine crusade. Doria sailed in with his Genoese galleys, Prince Louis of Portugal brought round from Lisbon his ocean-going caravels. From Genoa and Ostia, from Naples, Sicily and Southern Spain, Italian levies, Spanish veterans and German mercenaries converged upon the *rendezvous* at Cagliari. The galleys of the Pope and of the Knights of Malta fitly took part in the religious war. Charles, hoisting the Crucifix at his masthead, stood on his deck amid the nobility of the great crusading nation; the leader, he said, was Christ, and the Emperor His Standard-bearer.

Goletta, standing on the neck of land which flanks the narrow channel to the lagoon of Tunis, barred the Emperor's progress. After a month's desperate siege Goletta fell (July 1535). A week more and the troops half-dead, as Charles wrote, with heat and thirst struggled through the sand to Tunis. The Moors were beaten outside the walls, the 20,000 Christian captives rose within the city and opened the gates to Charles. At Goletta Barbarossa had lost 80 ships, here and at Tunis hundreds of cannon fell into Spanish hands; many, it was noticed, were stamped with the *fleur-de-lis*. It was a really great achievement. The campaign was fought in the full heat of an African summer; every barrel of biscuits, every butt of water, must be brought by sea from Sicily; there were no draught animals, the soldiers dragged their guns by hand.

Even now it would be no light task to find six weeks' supply for 30,000 men engaged with an African enemy equally well provided with artillery and munitions.

Muley Hassan was restored to Tunis under Spanish suzerainty, ceding to the Emperor Goletta, Bona and Biserta. Charles wished at once to sail for Algiers, but his army had suffered too severely. A little later he meditated a blow at head-quarters; he longed to head a Crusade, in concert with Venice, against the Porte. This was prevented by the Sultan's alliance with France, and by the inevitable outbreak of a fresh war in Italy. Charles for the first time visited his South-Italian Kingdoms. The pale-faced youth, who used to say little and count for less, was now the hero and the saviour of southern Europe. Francis I had taunted him as a stay-at-home, but the six weeks of an African campaign had eclipsed the two days' fight at Marignano.

In November 1535 died Francesco Sforza, and the duchy of Milan reverted to the Emperor. Francis I, in spite of the renunciation made at Madrid and Cambray, at once advanced the claim of his second son, the Duke of Orleans. The cession of Milan to a French prince, whose wife Catherine had claims to the possessions of the Medici, was for Charles impossible; yet refusal made war a certainty. The war, however, did not nominally arise from the demand for Milan, but from the French King's preposterous claims on Savoy. Hitherto the Dukes, closely connected with the French dynasty, had leaned towards France, whose troops had marched at will through Savoyard territory. This privilege was now refused, for Duke Charles III was under the influence of his spirited wife, Beatrice of Portugal, the sister-in-law and ardent admirer of the Emperor. In retaliation French troops occupied Savoy almost without resistance (March 1536), and crossing the Alps took Turin and great part of Piedmont.

Charles was still in Italy; it was impossible that he should overlook this outrage. Instead of attacking the chain of French posts in Piedmont he reverted to his old scheme for the conquest of Provence. He led his army in person across the Var. No French force of consequence met him in the field, but the whole country was devastated by the French King's orders, while the few towns still occupied were too strongly held to make attack possible or prudent. In November Charles was forced to a humiliating retreat; his army was ruined by disease; Leyva, the best of his old generals, had succumbed; the Emperor's Tunisian laurels were shrivelled by the chilling *bise* of Provence.

For two summers more the war dragged on in Piedmont and the Netherlands. For the first time the French more than held their own. The truce for the Netherlands which internal discontent forced the Regent to conclude in 1537 made the Emperor's position in Milan the more critical, for the whole French army could be thrown on Lombardy. The Pope earnestly intervened in favour of a general peace. For this Charles and Francis were too obstinate, but through Papal mediation a ten years' truce was signed at Nice (June 1538).

By this truce the hold of Spain upon Italy was seriously weakened. The Emperor, indeed, retained Milan, and his troops garrisoned one-third of Piedmont. The attempt of Filippo Strozzi and the Florentine exiles upon the newly appointed Duke Cosimo had ended in discomfiture. But the French now commanded the passes of the Alps and were firmly settled on the upper Po. They held, moreover, the protectorate of the little state of Mirandola, which became the focus of intrigue against Spanish influence, the sanctuary for exiles from Naples, Milan, Florence and Siena.

During the negotiations at Nice Emperor and King, though staying within a league of each other, had refused to meet. Immediately afterwards the world was astonished by their enthusiastic interview at Aigues-Mortes. All old grievances seemed to be forgotten. Definite shape was given to a project, long in the air, for settling Milan upon a French prince and a Hapsburg princess. Charles had previously professed himself willing to grant the Duchy to the King's third son, while refusing it to Henry of Orleans, the husband of Catherine de' Medici. By his elder brother's death Henry had become Dauphin, and negotiations were rendered easier; but this creation of a buffer Valois-Hapsburg state was not destined to be realised.

During the fit of friendship with Francis Charles had obtained leave to pass through France to punish his town of Ghent, which for reasons professedly financial, but partly religious, had rebelled against the Regent. After crushing Ghent Charles changed his mind with regard to Milan. He now proposed to marry his brother's daughter to the French prince, and to create for them a kingdom of the Netherlands and Franche Comté. In compensation Francis was required to resign all Italian claims, and to evacuate Savoyard territory. Nor was this all; Charles would settle for ever the question of Navarre by marrying the little heiress to his son Philip, while the French King should purchase the possessions of the house which lay northwards of the Pyrenees.

These were statesmanlike proposals, and, had they taken effect, might have saved Spain immeasurable calamities. She was strong enough to hold Italy, but not to hold both Italy and the Netherlands, and to assume all liabilities of war along the Franco-German frontier from Alps to Channel. But Francis could never forget his dream of Lombardy, the scene of his first great triumph and his subsequent disgrace. He taxed Charles with perfidy, and the delicate thread of amity was snapped. Francis ostentatiously married the heiress of Navarre to the Duke of Cleves, who had occupied Guelders, although this, under a convention with the deceased Duke, had reverted to the Emperor. Charles replied by formally investing Philip with Milan. Meanwhile, as in 1535, there was a lull before the storm; this Charles employed in the attempt to break Barbarossa's power in his own Algerian stronghold.

The capture of Tunis had ended in disappointment. Barbarossa was so little humbled that three months later he raided the Balearic Isles, and carried off the population of Port Mahon, including 5000 of the captives released at Tunis. Since then in French alliance he had scoured the coasts of Naples. A joint Spanish-Venetian expedition to the Adriatic foreshadowed the greater campaign of Lepanto. At Prevesa Barbarossa might have been crushed by Doria but for the time-dishonoured rivalry between "the two eyes of Italy," Genoa and Venice. The only result was the annihilation of the considerable Spanish garrison left in Castelnovo.

Time was ripe for a decisive blow against Barbarossa, but it was also overripe. Against the advice of admirals and generals Charles insisted on attacking Algiers late in the autumn of 1541. Yet failure seemed impossible. Barbarossa was absent; Algiers was weakly held by some 800 Turks and 5000 half-trained Moors and renegades. Charles's regular troops numbered at least 22,000 Spaniards, Germans and Italians. The fleet of 200 ships was commanded by Andrea Doria. With Charles sailed all his most distinguished warriors, Cortes, Alba, Santa Cruz, the younger Frundsberg, Ferrante Gonzaga. No sooner had the troops landed than disaster befell them. A phenomenal equinoctial gale blew down the tents, destroyed stores and ammunition, and finally drove the ships from their moorings to seek shelter to eastward. The garrison of Algiers, ably led, had a light task in completing the discomfiture of troops whose *morale* was already ruined. But for Charles's imperturbable courage on the retreat to rejoin the ships scarcely a man would have escaped. The very disaster made his reputation as a cool, seasoned soldier; it gave him probably his passion for fight. The great armada was yet further shattered by a recrudescence of the storm. All hope of success against the infidel was over for the reign of Charles.

Barbarossa died in 1546, but his son Hassan, the Anatolian Dragut, and the Jew Sinan successfully championed the Crescent against the Cross.

The misfortunes of Christianity were the opportunity of France. The murder of the French agents, Rincon and Fregoso, who were passing through Lombardy to the Porte, was attributed to the Marquis del Guasto, governor of Milan (May 1541). When six months later Charles's power seemed shattered at Algiers this murder served as a useful pretext for hostilities. War was declared in 1542. The French everywhere prepared to take the offensive. Yet in this last struggle between the two rivals Charles once more asserted his superiority. The Duke of Alba, inimitable in defensive warfare, drove the Valois from the walls of Perpignan. In June 1543 Charles left Spain for Italy, and journeying thence to Speyer threw himself on the generosity or credulity of the Diet. German aid enabled him to crush the Duke of Cleves and to annex Guelders before Francis moved a man to save his most valuable ally.

The Turkish fleet, after ravaging the Italian coasts, joined the French admiral in an attack on Nice, the last refuge of the luckless Duke of Savoy, and wintered in the friendly French harbour of Toulon. Yet the combined fleets met with no marked success, and the cry of Christendom rose loud against the hideous coalition. In Italy alone the French arms triumphed. At Cerisola, a Spanish general, Del Guasto, for once lost his head; the French lances under the Duc d'Enghien at length broke the Spanish foot. The exiles at Mirandola prepared to stir the embers of discontent throughout all Italy. But d'Enghien could not move from lack of funds; the exiles marching to his aid found Spanish garrisons always in their front. Francis must for once neglect Italy for France, for every man was needed for her defence. The King of England and the Emperor were both upon her soil.

The hostility between Charles and Henry had long been a

diminishing quantity. The fall of Wolsey, of Anne Boleyn, of Cromwell had satisfied any desire that Charles might have for vengeance. Catherine's death relieved him from his chivalrous obligations. Even before this he had urged his envoy to uphold her cause with non-militant discretion; he had been very cautious in pressing the claims of Mary. The English ministers he had long won; Henry's personal rancour had alone delayed an understanding. The old reasons for the Anglo-Spanish-Burgundian alliance still subsisted; it was an added gain if Henry could be withdrawn from a Franco-Lutheran combination.

Thus in 1543 an alliance actually came to pass, and in 1544 Henry VIII appeared before Boulogne, while Charles, invading France in person, spread terror to the very walls of Paris. Of a sudden peace was made at Crespy (Sept. 1544) in the full flood of Charles's fortune. The fall of Boulogne decided Francis, but the Emperor's motives are less certain. He was doubtless already influenced by his desire to settle the religious question in Germany. But his military position was by no means strong. Time had been lost upon a paltry siege; Henry VIII preferred conquest to cooperation. Hitherto Charles had relied upon composite armies; Spaniards and Italians, he would say, were the arms and legs of a *corps d'armée*, and Germans the stomach. He had with him few Spaniards or Italians; his troops were mainly German, of bad quality. Germans rarely fought without their pay, and Charles had little pay to give. A week's haggling or a day's mutiny might have placed him at his rival's mercy.

On the stage of Crespy the old play was once more acted with trifling variations in the lines. Charles engaged to give to the Dauphin's brother either his niece with the Netherlands or Franche Comté, or his daughter with the Duchy of Milan; within four months he must make the choice. The death of the French prince saved him from the wearisome alternative. There is little evidence that Charles had hitherto determined to incorporate Milan with the Spanish dominions; henceforth he seemed resolved to concentrate every inch of territory in the hands of Philip.

During the reign of Charles Spain spent most of her energy abroad; her domestic history is almost lost to view. In this, indeed, the defeat of the Communes at Villalar was the last striking event. The interest hereafter was mainly constitutional and economic. The nobles by their victory had expected to regain authority both with court and country. Before Charles's return they had clamoured for the confiscation of the rebels' goods or for compensation from the Crown. Charles was warned by his one noble *confidant*, the Marquis of Denia, to bring foreign troops. By so doing he secured his independence. Moreover nobles and communes still sullenly watched each other; in the defeated towns Charles might easily find defence against oligarchical pretensions. The consideration of the Crown, if not its popularity, was increased by the introduction of the more elaborate household, the more stilted ceremonial of the Burgundian Court. The expenses of the household, especially those of the table, were quadruple those of the Catholic kings.

In this expenditure the Crown found its gain. Of the eight Councillors of State only two were Spaniards, but the presence of 100 Spanish gentlemen at Court, each with his attendant suite, implied the formation of a royal party. Charles, after his return, frankly stated that Castile must be for Castilians: he did not repeat his error in granting the greater benefices to aliens. Yet he slowly learnt to be a Spaniard. As late as 1525 we read of mutual dislike between King and people. His manners were not young enough to make him popular. He was reserved and grave, untiring in public business, patient in listening, prudent in reply. His pleasures were few, he hunted a little, but was not inclined to women and other such frivolities. As compared with his predecessors he was thought stingy; extravagant as was his court, his personal habits, apart from his abnormal appetite, were unduly simple. Those who relied on the cast-off clothes of royalty were often unfashionably shabby. Yet as a ruler he had two virtues essentially Castilian; he had inherited his grandmother's high standard of justice and her fervent piety.

In 1526 Charles at length yielded to his subjects' wishes; he abandoned the idea of an English bride, and married his Portuguese cousin, Isabella, whose dowry was as attractive as her person. Marriages made for prudential reasons have a high average of happiness, and that of Charles increased this average. King and Queen were tenderly devoted to each other, and the Iberian union increased his popularity. Marriage, moreover, induced Charles to travel. As yet there was no capital in Spain, though Valladolid was the more usual residence of the Court. Castilians complained that Charles had seen so little of his kingdom. Now, with his bride, he made a progress through Andalusia and Granada. The old Moorish capital appealed to the artistic side of his nature, and here by the side of the Alhambra he began to build a renaissance palace, which still remains unfinished. The funds were drawn from a peculiar source; the Moors bought themselves free from the extreme rigours of the Inquisition. It was very rarely that Charles sold his soul, though more than once for diplomatic reasons he delayed or endangered its salvation.

In striking contrast to Charles's concession to the Moors of Granada was his extreme and personal severity towards those of Valencia. These latter had bravely defended their masters in the hour of peril; they had been forced to baptism by revolutionists since conquered and proscribed. They naturally reverted to their former faith and customs. The Inquisition held that they were renegades, and Charles upheld the Inquisition. All the experts, the Council of Aragon, the Cortes of Valencia pleaded for leniency, and urged the difficulties of compulsion. Charles replied that all great deeds were difficult. Threats of enforced baptism and exile drove the more spirited peasants into the Sierra. Hence they repeatedly drove back the local and royal forces, and were only in 1526 beaten by the German lanzknechts whom Charles had brought to Spain. It is possible that the difficulties of this savage little war contributed to the compromise with the Moriscos of Granada. The decimation of the Valencian peasantry completed the ruin of their landlords. The industrious East and South of Spain have paid dearly for the extravagant orthodoxy of the central provinces.

The decline of constitutional liberties in Castile is often dated from the defeat of Villalar. It is forgotten that the Catholic Kings had arbitrarily used or dispensed with their Cortes, and that during its revolt the third estate was laying claims to powers which it never had possessed. It is forgotten also that under Charles the influence of Cortes was still real and often freely exercised. The defeat of the Communes had little obvious effect on the relations of Crown and Cortes. Even in 1523 the deputies were peculiarly enterprising, insisting four times upon redress before supply, resenting the presence of the Chancellor at their debates, and the King's prescription as to the form which the instructions from their constituencies should take. Charles had a high sense of law and precedent, he would suffer no prejudice to the prerogative of the Crown. He therefore resisted the demand for the priority of redress, while the deputies themselves admitted that the limitation of their powers was by custom within his competence. The presence of the Chancellor at the debates was an innovation which was not repeated.

Charles showed respect for the traditional rights of the Cortes. His necessities, moreover, forced him to summon them with regularity; they met on the average every three years throughout the reign. However objectionable were his methods of raising money he never levied fresh taxes without consent. In one respect he conceded an innovation which should have proved a valuable constitutional safeguard, for he instituted, on petition, a standing committee drawn by lot from the deputies and resembling that of Aragon (1525). The function of this was to watch over the performance of promises made during the session. On two memorable occasions Charles submitted to a defeat. At the crisis of the war with Clement VII (1527) he called upon nobles and clergy for a patriotic grant. The nobles stood absolutely on their right of exemption; the clergy more delicately declined, and Charles must needs dismiss the Commons without obtaining supply.

In 1528, it is true, the towns proved more liberal, and at the Emperor's urgent demand they granted a subsidy for the war with France. Yet the memory of old parliamentary rights was still fresh. The deputies clamoured aloud for reform, as their predecessors had done on every occasion since the accession of Charles. No less than one hundred and sixty-six separate reforms were demanded. The old grievances of the inordinate aggregation of land in the hands of the clergy, and of its being tied up in perpetual settlement by the nobles, were aired once more with the same want of success as previously; the reform of the administration was urged, as were measures for increasing the trade with England and France, for avoiding the unjust pressure of taxation upon industry, for improving the food supply of the country, for the suppression of extravagance in dress, and many others. But the most important recommendation, as marking a change in public opinion since the Cortes of Toledo in 1525, was that a general amnesty should be granted to the Comuneros. Perhaps the Cortes saw already indications of the dry-rot which had entered into the parliamentary institutions which it was their duty to uphold. In any case this recommendation, like many others, was politely shelved by the sovereign[1].

Ten years passed and the Commons again proved restive. The Cortes of 1538 are very memorable. At a moment of great national danger nobles and clergy were once more sum-

---

[1] For this paragraph I am indebted to Major Martin Hume.—E. A.

moned. They were begged to assent to a *sisa*, an indirect tax on meat, which would affect all classes and thus produce a common interest between the three estates. Charles offered in return to place much of the financial administration under parliamentary control. The nobles desired a consultation with the Commons, but this, as contrary to precedent, Charles refused. They then again insisted on their privilege of exemption, and were angrily dismissed to their homes or to wherever they might be pleased to go. Even the Commons stoutly resisted the *sisa*, and only on the pledge that the subject should never again be raised was the usual subsidy granted. Henceforth the nobles were not summoned to the Cortes. The importance of this has been much exaggerated. The presence of the nobles had been exceptional, and had in no sense added to the strength of the Commons. Had they, indeed, accepted the liability for taxation the result might have been very different, but refusal was a foregone conclusion.

Thus the Cortes had so far held their own. Nevertheless it is true that in the reign of Charles their character began to deteriorate, and this was undoubtedly due in part to the defeat of the Communeros. It was not merely that possible progress received a final check, for in national life there can be no complete standstill. The fruits of Villalar were reaped neither by the victorious nobles nor by the vanquished democracy, but partly by the impassive Crown and partly by the lesser gentry, whose action, as a class, had been ambiguous. The latter seized the opportunity yet further to monopolise the municipal offices, and therefore indirectly the representation in the Cortes. The Moorish wars no longer gave employment, and the gentry could not trade; they therefore sought a livelihood in town service. Curiously enough this representation by official gentry prevailed at the moment when the towns reached the fulness of their prosperity, when trade became the chief interest and deserved the most ample representation in the national Council. The Cortes of 1538 proved how inadequate this was. The refusal of the *sisa* implied that extraordinary taxation would continue to be direct, and would fall exclusively on the non-noble classes, whereas the representatives themselves were exempt from liability.

In this municipal change there were several stages. The gentry first petitioned for admission to office in towns where they were hitherto disqualified. They then claimed a fixed proportion of offices, and finally demanded the exclusion of plebeians. While the members did not adequately represent their towns, the privileged towns less and less effectively represented the country. Even in 1520 Galicia had complained that the province had its mouthpiece in Zamora, a town outside its borders. Any extension of representation was opposed purely by the privileged towns. They resisted all requests for the admission of fresh constituencies on the plea of monopoly and privilege. Thus it is probable that the Cortes had no firm hold upon public opinion. The government, moreover, increased its influence over the towns through the *corregidores*, who, in spite of frequent petitions, were now appointed for all towns and for long terms. The pushing, active classes, occupied in feverish, commercial progress, seemed to ignore their political decadence.

It is difficult to resist the conclusion that the perpetual and ineffectual repetition of the same demands in Cortes was a mere sedative to popular discontent. They were seldom seriously pressed: they became, as so much in Spain, meaningless but solemn forms. The deputies urged the grievances of their constituents until their personal wants were satisfied. Thus the system of gratifications, by no means introduced by Charles, became under him or later an engine of corruption. The right of rejecting petitions had long been exercised, but Charles could venture to disdain the courteous formulæ which hitherto had decently veiled refusal. Castile had, as England in the eighteenth century, outgrown her constitutional machinery.

Under Charles the system of administrative councils was yet further developed. A more definite form was given to the Council of State, which seemed likely to become the highest consultative body, dealing with alliances, with peace and war, with appointments to embassies, viceroyalties and commands-in-chief. But there was still no fixed number and few official members; it consisted of men of experience from all the Emperor's dominions, who had risen to the top in Church and State. This Council was, perhaps, mainly of importance as entailing the growth of the Secretariate, though under Charles a single Secretary, Gonzalo Perez, performed all its functions. The trade of the Indies was already entirely regulated by the powerful *Casa de Contratacion*. But to Charles was due the Council of the Indies, which embraced every department of civil or ecclesiastical administration in the colonies (1524 and 1529). From the Council of Castile was detached a delegacy, termed the Council of the Chamber, for the bestowal of royal patronage. Finally in 1555 the Council of Italy was apparently separated from that of Aragon, while the same year witnessed the establishment of the Council of Flanders.

Charles had carefully watched the Castilian nobles; he gave them little effective power, but high and profitable appointments in his dominions; he treated them with honour and consideration. This is characteristic of his policy; he had early learnt his lesson, and was resolved not to risk a conflict with any section of his Castilian subjects. With Aragon he was somewhat less scrupulous. Contemporaries state that he tried to extort from the Cortes a surrender of national privileges, and that he begged the Pope to release him from his oath to maintain them. Once at least he committed a breach of the cherished privilege of *manifestacion* by denying the right of a defendant to place himself under the *justicia's* protection pending trial. In Castile he had retained a tight hold upon his clergy, yet after 1522 he kept it, with few exceptions, exclusively national. In Aragon he conferred two important sees upon Italian adherents. Yet even here, when pressed by the Cortes, he drew back and respected national prejudice and interest. In Spain Charles never pushed his absolutism to conclusions after his first lesson, and this is no small credit in a character by nature obstinate.

If constitutional independence dwindled, material prosperity advanced throughout the reign of Charles. On his accession the land was still mainly agricultural or rather pastoral. Silk manufacture was active among the Moors of the South, and there were cloth factories of repute in Central Spain. But the lower classes generally still lived on the produce of their homesteads, or on the wages of labour or service; the middle and upper classes on rents, salaries and the interest of the state debt. The sudden demand from the Indies changed all this. The settlers were not numerous, but they made their money easily, and would not labour to supply their needs. Whatever they wanted they must have, and at whatever price. European produce was also foisted by the colonial governments upon the natives, with or without their will. To supply these needs Spain had the exclusive right. Her agriculture and her manufacture must therefore alike be modified to meet an entirely new demand.

Thus it fell about that Spain became for a short space a manufacturing country. The very district which had been the scene of the rising of the Communes reached within a quarter of a century after their defeat the zenith of its prosperity. Medina del Campo, a phœnix from the flames, became the mart of the woollen trade, its fairs were the centre of the system of credit and exchange. Toledo, Segovia, Valladolid became busy manufacturing towns. Spanish life was being profoundly altered. There was a rush from the country to the towns, where wages were rising by leaps and bounds. The manufacturing hands in Toledo were quintupled between 1525 and 1550; in some towns beggars and vagabonds were forced into the factories. The cloth trade spread southward to

Granada; the silk manufacture spread northwards to Seville and thence to Toledo. We find the young Mary, Queen of Scots, receiving a gift of blue and red silk stockings from Valencia, as being of the finest quality in the world. A sure sign of the growth of manufacture was the differentiation of function. The small master-clothworker gave place to the capitalist manufacturer who employed some hundreds of hands, while the middleman undertook the shipment and distribution. Charles himself was deeply interested in the American trade; he believed it capable of indefinite expansion.

The fluctuations in agriculture were little less than those in trade. Hitherto tillage had been completely subordinate to pasture, but for the rest of the century there was a struggle between the two industries. The situation was the reverse of that in England. There sheep-farming was the modern encroaching element, and English conservatism called upon the legislature to check it. In Castile arable enclosures began to spread at the expense of the great sheep-rearing corporation, the *mesta*, and the more conservative bodies, the Cortes and the Council of Castile, were disposed to regard this as a breach of vested interests. The *mesta* hitherto had been all-powerful. It was a vast union, with its representative administration, its courts, its common chest. It forbade competition among its brethren, and so beat down the rents of pasture; it boycotted any landowner who dared to evict a member. Between the winter pastures in the sunny plains of Estremadura and the summer feeding grounds in the highlands of Castile lay a broad waste track over which no plough could pass. The Crown encouraged the *mesta* because its revenues depended on the tolls; the people tolerated it because the rents, though low, were certain and gave no trouble. And after all wool was Spain's most profitable product.

The colonial trade introduced a rapid change. The colonists cared only for gold; they would not till the soil. They drank largely, yet, except on the Pacific coast, they were forbidden to plant vines. Hence Spain must supply her colonies, and the area of wheat, vines and olives annually increased. Charles encouraged this tendency; his Ebro canal provided large stretches of Aragon with irrigation. A law was even passed forbidding the conversion of arable land into pasture. The Government raised the *maximum* price of grain; this encouraged the proprietors to sow and placed them in direct opposition to the *mesta*. In the South the agricultural interest split within itself, the growers of corn protesting against the extension of vineyards, which took bread from the poor. Once more, however, national traditions got the upper hand. The colonists had not acclimatised sheep, they regarded cotton clothing as degrading, and hence an increased demand for woollens. The pendulum swung back, and not only was fresh enclosure forbidden, but it was ordered that broken pasture belonging to the Crown, the Church and corporations must again revert to pasture (1552). Yet at the close of the reign agriculture was generally thriving; flax had been introduced, and the import of linen forbidden, to encourage the new industry.

Notwithstanding these roseate prospects the condition of trade and agriculture was not quite wholesome. The Cortes were in absolute ignorance of economic laws; they regarded it as the one function of government to protect the interest of the consumer, especially of the upper middle class consumers, who alone were represented in the Cortes. This was the meaning of the severe restrictions placed on native cloths to ensure quality and prevent fraud, of the governmental *maximum* fixed on the chief necessaries of life, of the so-called monopolies which, in order to eliminate the middleman, gave to individual producers the sole right of selling. Municipal granaries stored grain against bad seasons, and by their rights of preemption and of fixing prices were formidable competitors to private growers. The practical inconveniences arising from the want of currency, of horses, mules, leather, olive oil, breadstuffs.

were met by frequent laws prohibiting export. Spain was anything but a protective country, in spite of occasional protective regulations. In the interest of the consumer she encouraged imports. Her chronic difficulty was that she desired to buy without a corresponding willingness either to sell or to pay.

Prices throughout Europe were rising rapidly, and in Spain even faster than elsewhere. Foreigners attributed this to the indolence of the Castilian workman, who measured his wage by the disinclination with which he did his work. It was partly no doubt due to the inpour of precious metals, although the rise preceded any appreciable output from the Indies. In contradiction to this rise of prices there was throughout Spain generally an undoubted lack of currency. This was ascribed to the greed of Charles's Flemish suite upon his first visit to Spain. The superior purity of Spanish coinage undoubtedly encouraged its surreptitious export, but the main cause of the inconvenience was probably the backwardness of communications. Currency was badly distributed; it did not find its way beyond the great commercial centres, and, as commerce was much in the hands of foreigners, ultimately in spite of prohibition oozed away from Spain.

This rise of prices accompanied by a lack of currency horrified the Cortes, the official representatives of the consumer. They were in entire ignorance of the causes, and endeavoured to counteract the evil by a series of contradictory experiments which hampered both commerce and agriculture, and was ultimately destined to ruin both. At one moment they would forbid the export of breadstuffs, and force the price of wheat to its former level, regardless of the doubled cost of production. At another they strove to prohibit altogether the export of cloth, silk, leather and iron to the Indies, in order to compel the colonists to manufacture, and so, by stopping the drain upon the home supply, lower its cost for the home consumer. Yet again in the consumer's interest they opened the flood-gates to foreign imports manufactured at a far cheaper price than the rate of wages and produce in Spain could allow.

There were of course real difficulties. Nations, as individuals, have their opportunities too early or too late. Spain found her market before she was ready to supply it. Not only was she embarrassed by the feverish activity of the colonial trade, but her own gentry brought into contact with the wider European world learnt higher standards of comfort and luxury, and all other classes must imitate the gentry. Hence the supply never caught up the demand in a country where originally there was little capital and no habits of industry, and hence again the introduction of foreign capitalists who financed Spain at a ruinous rate of interest, and the competition of cheaper foreign goods.

A dislike for foreigners was common to all countries, but in Spain it was carried farther than elsewhere. Yet Spain, if she was to be equal to her new position, above all nations needed foreign aid. The Spaniard could conquer and keep down a huge subject population, but he had not the practical faculties necessary for trade and financial administration. Lacking the business talent himself he despised and hated it in others. The restrictions on foreigners were due not to Crown but to people. Ferdinand and Isabella had encouraged German, French and Italian colonies in Spain, although the people grumbled. When after Isabella's death the Cortes proposed to exclude foreigners from dealing in the necessaries of life and from municipal office, and to limit their residence to a year, Ferdinand frankly asserted that Spain could not do without them. Charles was for a time forced to yield to his subjects' wishes, but before long all the taxes were in the hands of Genoese, while the Augsburg house of Fugger farmed the revenues of the military orders and the mines of Almaden and Guadalcanal. The Cortes complained (1528) that the Genoese bankers had the monopoly of capital, that the trade in wool, silk, iron, steel, soap and all necessaries of life was in their hands. For centuries the harvest in Spain was reaped by Provençals and Auvergnats, who spent nothing and carried their wages back to France.

The American trade was at first confined to Castilians. Ferdinand admitted Aragonese, and Charles would gladly have opened it to all his subjects' ports. The German house of Welser did indeed contract for the colonisation of Venezuela, and the Fuggers for that of Chili and for the spice trade with the Moluccas. But Charles was beaten; the monopoly of Spain and especially of Castile was too strong for him. When he established the staple of the spice trade at Corunna the Seville merchants angrily protested. In 1529 Charles sold the doubtful Spanish claims to the Moluccas to his Portuguese rivals, and henceforth Seville reigned supreme. Her monopoly in early days was natural; Cadiz had similarly been the sole port for the Barbary trade. The seas swarmed with pirates, and the American ships must needs sail in company; the collection of duties was facilitated; the character of ships and crews and emigrants could be more closely watched. The trade was highly organised by the *Casa de Contratacion*, a Board of Trade with judicial powers, which regulated the number of ships and the bulk and value of their freights, received and distributed the precious metals and the merchandise from the Indies. All lines of traffic within Spain converged on Seville. Cadiz also throve because the bigger ships must anchor in her harbour. Hence sailed the galleons with their convoy for Porto Bello to supply Peru and Chili, and the *flota* which made for San Domingo and Vera Cruz. On the return journey the two squadrons joined company and arrived together. The privileged position of Seville and Cadiz drew all life from other Spanish ports; the monopoly was to become intolerable to Spain herself, to her colonies, to all Europe; the rigorous restrictions ultimately defeated their own object, and the bonds were burst by the growing maritime powers with the connivance of the colonists.

The Cortes, meanwhile, attributed the growing financial difficulties to the increase of taxation. This was of course mainly due to the recurring wars with France, but partly to the increased charges caused by the rise in prices. Contemporaries noticed that Charles was ever at his wits' end for money. Gold and silver began to flow in from the Indies, the extraordinary subsidy became regular and normal, and yet the deficiency grew apace. The dowry brought by the Portuguese infanta, the ransom for the French King's sons, the sum paid by Portugal for the monopoly of the Molucca trade, huge advances from German and Genoese bankers, were all poured into the bottomless vessel of a Danaid. Charles even resorted to the extreme measure of seizing the whole of the gold and silver brought by one of the American fleets, promising interest to the rightful owners until repayment. Nothing served to fill the void, and the King left behind him a huge debt of 20,000,000 ducats.

The economic errors of the Cortes and the fiscal oppression of the Crown were thus already present in the reign of Charles, and each succeeding reign exaggerated these evils. Had the manufacturing industry been fostered a prosperous future would have been in store for Spain, as her market was an exclusive one. But through a series of centuries every economic heresy, every wrong-headed experiment, every foolish nostrum was allowed to work its worst upon the national industries until they were ultimately strangled. The problem which constantly faced the successive Cortes was still the scarcity of currency accompanied by the continual rise of the prices of commodities; and the remedies, vainly repeated, were usually the restriction of the export of the latter, together with measures for the suppression of luxury in dress, principally against the use of bullion[1]. The constant drain of men

[1] A full treatment of the subject of Spanish sumptuary laws will be found in an Essay in Major Martin's Hume's volume, *The Year after the Armada*. E. A.

for the wars and by emigration rendered skilled labour increasingly dear, whilst the unwise fiscal arrangements which threw the greater burden of taxation upon industry, and hampered production by the arbitrary fixing of maximum prices in the supposed interest of the consumer, rendered the Spanish manufacturers of the more costly goods unable to compete with the foreigner; so that of the vast sums of money that came yearly from the Indies a large portion never got beyond Seville, where it was paid away to foreign merchants, in exchange for goods, for export thence to the Indies. Thus it came about that gradually the national industries were crushed, whilst the country was drained of its resources[1].

Spanish power had not been wholly occupied by attempts at expansion to the East and South. In Continental America the reign of Charles was the age of discovery, conquest, and settlement. Cortes conquered Mexico, and Pizarro Peru. Other leaders established themselves in Central America. Soto led his ill-fated expedition to the Mississippi valley. The contrast between the governmental settlements in Africa and those of the adventurers in America is very striking. The latter did not cling to isolated seaports which were held or lost at huge expense. They secured enormous territories in spite of resistance sometimes desperate and of civil war yet more dangerous. Even the original conquest is less marvellous than the imposition for all time of Spanish faults and virtues, language and religion on vast masses of hostile population.

In Charles's reign these conquests affected the mother-country directly in two ways, by the drain of population and by the inflow of precious metals. To the latter brief reference has been made. The effect on population is very uncertain, for evidence is conflicting. Some writers speak of severe restrictions placed on emigration, others ascribe the lack of recruits in Spain to the exodus of every able-bodied man to America;

[1] I am indebted for the last paragraph to Major Martin Hume. E. A.

a Venetian envoy describes Seville as being depopulated by emigration. Soto on his Mississippi expedition took 600 men from Spain. Usually, however, the conquerors levied their men in Cuba, but how far these were recent emigrants or older settlers it is difficult to decide.

The control which the home government asserted over the adventurers is very remarkable. Charles supported Cortes against his calumniators and covered him with honours, but he refused to combine the administrative with the military power, and created a Viceroyalty for Mexico with its *Audiencia* on the Spanish model. He was probably not sorry to see Cortes ruin himself with abortive expeditions towards the North-West, and allowed him to die in poverty. In Peru the danger was far greater. The first attempt to establish home control ended in total failure; Peru was within an ace of becoming an independent state, an example which the other colonies would speedily have followed. But Charles persisted, and Pizarro's house was crushed. The result of the reign was the establishment of the military, religious and judicial machinery which existed until the independence of the colonies, and in some respects survived it.

The intermittent war between Charles and Francis had closed with the peace of Crespy, and from this begins the last stage of the Emperor's career. Henceforth his activity is directed, to outward appearance, from the interests of Spain to those of Germany. It was at last possible to deal vigorously with religious revolt. The hands of Charles were freed by the shattered health of Francis, and by the Sultan's truce with Ferdinand. Pope and Emperor combined, not as of old for territorial Italian purposes, but for the restoration of Germany to the Church. The earnest of the league was the assembly of the long-deferred Council at Trent (1545). In the following year Charles took the field against the Protestant princes.

It was the Emperor's fortune to become the gaoler of each

of his chief enemies in turn. As he had captured the King of France and the Pope, so now the victory of Mühlberg entailed the imprisonment of his two inveterate foes, the Elector of Saxony and the Landgrave of Hesse. Paul III, indeed, startled at his early successes, and alarmed at the activity of the Council, had broken from him. Charles went his way regardless. Germany lay still at his feet. By the Interim he imposed upon the vanquished Protestants his own religious system; he humbled the free Imperial towns by war contributions and the establishment of municipal oligarchies; he bowed the princes to the ground by threats of confiscation. Charles was at length Emperor indeed, he was for a moment at the summit of his power.

The captivity of Francis I had led to the League of Cognac; that of Clement VII to the League of Amiens. The captivity of the Landgrave of Hesse was perhaps the most immediate cause of the treaty of Maurice of Saxony with the new French King. While Henry II seized the three Bishoprics, the military keys of Lorraine, Maurice, aided by the ill-concealed hostility of Catholic German princes and the indifference of Ferdinand, drove Charles headlong from Innsbrück. Then followed a momentary revival. Charles, once in the field, shook off the valetudinarian languor which had given Maurice his opportunity. Surrounded by Spanish and Italian veterans under the command of Alba Charles recovered a hold upon South Germany and laid siege to Metz.

As at Algiers, Charles paid dearly for his obstinacy in neglecting the advice of scientific soldiers. As in Africa the equinoctial gales, so in Lorraine the rains and snows of winter proved his ruin. The siege of Metz was raised; in the long wrestle between the two great powers the last fall was in France's favour; Metz for more than three centuries was lost to Germany. The defeat by France, the armed and unarmed protest of the German princes against his political and religious system, convinced Charles that he had failed. He left to

Ferdinand the responsibility for the legal recognition of the parity of the two religions.

In these chances and changes of fortune on German soil it is easy to forget that Charles was King of Spain. Philip's reign, indeed, within the Peninsula may be dated from the day when the Emperor left his son as Regent. Yet Charles's German triumphs and failures were vitally connected with his Spanish power and policy. To the last moment he had hesitated to abandon his hopes of religious reunion for religious war; his final determination was due to the pressure of Pedro de Soto, his Spanish confessor. The Spanish people, while complaining of their King's foreign interests, had long reproached him with his tolerance of German heresy. By Spain, and especially by the Spanish clergy, the sinews of war were supplied. In 1545 the Pope granted to Charles half the ecclesiastical revenues of Spain; he permitted also a large sale of Church lands. This principle, essentially Spanish, Charles wished afterwards to extend to all his dominions. Under the pretext of overthrowing heresy he would base his power on ecclesiastical property; he would make the Church throughout his dominions as subservient to the Crown as it was in Spain. This danger in no small degree contributed to the unfriendly neutrality of the German ecclesiastical princes towards Charles, when Maurice entered the lists against him in the name of German liberties.

Charles's victory was in great measure won by Spanish troops, led by Alba, the most characteristically Spanish of his generals. After Mühlberg Germany was held down by Spanish garrisons. Short, swarthy Spaniards, swaggering, superstitious and licentious, lorded it in Saxony, in the Palatinate, in Würtemberg. Philip of Hesse himself was never by night nor day out of the sight of his Spanish guards. Upon Alba was to be conferred the German principality of Neuburg. Hatred for the Spanish troops alienated all Germany from the Spanish King; here, as later in the Netherlands, this was the more popular and general cause of the revolt. Above all the victory of Mühlberg was followed by the definite attempt to foist Philip upon the Empire. Charles forced Ferdinand and his son Maximilian to consent that Philip should succeed the former. Germany would have become an annex of Spain, even as the Netherlands and Italy. Ferdinand was but little younger than Charles, and Philip long outlived Maximilian; Germany would therefore have fallen under Spanish domination. The success of Maurice scarcely shook the Emperor's resolve. But the resistance of the German princes, as manifested in the League of Heidelberg (1553), or, as Charles himself professed (Feb. 1554), the marriage of Philip with Mary Tudor induced him to abandon his scheme. He frankly surrendered all idea of uniting the Empire to the Spanish Crown, and this restored outward harmony between the two lines of Hapsburg. But the lukewarmness of Ferdinand and the outspoken indignation of Maximilian had contributed to Maurice's success. Germany could not tolerate a Spanish Emperor, and least of all Philip, whom Germans on his recent visit (1548) had learnt to know and hate.

Not only in Germany was Charles's later policy eminently Spanish. While he fought the Protestants on the Danube and the Elbe, his Spanish ambassadors and bishops fought the Papacy at Trent. Their numerical inferiority was compensated by their superior theological learning, their more genuine zeal for reform, their consolidation as a strong national Church, their subordination to the Emperor. The bishops were admirably led by Diego de Mendoza, the ambassador, a zealous churchman, but a diplomatist of high ability and wide modern learning. Stormy meetings preceded the transference of the Council to Bologna, which the Spaniards, remaining at Trent, refused to recognise. The Italian prelates resented the Emperor's pretensions, the Spaniards clung closely to their Crown. A Conciliar schism seemed inevitable.

Charles' scheme of Church reform was equally opposed to

Lutheran revolt and Papal conservatism. Once again his idea was Spanish. It was a return to the attempts of Spanish theologians, in the first days of the Reformation, to find common ground with Luther, not in doctrine, but in reform of disciplinary abuses. When Charles imposed the Interim upon Germany the victory seemed won for Spanish methods alike against German and Roman. Charles would be head of the Church in Germany as absolutely as he was in Spain. The settlement was peculiarly Spanish in being irrespective of the Papal protest; it was a revival of the ecclesiastical independence of Ferdinand and Isabella, a foreshadowing of that of Philip.

Not only on ecclesiastical questions were Pope and Emperor opposed. The resistance of the Curia to Spanish predominance in Italy was natural enough, but in restless territorial greed the Farnesi surpassed the Medici. Paul III's ambitions stimulated those of Charles's Italian governors; encroachment was forced upon them by the ever-present danger of Papal-French alliance. The Pope must needs found a state for his son and grandsons, be this Parma and Piacenza, or Milan, or Siena. The French King was still tempted by the old lure of Milan and Naples. To compass his desire he must intrigue with sullen nobles and turbulent democracy at Naples, galvanise Guelfic opposition in Lombardy, excite the exiles of Genoa and Florence against Doria and Medici, or hurl Turkish-African squadrons against the coasts of Sicily and Naples.

At Naples Don Pedro de Toledo ruled with a tight rein without provoking unnecessary scandal. At Milan the Marquis del Guasto had been succeeded by Ferrante Gonzaga, the personal enemy of the Farnesi (1546). The Pope had coveted the office for his son Pier Luigi or his grandson Ottavio, who had married Charles's bastard daughter. Gonzaga, although an Italian, was an Imperialist of Imperialists; while Charles was stifling independence in Germany, this cadet of the ruling house of Mantua outpaced him in Italy. Imperialist plots were hatched in Venetian Lombardy; a Spanish garrison terrorised Siena; Charles himself saved Genoa from Gonzaga, who would have overthrown its constitution and bridled it with a fortress.

Genoa, indeed, was the doubtful link in the Imperial chain. The exile Fieschi, thanks to a slippery plank, was drowned at the moment of seizing the city with French and Papal aid (1547). Gonzaga parried the thrust by murdering Pier Luigi and occupying his strong town of Piacenza. Paul III retaliated by affiancing his grandson Orazio to the Dauphin's bastard. A French garrison at Parma faced the Spaniards at Piacenza. Any power which held Parma and Piedmont was believed to control North Italy; Charles could scarcely have retained his hold but for the Pope's death and his grandsons' quarrel. Bastard daughters were useful pawns; Ottavio's marriage, in spite of his desire for vengeance, forced him back for a time to the Imperialist side.

Julius III, less noteworthy than any recent Pope, passed fitfully for an Imperial partisan. A Spanish subject, the Neapolitan Caraffa, succeeded him (1555), but it was left to Philip II to fight Charles's battles o'er again. The reign of Charles in Italy ended in success. Siena had revolted against its Spanish garrison (1552) and admitted a French force. Hence the Florentine exile, Piero Strozzi, could threaten the Imperialist Medici at Florence, and exercise pressure, not unwelcome, upon Rome. Alessandro de' Medici had been murdered by an equally disreputable cousin (1537): Charles conferred the Duchy of Florence upon Cosimo, a member of the younger line. The new Duke would gladly have succeeded also to his predecessor's widow, the Emperor's bastard. In this he was disappointed, but in return for a subsidy for the French War (1543) Charles withdrew the Spanish garrisons which temporarily held Florence and Leghorn. His confidence met with its reward. Cosimo's forces closed round the old rival,

Siena, and forced the French garrison to capitulate. Thus a large state, wedged between the Florentine and Papal frontiers, was annexed by the Spanish Crown. Early in Philip's reign Siena was ceded to Florence, but as a Spanish fief, and to Spain remained the Sienese seaboard, the so-called State of the Presidi, an invaluable halfway house between Genoa and Naples.

Nothing proves more conclusively the predominance of Spanish interests in Charles' policy than his settlement of Italy. The connection of Milan with the Empire was no mere theory. For Maximilian and the German princes its recovery had ever been the panacea for Imperial bankruptcy. The princes and towns of Northern and Central Italy had been forced to contribute to Charles' necessities on the ground of their relation to the Empire. If in the Italian campaigns the Spanish troops had proved themselves more efficient, the Germans had usually outnumbered them; the acquisition of Milan had cost more German than Spanish blood. The Imperial vicariate in Italy would naturally fall to the Hapsburg line which succeeded to the Empire. Yet Charles tossed aside all German claims, conferring upon Philip not only Milan and Siena, but the Vicariate with all its vague but dangerous pretensions. This was felt to imply the virtual incorporation of Italy with the Spanish Crown. Charles, whom the Spaniards would gladly have rejected, had learnt to see in Spain the centre of his power. He had abandoned all idea of a buffer-state in Northern Italy, and the old dream of a Burgundian kingdom. The long arms of the Spanish Crown must stretch over Italy and Flanders. Could they not also reach across the British Channel?

The reverses of Charles in Germany were not without their compensation. Far more important than the Empire to the ruler of Spain and the Netherlands was the friendship of England. It has been seen that in 1544 Henry VIII invaded France in concert with the Emperor. Even with the Protestant

government of Edward VI Charles had had no hostile relations.
When in 1553 Edward died and Charles' cousin Mary was on
the throne he determined with all his old fire and energy that
she should marry Philip. The Netherlands could then be
safely left to a son who was King of England. The old
alliance of Spain, Burgundy and England, seemed to be revived,
and set upon an infinitely firmer basis; the new national
rivalry between Spain and France should be reinforced by the
old traditional hatred between France and England.

For this transition Charles' own retirement was to pave the
way. His health was now completely broken; he longed only
for the rest to body and mind towards which in his laborious
life his eyes had often turned. Germany and Italy saw the
Emperor's face no more. The solemn transference of the
Empire to Ferdinand in March 1558 completed the cycle
of renunciations, but long ere this Charles had retired to
Yuste to dispel the gloom of recent years under the bright sky
of Estremadura. Out of all his wide dominions he found
himself at home in Spain. The Flemish alien had become
a Spaniard.

SPAIN:
ITS GREATNESS AND DECAY.

BY

MARTIN A. S. HUME.

CHAPTER I.

PHILIP II, 1527—1551.

At four o'clock in the afternoon of the 21st May, 1527, Philip of Austria first saw the light in Valladolid, the ancient capital of New Castile. An overpowering sense of the greatness of his coming destiny pervaded the birth of the Emperor's firstborn. His mother had ordered her face to be hidden from the light that no involuntary sign of her pain should be visible whilst the puny infant was being ushered into the world over which it was hoped he would rule in time to come.

To the remonstrance of her Portuguese lady attendants who urged her not to suppress the natural expression of her sufferings the Empress replied, "No. Die I may: but wail I will not." And not in the gloomy old palace alone was the importance of the event impressed upon the minds of men. The ruin which extended empire was to bring upon Spain had not yet proceeded far enough to be recognised by the ordinary citizen, and the pride of Spaniards was flattered by the idea that their monarch wielded sway over the greater part of Christendom, and indefinitely over heathendom beyond. So when the longed-for news came that the heir of his greatness had been born in the heart of Castile, and not in far-away Flanders like his father, gravity and restraint were thrown to the winds and the Spaniards went well-nigh crazy with joy. Throughout Philip's life fate decreed that his brightest hopes should always end in gloom and disappointment; and the circumstances of his birth were no exception to the rule. Suddenly the joy bells that greeted his advent were silenced by the dread news that only a fortnight before (6 May, 1527) the Emperor's troops had sacked Rome. In a moment the rejoicings of Valladolid were turned to mourning. All that the Emperor could do to demonstrate his grief at the event was done; but the citizens of his capital whispered in awestricken tones to each other that this was a bad augury for the newborn prince.

In March of the following year 1528 a special meeting of the Cortes of Castile was summoned at Madrid to swear allegiance to the infant heir to the crown, and though this time they granted the subsidy demanded of them (200 million maravedis = £65,789) they did so with a bad grace, and clamoured aloud for reform, as their predecessors had done on every opportunity since the accession of Charles; but on this occasion, as previously, their recommendations were politely shelved.

The education of Philip during the absence of the Emperor from Spain, from August 1529 to May 1533, was confided to the Empress, and to one of her Portuguese ladies, Leonor de Mascarenhas. Even thus early, he was a preternaturally grave and silent child, with a fair pink and white skin and silky yellow hair. From his earliest moments of intelligence he must have heard constantly around him prayers for the success of his father against the wicked heretics. The gloomy etiquette of the Castilian court, the atmosphere of grim devotion which surrounded the Empress, and the ever-recurring suggestion that his father was engaged in a great struggle on the side of the Almighty against the powers of evil, must have struck deeply into the nature of the infant. He was the descendant of a line of religious mystics, some of whom had crossed the border line of insanity, he sprang from the union of first cousins and the curse of epilepsy was in his blood, so that it is not wonderful that the effect of his ancestry and his surroundings were visible in him from his earliest years. On the Emperor's return to

Spain he appointed as his son's tutor, on the recommendation
of the Empress, a priestly professor of Salamanca named Juan
Martinez Pedernales, or Siliceo. He was a man of small
knowledge or energy and let the prince go very much his own
way. But Philip was an apt pupil in studies that attracted
him. He never was a proficient linguist but could read and
write Latin well at a very early age, and understood French
and Italian; whilst for mathematics he appears to have had
an extraordinary aptitude.

At the age of 12 he lost his mother (1 May, 1539). She
had borne to the Emperor two other sons who died of epilepsy
in their infancy, and Philip remained the sole heir of his
father's greatness. Wars and the cares of a vast empire kept
Charles away from Spain, except for three short visits, until the
end of 1541. Though still in the prime of life he was already
tired of the world, and the morbid mental lethargy which he inherited from his mother was dominating the physical vigour of
the burly Hapsburgs. He was eager thus early to indoctrinate
his son with the system of government of which he was to
continue the traditions, and he was delighted to find the boy
studious, grave and silent beyond his tender years. During
the time the father and son were together the great statesman
devoted a portion of every day to initiate his successor in the
task before him, and he found Philip ready for the lesson. In
the autumn of 1542 the Dauphin with an army of 40,000 men
overran Rousillon, which then belonged to the crown of Aragon,
and besieged Perpignan. The opportunity was considered a
favourable one for initiating the young prince in actual warfare,
and he accompanied the Duke of Alba to the relief of the
fortress; but he saw no fighting, for at the news of the great
reinforcements from Italy and Castile being on their way,
Henry of Valois abandoned the siege. But Philip's journey
was not fruitless. The Cortes of Aragon, Valencia and
Catalonia were in session at Monzon, and thither the prince
went to receive the oath of allegiance from them. Long ago

Jaime el Conquistador (1216—1275) had crushed the feudal power of the Aragonese nobles, and as usually happened in similar cases, had been obliged to depend largely upon the popular power in doing so. The Cortes of the Aragonese dominions possessed therefore far greater power than the Castilian Cortes and held with rough tenacity to the privileges they enjoyed. More than once Charles had met with resistance from them; in 1536, for instance, they had absolutely refused to raise taxes for the Emperor's need except in legally constituted Cortes where grievances could be first formulated. The Catalan deputies now took the oath to Philip as heir to the crown, only on condition that it should not be considered binding until it had been ratified in Barcelona. The oath of allegiance taken by the Aragonese to their kings at best was but a grudging one. "We recognise you as king," it ran, "so long as you uphold our privileges: and if not, not." The whole tendency of the policy of Charles and his successor was to concentrate and unify the national power, and no opportunity was missed of weakening, where possible, the autonomy of the stubborn Aragonese. But, like the English commons, they held the purse-strings and refused to vote supplies except on their own terms.

Charles's treasury was chronically empty, for the drain upon it was constant. He was now confronted with a fresh formidable coalition. On the side of France against the Emperor was the power of the Turk in the Mediterranean, the Pope (Paul III), and the sympathy, at least, of the Lutheran princes of Germany. On a former occasion when the Emperor was in the midst of his great struggle with France he had replenished his war chest with the rich dowry (900,000 crowns) of his Portuguese wife, and he now sought to repeat the operation by marrying his heir to his cousin the Princess Maria, daughter of John III of Portugal and of Charles' sister Catharine. Some years before Charles had projected the marriage of his son with young Jeanne d'Albret, titular

Queen of Navarre, whose ancestors' Spanish kingdom had been usurped by Ferdinand the Catholic; but Francis I had discovered and frustrated this dangerous intrigue, which would have brought the Spanish monarch over the Pyrenees as tributary sovereign of a large portion of southern France. Before Philip was wedded to the Portuguese princess his father was obliged to leave Spain for Germany, and encouraged by the precocity in statesmanship displayed by the young prince, he determined to leave in his hands the regency of Spain during his absence.

This was one of the most important junctures of Philip's life. He was barely sixteen years old and thus early was entrusted with Charles' secret system of government, which henceforward became his own and swayed most of the actions of his life. The two letters written by the Emperor on his departure, for his son's guidance, are of the utmost importance in providing a key to Philip's subsequent political action. Although the regent was entrusted with the ultimate decision on all points, he was to be guided by the opinion of some of Charles's wisest councillors, especially of Tavara, Archbishop of Toledo and the Secretary of State Francisco de los Cobos. Philip is privately informed that the reason they are appointed is that they are respectively heads of factions, and each one will prevent the regent from falling under the influence of the other. For the benefit of a young lad of sixteen, the Emperor mercilessly lays bare the faults and failings of the statesmen who are to aid him in his government. He is warned not to trust any of them separately. Their hypocrisy, their greed, their frailties of character and conduct are all exposed, and the prince is told that he must listen to them all, and then decide for himself. Even the Duke of Alba, the most eminent of Charles' Spanish subjects, is dissected for the benefit of the neophyte. He is, says Charles, ambitious, sanctimonious, and hypocritical; and perhaps even may try to tempt you (Philip) by means of women. But he is a grandee and must not be allowed to have any share in the interior government of the kingdom. "In foreign affairs and war make use of him and respect him, as he is the best man we now have." Quite as extraordinary are the more secret instructions given to Philip with regard to his social conduct and his coming marital relations, which are to be entirely ruled by his governor, Don Juan de Zuñiga. The great lesson enforced throughout both documents is self-suppression, patience, and, above all, distrust; the object being to play off one rival against another, and so by making all other men puppets, to concentrate power in the hands of the one man who held the wires. For the rest of Philip's long life these were his guiding principles, strengthening their hold upon him as he grew in age and experience.

With a heavy heart, overburdened with care, the Emperor left his son in the early spring of 1543. Before he set sail from Palamos (6 May, 1543) he impressed upon the young regent in a secret letter, meant for his eye alone, how utterly insufficient were his resources to meet the expenditure which he had undertaken, and urged him to provide money from Spain; "for if our subjects be not liberal with us I know not how we shall fare." Cobos was a great finance minister and lost no time in advising the regent to summon the Castilian Cortes for the purpose of providing funds in the urgent danger of the country: "the armies of the Turk and the King of France being in winter quarters so near us." Philip married his young Portuguese cousin in November 1543, and in January 1544 the Castilian Cortes assembled in Toledo. They were at first in no very yielding mood. They had no instructions from their constituents, they said, to go beyond the votes of the previous Cortes, which had promised 300 million maravedis[1] spread over the years 1546, 1547 and 1548, with 150 millions extra, payable during 1545. They had a large number of grievances, moreover, to be remedied before they would grant even this. First and most important they urged that peace

---

[1] 3040 maravedis were equal to one pound sterling.

should be made before the country was utterly ruined; and the reply to this was that nothing would please the Emperor better if it were possible. It was in fact already coming home to Spaniards that world-wide empire was an expensive luxury which a naturally poor country could ill-afford. The whole of the misfortunes of Spain sprang indeed from its apparent good fortune. When the nation was united under one sovereign at the end of the fifteenth century, it still consisted of many separate races and distinct territories. The work of consolidation and unification of its institutions, of the development of its resources, and the civilization of its peoples, might well have absorbed its energies for a century, especially if to this task were added the colonisation and domination of the New World. Eight centuries of struggle with the infidel had stamped their mark deeply on the character of the people. They were brave, hardy, and simple in their lives. Their strong religious feeling, engendered by the fact that they had long held the Christian outposts, would probably have saved them from the religious wars which ravaged the rest of Europe; the geographical position of the country rendered it unnecessary for them to take part in the politics of Central Europe; and probably if Spain had been occupied only in its own problems it would have become the happiest and most prosperous of countries. But as ruler of Holland and Flanders it was of vital importance that the King of Spain should always be friendly with England, as a counterbalance to France. Spain had to find resources to pay for most of the vast expenditure entailed by the foreign responsibilities of its sovereign, and by the time that Philip assumed the regency it was gradually being understood that the imperial connection, which had seemed at first so splendid, was a curse instead of a blessing. Charles himself, practically a foreigner, had always been unpopular in Spain, and hardly a Cortes met during his reign which did not clamour against the extravagance and injustice of the foreign officers by whom he was surrounded.

Thus it was that the Castilian Cortes of 1544 showed but little alacrity in voting fresh supplies for a war in which it was felt that the nation itself had but little concern. Their subsidy, such as it was, was supplemented by the Portuguese dowry and a loan from John III.

Philip as Regent of Spain was eminently successful. The Emperor through all his troubles and constant ill-health kept up a close correspondence with his son, who had answered his fondest expectations. Philip's wife died after one year and eight months of wedlock, leaving a sickly baby behind her, but Philip only allowed his grief to detain him in seclusion from his public duties for three weeks. He was already extremely popular with the Spanish people. His gravity, his preference for the Spanish tongue, and his reluctance to marry a French princess, as well as his piety and moderation, had even now gained him the affection of Spaniards, which for the rest of his life he never lost.

But the promise of his son, and the defeat of his enemies, once more aroused in the Emperor dreams of universal domination for the benefit of his descendants, if not for himself. It had been the intention of Ferdinand the Catholic that his elder grandson should succeed to his paternal dominions, the Empire and Flanders, whilst Ferdinand, the younger, should inherit Spain and Naples. Charles, however, had arranged otherwise, and made his brother King of the Romans, with the implied succession to the Empire. But he was determined that as little power and territory as possible should go with it, and he now proceeded to carry into effect the plan referred to (p. 97), of transferring to Philip the imperial vicariate in Italy, as well as attaching Flanders and Holland to the Spanish Crown; thus leaving the future Emperor in possession only of his Austrian dominions. Ferdinand of course did not like the arrangement, but was at last won over to it by the marriage of his son Maximilian to the Emperor's daughter Maria, and the Emperor's guarantee that on Ferdinand's death Maximilian should succeed him as Emperor. As soon as this was agreed to, the Emperor sent the Duke of Alba to Spain with a statement of the case for Philip's information. The Emperor's new policy was to result in untold trouble and suffering to future generations. The lordships of Flanders and Holland had not hitherto been regarded by Charles as necessarily attached to the Spanish Crown. The cession of the Netherlands to a French prince was one of the alternative conditions of the peace of Crespy; and since that had fallen through, Charles had discussed the advisability of handing over the Low Countries to his daughter Maria on her marriage with Maximilian. But the fatal step of making them the inalienable possessions of the ruler of Spain burdened the latter country with a new set of permanent interests, and rendered necessary a change in its foreign policy. Flanders once attached inalienably to the Crown of Spain could never fall into the hands of France; and the latter country would find itself almost surrounded by Spanish territory. If, moreover, the Spanish suzerainty over Italy were established French influence in that country would be at an end, and the papal power dwarfed. The whole balance of Europe would thus be changed, and France and the Pope forced into a secular struggle against Spain. The possessors of the Flemish seaboard had for generations found it necessary to maintain a close alliance with England, whose interests were equally bound up in preventing France from occupying the coast opposite its own eastern shores; the principal outlet for its commerce. But Charles' new policy transferred the vital need for a permanent English alliance to Spain itself as possessor of Flanders; and that at a time when such an alliance was daily becoming more difficult in consequence of Henry's attitude towards the question of religious reform. Spain was thus drawn permanently into the vortex of central European politics, to its own ultimate ruin.

The Emperor's new plans were not entirely to Philip's taste.

Having regard to Alba's correspondence with Granvelle upon the subject it is probable that the objection did not arise from motives of prudence, but rather from the ambitious promptings of Alba himself, who would point out to the young prince that the new arrangement would permanently cut him off from the succession to the imperial Crown. At his instance, therefore, the question of the suzerainty over Italy was left open; and with it what was doubtless Alba's real objection—namely, the ultimate succession of Maximilian to the Empire.

At the desire of the Emperor, Philip was to undertake a state progress through northern Italy and the dominions of the Empire to make the acquaintance of his future subjects, and gain the popularity necessary for carrying through the new plans. In pursuance of the policy of depriving the nobles of power in the state, Charles ordered that his son's household previous to his journey should be organised for the first time according to the pompous etiquette of the house of Burgundy, which has since been adopted in most courts. The proud Spanish nobility thus became attached personally to the household of the prince, in nominally domestic capacities, as chamberlains, equerries, ushers and the like; and the younger hidalgos no longer lived and hunted on their feudal estates, but surrounded the person of the monarch in silken and enervating idleness. The change was certainly not in accordance with Philip's personal character, for his tastes were simple, sober, modest and industrious; but he was a slave to duty, and thenceforward on state occasions moved in a constellation of splendour.

On the 4th April, 1548, Philip met the Castilian Cortes[1] at Valladolid and informed them of his approaching voyage, his

---

[1] Anciently 48 cities and towns were summoned to send representatives to the Castilian Cortes, but during the period under consideration the following cities only were usually represented, Burgos, Leon, Granada, Seville, Cordoba, Murcia, Jaen, Soria, Cuenca, Salamanca, Avila, Zamora, Toro, Segovia, Guadalajara, Valladolid, Madrid and Toledo. At the first

sister Maria, and her husband Maximilian, King of Bohemia, being appointed regents during his absence from Spain. The message was an unwelcome one for the Cortes. They at once despatched a letter to the Emperor, begging him not to summon Philip away from Spain. It was bad enough, they said, that the Emperor himself should live out of his Spanish dominions, but to deprive them of their prince as well was too bad. It had now become clear to the Spaniards that the dragging of them at the tail of the Empire was causing the ruin of the country, and they desired nothing so much as that Spain should be governed by a resident native prince, and should confine herself to her own affairs. "From your Majesty's absence," wrote the Cortes, "has resulted the poverty which these kingdoms are suffering, in consequence of the great sums of money which have been sent out. This has brought about a total lack of gold and a great scarcity of silver, and we are sure that if the absence of our princes continues, these kingdoms will become much poorer and more ruined even than they are."

Once more the Cortes formulated their list of grievances and protested boldly against disregard of former representations. Again they demanded that the Church should hold no more land; once more they urged the codification of the law, the purification of the judicial bench, and proposed a great number of domestic and administrative reforms, many of which Philip ratified before he left. What however troubled the Cortes most was the financial and industrial state of the

sitting of each Cortes a dispute for precedence always occurred between Burgos and Toledo, usually ending in the victory of the former and a protest by the latter. The members were paid by grants made by the King, four millions of maravedis being included for the purpose in the ordinary supply, but during the reigns of Philip II and Philip III considerable special grants and concessions were made to the members—both collectively and personally. In the latter reign a percentage on the supply 15 or 17 per cent. was sometimes given to them—a most vicious form of remuneration.

country. The economic heresies to which reference has been made (pp. 85—90) had already produced their baleful influence, and Spanish industry, heavily handicapped as it was, had to a large extent been supplanted by that of foreigners, even in Spanish markets. The remedy proposed by the Cortes was an extraordinary one. It was thought that, if the fine and costly textiles, mostly now the produce of foreign looms, were not shipped from Seville to the Spanish possessions, the money from America would remain in the Peninsula instead of being paid away to foreigners. The Cortes of 1548 therefore demanded that the export of cloth and silks to the Indies should be prohibited, but the petition was only partially granted.

On 1st October, 1548, Philip left Valladolid on his long voyage. By slow stages and followed by a great train of courtiers he rode through Aragon and Catalonia. Andrea Doria, with a splendid fleet of fifty-five galleys, met him in the Bay of Rosas and saluted him almost as a demi-god. It is no exaggeration to say that this intense and passionate devotion to Philip reflected at this time the general feeling in Spain, where he was regarded as the native born prince who would free his people from the crushing burden of the Empire. The qualities which made him popular in Spain had a contrary effect elsewhere. His reticence and gravity, his unconcealed dislike to the rough and boisterous pleasures, and the heavy eating and drinking, of the Germans and Flemings drew upon him the hatred of his father's foreign subjects. Through Genoa, Milan and Mantua, Tyrol, Germany and Luxemburg, the Spanish prince slowly progressed to meet his father in Brussels. Everywhere he was greeted by festivals, banquets, and tourneys, to a greater extent, said eye-witnesses, than ever had been seen before. He did his best, but such frivolity was not to his taste, and his journey certainly did not help forward the project of securing to him the succession of the imperial Crown. On the 1st April, 1549, he made his state entry into Brussels. Charles was still ailing,

but gathered new life with the presence of his beloved heir;
and for the next two years nearly every day Philip learnt from
the great Emperor the profound lessons of government which
were to rule his policy during the rest of his life. One of the
subjects, upon which the Cortes of 1548 had pressed the
Emperor, was that Philip should marry again. He had now
been a widower for four years, and had contracted a morganatic connection with Doña Isabel de Osorio, by whom
he had several children. His only legitimate child was the
lame epileptic Don Carlos, and during Philip's stay in Brussels
several matrimonial schemes were discussed between him and
the Emperor. Jeanne D'Albret was again suggested, but
Philip leant rather towards another Portuguese cousin, the
daughter of the old King Manoel and Charles's sister Leonora,
who after Manoel's death had married Francis I. But greater
affairs even than marriages were discussed at the same time—
nothing less, indeed, than the ultimate reversion of the imperial
Crown to Philip, and the exercise by him of the Emperor's
suzerainty over Italy even during his uncle Ferdinand's life.
When after infinite negotiation this had been agreed upon in
principle, Philip accompanied his father to the Diet of Augsburg,
and finally started in May 1551 on his voyage home to
Spain.

CHAPTER II.

PHILIP II, 1551—1560.

PHILIP arrived at Barcelona on the 13th July, 1551, and at once summoned the Castilian Cortes in Madrid to vote supplies. As usual, the long list of petitions for reforms was presented to the regent, and equally as usual, the consideration of the grievances was postponed; the Cortes being dismissed as soon as they had voted the ordinary subsidy of 404 million maravedis spread over three years. The Aragonese Cortes of the following year once more showed how much greater was their parliamentary power than that of the Castilians, since they insisted upon their grievances being considered before the subsidies were voted. The result was that a great mass of legislation of a popular character was passed, especially in matters relating to the liberty of the subject, together with the reform of judicial abuses, and a great sumptuary law prohibiting extravagance in dress.

Philip continued the negotiations for marriage with his Portuguese cousin, but he found John III less inclined to be liberal in the matter of dowry for his half-sister than he had been for his daughter, and the matter hung fire. Philip's bosom friend and favourite, Ruy Gomez—a Portuguese by birth—was sent in June 1553 to persuade the King of Portugal to loosen his purse strings; but during his absence from Spain an event happened which entirely changed the Emperor's

plans. It had been known for some time that Edward VI of
England was in failing health, but the extent of Northumberland's power and following was still uncertain; and Charles'
principal desire with regard to England had hitherto been to
keep on friendly terms with it. But the evil effects of attaching Flanders to the Crown of Spain were already working.
Without the strength of the Empire behind him, the possessor
of Flanders, with a covetous France on one side and Protestant princes on the other, was in an untenable position unless
he could depend upon England's co-operation through thick
and thin. When the events following on the death of Edward
VI proved that English loyalty was stronger than its attachment to the reformed religion, Charles suddenly seized the
opportunity presented. The hollow Crown of the Empire,
with its turbulent Protestant princes, might go. If England
could be joined in lasting union with Spain, then France
would be humbled and Spain supreme in Christendom.

Mary entered London on 3rd August, 1553, with the
imperial ambassador Renard by her side, and only four days
afterwards Philip's name was suggested to her as that of her
future husband. The English people themselves had fixed upon
young Edward Courtenay, and Mary was as yet uncertain how
far she dared thwart them. But she knew full well the French
plots to keep her out of her birthright, and longed for the
strong arms and subtle brains of her Spanish kinsmen to support her. She, too, was a grand-daughter of the ecstatic Isabel
the Catholic, a daughter of highly-strung Catherine of Aragon,
and a niece of Juana the Mad; and religious fervour aided
dynastic expediency in her choice of a spouse. Philip was a
dutiful son. He was 26 years of age, and his domestic arrangements with Doña Isabel de Osorio were on an established footing. But he was a politician and a patriot before all things:
personal pleasure was never his aim in life, and at Charles'
bidding, in a true spirit of sacrifice, he consented to marry
Mary Tudor. London was in a panic at the news, and Mary's

council made hard terms with the coming consort. They
had taken Renard's bribes willingly enough, but from stern
Gardiner downwards, they were determined that, come what
might, England should never be ruled from Spain. Renard
and his master subscribed to all the conditions, in the hope
that Philip's influence with the Queen after marriage would
enable him to have his way. What they failed to understand
was, that Mary herself was powerless against the will of her
Council, and against the English people, who dreaded and
hated the Spaniard. Philip was a gallant suitor to his elderly
bride, and more splendour was lavished over this marriage than
the world had ever seen. Charles was still at war with France,
and Philip brought with him from Corunna to Southampton,
where he landed (20 July, 1554), a fine fleet of a hundred sail
with 6000 soldiers to reinforce his father. He had been
warned to conciliate the English in all things, and he learnt
his lesson well. He conformed, as well as might be, to English
fashions and prejudice, offended his Spanish courtiers by
openly preferring English attendants, and prohibited the landing in England of a single soldier from the fleet.

In England he became personally not unpopular, for he
was always on the side of moderation, and studiously abstained
from publicly interfering in the government. His object was
to win over England by persuasion to the Catholic Church,
which would have led to the political domination of Spain.
But he and his father were politicians first and religious
fanatics afterwards; and on this occasion, as on many others,
the zeal of the Churchmen thwarted the Statesmen. Cardinal
Pole, the pope's legate, was stopped by the Emperor's influence on his way to England, until he had been persuaded not
to take any hasty steps in the matter of the restitution of
Church property confiscated during the previous reigns. Philip
and Renard prevailed upon him not to insist upon the return
of lands that had passed into private hands, and he was then
allowed to proceed to England. Mary's hope of progeny was

again and again disappointed, and Philip stayed on in vain expectation. The Emperor in the meanwhile was sinking into torpor and despair, yearning hourly for the coming of his son, who should take from his shoulders the burden they were no longer capable of supporting. In vain Renard told him that as soon as Philip left England the bigots in Mary's Council would carry to its bitter end the persecution which King Philip's influence alone had hitherto kept in check. But, at last, Charles would wait no longer and peremptorily summoned his son. By August 1555 the rogations to the Almighty for the birth of an heir were discontinued, and the great plan of the dynastic union of Spain and England was seen to be a failure. An Anglo-Spanish power ruling England, Spain, Holland and Flanders, supreme over most of Italy, and the Mediterranean, with the riches of the Indies in its hands, would have dominated the world. France, shut in on every side by land and sea, could have progressed no more; and Spain would have become paramount more completely than if the Emperor's first plan of universally extending the power of the Roman-Austrian empire had been realised. But it was not to be, and Philip made the best of it, with all courtesy and gentleness to his disappointed wife, whom he left, sick at heart and failing in body, on the 26th August, 1555. She watched him from the window of her palace at Greenwich as his boat dropped down the river to Gravesend, and thenceforward, powerless alone to stay her bigoted councillors, was constrained to consent to the lighting of the hellish fires of Smithfield, which will for ever cast a baleful glow upon her wretched reign.

From Flanders Philip sought to restrain the persecution, which was entirely against his political interests. What he wanted was the aid of English ships and men against the French. Here the English Councillors were not so ready, for of all things they feared to be dragged into a war with France, and such help as they gave was obtained by Philip on specious pretexts, and granted with grudging unwillingness.

The Emperor was falling a prey to the last extreme of senile mental and bodily depression when Philip arrived in Flanders. "Fortune is a strumpet," he said after the disaster of Metz, "and reserves her favours for the young"—and to the shoulders of his son he determined to shift his burden. He had already, on Philip's marriage in Winchester cathedral, conferred upon him the kingdoms of Naples and Sicily, and had confirmed to him the duchy of Milan, the latter a fief of the Empire. He now determined to hand over to him the sovereignty of the Netherlands. The scene, one of the most dramatic in history, took place in the great hall of the palace of Brussels, on the 25th October, 1555. All that could add impressiveness and solemnity to the ceremony was done to mark the greatness of the occasion. The prematurely aged Emperor leaning on the shoulder of the youthful William of Orange, in a voice broken with tears took a last farewell of his Flemish subjects whom he loved best. He was a Fleming at heart, and the leavetaking was an affecting one on both sides. The Emperor prayed his son to treat his new vassals well, but the Flemings knew that their new Sovereign's heart was for Spain alone, and that though Philip might be their ruler, he could never be their father and friend as the Emperor had been. For once Philip's own self-control gave way at the affecting scene, and it was only after some delay that he could summon sufficient composure to speak—and then alas! only to say that he was unable to address his subjects in their own tongue, and must depute the task to another, Antoine de Perennot, the bishop of Arras (Cardinal de Granvelle).

On 16th January, 1556, the crowns of Spain were also transferred to Philip, and Charles remained Emperor only in name, until the German electors were prepared for his abdication in favour of his brother Ferdinand. Before he turned his back upon the world for ever, and went to fret his life away in the cloisters of Yuste, he arranged (February 1556) a truce for five years with his old enemy the King of France, who by the treaty of Vaucelles was thus for a time separated from his ally the Pope.

Philip now stands on the stage alone, the most powerful monarch in the world. He had from his very childhood adopted the statecraft of his greater father, and held by it slavishly for the rest of his life. By nature reticent and distrustful, slow and secretive, his qualities had been accentuated by the schooling of his mentors. His inherited religious exaltation, and belief in his divine inspiration, made his methods rigid and unadaptable. He was pitted against opponents whose opportunism and elastic consciences gave them an enormous advantage over him, and the task which he inherited could hardly have had a more unfortunate champion than the monarch who led it to defeat. His sense of duty was overwhelmingly great. He was modest, laborious and conscientious, almost to a fault; a good husband and father; and he strenuously did his best through life, according to his limited lights. He accepted his great inheritance as a sacred trust, but his qualities were not equal to his task, and he was a splendid failure. It cannot be too often repeated that, although he was personally pious, his aims were in the main political rather than religious. The irony of events decreed that the very first task to which he set his hand should be to fight the Holy See. The policy of his father had wrested from one pontiff after another their rights over the Spanish clergy, until at last the vast revenues of the Church were used mainly as an instrument of governmental policy; and the priests were made to understand that they depended for promotion, not upon the Pope, but upon their sovereign. The royal council claimed the right of supervising the ecclesiastical courts, and of withholding the circulation of the papal bulls in Spain. The Inquisition itself was quite as much a political as a religious institution, and was jealously regarded by Philip as being under his immediate control when it suited him.

Philip's anomalous position in Italy rendered still more

difficult his relations with the Italian popes, whom he never regarded otherwise than as tools to be used for the furtherance of his political objects, notwithstanding all the exaggerated lip-deference with which he treated them. The Spanish encroachments in Italy, and the claims of the Spanish monarchs to exclusive control over the temporalities of the Church in Sicily and Naples, which had been suffered with a bad grace by previous pontiffs, aroused the Neapolitan Paul IV (Caraffa) to fury. He launched the most violent invectives against the Emperor and Philip. The Spaniards, he said, were the vile and abject spawn of Jews, the dregs of the world, and must be expelled, neck and crop, from Italy. The aid of the Sultan Solyman was invoked by the Christian pontiff, while Henry II was inflamed by exhortation and reproach beyond measure, and was at last induced to break the truce of Vaucelles in June 1556, only four months after it had been signed. Then the Pope broke through all bounds of decency and decorum, for he thought he had Philip at his mercy. A violent bull of excommunication was issued against the Emperor and his son. The latter is addressed as "the son of iniquity, Philip of Austria, offspring of the so-called Emperor Charles, who passes himself off as King of Spain; following in the footsteps of his father and rivalling him in iniquity."

The position was a difficult one for Philip. He could not afford to degrade the papacy, upon which he looked as one of his principal levers, and yet he must fight the Pope, or lose his Italian states. He was Duke of Milan, a fief of the Empire, his troops had occupied the principalities of Parma and Piacenza, whilst he was independent sovereign of Sicily and Naples. The French still occupied Piedmont, and during the first campaign before Philip's accession had ousted the imperialists from Siena. The imperial troops in Milan had been hitherto a coercive power over the other imperial fiefs, but under Philip they could no longer be so regarded, as they were the forces of a Spanish prince, who himself was in Milan a

tributary of the Emperor. On his accession Philip had sent
Alba from England with very full powers to exercise all his
sovereignties in Italy, an appointment not to the taste of the
Emperor, but probably prompted by a desire on the part of
Ruy Gomez, who was the leader of the party of peace and
diplomacy in Philip's councils, to remove the warlike old
noble from his master's side. On the second coalition against
Spain after the rupture of the truce of Vaucelles, Alba invaded
the papal states, and nearly captured Rome itself, but he was
well matched by Guise, who commanded the Franco-papal
forces. Suddenly Henry II found a powerful army from
Flanders marching upon Paris, and Guise had to be recalled
to France. By the aid of the Doge of Venice a peace was
patched up between the Pope and Philip, and Alba sulkily
entered Rome, not as a conqueror but as a pretended penitent.
Paul IV was conciliated with futile concessions, and Philip was
left face to face with France.

It was vital for him that he should obtain English aid—the
last and only benefit he was ever likely to get now from his
marriage with Mary, who was sorrowfully wearing herself into
her grave. The English Council were determined not to serve
purely Spanish aims, or to allow themselves to be diverted
from extirpating heresy; so the King, sorely against his will,
had again to go to England, and exert his personal influence.
He arrived on 20th March, 1557, and found his wife ready
enough to be avenged upon Henry and his ambassador de
Noailles, for their intrigues against her. But the English Council stood in the way. They had always dreaded this result
of a Spanish match, and had no special quarrel with France.
The French King however sought to counteract Philip's influence in England, by aiding the discontent of the English
Protestant refugees in France, and promoting Stafford's foolish
attempt on Scarborough. This act of hostility gave Mary an
opportunity of persuading her Council, and war between England and France was declared on the 7th July, 1557. On the

3rd of the following month Philip bade a last farewell to his wife, and returned to Brussels, well contented with his success. 8000 English troops were got ready and sent to join Philip's force of 50,000 men in Flanders, under his gallant young cousin Emmanuel Philibert, Duke of Savoy. By a series of rapid and masterly movements Savoy managed to outwit Coligny and Montmorenci, who commanded the French forces, and won the great battle of St Quentin on the 10th August. 6000 of the French troops were killed, as many more captured, with all the artillery, and Montmorenci himself taken prisoner; Coligny held out inside the town of St Quentin until 27th August, when the place was taken by assault, amidst scenes of heartless carnage and horror, mainly the work of German mercenaries, which will for ever remain one of the most dreadful episodes of modern warfare. After the destruction of Montmorenci's force nothing stood between Philip's victorious army and Paris. This was his great chance; and he missed it. Overcaution was almost a mania with him, and he refused Savoy's request to be allowed to march on the French capital. When the Emperor heard in his cloistered seclusion the news of the great battle, his first question was whether his son had arrived in Paris. The Spaniards complained that the English had behaved badly at St Quentin; the English were sulky and discontented; and soon the same spirit was seen in the rest of the force, consisting, as it did, of many jarring nationalities distributed idly amongst the French captured towns. Wages were in arrear, the German mercenaries quarrelled and deserted, the English clamoured to be sent home, and Philip dreading unpopularity in England let them go. Thus his force dwindled, and in a few weeks the fine French army under Guise marched back from Italy. The English fortress of Calais was known to be neglected. Suddenly Guise appeared before it, stormed the crumbling undermanned outworks (2nd and 3rd January, 1558) and finally captured the citadel on the 8th of the month. Lord Wentworth was in command, but the forces at his disposal were utterly inadequate to defend the place. As a natural result of the fall of Calais the other English fortress of Guisnes was captured from Lord Grey a few days afterwards, and the last foothold of the English in France was gone. In England counsels were distracted, the war was unpopular, and men were thinking rather of what was to come when the Queen died, than of passing events. When Feria, Philip's friend and ambassador, saw the Council in Pole's chamber (28th January, 1558) to beg for further English aid, they were tearful, apologetic, but despairing, and begged for mercenary Germans to be sent to England, instead of sending Englishmen away. Philip assented, and the money was drawn from England to pay for the German levies; but they were eventually utilised by Philip, as no doubt was intended from the first. The English Council, too, were deluded into the belief that an attempt was to be made to recover Calais, and fitted out a fleet; but this also was made use of in the Spanish interests, and at a critical moment (13 July, 1558) turned the tide of victory against the French at Gravelines, preventing an intended march upon Brussels, and compelling Guise to stand on the defensive.

Philip's treasury was empty; he was deeply in debt, his troops mutinous, and he hated war. Henry II was in similar straits, and was already looking with dread upon the growth of the party of religious reform in France. Both parties were tired of the struggle, and peace negotiations were opened, Granvelle, Alba, and Orange, representing Philip, Cardinal Lorraine, Montmorenci and St André, the French King; English interests being safeguarded by the Earl of Arundel, Dr Thirlby bishop of Ely, and Dr Wotton. Soon after the negotiations commenced Mary Tudor died (17th November, 1558). Feria had hurried over to England, but the Queen was almost unconscious when he arrived, and he at once set about propitiating Elizabeth at Hatfield. England had slipped through Philip's hands, but it was vital to his power that it should remain friendly to him. If Elizabeth could be married to his nominee all might still be well: but the new Queen showed Feria in her first interview with him that she declined to be patronised. Savoy, who had always been the Spanish candidate for her hand, was again suggested but dropped, for the English dreaded that he might drag them into war to recover his territory from the French. Then Philip himself was tentatively brought forward by Feria, but Elizabeth was coyly irresponsive, and proved herself fully a match for the diplomatists who sought to pledge her to a marriage that should bind her to Spain. Such a marriage, indeed, could only have been possible on conditions that would have vitiated her own claim to the throne. So long as there seemed to be any prospect of his being allowed to influence English policy, Philip stood by the side of the English envoys in demanding the restitution of Calais as a condition of peace, but when Elizabeth's attitude was defined he gave her clearly to understand that, if peace could only be made with the loss of Calais, then Calais must go. Elizabeth was not in a position to go to war with France alone, for her own position was uncertain, and her treasury empty; so at last the bitter pill had to be swallowed, and the peace of Cateau Cambresis was signed (2 April, 1559), Calais remaining in the hands of the French.

This was an important juncture, upon which the future of Spain was mainly to depend. The keystone of Philip's policy was a close and constant alliance with England: a policy imposed upon him by his inheritance of the Netherlands, but which the circumstances of Elizabeth's birth and her personal character made well-nigh impossible, whilst she remained Queen of England. There were even thus early two well-defined parties in Philip's Councils, for this was part of his cautious method of having every question debated from both points of view. The nobles and soldiers of the Alba school ceaselessly urged upon him that he must overturn Elizabeth, by force of arms if necessary, before she had time to consolidate her position; above all things, they said, no time must be lost. The people of England were mainly Catholic at heart, many of the principal nobles and councillors were in the pay of Spain, and Philip must strike with promptitude and boldness. But Philip was timid and slow. Ruy Gomez and the bishop of Arras (de Granvelle) were by his side to advise moderation and diplomacy, and though Feria might sneer, the King would not be hurried into violent action. As usual, he pondered until it was too late, and the opportunity had slipped away, to the dismay of those who had always held as an article of political faith that the possessor of the Netherlands must live in close amity with England. Philip's own alternative combination was characteristic of his peaceful methods. One of the principal reasons why Henry II was anxious for peace in 1558 was, as we have seen, his dread of the growing power of the religious reformers in France. Philip at the time was not actively responsive on the point, as the religious agitation in the Netherlands had not become acute, and the position of England was undefined. But now Elizabeth's firm attitude had changed the problem. By the draft treaty of Cateau Cambresis Henry's eldest daughter was betrothed to Philip's only son Carlos, who was now fourteen, the bride being three months younger. Philip decided to marry the young princess himself, and so to unite France and Spain in close bonds, to the confusion of Elizabeth and the Protestants throughout Europe. His policy towards England was not aggressive: he only sought to render her innocuous. The next heir after Elizabeth was Mary Stuart, the dauphiness of France, and practically a Frenchwoman. Better a thousand times for him that the heretic Elizabeth should remain Queen than that France, Scotland and England, should be ruled by the same hand. Then indeed would the Netherlands be in jeopardy; and Philip doubtless thought that it would be easier to prevent such a consummation from the inside, than from the outside. So Alba with a splendid train entered Paris late in June 1559 to marry by proxy the beautiful little princess (Elizabeth of the Peace as the Spaniards called her) for his master King Philip. The union began unhappily, for Henry II was accidentally killed by a thrust in the eye, by the lance of Montgomerie the captain of the Scots Guard; but the beautiful French princess became one of the most beloved of Spanish Queens, and her sweetness, wisdom and goodness completely won Philip's heart.

The King was yearning for his darling Spain. It had not taken long for his policy of personal concentration of government to bring the storm clouds over his Netherlands. The Emperor, a Fleming himself, might do much and be forgiven by the sturdy burghers, but Philip was Spanish, and unsympathetic to the core, and a measure which would have been popular from a native sovereign was from him the reverse. His proposal to reconstitute the Flemish hierarchy, and create fourteen new bishoprics and three archbishoprics, was looked upon by the Netherlanders with sulky disapproval, and the presence of 4000 Spanish troops in the country aroused the fear that Spanish views both of government and religion were to be forced upon the autonomous States at the point of the pike. Philip had to listen to some bold talk at the farewell meeting of the States, and a petition was presented to him begging that the Spanish troops might be withdrawn, signed by the principal nobles of the Netherlands, Orange and Egmont amongst them. As was his wont, however, he dissembled, though he must already have decided in his stealthy way, that this manifestation must be crushed ruthlessly, if these stubborn States were to be ruled according to his centralising notions from Spain. He left the difficult task of governing the country to the Duchess of Parma, a daughter of the Emperor by a Flemish lady, and now married to Ottavio Farnese, whose principalities had been taken, and subsequently restored to him, by the imperial troops. The choice of a Regent was not an unpopular one, but all the hatred and resistance of the Flemings fell upon the man whom Philip designated as his sister's prime adviser, Antoine de Perennot, Cardinal de Granvelle, a Franche-Comtois and a foreigner, whose very appointment was regarded by the Flemings as a violation of their rights of self-government. When, therefore, Philip sailed for Spain (August 1559) he left behind him an atmosphere charged with trouble, which very soon was to develop into deadly strife.

In his absence Spain had been governed by his widowed sister Juana, whose young husband, Don João of Portugal, had died just before her appointment, leaving her with an infant who afterwards became the unfortunate King Don Sebastian. In May 1555, less than a year after Philip's departure on his matrimonial errand to England, it became necessary to summon the Cortes of Castile to vote supplies. Their parliamentary powers were in process of extinction, but they made some show of asserting them. When they conveyed to the regent the intelligence that they had voted 404 million maravedis for three years' supply, they presented 133 petitions for reform and remonstrated mildly against the disregard of similar presentments from previous Cortes. Once again they begged for a codification of the law, clamoured against the encroachments of the clergy, against luxury in coaches and dress, against the unjust incidence of taxation, the abuses of criminal procedure: in fact, they brought out all the old grievances, as fruitlessly as heretofore,—for they had voted the money first. Amongst other subsidiary petitions they begged that bull-fights should be abolished and that the household of the Prince Don Carlos should be arranged on the old Spanish lines, and not in the pompous new-fangled way of the house of Burgundy. But whilst they were clutching at these shadows, the very substance of their parliamentary rights was being haughtily taken from them. It had been a rule of the old Cortes that laws made by them could only be repealed by a vote of Cortes. In pursuance of the centralising system introduced by Charles, decrees had been issued by him abrogating parliamentary statutes, and the Cortes of 1555 begged that in future the old legal course should be followed. No answer at all was vouchsafed for three years, and then Philip gave one which fittingly foreshadowed the spirit in which he meant to govern. "If I please," he replied, "I shall annul without the Cortes the laws made in Cortes. I shall legislate by pragmatic, and I shall repeal by pragmatic." A meek protest was also raised, both in the Cortes and by the persons interested, against the arbitrary seizing for national purposes of the money coming to Seville from the Indies, on account of private merchants; but the leaders of the protest had been loaded with irons and cast into prison, and henceforward the trading and industrial classes bore the vast burden of national expenditure, with hardly any audible murmur.

In matters of religion, however, the position even in Spain was not so tranquil. The steady policy of Charles and Philip was to bring the Spanish Church under subjection to the monarch. The rich ecclesiastical preferments were now all in the King's hand, and the clergy mainly subservient. During Philip's absence and his struggle with the Pope, the Spanish council had forcibly excluded the papal bulls from Spain, and the regent had imprisoned the messengers who bore them. It was seen that, however ceremoniously Philip might treat the papacy when it suited his political objects, he looked upon it, like all else, as a tool for his semi-divine mission; and that the holy Church was to be no exception to his determination that all power, temporal and spiritual, in his dominions, should be centred in himself. The Inquisition, especially, had been guarded against any effective interference from Rome, and had already begun to assume its character as a great political agency in the hands of the monarch, working behind an ecclesiastical mask. So far as Philip's personal experience extended, all resistance to authority arose from religious divergence, and with his views as to the identity of his interests with those of the Almighty, it was obviously his duty to crush ruthlessly all manifestations of a spirit of religious independence that might lead to rebellion against his authority. The Inquisition was a convenient means for this purpose, and it became necessary for him to strengthen its authority by supporting it through thick and thin. Whilst Philip was in Brussels, he had appointed to the archbishopric of Toledo, the richest see in the world, his confessor Bartolomé de Carranza, who had made himself conspicuous by his eloquent attempts whilst in England to refute the views of the reformers. The archbishop arrived in Spain in time to stand at the deathbed of the Emperor at Yuste, and in August, 1559, was suddenly summoned from Alcalá by the regent. He knew that the spies of the Inquisition had been following him from his first landing in Spain, and fearing the meaning of the summons, tried diplomatically to delay his journey until the expected arrival of the King. He was however suddenly dragged from his bed, and carried off to the prisons of the Inquisition at Valladolid. His arrest caused the greatest consternation and indignation throughout Spain. He was accused of heretical writing in a certain commentary of his on the Catechism, which writing was unanimously approved by the Pope and the Congregation of the Index in Rome. Public opinion in Spain made no secret of its belief that he was a victim to the jealousy of Valdés, Archbishop of Seville, Inquisitor-General, who resented his elevation to the primacy. If Philip had arrived in time to prevent his arrest he would no doubt have escaped, but matters assumed another appearance when the Archbishop was in the hands of the Inquisition. Philip was friendly with Carranza, and had no reason for desiring his ruin; but the Inquisition must be supported at all risks; and so for many years it became a pitched battle between the King and the Inquisition on the one hand, and the whole Catholic Church on the other. The Pope Pius V in 1566 sought to exert his influence, and threatened to excommunicate Philip unless Carranza were sent to Rome; but the great struggle ended at last, practically in the victory of the Inquisition, for although Gregory XIII condemned Carranza to only a slight penance, he died an exile from his diocese and from Spain, in May 1576.

Philip arrived in Spain on the 8th September, 1559, and almost his first act was to mark his personal participation in the effort of the Inquisition to extirpate heresy in Spain. Before his arrival the regent Juana and his son Don Carlos had sat in the great square of Valladolid (21st May, 1559) whilst three Spanish priests and others convicted for heresy were burnt at the stake. The Cortes of Castile were sitting in Valladolid at the time, and a great multitude came from far and near to see the grand sight, the first auto da fé that had ever been witnessed in state by a prince of the house of Spain. But this show was surpassed when on October 18th Philip himself sat in his splendidly decked balcony opposite the Church of St Martin at Valladolid, surrounded by a great multitude, frantic with joy to see their beloved prince again, and to enjoy a brilliant holiday and obtain the forty days' indulgence with which the Church rewarded them for their attendance. In their presence Philip swore solemnly to maintain the purity of the faith, and to support the Holy Office, and as the condemned wretches passed his balcony on their way to death, one noble, Don Carlos de Sessa, crippled in all his limbs by the tortures he had undergone, demanded of Philip, "as from one gentleman to another," why he had submitted him to such indignity as this. Philip answered him in the ominous words, "If my son were as perverse as you, I myself would carry the fuel to burn him."

It is probable that Philip's object in thus celebrating his return home, was to strengthen the prestige of the tribunal which henceforward was to be used as a main instrument for keeping his country from the civil and religious dissensions, which he saw spreading over the rest of the world. In any case, the attitude he adopted, and even the Inquisition itself, were not unpopular with Spaniards. It must not be forgotten

that the country had been fighting for many centuries with the
enemies of the Christian faith, and that the great majority of
Spaniards exulted in the idea that their nation, and especially
their monarch, had been selected to make, as they and he
thought, common cause with the Almighty for the extirpation
of His enemies.

In the meanwhile Philip's plans for the isolation of
England, by the close union of Spain and France, were progressing amidst many difficulties. The two countries had
been enemies and rivals for many years, and the deepest
distrust still existed between them. The lovely young
princess, whom Alba had wedded as the King's proxy, slowly
travelled through France, amidst the lamentations and pity of
her brother's subjects. Both they and she knew that she was
to be handed over as a mere chattel to the Spanish King
whom they feared and hated. At the frontier endless questions of etiquette and mutual jealousies had to be settled
before she was allowed to cross the Pyrenees, and it was not
until the 30th January, 1560, that Philip met his child-wife at
Guadalajara. Their first interview was not propitious. Philip
was 33, and looked older, with his grave face; the Queen was
only 14; and as she gazed in nervous silence at her new
husband he asked her roughly whether she was looking for his
grey hairs. But they were, withal, well matched, and in a
domestic sense the next few years were the happiest in
Philip's life; though in his home circle, and with his servants,
he was always just, considerate, and beloved. The new
Queen fell ill of smallpox immediately after the marriage at
Toledo, and regardless of the remonstrances of those who
feared for his own health, her husband hardly left her during
her long illness and convalescence. Much depended upon
her life apparently, especially for her mother. Catharine de
Medici, after years of neglect, found herself by the death of
her husband practically arbitress of France, and henceforward
she meant, if she could, to keep the balance of power in her

own hands. For the moment the Guises were paramount, for the Queen-Consort was their niece Mary Stuart, but the Vendomes, the Montmorencys, and the Protestants, were ever on the watch, and if Catharine, through her daughter, could secure a hold upon Philip, she might be mistress of France, whatever faction was uppermost.

The young Queen was therefore well schooled in her lesson by her clever mother. Her task was to win the cold heart of her husband, at any cost or sacrifice, and to draw the dynasties of France and Spain closer together. The Queen played her part with infinite tact and prudence. Almost daily letters from her mother kept her from the natural mistakes of her youth; and in the inevitable bickerings between the French and Spanish courtiers who surrounded her she so bore herself as to increase her popularity with both parties. Her personal charm compelled the love of all who approached her and she did her best. But circumstances are stronger than individuals and she was sacrificed in vain.

CHAPTER III.

PHILIP II, 1560—1568.

WITH the return of Philip to Spain in 1559 may be said to commence the long period of his personal government, which left indelible traces on the history of his country. We have already glanced at his personal limitations, and the exterior problems which he inherited; we will now consider the interior condition of Spain itself, in order that we may be able at a later stage to understand the effect of the policy which he inaugurated. The representative institutions of Castile had been undermined by Charles, during whose reign the nobles and clergy were excluded from the Cortes. Under Charles and Philip the municipal life of the country, which had been so vigorous, was completely destroyed, the corregidores of the towns becoming simply magistrates appointed by the royal authority and subservient to the Council of Castile. The town councils had in former times been the basis of parliamentary representation, and with their degradation, and the subsequent corruption introduced, the Cortes became merely an institution for legalising the exactions demanded by the sovereign of the people. The administration of the country was nominally confided to eleven councils, the principal of which were the Council of State, the Council of Castile, the Council of Finance, and the Council of War. The first of these had in the earlier reigns practically assumed nearly all the executive power, but under Philip and his father it became a consultative body of favourites appointed by the King, every subject touching the international relations of the country being submitted to it for infinite discussion and report to the King by the Secretary of State. The Council of Castile was concerned in the administration of justice and the interior government, whilst the functions of the Councils of War and Finance are indicated by their names. Practically, however, every matter was now brought under the consideration of Philip himself. Early and late he toiled at his desk, copiously annotating the reports of the councils brought to him by his secretaries, reading letters and drafting replies. Matters of the gravest moment were delayed, almost indefinitely, whilst the councils were discussing and rediscussing every aspect of them, and reporting, again and again, to the King. Ambassadors and Viceroys were frequently driven to despair whilst their important letters were left unanswered month after month. Concentrated personal government, which had been the ideal of the Emperor, became a reality under the reign of his son. Men of initiative and power were not sought, or required: the ideal minister was a diligent clerk, and it was part of the system that none but men whom the sovereign had raised from the mire, and who could be cast down again by him should have real power in the central government. The nobles, divested of legislative power, had been encouraged in lavish expenditure about the court. Idleness had sapped their vigour as a class, and during the reign of Philip their vast entailed estates were heavily overburdened with debt. In pursuance of his invariable system he did his best to promote jealousy and division amongst them; and although the number of small nobles holding seignorial rights over towns was largely increased by the purchase of seignories from Charles and Philip, the Crown lost no opportunity of curtailing their privileges and favouring their vassals in all appeals against them. Only in foreign wars, viceroyalties and diplomacy, did Philip consider it safe to employ great nobles.

The material condition of the country was positively disastrous. The constant demands made by Charles and Philip for vast sums to carry on the foreign wars entailed by the fatal inheritance of the house of Burgundy fell mainly upon commerce and industry. By far the greater part of the land was tied up in possession of the clergy and great nobles, and almost escaped taxation. The clergy, indeed, were exempt from the payment of the dues which fell upon the rest of their countrymen, and only intermittently were attempts made, with very limited success, to make them bear any share at all in the national burdens. The nobles were fleeced by forced loans or the imposition of costly missions, but the main revenue of the country was drawn from the *alcabalas*, a tax of 10 per cent. on the sale value of everything which changed hands by purchase. The utter unwisdom of such a tax is obvious, and was luridly exemplified when Alba tried to impose it upon the Netherlands. Attempts were made to counteract its disastrous effects in Spain, by eliminating the middleman, by the placing of restrictions of all sorts upon the resale of goods, especially provisions (an innkeeper, for instance, not being allowed to sell the food he cooked for his customers), by the arbitrary limitation of prices by decree, by the establishment of municipal pre-emption, and the like. In addition to this suicidal source of revenue (the *alcabalas*), there were the King's share or royalty of the silver and gold remittances from the Indies, import and export duties upon goods, varying with the commercial theory of the moment, the *sisas*, a tax upon certain articles of food (which afterwards developed into the detested excise called the "millions"), the sale of titles and offices, the revenue from the sale of indulgences granted by the Pope and known by the name of the *cruzada*, the State monopoly of salt, etc. and the revenues from the royal patrimony. To add to the oppressive nature of the taxation it was usually farmed out for years ahead, in return for loans at ruinous rates from Genoese, German or Flemish bankers.

In these circumstances the chronic scarcity of currency is not to be wondered at. The temporary flash of prosperity in the cloth and silk weaving industries, which the sudden demand from the colonies had caused, was already on the wane when Philip came back to Spain. The *alcabalas*, added to the heavy municipal tolls, had so hampered the interior traffic, and conjointly with other causes had so greatly raised the price of textiles, that it was found impossible to compete with foreign cloth. It had been sought in 1549 to prevent the further rise in prices by prohibiting the weaving of finer cloths, so as to turn all hands to the textures required by the common people. It happened that the finer qualities were the only kinds in which the Spaniard could still hold his own for the foreign market, and the export trade that remained was ruined. This was seen in the following years, and the prohibition was withdrawn. At one time an attempt was made to cheapen prices by allowing the free introduction of textiles from abroad, whilst native goods were handicapped with all sorts of restrictions. At another time export was encouraged; but the measure came too late, and by the time of Philip's return nearly all the finer and more costly goods used in Spain and the Indies were of foreign make. Every nostrum was adopted to reduce the cost of production and to promote manufacture, except the obvious one of relieving industry from the crushing burden of unproductive taxation, and from the trammels which impeded the circulation of food and manufactured goods. The constant drain upon the population through foreign wars and emigration to the Indies, the enormous number of ecclesiastics, and the discouragement of industrial pursuits, which, moreover, came to be looked upon, in Castile at least, as undignified, naturally produced a considerable diminution in the number of valid citizens, both in town and country, for agriculture was as much hampered by the *alcabalas* as any other industry; and the whole population of Spain at the beginning of Philip's reign certainly did not exceed eight million souls, although in ancient times the number of its inhabitants must have been much greater. Philip's only remedy for the crushing distress of his people was to make of himself a benevolent but purblind providence. His one idea of government consisted in the abject subservience of all men to him, whilst he laboured like a very slave, settling, down to the smallest detail, everything which he thought would be for the benefit of his people. The nation gave him credit for all his laborious good intentions in its behalf, and loved him accordingly; but it credited him with a wisdom which he did not possess. No country in the world has ever been so completely ruined as Spain was by the avoidable faults and follies of its governors.

When Philip met the Cortes at Toledo in 1560, one of the subjects upon which they pressed him most was the desolation and ignominy suffered all along his coasts by the insolent incursions of Moorish pirates. He could only answer that he was doing his best. The position of Spain—even of Christianity—in the Mediterranean was, in fact, hanging in the balance. When in 1558 Paul IV and the King of France had invoked the aid of the Turk, a hundred galleys from Constantinople under Piali Pasha, with the famous Barbary pirate Dragut Reis, had scourged the coasts of Sicily and Naples, overrun Minorca, attacked Nice, and captured Tripoli, which belonged to the Knights of St John of Malta. After Philip had made peace, the Grand-Master begged him for help to recover the fortress. Philip was told that the enterprise would be easy, and he consented. Medina Celi, his Viceroy of Sicily, was to command the Spanish force, and Doria the galleys. Delay after delay was experienced in organising the force. Philip's system of doing everything himself was already paralysing his administration; but at last, in November 1559, a force of 12,000 men was assembled at Messina. The Grand-Master had originally made promptitude a condition of success, but six months had passed, and whilst Philip was tardily sending cautious dispatches to his officers, the Turk was crowding the Mediterranean with great galleys, and Dragut Reis was on the alert. Before the Spanish fleet sailed, 3000 of the men in it had died or deserted, the food was rotten, the water scarce, and the crews mutinied as soon as they left port. The fleet reached Malta on the 10th January, 1560, and shipped fresh men and provisions, sailing thence, 100 sail, a month afterwards. They captured the small island of Los Gelves in the Gulf of Khabes, but the day afterwards a fleet of 74 Turkish galleys full of janizaries, with 12 others under Dragut, from Tripoli, appeared. Medina Celi and young John Andrea Doria lost their heads. A hideous panic ensued in the Spanish fleet. The commanders fled shamefully, and 65 vessels and 5000 men fell into the hands of the infidel. The Spaniards entrenched on the island of Gelves, 8000 brave fellows, almost without provisions, stood out against terrible odds for six weeks, under Alvaro de Sande, and then all that were left of them, about 1000, stood starved and naked in the breach, to be slaughtered by the victors or carried to Constantinople to a less worthy fate.

The blow was a terrible one for the Spanish power. The only considerable Christian force in the Mediterranean had disappeared, and the victorious Moslem was practically supreme. By a great effort, and on borrowed money, Philip managed in the following year, 1561, to send out a fresh fleet of 70 hired galleys to face the Turk, and restrain his incursions; but the whole force was scattered, and mostly lost, before it left the Spanish coast, and the complete domination of the Mediterranean by the Turk appeared inevitable.

For the next three years the struggle dragged on. The coasts of Spain and Italy were ravaged almost with impunity, the Spanish fortresses on the north coast of Africa especially being the object of attack. At Mers-el-Kebir in the spring of 1563 the little Spanish garrison of 200 held out for months against a Turkish force of 20,000, and although they were almost within sight of the Spanish coast, so cumbrous was

Philip's administration that it took over two months before any relief could reach them. In the autumn of 1564 Don Garcia de Toledo managed to capture Peñon de los Velez, one of the principal nests of pirates in the kingdom of Fez. But withal the Constantinople Turk was untouched, and it was known that he was fitting out a great expedition which was to capture Malta, and finally crush Christian predominance in the Mediterranean. The Grand Master of St John, a Frenchman named Parisot de la Valette, appealed to Philip to save Christendom from the calamity which threatened it. There was no one else to whom he could appeal. France was powerless in the face of its religious dissensions, besides which it had always been the friend of the Turk against Spain: the Emperor had neither money nor galleys, and the Pope, Pius IV, could do but little and was on bad terms with Philip. The occasion was pressing, but no hurry could be expected from Philip. His treasury as usual was empty, his own kingdom of Naples was almost in open revolt against the dreaded Inquisition; and clamour as Parisot might, aid from Spain would come, it seemed, too late, if it came at all. Before the end of his reign Philip's system had paralysed all his subordinates, but at this time (1565) it had not yet entirely crushed them. Don Garcia de Toledo, the Viceroy of Sicily, was nearer to the danger than his master was, and soundly, almost rudely, rated the slow methods of the King in so great a crisis. The Turks, he knew, would not wait whilst Philip was pondering, and he took the matter in his own hands so far as he was able. Sicily and Corsica were scoured for men to replace the Spanish troops to be sent to Malta; the coasts of his Viceroyalty and of Naples were prepared for defence; reinforcements were sent to the Grand-Master, and by the time that Piali Pasha and Dragut Reis appeared before Malta with 100,000 men (19th May, 1565) there were 10,000 Christian soldiers on the island. The brunt of the Turkish attack fell upon the isolated fort of St Elmo, with a garrison of 600 men. As the defenders fell, their places were filled up with the best troops from the main island. After a month of ceaseless battery the Turks stormed the fort, and found only nine of the Christian defenders left alive.

The island, closely beleaguered, short-handed, and stricken with famine, still held out gallantly. Fresh prayers went forth from the Grand-Master to distant Philip, and to determined Toledo. Strong swimmers bore beyond the Turkish galleys beseeching letters, saying that for twenty days more at most the garrison could hold out, and after that the infidel must rule the Mediterranean. Sixteen thousand cannon-shots had been fired at the Christian forts in one month, and the end was now in view. All Christendom looked on aghast whilst Philip was spending his time in processions, fasts, and rogations, for the delivery of Malta. Don Garcia's activity to some extent made up for his master's tardiness, and, mainly owing to his continued help, Malta was still able to hold out month after month. A relief squadron of 28 galleys and 10,000 men was finally collected in Sicily. Tempest scattered it again and again, and it was September 1565 before it approached Malta. The defenders of the island had reached their last hope, but the appearance of the relief gave them new life. Don Garcia himself came with a second reinforcement of men and stores, and the Turks began to lose heart. A last attempt was made to storm the stronghold and failed; then they abandoned the siege, one of the most terrible in history, and the Christian power in the Mediterranean was saved; thanks mainly to the heroism of the Knights and the Grand-Master Parisot de la Valette.

In the meanwhile Philip was, by every means in his power, strengthening his favourite tribunal, the Inquisition. His attempt to introduce it in the Spanish form in Naples nearly lost him the realm, and even in Spain some opposition was manifested. In his address to the Castilian Cortes in February 1563, he rejoiced that owing to the aid and favour he had shown to the Holy Office, "not only had the evil (i.e. heresy) which had shown itself in the realm been extirpated, but such precautions had been taken, that it was hoped, by God's help, it would remain in future in true and pure obedience to the Catholic faith and the Roman Church." In the reply of the Cortes complaints were made of the abuses of the ecclesiastical judges, to the detriment of the ordinary judicial procedure, and the utilisation as evidence of the private reports of friars. The King's retort to this was, simply, that no change was desirable.

As usual, however, the Aragonese Cortes in the following year was much more outspoken. The members were fractious about the interference of the Castilians in their affairs. But, as Philip had told the Castilian Cortes, "the ordinary revenues were nearly all sold and pawned, the past and present supplies voted by the Cortes all spent, and every possible source of revenue consumed and anticipated, so that the King had nothing whatever with which to meet the ordinary expenditure for guarding the frontiers, the maintenance of the royal establishment, and the payment of necessary salaries." He therefore had to put up with some bold speaking from the Aragonese, who understood "grievance first." But when they roundly attacked the Inquisition an explosion nearly resulted. The ministers of the Holy Office, they said, committed all sorts of abuses and injustice, interfered in matters not relating to the faith, secured immunity for misdeeds, by appointing crowds of nominal familiars, who were absolved from civil jurisdiction ; and much else of the same sort. Philip endeavoured to shelve the question as usual; but the Aragonese would have no evasion. Philip fell ill with rage, but in the end promised that an official enquiry should be instituted by Aragonese officers : and the effect was that, after long negociations, an Act was agreed to in 1568, which, so far as Aragon was concerned, remedied some of the encroachments of the ecclesiastical tribunal in civil causes. But it went sorely against Philip's grain, and the French ambassador wrote at the time to Catharine de Medici, that he meant on the first opportunity "to cut their claws, and limit the privileges which made them so insolent, and almost free."

That Philip's plans in strengthening the Inquisition were understood, is clear from the remark in another letter from the same ambassador. "The King intends," he wrote, "principally to establish obedience to him by means of the Inquisition;" and soon the Church itself took fright at the power of the Holy Office. The Council of Trent, after many years' suspension, had met again in 1562. The French and German bishops endeavoured to unite Christendom by proposing radical reforms in the Church. They proposed that priests should be allowed to marry, and that the sacrament might be administered in two kinds. Perhaps this encouraged the Spanish bishops, or the persecution of the primate Carranza may have shown them that there was no safety even for prelates. They had been willing to aid the sovereign to strengthen his power over the Church, but when it meant placing their own lives at the mercy of an institution working for civil ends, it was another matter, and they sought in the Council of Trent to extend the papal control over the Inquisition. Philip haughtily forbade the subject to be mentioned in the Council, and his ambassador Vargas asked the Pope, Pius IV (Medici), to prevent the Council of Trent from interfering in any way. There were limits even to the patience of Pius IV, and he remonstrated with Philip for his meddling, whereupon the pontiff was arrogantly scolded by Vargas. Matters became more and more embittered. "Never was a Pope so ill treated before, as he had been by the King of Spain and his ministers," said Pius. "In Spain you all want to be Popes, and to bring the King into everything. The King may be King of Spain, but whilst I live I will be Pope." Philip threatened to withdraw Vargas, and the Pope retorted that he would cancel the right of selling the crusade bulls, from which Philip drew a considerable revenue. The religious settlement in France however caused many of the French bishops to return home, and by bribes and threats Philip once more got the upper hand in the Council of Trent. But withal, a decision was arrived at which seemed distantly to infringe upon his omnipotence over the Spanish Church. It gave the right to provincial synods, and (as a last resource) to the Pope, to enquire into the moral character of the recipients of benefices in Spain. Philip's ambassador called such resolutions "works of the devil;" and for over a year the decisions of the Council of Trent were not allowed to be promulgated in Spain. When they were finally published it was with the saving clause that nothing in them should infringe upon the King's rights over the clergy, the benefices, or the tithes.

The position in the Netherlands grew more and more threatening as time went on. The want of sympathy between the sovereign and the people had begun the breach; and Philip took no trouble to mend it. He was rigid and unadaptable, as beseemed a man who thought he was the chosen instrument of the Almighty for promoting His cause. He had probably no desire to offend the Flemings at first, but for him there was only one possible way to govern, and if the Flemings were blind enough to dislike it, that was their misfortune. That he or his system could be wrong was of course out of the question. The presence of the Spanish troops in Flanders galled the Flemings, and the rough demand of the States that they should be withdrawn hardened Philip's heart; besides he had no money to pay them, and without their wages they would not budge. It was only by using the first half of his French wife's dowry of 400,000 ducats that the troops were sent away partially satisfied early in 1561. But by this time the evil seed was sown, and Philip was reminded in every letter from Flanders of the rights which he had sworn to uphold in the several States. Most of the unpopularity fell upon de Granvelle, a foreigner, who returned the dislike of the Flemings with interest, and in pursuance of Philip's system only consulted the Flemish Council when it pleased him. Orange, Egmont and other nobles, resented this, and wrote remonstrating with Philip, who returned a temporising answer only after long delay, when matters had gone too far for conciliatory words alone and the hate towards de Granvelle had become deep and general. The Regent Margaret to some extent sympathised with her countrymen, and had no desire to share in de Granvelle's unpopularity. When, consequently, Orange begged her to summon the States General, which she could not do against de Granvelle's advice, she consented to call together the Knights of the Golden Fleece, or, in effect, the higher nobility of Flanders. The pretext of the assembly was a demand on the part of Philip that troops should be raised to aid the Catholic party then in arms in France. It was soon evident that the nobles would not trust de Granvelle with troops, and the Regent hurriedly dismissed the assembly.

Soon the religious element began to ferment. Prosperous, industrious Hainault had largely imbibed Calvinism from its French neighbours. This, said Philip, must be put down sternly. But the Flemish ministers refused to carry out Margaret's orders and torture their fellow-countrymen, in defiance of their provincial rights. Margaret threatened and imprisoned the magistrates; the people of Valenciennes took the matter into their own hands, broke open the prisons, and set the accused free. Philip and Margaret were indignant, but the Marquis of Berghes, the Governor of Hainault, was a great Flemish noble, and refused to allow any infringement of the rights of the people. Upon him de Granvelle cast the responsibility, whilst Egmont, Orange and Horn ceaselessly blamed the unpopular Cardinal, and urged the King to dismiss him. Philip was cool and temporising, as was his wont, but Alba stormed at the insolence of the Flemish nobles. "Every time I read their letters," he told the King, "I fall into such a rage that if I did not make a great effort to control myself

your Majesty would think me frantic"; and de Granvelle
fanned the flame by assuring the King that "they wanted to
reduce the country to a sort of republic, in which the King can
do no more than they like." The Regent herself told her
brother that if de Granvelle were maintained against the will of
nobles and people a revolution would result. Philip stood out
for a time, but at last, with an elaborate pretence of reluctance,
he hinted to Granvelle that a short temporary absence on
pretext of family affairs would be advisable. De Granvelle
left Flanders in the spring of 1564, to the open joy of all classes,
from the Regent downwards, and, though he did not suspect it
at the time, he was allowed to return to Flanders no more.
He had, however, only been a scapegoat, and Philip's policy
was not varied a hairbreadth in consequence of his departure.

The King was full of kind words and soft assurances to
Egmont, who went to see him in Madrid, but he had even now
made up his mind to break the spirit of the stubborn Flemings,
and stamp out once for all the talk about the rights and
privileges which he had sworn to respect. "For the interests of
God and his Majesty,"—now the invariable formula,—Flanders
must be governed like Spain, and that was enough. Thousands
of industrious citizens were flocking across to England, taking
their looms with them, and English Protestants looked more
bitterly than ever upon Philip and all his works. Holland
and Zeeland were full of Lutherans, who were determined to
stand to their faith; and Margaret told her brother plainly
that she was powerless to coerce them, for, she said, "the
governors of the provinces will not allow me to cast 60,000 or
70,000 people into the flames." Hitherto the resistance had
come mainly from the great nobles, Catholics to a man, who
had merely asserted the time-honoured constitution of the
States. But now Protestants like St Aldegonde and others
swore to resist the proceedings of the Inquisition, and to stand
up against "the gang of strangers"; and then the little
gentlemen and burghers under Brederode threw down the

gauntlet, and the "beggars" were born at that sottish banquet at the house of Culemburg (April, 1566), to be quelled no more till the country which their own fathers had rescued from the sea was free from the Spaniard for evermore.

The great nobles hung back now—all but Orange, who bode his time in spite of Philip's blandishments—but Protestant fervour and national patriotism blazed out irresistibly. The Regent was powerless; she could not punish all Flanders, and she ceaselessly urged gentler methods upon her brother. His action at this juncture was characteristic of him. He authorised Margaret to suppress the Inquisition and pardon the confederates; and with soft words tried to win Orange to his side. And then a week later he suddenly threw off the mask; signed a solemn declaration that he was not bound by his promise, and swore that he would rather lose his dominions and a hundred lives, if he had them, than allow any backsliding in religion; "for I will never be a ruler of heretics." Then began the tumults, the wrecking of Catholic churches, the desecration of shrines, the mob violence which dismayed the Regent. The Catholic nobles did their best to stem the tide of disorder, the Regent made such concessions as she dared; but Alba in Madrid was fuming with rage at Philip's slowness in crushing such insolence under the iron heel. At length Orange reverted to the Protestant faith of his fathers, openly sided with the revolted Flemings, and promised to lead the cause of reform when the time came. The tumults ceased as if by magic. Orange had gone to Germany to raise his forces, and the cry went out that he had abandoned the cause. The Protestants lost heart. Thousands of them fled to England, many submitted, and many others suffered martyrdom. Margaret entered Antwerp in state, and all rejoiced but those who were led to the stake for the sake of "God and his Majesty." But the calm did not deceive Philip. He knew that Orange was in earnest, and that to make Flanders a province of Spain he must utterly crush the national feeling and the nobles who led it. So he determined to go himself, with Alba by his side, to conduct the operation. At least he announced his intention of doing so, and fitted out a great fleet for the purpose. All was quiet now, said Margaret, and no more punishment was needed. In that case, replied Philip, he would come personally to thank those who had brought about so happy a change.

When all was ready, and the force collected, no longer an escort, but an avenging army, it was decided that Alba should go alone. In vain Margaret protested. The Duke, she said, was so detested that his mere coming would make all Spaniards hated. She threatened to retire if Alba came, and she was allowed to do so, with every sign of disgrace. Europe understood now what was to be expected, and Protestants of all nationalities closed their ranks, in face of what was seen to portend a systematic attempt to crush religious freedom throughout Christendom. Alba left Spain in April 1567, to march through Italy on his fell errand to the Netherlands. Alba and the fanatic churchmen had for once overborne in Philip's councils the peace party of Ruy Gomez and the mild remonstrances of the Marquis of Berghes and Florence de Montmorenci, lord of Montigny, two Flemish nobles who had been sent to Madrid on behalf of their countrymen, and who were on various pretexts detained there. But the determination adopted by Philip was not carried out without considerable friction amongst his councillors; and the departure of Alba gave rise to an incident which culminated in the greatest domestic sorrow of the King's life. His only son Don Carlos (born 8th July, 1545) had always been stunted and malformed in figure, imperfect in speech, and vacant in mind, but his prospects made him the greatest match in Europe. Catharine de Medici had secretly instructed her daughter Elizabeth, when she had gone to marry Philip in 1560, to endeavour to bring about a marriage between Carlos and Elizabeth's sister Margaret, who was afterwards the famous wife of Henry of Navarre. This was in order to prevent the Emperor Maximilian from getting the heir of Spain for his daughter, which would have been distinctly against French interests. Every Cortes for years past had urged that Carlos should be married, and the succession assured; and French and Austrian intrigue was busy, but to all approaches Philip replied with bland evasion.

The best match for his policy would unquestionably have been that with the widowed Mary Stuart, for by this means Scotland and England, too, might have fallen again under Spanish influence. But tempting even as this was, when proposed on Mary's behalf, before she drifted into marriage with Darnley, Philip neglected to seize it. Rumours began to run that Carlos was neither physically nor mentally in a condition for marriage. He had been brought up by his aunt, the widow Doña Juana, to whom he was extravagantly attached; and when Elizabeth of Valois found she could not get him for her sister, she endeavoured to bring about his marriage with his aunt, and the Cortes of 1563 addressed the King in favour of the match. Exactly a year before (April 1562) Carlos had accidentally fallen down a flight of stone steps at Alcalá and had suffered a concussion of the brain. He was unskilfully treated by the doctors, ghastly superstitions were resorted to instead of proper surgical treatment, and he lay unconscious, blind and partially paralysed, until an Italian surgeon trepanned him, and he then apparently recovered. He was a congenital epileptic before: he now became at intervals a lunatic. His hatred of his father was intense, whilst his attachment to his aunt and his stepmother was an infatuation. He was a prey to constant fever and agues. As he grew up his mad humours became more unrestrained and unconcealable, until his violent and disgraceful behaviour, even in the street, provoked public scandal. He respected neither age nor rank, and attempted to murder his Governor Don Garcia de Toledo, Cardinal Espinosa, the Inquisitor-General, and many other persons of high degree. At last Ruy Gomez, Philip's dearest friend, was appointed his Governor. It is quite probable that he may have instilled into the Prince his views as to the advisability of a conciliatory policy with the Flemings, and it is certain that some sort of communication was addressed to him by the Flemish nobles then in the Spanish Court, though the often made assertion that he embraced the Protestant views appears to rest on no solid foundation. In any case he was violently bent upon accompanying his father to Flanders, and when he found that Alba was to go alone his fury passed all bounds, and he attempted to stab the Duke when he went to bid him farewell, and shrieked that he, and not the Duke, must go to Flanders.

From that time his father was estranged from him, and his conduct grew worse and worse. At Christmas 1567, he spoke wildly to his young half-uncle, Don Juan of Austria, about escaping from Spain and killing a man with whom he had quarrelled, and in the confessional the Prior of the Atocha drew from him the avowal that the man was his father. Word was sent to Philip at the Escorial, and the Prince was closely watched. In the middle of January 1568 he made arrangements for flight. Suspecting that Don Juan had betrayed him, he tried to kill him, and on the same night (18 January) Philip himself, dressed in armour, entered his son's room with his guards and arrested his son. Through all the bitter trial Philip had never lost his marble serenity, but his pride and domestic affection, for he was a fond and loving father, must have been pierced to the heart. He made the mistake of trying to hide the real cause of the arrest by vague generalities, but the case was too important to be glozed over, and gossip soon became rife throughout Europe. Henceforward Carlos was kept in close confinement. Neither his aunt nor his stepmother was allowed to see him. Some sort of trial or examination of him dragged on for months, and Philip's many enemies were busy with rumours that the Inquisition were to sacrifice him for heresy. There is however no evidence that this was the case; and certainly those best likely to know do not suggest it. Positive it is that the Prince's madness grew. He often refused food for days together or swallowed inedible substances. On 21st July, 1568, the French Ambassador wrote that he was dying of weakness. "The King," he says, "is much grieved because if he die the world will talk."

The next day the Prince died. Philip's bitter foes—and particularly the traitor Antonio Perez—positively stated that Carlos was murdered by the King's orders. The whole balance of evidence, however, goes to show that he died of his own maniacal aberrations. On the 3rd October in the same year Philip's third wife, Elizabeth of Valois, died in childbed, through the unskilfulness of the Spanish physicians, leaving Philip with two children, both girls, to whom he was devotedly attached, as he had been to their mother. Henceforward till the hour of his death the elder of these two children, Isabel Clara Eugenia, was his chosen companion and solace through all his trouble—and he had a greater share than falls to the lot of most men—borne with the dignified patience that was to be expected from one who sincerely believed that the Almighty was working through him for His own inscrutable ends. Once only during her married life was the object for which Elizabeth of Valo was sent to Spain within reach of accomplishment. When the English Queen and the Huguenots began to draw closer and aid the Protestant Flemings, Philip arranged an interview between his wife and her mother (1565) in order to bind Catharine hard and fast to the Catholic cause. Elizabeth of England at once met this by close professions of friendship to France, and opened negotiations for her marriage with Charles IX. When Alba made it clear to Catharine at Bayonne that she would have to pledge herself to exterminate Protestantism root and branch in France, she saw that the terms would not suit her; and though she affected to consent, she brought forward new conditions which made the arrangement impossible, and it fell to the ground. By the time that his third wife died, therefore, Philip recognised that he would

have to face and destroy religious reform alone, throughout the
world, or be himself destroyed.   Even now, a policy of toleration and the abandonment of his fetish of centralisation of
power would have enabled him to become friendly with
England; and he and his country might have been saved from
ruin.   But his slow mind was incapable of initiating policies.
He had inherited his system, as he had inherited the difficulties
which his system could not conquer; and all he could do was
to plod on laboriously, a slave to duty, in the besotted certainty
that he could not fail in the long run, because, forsooth, his
cause and that of the Almighty were indissolubly linked together.

CHAPTER IV.

PHILIP II, 1568—1581.

Though Philip might boast that the Inquisition had absolutely cleared Spain of the virus of Protestantism, he had religious questions of another sort to deal with in his own country. On the capture of Granada full religious toleration had been promised to the Moors, but the bigoted zeal of the churchmen had subsequently prevailed, and uniformity of faith and customs had gradually been forced upon the Spanish citizens of Moorish descent. Nearly all the south of Spain was inhabited by peoples of pure or mixed Moorish blood; industrious, thrifty, and peaceable, outwardly conforming to the Christian faith, garb and manners, but to a great extent secretly following in the footsteps of their forefathers. They were in gradual process of amalgamation, and if they had been left alone they would in time have been merged in the rest of the population. Their thrift and industry, however, were a source of jealousy to the Christians, who constantly accused them of sympathising with the Turk in the Mediterranean, which they probably did. Some of the Emperor's edicts against them had been allowed to fall into abeyance during his long absence, but as soon as Philip returned to Spain the Cortes began to clamour for fresh restrictions on the Moriscos. First, in 1560, the importation of slaves from Africa was forbidden. In 1563 the Moriscos were prohibited from possessing arms, an enactment which caused much discontent. When Cardinal Espinosa became a power at court, and was made Inquisitor-General, the systematic oppression of the poor people was commenced. In 1567 they were forbidden to wear any distinctive garb, and the women were to appear with their faces uncovered. They were not allowed to have locks to their doors, their warm baths were made illegal; and above all, they might use no other language but Castilian, and acknowledge no other faith but the Christian.

All this was to be enforced with brutal penalties, thanks to the efforts of Espinosa in Madrid, and Deza—afterwards Cardinal—in Granada. In vain the Ruy Gomez party protested and expostulated; in vain the Marquis of Mondejar, the governor of Granada, pointed out the impossibility of carrying out such decrees suddenly; the churchmen would have no half-measures, and at length (Christmas, 1568) the inevitable storm burst. Up in the savage Alpujarras the revolt against the edict was first organised. A youth named Aben Humeya, said to have been a descendant of the prophet, was proclaimed King of Granada, and appeals for aid were sent to Barbary and Constantinople. On the night of 26th December, 1568, the mountain Moors suddenly pounced upon sleeping Granada, and called upon the men of their race to strike against the tyrant. Sacking, plundering and desecrating the Christian shrines, the mountaineers swept through the city; but the large Morisco population, cowed by terror, made no move. Through the fertile plain of Granada the revolutionaries passed without resistance, carrying torture and murder with them. Blazing villages and murdered country folk— three thousand of them on the Vega of Granada alone—rapine and ruin over all the smiling land, told once more of the irresistible blood-lust of the slave rising against his oppressor. Through all Andalucia the fever for freedom spread, and centuries of hate were concentrated in a week of slaughter. The governor of Granada (Mondejar) raised what force he could, and defeated the revolutionists in the pass of Alfajarali; and then the massacre began on the other side. The Marquis de los Velez with another hastily mustered force set out in the early spring of 1569 on a mission of massacre. Slaughter without pity or distinction of age or sex was the order of the day, until slaughter itself palled. On one occasion Velez's soldiers killed 6000 women and children in the course of a few hours, and kept 4000 more as slaves. Soon the Spanish force became demoralised and began to melt away, breaking up into separate bands devoted to private plunder.

Deza in the meanwhile sent constant complaints to Madrid of the moderation of the governor (Mondejar) and it was decided to send thither the brilliant young natural son of Charles V, Don Juan of Austria. He had been brought up in the tenets of Ruy Gomez and Secretary Antonio Perez, and it was no doubt hoped that he would smooth matters over. He was however dashing, ambitious, and romantic; and diplomacy was not his strong point. He was sent to Granada in 1569 with strict orders to take no personal part in the mountain warfare, but to report diligently to Philip the real position of affairs. He began to chafe at his mission as soon as it began and begged for more active work, only to be told that he must obey orders. The remedy of the bigoted churchmen was to expel every person of Moorish blood from Granada, and the distasteful task fell to Don Juan. Thirteen thousand of them, mostly quite innocent of participation in the risings, were sent to labour in the galleys or the mines, or more mercifully hanged, whilst the women and children were sent to slavery in frowning Castile. Beautiful Granada was ruined, and Mondejar's heart well-nigh broken; but Deza, Espinosa and the other churchmen had no pity. In the meanwhile the revolutionists in the mountains were weakened by dissensions; Aben Humeya was murdered, and a stout blow struck now would have ended the revolt. But los Velez's force had become simply a mob of marauders, unpaid and mutinous, and no service could be expected from them. At last Philip listened to the prayers of his brother, and gave him a free hand.

Round the one regiment of veterans he grouped a fresh force, his energy and popularity more than supplying his want of experience. With 13,000 men he besieged Galera and took it by assault on the 16th February, 1570. Once more massacre and pillage demoralised the Spanish force, and only a few days later the victors were routed by an absurdly inferior force of Moors at Seron and became once more an uncontrollable rabble. But the rising now was practically at an end, and the Moors sued for terms. Don Juan himself advocated an agreement, and begged for clemency for the vanquished. But the fanatics would not hear of it, and to Don Juan's indignation he was ordered to expel from Andalucia—the smiling land which their forefathers' labour for centuries past had turned into a garden—every soul who bore the taint of Moorish blood. To slavery or death, without truce or mercy, the poor creatures were driven forth. "It is," wrote Don Juan to Ruy Gomez, "the saddest sight imaginable to see the depopulation of a whole kingdom," but notwithstanding his protests, by the end of 1570 the patient, thrifty, industrious Morisco citizens of Andalucia had left their native land, and with them had gone for many a long year its productiveness and prosperity.

Calamity crowded on Spain from every side, and each Cortes in succession pressed upon the King the utterly exhausted condition of the country. Alba's policy of blood and fire in Flanders drained Spain both of men and money. Privateers, or pirates who claimed to be such, English, Huguenot, and Flemish, crowded the seas, and almost annihilated Spanish shipping. The Turk was busy in the Mediterranean, and Philip was at his wits' end for money. The Cortes of Castile in 1566 plucked up courage to protest against the imposition of fresh burdens without parliamentary authority, and the King apologetically explained that, the treasury being absolutely exhausted, he had been forced to raise money as he could. The soft answer, however, did not satisfy the members, and for a time a dead-lock occurred, the

Cortes refusing to vote fresh supplies unless a pledge were given that no similar illegal taxes should be imposed in future; a pledge which ultimately had to be given by the King, after the ordinary supply of 304 millions of maravedis in three years had been voted, but before the extraordinary vote of 150 millions was passed. At the end of 1569 Philip's difficulties were still further increased by the seizure by Elizabeth of £31,000 in money which was being sent to Flanders, the ships conveying it being forced into English ports to escape privateers. The amount had been borrowed on onerous terms from Genoese bankers to pay Alba's troops, and its loss led to further humiliation for Philip. His ambassador, De Spes, was expelled from England with even more indignity than Philip had used in the expulsion of Dr Man, the English ambassador, from Spain in 1568; and the seizure of English shipping and property in Spain and Flanders led to reprisals in England by which the commerce of Spain suffered more severely still, for the wines and oils and other products of Andalucia rotted in the stores for want of ships in which to export them.

Thus, when Philip met his Cortes in 1570, both he and his subjects were in greater straits than ever. In the King's opening address he said that, "The royal treasury was quite exhausted, all the patrimony drained and consumed, the royal revenues spent, sold, pawned, and transferred, and his Majesty absolutely unable to meet even the ordinary expenditure for the maintenance of his royal state—much less the important extraordinary calls upon him. Although his Majesty, with his invariable desire to relieve these kingdoms, has endeavoured to resort to other means of raising money, he has been unable to get the great sums he needs, and all he has obtained has already been spent." He concluded by saying that unless his people were liberal, both religion and the state would be in danger. But withal the vote was no larger than usual, and the members for ruined Granada protested

that their constituency could pay nothing at all. This did not
satisfy the King, who urged them to consider what new taxes
were possible. They reported in March 1571 that the condition of the country was so disastrous that the Cortes dared
not burden it further, and in this they stood firm until they
were dismissed. But before they separated they adopted
another spirited remonstrance against the illegal raising of
taxes by the King without the authority of the Cortes. A
similar course was followed by the Cortes of 1573, where
again, the ordinary vote of 304 millions of maravedis (*i.e.*
300 millions for the King and 4 millions for the members of
the Cortes), with the usual 150 millions extra, were all that
Philip could obtain. The provinces of Granada, Murcia,
Jaen, and Granada again protested that they were utterly
unable to pay anything at all. The parliamentary rights of
the Castilians however went no further than protests now, and
they received an additional blow in this Cortes of 1573. The
sturdy Aragonese took care, on each occasion that they voted
supplies, to state distinctly that they did it of their own free
will, and that their vote must not be taken as a precedent.
The Castilian Cortes had continued to vote their 300 million
maravedis each three years, without taking this precaution;
when therefore on this occasion they began discussing the vote,
they were told on behalf of the King that the 300 millions were
a tribute that they were obliged to pay to the King, the voting
being a mere matter of form; and henceforward it apparently
became so. Money however had to be obtained somehow in
larger quantities, and without parliamentary sanction the King
again raised the taxation upon salt—which had been created
a royal monopoly—wool, and various other merchandise.
Against this the Cortes of 1576 once more protested, and also
against the continued alienation of the seignories of the Crown
over towns and villages; but in both cases fruitlessly, for the
King, in effect, replied that necessity overrode the law.

In these circumstances it may well be believed that the

Catholic party in England could obtain but little effective help from Philip in the interests of the imprisoned Mary Stuart. Vague approval, conditional promises, small sums of money, were doled out in aid of Ridolfi's plot, of Norfolk's treason, of the rising of the Northern lords: but Philip was far too hardly pressed to come to open war with England, and fiery Alba himself frankly told him as much in February 1569. Philip's timidity and slowness had brought him to this pass in fifteen years of rule. He and his people were bankrupt, his shipping nearly swept from the sea, his treasure taken, and his rebel subjects upheld against him by the English Queen; and yet he was unable even to retaliate, except by the subornation of secret murder. To prevent the utter ruin of the Andalucian producers and shippers Philip was forced to connive at the violation of his own edicts forbidding trade with England, while proud Alba was brought to his knees in 1573 and opened again the markets of Flanders to English cloth. For Flanders by this time was far on the road to utter exhaustion under Alba's rule of blood, and the old Duke himself was heartsick and weary of a task, in which he could not help seeing that he had failed.

There is no doubt that when he went to Flanders in 1567 it was for the set purpose of stamping out the Flemish national feeling, striking first at the nobles who led it. Montigny and Berghes were in Spain and Philip looked after them, but Orange, Egmont and Horn, were to be disposed of as soon as Alba arrived. The two latter fell into the trap, and were captured after the grim dinner-party in Brussels (9 September, 1567), whilst Orange's caution alone saved him from a similar fate. The persecution was at first not a religious one, for the nobles were Catholics, and the monks were the first to fly on Alba's advent, followed by the rich burgesses, also Catholics almost to a man. They fled because Alba's troops respected Catholics no more than Protestants, and were quartered on all citizens alike. There was in Flanders itself no resistance on religious lines at first. "The citizens flocked to church," said Alba himself, "like Spaniards in jubilee time." But when the people began to hurry away in shoals to England, Alba brought down his hand and began by hanging 500 citizens who were suspected of an intention to run away. On the flight of Orange's mercenary Germans at Heiliger Lee, and the collapse of the revolt for a time, Alba's deliberate holocaust of innocent citizens all over Flanders was intended to strike terror to such an extent that Flemish patriotism should never again raise its head. It was successful for a time, and on the 1st July, 1570, Alba could announce his amnesty of forgiveness for all faithful Flemish subjects of the King.

It was not religion, it was not even patriotism, which finally aroused the Flemings to fury and made them join hands with the Protestant Zeelanders. It was the "eternal lack of pence" which afflicted Philip's treasury. The *alcabala* of 10 per cent. on every sale and purchase was suffered in Spain because its effects were not understood, but in commercial and industrial Flanders, where economical questions had been studied for centuries, its impossibility was seen at once. The "tenth penny" did what patriotism and religion themselves could not do: it welded all Netherlanders of the trading and industrial classes into one. The first result was the bankruptcy, real or pretended, of the Flemish bankers, upon whom Philip largely depended for loans. Philip's council remonstrated with Alba. Bishops, councillors, confessors, Flemings and Spaniards too, protested against the tax; Philip himself was more than doubtful. "Everybody turns against me," wrote the Duke, and he was right in this. But he stuck to his guns. He was face to face with a stubborn people, fighting not alone for autonomy now, not alone for religion. They were fighting for their money bags—for their industrial existence—and they fought sturdily. For a time the spirit of the southern Flemings was utterly cowed by fierce brutality, almost unexampled in civilized history; the French Huguenot sympathisers were massacred without mercy; and throughout Flanders submission the most abject was the only alternative to slaughter. But what cowed Walloons and Brabanters only made stubborn Dutchmen the more stubborn, and Holland and Zeeland still stood firm. By 1573 Philip himself was tired of Alba's fruitless cruelty, against which all Christendom was crying. Cardinal Espinosa had died of sheer fright when the usually impassive King roughly told him that he lied as to the effect of Alba's proceedings (September 1572). The Ruy Gomez party was now paramount, and plausible Antonio Perez, Alba's deadly enemy, was always at the King's ear.

Philip was not a cruel man by nature, though no consideration of human suffering was allowed for a moment to influence his policy. In his view success in the object justified carnage, but unsuccessful or wanton carnage was distasteful to him. So the old Duke, whose hard heart was nearly broken by his failure, was recalled, and a new era of moderation and conciliation commenced under Don Luis de Requesens y Zuñiga (September 1573). He had to struggle against the hatred aroused by Alba's cruelty, but withal he was not unsuccessful in calming the Catholic south. But the Hollanders held their own, and Requesens died before his work of pacification was done (March 1576). Like all Philip's officers he had prayed constantly for money—and prayed in vain, for, as we have seen, Spain was well-nigh squeezed dry. The troops in Flanders were unpaid, a murderous, mutinous rabble, and the King was given clearly to understand by his friends in Flanders that, unless these ruffians were withdrawn, Catholic Brabant, Hainault and Artois, would follow Protestant Zeeland, and slip from his grasp. His position was such that it was absolutely impossible for him to carry on war any longer, and he bent to the inevitable. The decision to pacify the Netherlands, at almost any cost, also relieved him of another difficulty which had caused him endless anxiety and worry.

When the Turks had abandoned the siege of Malta they

did so with their great naval power still intact, and this the new Sultan Selim determined to turn against the Venetians, the great trading power in the Levant. The interests of Philip and the Venetians had usually been divergent, and when the republic found that its island of Cyprus was being attacked (1569) and that the Cypriotes were welcoming the infidel, the seigniory first appealed to the Pope for help. Pius V promptly summoned Philip to join in crippling his old enemy the Turk. The proposal reached him when he had just succeeded in crushing his own Moriscos, and when Alba's short and fallacious calm had been attained in Flanders. Young Don Juan was by Philip's side, fresh from victories over the Moriscos and aflame to cope once more with the infidel. His persuasions, backed by those of the Nuncio, prevailed; and after three days of prayer for guidance at the shrine of St Fernando in Seville the King decided to put away his unfriendliness to the merchant republic and join it in beating the infidel. This was in the spring of 1570, but before the Spanish and Papal galleys could be ready Nicosia had fallen, and the Venetians were negotiating with the Turk for a separate peace. This was a danger which had to be avoided: the Venetians must be brought back to the league, which was intended to be a permanent one to break the power of the Turk in the Mediterranean. Philip lost no opportunity of advancing his own political interests, and the alliance was made a pretext for extorting from Pius V a promise to abstain from interfering again with the Inquisition in Spain—as he had made some slight attempt to do recently at the request of the Catalan Cortes: he also renewed the King's right of selling the "Crusade" bulls in Spain.

It was therefore late in the summer of 1571, before the great combined fleet of 208 galleys, 6 galleasses and 50 small boats, with 29,000 men at arms, and 50,000 sailors and rowers, collected at Messina, under the supreme command of Don Juan. The Turks had captured Cyprus, and were ravaging the coasts of the Adriatic. Christian fervour had been worked up to a point of frenzy. The Pope had sent the sacred banner to Don Juan, and prayers were offered throughout Catholic Christendom for the new Crusade. The handsome and splendid young prince was a hero of romance in the eyes of men and women alike. It was the age of chivalry, be it remembered, when Amadis de Gaul, and the adventures of Arthur and his knights, formed a main part of the literary life of the people; and Don Juan was hailed as the Christian champion who was to raise for ever the Cross over the Crescent. Every free man on the fleet, high and low, was inflamed with religious fervour: prayers, fastings and penitence took the place of soldiers' oaths and sailors' roystering; and when at dawn on Sunday, the 7th October, Don Juan sighted the Turkish fleet in the bay of Lepanto, every man knelt before the crucifix, and was absolved by the monks who crowded the ships. Through his fleet Don Juan was rowed in his pinnace, crying exhortations to his men, "The hour of vengeance has come. Christ is your leader. This is the battle of the Cross!" With such a feeling as this the Christians were irresistible. Doria and other experienced commanders were for avoiding an engagement, but Don Juan could not be held back. The Turkish fleet was swept from the seas and the naval power of the Sultans broken for ever.

Much of the credit for the victory must be given to the cool old hero Santa Cruz for his support at a critical moment, but brilliant young Don Juan, with his handsome face and his dress of white velvet and gold, was made the idol of victory, and all Christendom rang with adulation of him. Prudence and restraint were forgotten. Don Juan was to conquer anew the empire of Constantine and become the ruler of the Christian orient; and with the encouragement of Rome the prince kept his fleet together, praying Philip constantly for money to carry out his vast projects. But, as we have seen, Philip had no money to send, and dared not allow himself to be dragged into fresh schemes for the benefit of his base-born brother.

Nevertheless, in October 1573 Don Juan sailed and captured Tunis, which he hoped to make the nucleus of a Christian empire of North Africa. Philip and the peace party of Ruy Gomez and Perez began to see now that Don Juan was a dangerous person, and orders were sent to him to dismantle Tunis. These orders he disobeyed, and Philip cut off supplies. De Granvelle, too, who was now viceroy of Naples, adopted a similar attitude, and for want of support Tunis and La Goletta were recovered by the Turk within a year, 8000 Spaniards being slaughtered. Don Juan was clamorous and indignant, and was rapidly getting out of hand. His projects of empire were unappeased, and he was claiming the full privileges of a prince of the blood. Philip was always distrustful and suspicious, but he was averse to violent measures, and on the advice of his principal secretary Antonio Perez (Ruy Gomez being recently dead) sent one of his own secretaries named Escobedo, a member of the peace party, to be a mentor to Don Juan, and, if possible, to bring him down from the clouds. But Don Juan's enthusiasm was contagious, and soon Escobedo surpassed his new master in highflown schemes for Don Juan's future aggrandisement.

It was at this juncture that Requesens died in the Netherlands (March 1576), and Don Juan was ordered to proceed thither to pacify the country, on any terms consistent with Philip's sovereignty, and the maintenance of Catholicism. The Spanish troops were to be withdrawn, and the Flemings conciliated, come what might. This seemed to be an excellent pretext for getting Don Juan away from the dangerous neighbourhood of the Mediterranean. But Philip and Perez had reckoned without Don Juan. He and Escobedo were full of another plan now. With the Spanish troops to be withdrawn from Flanders, Don Juan was suddenly to swoop down on the English coast, and with the aid of the Catholic party there, liberate and marry the captive Mary Stuart, and rule over a Catholic Great Britain. The new Pope, Gregory XIII, had urged the idea upon Philip, but the latter could not allow his policy to be dictated by others. None knew his difficulties so well as he himself; and he had plans of his own, to be mentioned presently, to which this new project would have been fatal. So Don Juan was ordered to proceed directly from Italy to Flanders on his distasteful errand of conciliation, without a day's delay. Again he disobeyed orders, and suddenly appeared in Madrid, with Escobedo, to press his own views. Philip kept his temper, calmly evaded his brother's claims, and sent him to Flanders as soon as possible. But Philip's only idea of government was that all men should obey him absolutely; and henceforward he knew that his brother was not to be trusted. The prince had now quite broken with the peace party, of which Perez was the leader since Ruy Gomez's death, and it was policy for Perez to undermine the influence of one who would be so powerful a political rival to him. He had learnt that, notwithstanding the King's orders, Don Juan still cherished the scheme of invading England from Flanders, and both the prince and Escobedo kept up a close confidential correspondence with him. All they wrote was shown to the King, and his distrust still further aroused. Hasty and disparaging expressions of Don Juan were twisted to a treasonable meaning, until Perez had the satisfaction of seeing that the flighty romantic young prince was hopelessly ruined in the estimation of his brother the King.

Don Juan's disobedience and delay had ruined his mission. Before he could arrive in Flanders the "Spanish fury" had fallen upon Antwerp (4 November, 1576). The unpaid mutinous Spanish soldiery had killed 6000 unarmed citizens, had burnt and plundered 12,000,000 ducats'-worth of property, and Netherlanders of all creeds were united to withstand their unbridled rapine. Even those who through all had stood faithful to Spain, joined the cause of order now. The De Croys, Champigny, De Granvelle's brother, and the like, were at one with Orange; and Don Juan when he reached Luxemburg, was told that he could only be received on certain terms, to be dictated to him by the States. Above all, the brutal Spanish soldiers must be withdrawn at once, *and by land*. He was in despair. Again and again he begged that Philip would intrust the task of submission to other hands than his—a woman would do it better, he said. Wild and foolish threats of suicide, and other desperate courses still further steeled his brother's heart against him, and the breach between them became wider. The troops would not move without their pay, and Philip sent no money; he had, indeed, none to send, nor, as Escobedo rudely told him, was his credit good enough to borrow on, for in 1575 he had simply repudiated the debts he owed abroad. But by the spring of 1577 Don Juan, through Escobedo, had borrowed on his own credit of the merchants enough to induce the troops to march, and thereupon made his "joyous entry" into Brussels—joyous for all but him, for disappointment and disgust were raging in his heart, and he loathed the Flemings who welcomed him. He had threatened for months to return to Spain in defiance of orders, but in the summer of 1577 he sent Escobedo instead, to press his schemes and make arrangement for payment of the loans he had raised.

Shortly after Escobedo's arrival in Spain, where he and his mission were unwelcome, Philip secretly ordered Perez to have him killed—the accepted idea then being that as the King was the fountain of all law, he could order a private execution without judicial process. Soon afterwards news came that Don Juan had broken with the States and thrown himself into Namur, and that a fresh war was in progress, in which, for the first time, Orange and the Catholic Flemings were making common cause. The blow was a bitter one for Philip, and he let his turbulent brother rage his heart out almost unsupported. Philip's nephew, Alexander Farnese, was sent with an army to conquer the States and afterwards to conciliate the Catholics. He and Don Juan together gained the battle of Gemblours (31st January, 1578), but Don Juan's spirit was broken. His faithful Escobedo was found stabbed to death in the streets of Madrid (31st March, 1578). He knew that he would never be allowed to rule in Flanders, or elsewhere, that Philip would not have him in Spain, that he was distrusted, hated, and ruined. His vague ambitions gone, without the keen wit enough to free himself from the toils that artful Perez had wound about him, he died brokenhearted, on the 1st October, 1578, of malignant fever. His death relieved Philip from an intolerable position, and the military skill and diplomacy of Alexander Farnese gradually introduced division again between the Protestant Hollanders and the Catholic Flemings.

Meanwhile all Philip's indirect attempts to bring trouble upon Elizabeth, and to prevent her from supporting the Netherlanders in their struggle, had failed ignominiously. She was well served with spies, his cumbrous and tardy action was always anticipated. He was not ready yet for open war with England, for Catharine de Medici still held the balance in France, and was looking covetously at Flanders as a future dominion for her youngest son Alençon. The opportunity of an open struggle with England would certainly have been taken by Catharine still further to hamper him; but it was vital for him, if possible, to keep both Elizabeth and Catharine busy without open warfare with them, whilst he carried out a plan which he fondly hoped would render him powerful enough to withstand them. He patronised and mainly defrayed the cost of an invasion of Ireland under the Pope's banner, by expeditious sailing from a Spanish port in aid of the Desmond rebellion 1579 and 1580; but the whole force, 800 men, was massacred at Smerwick (November 1580), and he dared not attempt to avenge them by an open declaration of war. His method of rendering Catharine innocuous to him was similar. He drew closer to the Guises, and promised them support against the Huguenots, who, under Elizabeth's patronage, were promoting Alençon's scheme for obtaining the sovereignty of the Netherlands.

Philip's object was a far reaching one. His young nephew Sebastian, King of Portugal, as fervent and romantic as Don Juan, had fallen in the battle of Alcazar, in his hairbrained crusade against the Moors (7th August, 1579); and his successor on the throne was the aged childless Cardinal Henry. He was only a stop-gap, and as soon as he succeeded Philip began to intrigue for the Portuguese Crown. With the fine harbour of Lisbon, the great Portuguese commerce, and the wealth of the East as well as the West, he could work well, he thought, upon his enemies. The claimants to the Crown were many. Philip was the son of King Manoel's eldest daughter Isabel, the Duke of Savoy was a son of a younger daughter Beatrix, the Duchess of Braganza was a daughter of Manoel's son Duarte, and Alexander Farnese had married her younger sister. The popular claimant was the Prior of Crato, a doubtfully legitimate son of Luis, a younger son of Manoel. Foreigners were supposed to be ineligible for the Crown, but Philip contended that a Spaniard could not be considered a foreigner in Portugal. The Portuguese, however, hated the Castilians, and notwithstanding Philip's bribes and intrigues, the first movement of the Portuguese people was to proclaim Antonio King on the death of the Cardinal. The council of regency, however, had been gained to the side of Philip; and with the knowledge of this he determined to take Portugal by force of arms if needful. Alba had been disgraced long ago by the machinations of Perez on an utterly inadequate pretext, and old De Granvelle had been kept away from the government of Spain, but Perez, for reasons presently to be explained, was already a waning force, and in any case his glib tongue and ready pen were not the desiderata in the present juncture. So the old soldier Alba was summoned from his retreat to lead Philip's army to the conquest of Portugal, and the old statesman De Granvelle was recalled to govern

Spain whilst his master took possession of this new kingdom.

Alba's task was comparatively easy. There was no religious question to make men obstinate, the Portuguese nobles had all been bought, or forced into exile; the people were poor and cowardly, without leaders or resources; and Alba rode roughshod over them, with but small resistance. King Antonio was beaten at Alcantara and Viana and fled; after eight months' wanderings he escaped to France, and thence to England; whilst Philip travelled by slow stages with all his court from Madrid to Lisbon. With him went his fourth wife Anne, daughter of his sister Maria and of the Emperor Maximilian, whom he had married in 1570. By her he had had several children, three of whom he had left in Madrid with his two elder daughters. At Badajoz in the Autumn of 1580 he fell ill of what we now call influenza, and was like to die. His wife, devotedly attached to him, as all his wives had been, prayed that her life might be taken instead of his. Her prayer was answered, and she died (25 October, 1580). In deepening gloom he moved on, and on the 1st April, 1581 he received the oath of allegiance from the Portuguese Cortes at Thomar. Soon afterwards two out of the three children by his fourth wife followed their mother to the grave, leaving only one son, Philip, an infant, to inherit the wide dominions of Spain and the Indies.

Philip II was a man of devoted domestic affections, loving and beloved in his home circle, and the misfortunes during his absence in Portugal left indelible traces upon him. His yellow hair, hardly grizzled before, turned white, and for the rest of his life he dressed in deep mourning, shrinking more than ever from the public gaze, his only distraction from his endless round of drudgery and rigid devotion being the building of his vast granite monastery-palace of St Lorenzo of the Escorial in fulfilment of a vow made at the time of the battle of St Quentin, where a church dedicated to St Laurence had been destroyed. Philip's system of administration had now been crystallised into a habit. His eye for microscopic detail kept him at work early and late over his papers, nothing, however small, being omitted from his purview. Everything was done by correspondence, even with his own secretaries. Every letter, however insignificant, had to be ciphered and deciphered, considered by the Council of State, and a report and recommendation thereon in writing presented to the King by one of the Secretaries of State. Upon this recommendation the King scrawled his orders; or more frequently made suggestions for future consideration and report by the Council of State, or by the special council to which the matter referred to appertained. Every reply before it was sent had to be submitted in draft to the King, who often at great length criticised words; or again sent the matter back for consideration—and so on almost infinitely. In these circumstances it may be well understood that all independent judgment and initiative on the part of executive officers became impossible. No one dared to act on his own responsibility; the King was never in a hurry, and the wheels of the public service were clogged hopelessly. In vain each successive Cortes presented scores of pressing petitions for reform of civil, financial or judicial administration. Year after year the old abuses continued, for the King was for ever immersed in small detail; and questions of broad principle were obliged to wait. De Granvelle complained and remonstrated, but to no purpose, for Philip was now too old to change. Around him henceforward were no great statesmen, but men with the minds of superior clerks, Juan de Idiaquez, Cristobal de Mora, and Mateo Vasquez; who with the Count de Chinchon, formed the famous "Council of night," which after De Granvelle's death (1586) was Philip's principal advisatory board.

In the meanwhile the absence of the King from the social life of his capital was producing its natural result. His court had always been dominated by gloomy devotion, and in his later years became like a monastery. But the morals and manners of his people went from bad to worse. The most abject sanctimoniousness went hand in hand with horrible licentiousness, the immorality of the clergy being a crying scandal. Whilst the public treasury was, as we have seen, chronically empty, scandalous corruption was at work, by which the public officers and contractors became immensely wealthy. The Spanish ladies, even, who had in former reigns been models of piety and modesty, became for the first time notoriously loose and immodest in their behaviour, and their shamelessness became a by-word and a wonder to foreigners for the next sixty years. The most appalling poverty of the common people, sunk now into idleness, went side by side with a lavishness in dress on the part of the higher classes which formed a stock complaint of the Cortes for many years, and which repeated pragmatic edicts were quite powerless to check, notwithstanding the severity of the penalties for infraction. Philip toiled for ever at his papers, assailed already with the gout which ultimately killed him. But whilst he was cavilling with Idiaquez about an insignificant word in an unimportant letter, or wrangling with the Pope as to whether Spanish bishops should be called simply "lordship" or "ilustrisima," Drake was harrying the Spanish colonies in the west, and the privateers, which had well-nigh destroyed Spanish shipping, regularly intercepted the silver fleet every year off the Azores. Holland and Zeeland had slipped from Philip's grasp for ever; England and France insulted and injured him with impunity; and his own beloved Spain, whose honour and prosperity were the object of his ceaseless toil, was rapidly bleeding to death, with ruined industries, and commerce, a dwindling population and an empty treasury. To this pass had personal centralisation reduced Spain under sixty years' rule of the house of Austria.

CHAPTER V.

PHILIP II, 1580—1598.

PHILIP returned to his capital in 1583 an old and broken man. Trouble overwhelmed him on every side. During his absence, death had removed his wife and two children, and a French prince (Alençon), with the countenance of Elizabeth, and the tacit consent of the King of France, had been crowned sovereign of the Flemish patrimonial domains of the house of Burgundy, with the Protestant Orange at his side (February 1582). Naples was in chronic revolt against the intolerable oppression and extortion of its Spanish masters. Not only was a sum of 2½ million ducats sent to Spain every year as tribute, but nearly the whole country had been sold to feudal nobles—princes and dukes literally by the hundred—who squeezed the wretched people dry, only to be themselves drained in their turn almost to the last ducat. Nobles and people were therefore at one against the foreigner, and were only kept in check at vast cost, and by mere terrorism. Portugal was conquered, but riddled with disaffection, and though Santa Cruz had beaten, off the Azores, the French fleet under Strozzi (July 1582) in the service of Don Antonio, the whole of the islands outside the forts of St Michael's and Terceira still stood faithful to their native King against the Castilian.

Above all, Philip's lifelong struggle with the papacy for supremacy over the Church in Spain had reached an acute stage which, as he himself wrote to de Granvelle, was exhausting even his boundless patience. The encroachments which had been made upon the papal control over ecclesiastical jurisdiction in Spain had, generally speaking, had the sympathy of the Spanish clergy, especially of the order whose interests at the moment were not immediately touched. The bishops, as we have seen, in the Council of Trent, endeavoured to promote an appeal to the Pope in cases where the Inquisition had to deal with a prelate, but both they and the Council of Trent were willing enough to confirm the King's claim that the bishops should have control over the cathedral chapters, which had become notoriously corrupt. This claim the chapters and the popes had always strongly opposed. But even more bitterly had they resisted the right of Philip to have a lay representative of his own present at the meetings of all provincial synods. Against the resolutions of the provincial synod of Toledo so constituted (1581) the chapters of the province protested to Gregory XIII; and a conflict began which continued for years, the Pope using all the weapons in his armoury, but finally without result, as Philip had on his side his own bishops, and most of the beneficed clergy outside of the chapters. The struggle was precipitated by the Nuncio (Taverna, bishop of Lodi) who had been sent (1581) by Gregory with the stated purpose of resisting royal encroachments on the rights of the clergy. An opportunity was not long in presenting itself. Philip, who was in Portugal, had recently ordered the bishop of Calahorra to pay a visit of inspection to his chapter. The Nuncio at the instance of the chapter forbade him to do so, and the bishop appealed to the Council of State. Granvelle was at the head of affairs in Madrid, and acted firmly, and an order of Council was sent to the Corregidor of Logroño to seize and sequestrate the property of those who had opposed the bishop's authority. The Nuncio thereupon insolently caused to be fixed upon the doors of the Cathedrals of Calahorra and Logroño three great placards, one excommunicating the Corregidor of Logroño and his officers, the second dismissing the bishop of Calahorra and confiscating his revenues, and the third containing the famous bull "*in cæna Domini*," the promulgation of which in Spain had been expressly prohibited by Philip. The King kept his temper, and instructed Granvelle to conciliate matters if possible, but the Nuncio stood firm. Immediately on Philip's return to Madrid, he therefore had to take the extreme step of expelling the Nuncio, who was as deaf to the King, as he had been to De Granvelle. This vigorous step brought the Pope to his senses, and Philip had his way; but the latter was full of bitterness, that the Pope and Cardinals, most of whom he had bribed and favoured, should tend rather to favour the shifty half Huguenot King of France Henry III than him whose life was spent in struggling for the Catholic cause. But the keen churchmen saw what, perhaps even Philip himself hardly realised, that his championship of Catholicism was only a means to an end, and that his main object was the political supremacy of Spain and his dynasty.

In addition to these various sources of trouble, Philip was gradually evolving from his slow mind a great plan, which at one stroke, should avenge him upon his foes and redress all the misfortunes which his mistaken policy had brought upon him. Catharine de Medici's hostility towards him, with regard to the Netherlands and Portugal, had been answered by a closer understanding between him and her enemies the Guises. The aid sent by Elizabeth of England to his rebel subjects had been similarly met by the promotion of revolt in Ireland, but he had always dreaded an open war in which England and France might join against him. Although he had on several occasions listened with sympathy to appeals made to him on behalf of Mary Stuart by the English and Scotch Catholics, he had two reasons for not proceeding to extremes towards Elizabeth. First he distrusted Frenchmen, and had no wish to place Mary on the English throne, under the tutelage of her French kinsmen the Guises; and next he feared that if he attacked

Elizabeth Catharine might, by one of her sudden movements, temporarily patch up the differences between the Huguenots and the Catholics in France, and unite the country against him.

Suddenly an event happened which banished both fears. The Guises began to see in the condition of France a better chance of satisfying their ambition than by attempting to interfere in England. Guise was popular, especially in Paris; the Catholics in the country were numerically in a majority; Catharine, the balancing power, was old and failing; by the aid of Spain the Duke of Guise might become king of all, or part, of France.

In 1580, accordingly, Mary Stuart sent a message to Philip saying that with the advice of Guise she had decided in future to throw herself, her son and her country, entirely into the hands of Spain, while at the same time Guise took measures to let Philip know that he, too, would in future be his humble servant. This made all the difference. If Guise and Mary were Spanish in all things, Philip had nothing to fear by the substitution of Mary for Elizabeth in England, nor could Catharine unite France against him, whilst Guise and the French Catholics were in his pay. Seminary priests flocked over to Scotland and England, an active propaganda was commenced, and Lennox in Scotland was drawn into a conspiracy for an invasion of England simultaneously from Scotland and France, with Spanish and Guisan forces. Whilst Philip was in Portugal the plan was matured, but before he returned to Spain it had fallen through, thanks to Lennox's incompetence, and the political ineptitude of the Jesuits who were interested, and whose prime object, naturally, was rather the advancement of their religion than of the political interests of Spain. Guise, too, had shown himself to be a bad conspirator, whose lesson of complete submission had not yet been learnt to Philip's satisfaction. So the matter was allowed to rest for a time, whilst Guise was gradually pushed into the background, and warned, not without some resistance on his part, that in future his attention must be confined to France. The Raid of Ruthven, the flight of Lennox, and the subjection of James VI to the Scottish Protestant party, convinced Philip that with such a successor as James to follow his mother, no permanent benefit would accrue to Spain or Catholicism by placing Mary Stuart on the English throne. Another element also came into play. Dr Allen, Father Parsons, Sir Francis Englefield, the Duchess of Feria (Jane Dormer) and the other English Catholics in Spanish interests were strongly averse to the establishment of a Scottish King in England, and ceaselessly urged upon Philip that his own claim to succeed Mary Stuart—as descendant from John of Gaunt, both on his father's and his mother's side—was a good one if James became ineligible in consequence of heresy. He was assured again and again, that English Catholics would a thousand times rather welcome a Spanish ruler than allow a Frenchified Scot to reign over them. It was not difficult to persuade Philip that this was the case, and here the interests of Guise, the Scots, and the Vatican, became divergent from those of Spain. Guise endeavoured to force Philip's hand more than once by proposing vague plans for the invasion of England from France, under his leadership, and prompted James to pretend a desire to become a Catholic. The Scottish Catholic party and the French and Scottish cardinals and priests in Rome also made strenuous efforts to bring about an apparent conversion of James; but Philip's clever diplomacy in Paris and in Rome, and heavy bribes on all sides, always counteracted the idea, and discouraged the attempts of Guise and the churchmen to stand in the way of Spanish aims.

The plan of the English Catholics in Philip's counsels was for Philip to invade England itself, either from Flanders or Spain; whilst the Scottish party were desirous of the invasion being attempted over the Scotch border, the port of Leith and others being offered by them to Philip as places of landing for the Spanish force. Their offer was not rejected. Encouraging messages and promises of money were sent from Spain, and from Farnese in Flanders, to Huntly, Morton (Maxwell) and Claud Hamilton, but Philip's plans had now, after thirty years of hesitancy, taken definite shape, and he had no intention of serving as a cat's-paw for so shifty a creature as young James Stuart. The intention, therefore, was to use the Scottish Catholics merely as a diversion, whilst England was invaded direct from Spain. The project had been urged upon Philip ever since the accession of Elizabeth. At first it might have been easy, but he had tried by diplomacy and patience—and sometimes by suborning assassination—to bring about again the close alliance with England which was vital to him. With any other sovereign perhaps than Elizabeth he might have succeeded; but her circumstances, as well as her character, were peculiar, and she could not acknowledge the papal supremacy—without which her alliance would have been useless to Philip—except on conditions which would have illegitimised her birth and vitiated her claim to the Crown. Immediately after his second victory over Don Antonio's French fleet off Terceira, Santa Cruz wrote to Philip (9 August, 1583) begging his permission to make a sudden descent upon England. But Philip was not ready yet. If the thing were to be done it must be done once for all, and effectually. Religious disturbance must be raised in France to prevent the Huguenots from aiding Elizabeth, or Guise from interfering in favour of his kinsman the King of Scots. The Pope must be conciliated and, above all, a vast sum of money raised. This, as usual, was Philip's greatest stumbling-block. Each Cortes that had been held had re-echoed the utter exhaustion of the country, and had persistently prayed that the incidence of taxation might be reformed, and that no fresh burdens should be imposed; but little attention was paid to their prayers. On the contrary, the selling of the royal patrimony, the pawning of the public revenues at ruinous rates, the raising of forced loans, and the imposition of illegal taxes, increased rather than diminished.

The amount needed for the invasion was a vast one. Santa Cruz's original estimate made in the spring of 1586 was 3,800,000 ducats[1]. He proposed that the whole force should be raised in Spain itself. There were to be 150 great ships, 320 smaller craft, from 50 to 80 tons each, 40 galleys, and 6 galleasses—besides 240 punts and pinnaces. The number of seamen was to be 30,000, and of soldiers 63,890, with 1600 horses. Philip saw that, in any case, this would be beyond his means; and the raising of such a force in Spain would be impossible under some years, during which time all Europe would be on the alert. After 30 years' delay he was now in a feverish hurry, and adopted the unfortunate resolution of ordering Farnese to collect 30,000 soldiers in Flanders. This divided the forces and was a main cause of the subsequent disaster.

All round the coasts of Spain, Portugal and Naples shipwrights, armourers and victuallers, were hard at work. Diplomatists, spies and agents, were plotting and planning in every part of Europe; but the threads that moved them all were held by the austere, reticent, old man, toiling night and day over his endless papers in the heart of arid Spain. Nothing was to be forgotten, nothing overlooked. The cumbrous machine was to work with the crushing irresistible force of a glacier, and the impious enemies of Philip annihilated by God's thunderbolts cast by the hands of His chosen instrument. Pope Sixtus V had no desire to serve purely Spanish ends, and when he had been appealed to by Guise and James Stuart to subsidise a Catholic Scottish attempt on England, he consented to do so to a moderate extent. But the Spanish ambassador, Olivares, warned him, in Philip's name, that if England were to be brought back to the Church it could only

---

[1] These were the so-called copper ducats worth about 2s. 5½d. each.

be done with Philip's overwhelming force, and that the Pope must find not a small subsidy, such as Guise demanded, but a great sum of ready money. Sixtus V (Peretti) was prudent and frugal, and had no love for Spain or haughty Olivares. But many of the cardinals were in Philip's pay, and Sixtus was ultimately cajoled into promising to subscribe a million gold crowns[1] to the enterprise. But he always distrusted Philip, and no pressure could prevail upon him to pay a single crown until a Spanish force was actually landed in England; and with this Philip had to be content; although Olivares obtained a half promise of another million by way of loan on certain conditions. The matter of the investiture of the English Crown was even more difficult of arrangement. As long as possible Sixtus was kept in the dark as to Philip's own claims. Only cautious hints were dropped by Allen as to the English dislike to Scots, and the descent of Philip from Edward III; whilst Olivares told Sixtus that it was absurd to suppose that Philip would go to so vast an expense for the sake of putting a heretic on the throne. At last, after infinite haggling, the Pope was induced to promise the investiture of England to the person to be subsequently indicated by Philip. Although the Pope did not know it at the time, the person whom Philip intended to nominate was his beloved elder daughter Isabel; the younger, Catharine, having been married in 1585 to the turbulent young Duke of Savoy, Carlo Emmanuele, whereby he was gained to the Spanish interest for a time.

But side by side with the plot in Rome, another intrigue was being conducted from Paris, by Philip's astute ambassador Mendoza. He was deep in the confidence of Mary Stuart, and all of her agents and advisers were in his pay. Every argument was used to inflame her religious zeal, and to induce her to disinherit her son for heresy. She was a prisoner, and her only hope of reigning was through Spanish help. At last

---

[1] The Roman gold crown of the period was worth 6s. 8d.

she was convinced, and in June 1586 she wrote to Mendoza saying that she had by her will made the King of Spain her heir. Shortly afterwards she fell into the trap of the Babington plot and her doom was sealed.

When the Cortes of Castile met in the autumn of 1586, once more the dismal story was told of the distress and penury of the country, but the usual 450 millions of maravedis in three years, 1585—7, were voted readily enough, for nearly every member presented a petition for some personal favour to himself, and every one was granted. But this vote was a mere drop in the ocean of the demands to be met. Every device was adopted. The clergy and nobles were bled freely; forced loans from merchants in Spain, and loans from foreigners at heavy interest were resorted to; the Italian princes were put under contribution, and the coast towns of Spain and Naples made to supply ships and provisions free. But, withal, when the Cortes met in Madrid in April 1588, the Armada being almost ready to sail from Lisbon, Philip, in spite of the misery of the country, demanded an extraordinary vote of 8 millions of ducats. The members were aghast. Such a sum had never before been heard of, and protests were boldly made by the members. But Philip had learnt now how to overcome their scruples. Secret orders were sent to every prelate in the country to use the influence of the confessional, the pulpit, and the Church, to persuade the constituent town councillors and others in favour of the vote, whilst the members of Cortes themselves were bribed again almost to a man. The great sum of course was granted, and in 1590 the excise on certain articles of food was accordingly increased and developed into the hateful tax called the "millions," which for over 200 years weighed on wine, vinegar, meat, and oil, the principal food of the people. Santa Cruz died in February 1588 broken-hearted at the failure he foresaw as a consequence of the King's impatient indifference to his experienced advice with regard to the great expedition to England. He saw the paralysis that had resulted from Philip's methods. When Drake had suddenly appeared before Cadiz (29 April (N.S.) 1587) and burnt all the shipping and naval stores, not a man had initiative enough to attempt resistance; and Santa Cruz himself had sadly to confess that, if Drake had entered the Tagus, he might have destroyed the whole Armada, as there were no men or guns on the ships to resist him, although the expedition was expected to have sailed that summer. Philip was far away and inaccessible, a mere abstraction to most of his officers. Responsibility was hard to fix and easily shifted, and peculation, laxity and corruption, were universal.

To succeed Santa Cruz the most unfit man in Spain was chosen—a great noble, the Duke of Medina Sidonia, with all the coast of Andalucia under his rule, but timid, weak, utterly inexperienced, and, above all, incompetent. He protested in vain his own insufficiency. Philip insisted, and he reluctantly, and under protest, accepted the command of the Armada. The reason of his appointment was probably that Philip thought that his rank would ensure obedience to him, whilst his character would prevent him from thinking or acting for himself. The King doubtless hoped to command the Armada from his cell at the Escorial. The danger always was the division of the command. Farnese was to be supreme on land, and Medina Sidonia at sea. The fleet was to protect Farnese's passage across, and reinforce him with 6000 veteran Spanish infantry. But the two commanders were at issue from the first. Farnese was desperately short of money, and twice over he had mustered his men at great cost only to be disappointed at the non-arrival of the fleet. His men deserted and fell sick. He himself was doubtful of success from the beginning, but when he found his army reduced from 30,000 men to 17,000, he wrote to Philip earnestly advising him to allow him to make peace in reality with Elizabeth's commissioners at Ostend, whom he was beguiling with feigned negotiations (March 1588). Medina, on the other hand, began, as soon as he sailed, to cavil about letting Farnese have the 6,000 men, and to Farnese's great indignation talked about the latter coming out and meeting the Armada. In answer to all this, Farnese continued to insist upon the exact carrying out of the promises given to him. He must have the 6,000 men, and the Armada must clear the Channel of enemies, before one of his flat-bottomed boats could come out of Dunkirk.

The Armada sailed from Lisbon (30 May, 1588) with its failure assured, except under an exceptional combination of favourable circumstances. For nearly three weeks it beat and drifted about the coast, and was on the 19th June scattered by a storm, 40 ships following the Duke into Corunna and the rest seeking shelter elsewhere. They had already discovered that the victuals were mostly rotten, the water foul and short, the morale of the men bad, the officers ignorant and lax, and the ships cumbrous, unhandy and slow. On the 24th June the Duke wrote to the King telling him all this, and advising him to abandon the expedition. The King scorned the advice, and the great fleet left Corunna on Friday 22nd July (N.S.) 1588. The total force consisted of 131 vessels, carrying 24,000 effective men—7,000 sailors and 17,000 soldiers. There was a somewhat larger proportion of great ships in the Spanish fleet than in the English, but the superiority was more apparent than real. The great height of the castles of the Spanish ships caused them to look more imposing, but made them slow and crank. Their lines, moreover, were very clumsy, and the best of them could only work to windward with difficulty. Before the Armada reached the Channel all the four galleys, and several other vessels, had fallen off, and the full strength that sighted the Lizard on Saturday, 30th July, could not have exceeded 122 vessels, of an aggregate tonnage of 56,000 tons, and armed with 2,400 cannon. About 70 of these were victuallers, unfit for fighting, but carrying a number of soldiers for defence. The English fleet under Howard consisted in all of about 100 sail, whilst Lord Henry

Seymour was watching Dunkirk with nearly 40 ships, and Justin of Nassau, with the Holland fleet, was lying off the mouth of the Scheldt, ready to help if needed. The English ships were more heavily armed with guns than the Spanish, and of course less cumbered with foot-soldiers. Despite of all experience and warning, the Spaniards had continued in the old-fashioned tactics of grappling and boarding the enemy, looking upon artillery as an undignified arm, and depending mainly upon small-arms and infantry.

Medina Sidonia was outmanœuvred from the first. He sighted the enemy on Sunday morning (July 31), abreast of Plymouth, and to his dismay found that the English ships could sail round him as they pleased; their finer lines and smarter working enabling them to haul much closer to the wind than the towering round-bowed galleons. Howard and Drake attacked with artillery, keeping out of small-arm range. In vain the Spaniards tried to close, and yelled that the English were afraid, but as they realised their powerlessness their spirits fell, and the little-hearted Duke grew ever more despondent; for the English gained the wind and kept it. To add to their confusion, on Sunday evening, one of the finest of the Spanish ships under Don Pedro de Valdés, with a great treasure on board, fouled another vessel, and became crippled. The weather was heavy, the night coming on, and the English hanging on their flanks. A half-hearted attempt was made to take Valdés' ship in tow, and failed: and then Medina Sidonia shamefully abandoned her to her fate, and she was captured by the English. The same evening Oquendo's vice-flagship blew up, and was also abandoned, with hundreds of maimed and scorched wretches on board. And so for a week the Armada sailed or drifted up the Channel a helpless target to the enemy, who kept the wind and would not close. Medina Sidonia could only write, as he did daily, agonising appeals to Farnese to come out and help him. Farnese was furious. The wind was blowing dead into the poor little harbour of Dunkirk; his boats were mostly canal punts; and he stood firmly to his conditions. He must have 6,000 Spanish infantry from the Armada, and the Channel must be cleared of foes before he would move.

The Flanders coast is shoally and dangerous for big ships: the currents are strong, and the wind was blowing up-Channel. If the Armada sailed past Dunkirk it was clear it could not get back again. So the Duke decided to anchor off Calais till he could obtain word of Farnese. On Sunday night, 7th August, he heard to his despair that the Flanders force was all unready; a fact which Farnese subsequently denied. At midnight seven or eight English fireships came flaring down the wind straight on to the Armada. Panic, utter and uncontrollable, seized the Spaniards. Cables and anchors were slipped to the bottom of the sea, and the greatest fleet that ever sailed became a hustling mob of ships trying to get away. A great galleass ran ashore in the confusion, and was lost, the rest sailing with the wind towards the fatal sandbanks, with the English fleet always to windward. Medina Sidonia with 40 of his best ships anchored off Gravelines, and at early dawn was attacked by the united English fleet. All day long the battle raged. The Spaniards fought desperately, but hopelessly, for they were fighting a lost battle and they knew it. They were now outnumbered, their men starved and sick, their ammunition short, and their leader an incapable poltroon. When the English drew off at night, the Spanish ships that had been in action were simply riddled, blood-drenched wrecks; a heavy wind was blowing dead in-shore, the sandbanks were to leeward, and it looked as if nothing but a miracle could save the whole fleet from destruction. Two great galleons drifted ashore and were lost, but a providential shift of wind enabled the rest to weather the shoals, and stagger up the North Sea. Some of the sailors were for turning and fighting again, but Medina Sidonia and the soldiers had had enough; and with curses on their lips, and rage in their hearts, they determined to run up to the latitude of the Orkneys, make a long westerly tack far into the Atlantic and thence set a course for Spain. Only 65 battered wrecks ever reached home. Beset with famine, drought and pestilence, pursued by appalling weather, the rest went down unnoted in the wild Atlantic, or were dashed to pieces on the coasts of Ulster and Connaught, where thousands of poor starved shipwrecked creatures were slaughtered by the English garrisons and the wild Irish peasantry. The blow to the power of Spain was never recovered; but Philip was patient and resigned through it all. He and his country were utterly beggared, and his enemies victorious all along the line, but he never lost heart or faith. He was, he thought, only the instrument for fighting God's battles; and in the long run victory surely must crown such a cause as his.

Don Antonio had continued to be a thorn in the side of Philip. Alternately Elizabeth and Catharine de Medici had cherished and abandoned him as it suited them. On several occasions unsuccessful attempts had been made to assassinate him by men in Philip's interest. The Portuguese populace and clergy were almost unanimously in his favour; but the nobles had all been bought or deported, with the exception of a few at Antonio's side in England. The idea of avenging the Armada-attack, dispossessing Philip of Portugal, and making the country practically a tributary state to Elizabeth, whilst rendering impossible any attempt on the part of Spain to renew the invasion of England, was too tempting a one to be missed. Thanks to Don Antonio's sanguine importunities, and the eagerness of Drake to " singe the King of Spain's beard " once more, the Queen consented to an expedition being despatched from Plymouth to Lisbon in the interests of the Portuguese pretender. She contributed herself £20,000, and seven ships of her navy; but most of the cost was defrayed by a joint stock undertaking, in which the shareholders hoped to be recouped by the plunder, and Don Antonio's gratitude. The expedition was disastrous from the first. Delay and mismanagement of all sorts accompanied it. The men on the expedition were mostly idle, unruly and undisciplined, and the ten days well-nigh wasted at Corunna, against the Queen's positive orders, in attacking and pillaging the town, and burning a few ship-loads of stores, enabled the Archduke Albert, Philip's nephew and Viceroy, to organise the defence of Lisbon, and to terrorise the Portuguese. Norris, in command of 11,000 soldiers, marched overland from Peniche, against Drake's advice, without siege artillery or baggage train. He found the native inhabitants utterly cowed, and none but a few monks and peasants rallied to Don Antonio. After a few days of inglorious fighting he retired and joined Drake's fleet at Cascaes. Of the 18,000 men who sailed from Plymouth (23rd April 1589, N.S.) less than 12,000 returned. The attempt was acknowledged to have been a failure, demonstrating that the superiority of the English was in their ships and seamen, rather than in land fighting; which was natural in the case of a country in which more or less overt piracy had been the principal seafaring industry for more than twenty years.

An adverse fate appeared to beset Philip's cause. We have seen how the possession of Flanders made it necessary for him to keep friendly to England, whilst Elizabeth's position made such a friendship impossible; we have seen how he was forced to intervene in French politics and subsidise the Guises, in order to promote division, and to prevent the country from becoming officially Huguenot and making common cause with Elizabeth and his rebel Hollanders. Such a result would have isolated and ruined him; and yet from the mere force of circumstances this result seemed inevitable. The Duke of Anjou, the last of the French King's brothers, died in June 1584. Henry III himself was childless, and the next heir was Huguenot Henry of Navarre, son of that Jeanne d'Albret, to whom, in his early youth, Philip himself was to have been married. Insidious attempts were made to conciliate Henry of Navarre himself, but he, like Elizabeth, was determined to be a national sovereign, depending upon the French people, and not upon the King of Spain. And yet, at all costs, Philip must prevent France from being ruled by a Huguenot. The popular idol Guise, head of the Catholics, was already in Philip's pay; but he became henceforth a much more important personage for Spanish ends. The bases of the Holy League were settled early in 1585, ostensibly with a purely religious object, but Philip's ends were, as usual, political. The dismemberment of France would have been a master stroke. If Navarre could be forced or cajoled into being content with Béarn and the south-west, Guise might have the centre and east; Provence could be occupied by Philip's son-in-law Savoy; Philip's eldest daughter Isabel would inherit, in right of her mother, Brittany, where the Salic law was inoperative; and Philip himself could add Picardy and French Flanders to his own dominions. But Navarre would have all France or fight for it. An attempt to ruin him in the eyes of the French people was made at Philip's instance, by the famous bill of excommunication (September 1585). But the Béarnais gave Sixtus V a good answer. "The man who calls himself Pope Sixtus is himself a liar and a heretic": and henceforward it was war to the knife between them.

Henry III had been already coerced by the league into signing the treaty of Nemours, withdrawing religious toleration from the Huguenots, but he bitterly hated Guise, his hard taskmaster. He fled from his capital, and anarchy and war thenceforward ruled throughout France; whilst Philip looked on, satisfied with the success of his schemes, which made the unity of France appear impossible. The wretched Henry III, contemned by all parties, a mere cipher, had Guise and his brother murdered in his own palace at Blois (23 December, 1588); and then for a short time it seemed as if Philip's plans in France were to be as unsuccessful as his attacks on England. But Henry's exultation was short-lived. "At last I am King of France," he said to his mother. "You have cut out the garment," she replied, "but you have not wit enough to sew it together." And she was right. Denunciations of the royal murderer rang through France. The doctors of the Sorbonne declared the crown forfeit and the subjects relieved of their allegiance to Henry of Valois. A council of government was erected in Paris, with Guise's brother Mayenne at its head, and soon the League was the only organised governing power in France. But Mayenne was weak and vaguely ambitious. He had no one to turn to but Philip, and he cast the predominant Catholic party in France at the feet of the King of Spain. Henry III with the aid of Navarre was ably to rally to his side the Huguenot and moderate party, and those Frenchmen whose patriotism was stronger than their religious bias, and with 40,000 men he besieged Paris, now in the hands of Mayenne and the League.

In August 1589 the wretched Henry III fell under the dagger of Jacques Clement, the fanatic monk. Philip's friends acclaimed the murder as an act of divine vengeance, but to the King of Spain himself the event was an untoward one. The rightful heir Henry of Navarre proclaimed himself King, and it was evident now that if the League were to succeed it could only be by reconquering the country with the national forces of Spain. The first suggestion of the council in Paris was to proclaim Philip King of France, but Mayenne had succeeded to his brother Guise's pretensions, and caused the adoption of the aged Cardinal de Bourbon, Navarre's uncle, as King to serve as a stopgap. The so-called Charles X was in the hands of his nephew and was a mere figure-head, as Henry of Portugal had been. If Spain was not to be utterly ruined France must be prevented from becoming officially a Protestant country, and Philip was again driven into the position he had been forced to adopt in the case of England. He must conquer the country himself in order to keep it Catholic: and again he thought, that if Spanish doubloons and men-at-arms won the prize the King of Spain must keep it.

So he dropped for a time the policy of dismemberment, and adopted that of conquest. This gave to Henry IV the inestimable advantage of championing the national cause against the foreigner, and rendered even Mayenne sulky and halfhearted in a struggle which could only make a Spaniard King of France, and leave the Guise ambition still unsatisfied. With the aid of subsidies from Elizabeth, Henry's dash, energy and military skill swept through northern France from Normandy to Paris, beating Mayenne's armies again and again and beleaguering the capital. A Spanish force was holding Paris for the League, and another Spanish army from Flanders under Egmont was advancing to take the Béarnais in the rear. They were met by Henry at Ivry on 14 March, 1590. They were mostly Walloons and mercenary Germans, utterly unable to withstand the splendid rush of the 2000 horsemen, the chivalry of France, which followed the white plume of gallant Navarre. The Leaguers fled in hopeless disorder, and Paris again was closely surrounded by the national forces.

The Spaniards were soon convinced that Mayenne was not to be trusted, and that if France was to be won it must be by sheer fighting, Spaniards against Frenchmen. Philip was old, ill and weary, overwhelmed as usual with financial and other troubles, but he was forced to struggle whilst he lived against France becoming a Protestant power; and Farnese was ordered to take the field against Henry of Navarre, with the avowed object of placing the Infanta Isabel on the throne, as the elder daughter of Elizabeth of Valois—for Philip made as light of the Salic law in France as he had of the rights of the house of York in England. Farnese refused to undertake the command unless with a force which he considered sufficient; and with infinite difficulty Philip provided him with resources to raise 13,000 men, with whom he joined Mayenne at Meaux on the 23 August, 1590, and marched to relieve Paris. He succeeded in partially raising the siege, and entered Paris in September. Almost immediately Mayenne began to show his teeth. Dissensions arose between the Spanish and French leaguers. Farnese was not conciliatory, and to prove that Mayenne was powerless alone, simply marched away and left Paris to its fate. The Catholic zealots in Spain once more began to whisper in Philip's ear that Farnese was disloyal and unorthodox, as they had done at the time of the Armada. Philip's plans again underwent a change. It was clear that he could not coerce the French nation into acknowledging him or his daughter as its sovereign, but Navarre might be driven into accepting terms which should render him powerless for harm. Spanish troops were accordingly sent under Don Juan del Aguila to aid the Duke de Mercœur in Brittany, where they seized and held Blavet on the coast in spite even of the Leaguers. Savoy entered Marseilles with a strong force, and 4000 Spaniards garrisoned Toulouse. Elizabeth retorted by sending 3000 Englishmen under Essex to the north of France, and so the struggle became general all over the country. Farnese himself was ordered to make a last great effort, and re-entered France. He raised the siege of Rouen in April 1592;. but Mayenne and the French Leaguers now hated and distrusted the Spaniards almost as much as the Huguenots and gave but little help. Farnese soon found himself hemmed in by Henry's forces at Rouen. Ill and wounded, resentful of Mayenne's jealousy, he escaped with difficulty, and returned to Flanders, with the loss of half his force, only to die there broken-hearted in December of the same year, 1592. He was the last of Philip's great officers; and, like the rest of them, had been sacrificed to the blighting system which had sought to reduce him—a man of the highest gifts—to the position of a mere machine; to whom cold half-confidence and semi-veiled distrust were given in grudging return for slavish obedience to the orders of an anchorite a thousand miles away.

The selfish objects of the Spanish King were evident now, even to the Leaguers, and it was seen by all that his cause was desperate. A promising proposal had been made to marry the Infanta to the young Duke of Guise and make the latter King, but Mayenne had selfishly stood in the way; when, however, the Estates met at the Louvre in January, the solution was once more brought forward by the Duke of Feria, Philip's representative. But it was brought forward too late, for during the weeks Feria lost in presenting and pressing the Infanta's impossible claim, the clever Béarnais outside the walls was winning the Estates, posing as the patriotic Frenchman, and allowing himself to be persuaded to take his final step of policy and to become a Catholic. Paris, he said, was worth a mass; and to mass he went in St Denis on the 23 July, 1593, entering Paris as King in March 1594. The Spanish troops marched out next day, and Philip's hope of dominating France was gone for ever. But he had so far succeeded that France was not a Huguenot power. The war flickered on languidly in Picardy until 1598; only pride on the part of Philip, and the conditions of Henry's alliance with the English and Dutch, preventing peace being made before. But at last Henry left his allies in the lurch and made peace with Spain alone. He earned the opprobrium of the English Queen and his own extreme Huguenots, but he made France once more a united nation, and thus ended a fratricidal strife of nearly forty years.

It has already been related that Escobedo, the secretary of Don Juan of Austria, had been assassinated by men in Antonio Perez's pay at the end of March 1578. The King had authorised his assassination six months before, but when the deed was done the reasons for it had disappeared, for all hope of conciliating Flanders had then vanished, and Philip was pledged to another war. It had always been Philip's policy to maintain jealousy between his secretaries; and Secretary Mateo Vasquez lost no time in telling him that the gossip of the capital connected with the murder the names of Antonio Perez and Ruy Gomez's widow, the Princess of Eboli. It was inconvenient, for Philip had no wish for a scandal; particularly as the murder when it was done was no longer necessary, and probably surprised him. But the princess was a quarrelsome virago, and Perez a spoilt favourite, and when they learnt that Mateo Vasquez had been talking about them, they continued to clamour to the King for his punishment. Philip did his best to calm them for a time, but at last lost patience, and had Perez and the princess both arrested in July 1579. The princess never regained her liberty, but Perez was only nominally confined, received repeated reassuring messages from the King, and was soon after restored to office. But when Portugal had to be conquered, and the Alba party became paramount, Perez's doom was sealed. Gradually Philip's eyes were opened to the fact that, for his political ends, Perez had deceived him and poisoned his mind against Don Juan, and that the King's order for Escobedo's murder had been executed, when no longer needed, simply to satisfy the vengeance of the princess, with whom Escobedo, an old adherent of her husband, had remonstrated for her indecorous relations with Perez.

In 1584 Perez's papers were seized, and he was sentenced to two years' imprisonment, ten years' deprivation, and a fine of 30,000 ducats, for tampering with state papers. He escaped to sanctuary, and was recaptured. In 1588 he was put on his trial for murder, and tortured to make him confess why the murder was committed when it was. Fearing a trap he refused, until the rack tore a promise from him that he would tell the reason for Escobedo's assassination. At that day no one could understand Philip's action in persisting thus in the persecution of Perez for the commission of a crime, for which, it was acknowledged, he had the King's warrant. Philip gave his confidence slowly, but he was implacable when he was tricked and deceived, and Philip now knew that he had been made to distrust and betray his own brother by Perez's lies, and that his secret orders had been divulged to an infamous woman, who had used them to wreak her private revenge. Philip dared not explain this at the time, and some of the highest people in Spain thought that Perez was being badly used. With their aid he escaped to Aragon, and appealed for protection of the Aragonese courts, in which torture was not allowed, and over which the King had no control; for the chief-justiciary was irremovable. But Perez had possession of all Philip's secrets, and orders were sent to capture him and send him to Castile, in spite of Aragonese liberties. The people rose in revolt and rescued Perez, who was lodged in the Aragonese prison, where he was safe from summary process. When Philip found that he could only appear in court as an ordinary prosecutor, and would have to divulge the whole story, he abandoned the prosecution. In prison, vain and boasting Perez had threatened Philip that he would bring Henry of Navarre into Aragon, that he would make it a republic, and much else; but above all, he had ventured to sneer at Philip's religion. The spies of the Inquisition heard him, and the Holy Office took him from the Aragonese prison to its own dungeons. The consequence was a formidable popular rising. The Inquisition was threatened, its dungeons opened, its prisoners released, the King's representative nearly murdered, and all authority defied. At length at the end of 1591, after much violence and disorder, Perez escaped to France and England, to be caressed by Henry of Navarre and Elizabeth, to live in luxury in Essex House, to sell his country to its enemies for the rest of his worthless life; and at last to die (1611) scorned and forgotten in abject misery in Paris.

Philip had always hated the sturdy liberties of the Aragonese. His army under Alonso de Vargas had now (1591) a pretext for severity, and made the most of it. Whilst the pikemen cowed the towns, the Inquisition spread its net far and wide. Swift and exemplary vengeance fell upon the heads of the revolt. Philip had sworn to respect the constitution, and he could not openly break his oath. No change but an extension of the royal power in criminal cases was made by the Cortes of Tarazona (1593), but with the iron heel of Castile upon their necks, the Aragonese were made clearly to understand that in future their autonomy must not be exercised against the sovereign's will—at least during Philip's life.

In the meanwhile the intrigues had continued between the English Catholics who wanted the Infanta for Queen on Elizabeth's death, and the Scots Catholics who hoped to gain the Crown for James; but with an exhausted treasury and depleted forces Philip could do no more now than hamper Elizabeth by encouraging rebellion in Ireland. Tyrone and O'Donnell had sought his aid some time before they made an attempt to rise, and he had sent more than one little mission to report upon their position. He could not do much for them, and his aid was always scanty, tardy, and ineffective. But Perez was busy in England, and magnified it as much as possible. Essex was ambitious and warlike, as usual, and between them they made the Queen believe that a really dangerous expedition was fitting out in Spanish ports. The result was the raising of the fleet under Essex, which, after much misgiving on the part of the Queen, sailed from Plymouth on the 3rd June 1596. It consisted of 17 royal ships, 76 freighted ships, and a Dutch squadron of 24 sail. What was left of Philip's strength was concentrated in Cadiz, and before that port Essex's fleet suddenly appeared on the 20th June. The city was panic-stricken. No strength or resource was to be expected from Philip's officers, and the war-ships were withdrawn after the loss of two of them to the end of the bay (Puerto Real), where there were 40 rich galleons loading for the Indies. The city was taken almost without resistance. For 15 days the richest port in Spain was subjected to a systematic sack, and was left a heap of smoking ruin. The whole of the fleet and the 40 galleons were burnt by the Spaniards, with 11,000,000 ducats' worth of merchandise, and Essex sailed out again practically unmolested. This was the last blow to the naval supremacy of Spain, and showed to the whole world that, under Philip's system, his country had become effete. He himself was sinking to the grave, condemned to agonised helplessness by the gout. At the end of June 1598 he was carried in a litter to the Escorial, the great granite palace on which he had squandered the vast sums wrung from his miserable people. Repulsive sores covered him. His pain was so intense that his wounds could not be washed or tended. Antiseptic science was undreamed of, and the King for fifty-three dreadful days lay slowly rotting to death, under circumstances of appalling horror too hideous for relation. But through it all he never lost his supreme faith and resignation. Fervent, almost frantic, appeals to God for forgiveness were for ever on his lips, and in the grim forbidding cell in which he died the intercessions of the Church went ceaselessly on night and day. In his last interview with his only son Philip, he enjoined him to be pious, just, and merciful to his subjects, and bade him see how the monarchies of the world ended. To his beloved daughter, Isabel, he left the sovereignty of the Netherlands, in union with her cousin the Cardinal Archduke Albert, whom she was to marry; and then he bade farewell to mundane affairs and prayed until he died (13 September, 1598). He was born to a hopeless task. His only chance of success under the circumstances was to adopt an easy opportunism, such as that by which his rivals beat him. He had to cope with Elizabeth, Catharine de Medici, Orange and Henry of Navarre, whose religious convictions sat lightly upon them, whilst he was burdened with an hereditary system of government and conduct, from which he had not sufficient quickness of wit to free himself, and he was borne down with the greatness of a task, for which his qualities and training rendered him unfit.

When he succeeded to his father Spain was already well-nigh ruined by the drain of the Emperor's wars, imposed upon him by the inheritance of Flanders and the Empire. It would be unfair to blame the monarch for the folly of his financial measures, as the science of political economy was yet unknown; but their persistent perversity seems almost systematic. When no further supplies could be wrung from the Cortes, funds were raised by the seizure of the money which came to merchants from the Indies in payment for goods, by forced loans from nobles, prelates or wealthy burgesses, by the sale of seignorial rights over villages and towns, and of the royal patrimony, by repudiating debts, reducing interest, and hampering commerce and industry.

The maladministration arising from the evil system of pledging and farming future resources was never reformed, the squalid lavishness of the Court expenditure was never reduced, a conciliatory policy in order to avoid the cost of war was never adopted: the only steps which appear to have occurred to the financial advisers of Philip were those which undermined public confidence and security, which blighted the national industries and which killed future resources for the sake of present advantage. The sumptuary laws to reduce the expenditure of the lieges and the method of reducing prices by prohibiting the export of Spanish goods strangled the industries by which many taxpayers lived; the ineffectual attempt to prevent the export of bullion hampered the introduction of foreign goods through the custom houses and encouraged contraband, besides raising the cost of labour in Spain by the depreciation of metal. Concurrently with these disastrous measures, other operations no less destructive were at work. The continued aggregation of land in the hands of the Church, and tied up in perpetual entail, and the expulsion of the Moriscos from Andalucia, had well-nigh ruined agriculture. To prevent whole provinces from starving in the finest grain country in the world immense quantities of wheat had to be introduced from abroad, and the *alcabala* suspended on breadstuffs imported into Seville. Constant wars and emigration, the association of the Moriscos with industry, and the immense number of Church holidays, moreover, made the ordinary Spaniard contemptuous of work, and scanty in his aggregate production. And so the vicious circle went on, and the curse of far-reaching dominions in the possession of an imperfectly unified and organised country had in seventy years reduced Spain to the last depth of misery and penury. To some extent this may, of course, be attributed to Philip's qualities and limitations; but it was mainly owing to a system, and to circumstances, which were originated before his birth, and which neither his training nor his character enabled him to vary.

CHAPTER VI.

PHILIP III, 1598—1621.

PHILIP II had nearly ruined Spain, but his dream of centralisation of authority and uniformity of faith had been realised; and Philip III succeeded to the throne a purely Spanish monarch of a united Spanish nation, to a great extent unhampered by the traditions of the imperial connection. The possession of Flanders, the origin of much of Spain's misfortune, passed to the Infanta Isabel and her husband, to revert to the Crown of Spain in case of their having no issue; but even thus lightened, the burden was a heavy one. Philip was in his twenty-first year when his father died, and already the astute old King had seen that he would be but a degenerate successor. Philip II had laboriously endeavoured to instil into his son those profound maxims of state which he himself had so early learnt of the Emperor. But there was no application or industry to be got from young Philip. Well-meaning, amiable and weak, not a fool, but idle and careless, he was destined to be the mere tool of favourites all his life. Against this his father had always stood, and just before his death he sighed out to his faithful de Mora, "Ah Don Cristobal, I fear they will rule him!" Concentration of all power in the person of the monarch had been Philip's aim, but the possibility of the transfer of the power entire to an interested favourite was the weak point of the system, and it must have added to the bitterness of Philip's last moments to foresee this result of a lifetime of plotting and planning. The Secretary of State, Don Cristobal de Mora, immediately after Philip II's death carried to the new King a number of documents for consideration and despatch. With a sign of the hand the King told the old minister to place them on a sideboard, where the Marquis of Denia (Don Francisco de Sandoval y Rojas, afterwards Duke of Lerma) would attend to them. This was the first act of Philip III as King, and it was prophetic of his reign. To Lerma was handed almost every royal prerogative. The old ministers and officers of Philip II were unceremoniously removed, to be replaced by friends and hangers-on of Lerma, and thenceforward for twenty years the favourite was, in all but name, King of Spain.

Before Philip II died he had arranged the marriage of his son with Margaret of Austria (daughter of the Archduke Charles, the aforetime persistent suitor of Elizabeth of England), and of his daughter Isabel with the Archduke Albert. Margaret and Albert came together through Italy, with all the pomp of their imperial house; and the two marriages were celebrated by proxy in Ferrara by the Pope on the 13th November, 1598. Philip was to meet his bride in Valencia, but before he could start from his capital with fitting magnificence money had to be obtained. During the reign of his predecessor the power of the Cortes had been almost entirely sapped. The constituents were tampered with, the members bribed, and latterly Philip II had postponed indefinitely the consideration of the presentments, keeping the same parliament in existence for many years. When Philip II died the Cortes of 1593 was still undissolved. He had asked them for 500,000,000 maravedis; but corrupt as they were, they replied that it was useless to vote it, for the people could not pay it. No blood could be got from a drained body, they said: "No one has either money or credit, and the country is utterly ruined. Any money that is made is hidden away, and the owner lives poorly upon it, until it is gone....Commerce is killed by the *alcabala*. Where 30,000 *arrobas* of wool were manufactured there are not now 6,000, and in the principal cities most of the houses are closed and deserted." But the confessional, the pulpit, official and court pressure, were once more brought into play; and the 500 millions were voted. By the time Philip died, however, all that could be collected of it had been spent, and the finances were more embarrassed than ever. Philip III called a new Cortes together on the death of his father, and begged for a new vote of 18 million ducats in six years (£2,200,000). He had not, he told them, funds, resources, or property of any sort to meet his daily expenditure. With many groans the Cortes voted provisionally the sum demanded, pending an appeal to their constituents. Instead of adopting some measures of economy, reducing the enormous expense of the palace, or dismissing some of the army of idlers, Philip and Lerma launched into a perfect frenzy of extravagant splendour. The progress through the ruined country to Valencia, to meet the new Queen and the Archduke, surpassed in magnificence the greatest displays of the Emperor. The obedient Cortes had also voted an extraordinary supply of 150 million maravedis for the King, and a similar sum for the Queen's "pattens," or pinmoney; and Lerma himself spent 300,000 ducats on the festivities.

From Valencia after the marriage Philip and his bride went to Aragon, where he gained for ever the love of the Aragonese by granting full amnesty to all the surviving offenders in the late troubles. Money and caresses were showered upon him and his wife; but when the Aragonese asked for the abolition of the Inquisition, Philip had to say that he would consider the matter later. By the time Philip had returned to Madrid he had by the advice of Lerma given away more knighthoods than his father had done in ten years. Grandeeships and titles were showered right and left, to fill Lerma's coffers and to conciliate partisans; whilst upon the favourite himself and his family offices and honours were lavished to his heart's content. The craze for waste and prodigality in the Court was now beyond all precedent. Philip II had lived like a hermit, and for years had dressed in mourning, but with the coming of a new young King and Queen an era of shameful extravagance in dress and living began. Pragmatics of the most severe character were published against luxury in 1600, but the example of insolent splendour was set by the Court, and could not be put down. The common people were starving, the looms were idle, the fields untilled: nearly all the finery came from abroad: the prices of commodities continued to rise; and Old Castile, especially, was rapidly becoming a wilderness. The Cortes attributed the general ruin mainly to over-taxation, and proposed measures of economy. This however did not suit Lerma. His remedy was to transfer the capital from Madrid to Valladolid, which was done early in 1601, with disastrous results. Madrid was ruined, whilst Valladolid and Old Castile did not benefit. The price of necessaries was higher than ever, and widespread misery resulted. The continued rise in prices was accompanied again by a scarcity of currency, notwithstanding that vast sums of bullion came every year from the Indies. Davila says that in the year 1595, 35 million ducats in gold and silver came to Seville, and an ordinary amount in gold alone was 12 millions; but much never got beyond Seville, where foreign merchants received it in exchange for goods, and the rest was mostly hoarded, or conveyed to places of safety, where the rapacity of the tax farmer could not reach it. It was not so much scarcity of currency, as the obstacles to its circulation which caused the trouble. Lerma himself, by a stroke of genius, conceived another theory. It was, he said, the waste of silver in making Church and household plate which caused coin to be so scarce. So in April 1601 sudden orders were sent throughout Spain, for official inventories to be made of every piece of silver plate in private houses and churches, and all this was to be kept intact until orders were received for its utilisation. This was too much. Bishops and clergy thundered from the altars and pulpits against such sacrilege, and in August a humble apology was given and the order cancelled. But something had to be done. The Cortes now might vote what they liked, but the ruined people could not pay it; and the next device was an appeal *ad misericordiam* to bishops, nobles, officials, and others, to give what money and plate they chose. The Archbishop of Seville contributed his plate and 30,000 ducats in money, and others gave in proportion. But there was a lower depth still. Officers were appointed to go from door to door accompanied by the priest of each parish, to beg for alms for the King, the smallest sum received being fifty reals. To this had Spain fallen. The master of the New World with its countless treasures had not money to pay for his household servants, or to set forth the meals for his own table. More disastrous still was the measure adopted of doubling the face value of the copper coinage. This was mostly used by poor people, and the measure of course, at once, more than doubled the prices of articles of prime necessity, besides which immense quantities of copper counterfeit coins were introduced from abroad, and rapidly exchanged for silver. The natural result was the disappearance of silver from circulation, and another blow was dealt to the national welfare.

Amidst all this disorder the pompous pretence that Spain was the most powerful nation on earth was still kept up, and for many years to come was to some extent accepted by foreigners as the fact[1]. As a result of this tradition it was still looked upon as being incumbent on Philip, pauper though he was, to interfere in the affairs of England, which under Elizabeth had grown to be immensely more prosperous and powerful than Spain in reality. When Philip II died, ominous news was already rife of another intended English descent upon

[1] In one of his moments of debasement with Gondomar (1617) James I said, "Of course I know that, so far as greatness is concerned, the King of Spain is greater than all the rest of us Christian Kings put together."

Portugal, and fleets were being prepared to withstand them in Seville, Lisbon and Corunna. The English Catholic refugees in Spain and Flanders had continued to urge that England should be dealt with direct, whilst the Scots still advocated the invasion through Scotland, and agents from Tyrone were unceasing in their prayers for the help of Spain to the Irish cause. The first course appeared most flattering to Spanish pride and interests; and with great effort the fleets were concentrated in Lisbon in the summer of 1599, with the object of invading England under the Adelantado of Castile, Don Martin de Padilla. His own account of his object, quoted by Davila, shows the change of feeling which the fate of the Armada had brought about. He was inflamed, he said, purely by religious zeal, and neither he nor his force would take the value of a penny from England. To punish Jezebel and bring England to the Church was all he sought, and he would do it if possible, by mildness, persuasion, and presents. He was a romantic and quixotic bigot, and the corruption, penury, and delay, more than once made him despair of ever being able to sail at all. When at last he did so it was only to have his fifty ships scattered by a storm, and beaten back into Spanish ports.

At the same time a supreme effort was made with the galleys from Naples, Genoa, and Cataluña, to free the coasts of Spain from Moorish pirates. Great levies of soldiers were ordered to be made in Spain, Portugal and Italy; for notwithstanding that the Low Countries had been handed to the Archduke, his resources were utterly inadequate to maintain the 70,000 men required for the war. The Duchy of Milan too was unquiet, and the turbulent Duke of Savoy was discontented at being made to serve purely Spanish interests. Troops were first hurried off to Italy, and then a supreme effort was made to send a force to the Archduke. Isabel and her husband had arrived in their new sovereignty in September, to find that in their absence the Archduke Andrew and

Juan de Mendoza (Marquis de Guadalete) had occupied the neutral territories of Cleves and Westphalia, and that now the Protestant princes had made common cause with Maurice of Nassau and his Dutchmen. The Spanish and Walloon troops, as usual unpaid, mutinied, and the Archduke as a last resource opened negotiations with Nassau and the Queen of England. When the plenipotentiaries met at Boulogne it was soon evident that the claims of the Spaniards were still inflated and absurd; and the conference broke up (May 1600). Maurice of Nassau was no sluggard, and without delay marched into Flanders and besieged Nieuport. Isabel did her best, rallying her mutinous rabble of an army at Bruges, and sent them under her husband to meet Maurice. The Archduke was as brave as befitted a prince of his house, but was utterly out-generalled and routed, and the only armed force upon which his sovereignty rested disappeared. But Nieuport still held out; and Maurice, who was more concerned for the moment in holding Holland than in conquering Flanders, returned home, and thence went to Cleves to regain the places held by the Spaniards (July 1601). If the hold of Spain over Flanders was to be maintained now was the time for a supreme effort, and it was made. Troops and war material were crowded into all the ships which could be seized at Lisbon and along the coast. But before the force was ready Savoy and the Italians were sufficiently conciliated for troops to be sent to the Archduke from Italy.

For several years past close communication had existed between Tyrone and Spain. Tyrone's "ambassador," Hugh Boy, and the Irish friars at Madrid had never ceased to beg for help. Money, arms, and experienced officers had often been sent to Ireland, but what was wanted now was a large force. Just as the great preparations in Lisbon for the Archduke were found to be unnecessary (summer of 1601), there arrived in Spain the Spanish archbishop of Dublin (Mateo de Oviedo) and Don Martin de la Cerda, who had been sent from Spain to report. If, they said, a good force were sent now, the English would be driven out of Ireland, and Spain might be supreme. Tyrone and O'Donnell were losing heart. This was their last prayer, and if it were not granted they would abandon the struggle and accept the fair terms offered by the English. Lerma listened and consented. The Cortes voted an extraordinary tax of 24,000,000 of ducats spread over six years—which became permanent—to be raised by increasing the "millions" on articles of food; and the fleet sailed from Lisbon for Ireland early in September 1601. Diego Brochero was the admiral, with 33 ships—thirteen of them seized from private owners. A force of 4500 men at arms under Don Juan del Aguila was carried, and a large quantity of war material. Nine vessels with 650 soldiers on board were driven back to Spain by a storm, but the rest of the soldiers under del Aguila landed in Kinsale. His men were now but few—for already sickness had further reduced their number; and he begged Tyrone to come south and join him, whilst to Spain he sent for more men and food. But the reinforcements arrived too late (11 December, 1601), when Mountjoy the Viceroy had beleaguered Kinsale, and the Irish under Tyrone were scattered like chaff before the wind, the 200 Spaniards sent from the relieving force to help them being killed, except those who took refuge in Baltimore.

Del Aguila's position was now hopeless. No help could be expected from Tyrone or the Irish; and to conquer the country alone was an impossible task for Spain, though the Irishmen in Spain unweariedly tried to persuade Lerma otherwise. The reinforcements sent to del Aguila in December found him surrounded, and were landed (650 men) at Castlehaven, Baltimore and Dunboy, where they were joined by the remnants of O'Donnell's men, O'Donnell himself escaping to Spain in the ships which had brought the reinforcement. Early in 1602 del Aguila made terms with Mountjoy and sailed away to Spain, leaving to the mercy of the English the territories of Dunboy (O'Sullivan Beare), Castlehaven and

Baltimore (O'Driscolls). O'Donnell died in Spain shortly afterwards in despair, the O'Sullivans became great Spanish nobles, and of the O'Driscolls some remained in Spain praying still for aid and some subsequently returned home. But the English in Madrid, who had always frowned on the Irish aid, were still urging the King and Lerma to take measures, at least to ensure the succession of the Infanta after the Queen's death. Father Creswell in Madrid, and Father Parsons in Rome, were unwearied in their persistence; whilst the Earl of Bothwell (Francis Stuart) and Colonel Semple were as energetic in pressing the Scottish view. But the Archduke and his wife were cold. They were straining every nerve in the memorable siege of Ostend; they were never likely to have children, and had no desire to enter into the hopeless task of conquering England. At length, in March 1603, Philip and his Council agreed that Spanish arms and money should be at the service of any English candidate for the Crown whom the English Catholics should choose for Elizabeth's successor. There was still some bombastic talk about holding the Isle of Wight as a return, but the decision practically meant that Spain, after fifty years of failure, abandoned her attempt to coerce England. The person to be selected by the English Catholic and anti-Scottish party was Arabella Stuart, and if Philip's decision had been taken a year earlier, she might have become Queen of England. But Elizabeth died (24 March, 1603) before any preparations could be made in Spain. Robert Cecil had made all arrangements for James' succession, and the last chance of making England Catholic in the interests of Spain had fled for ever.

It has already been pointed out that much of Elizabeth's animosity against Spain was personal. James I had no such feeling. He was base and truckling by nature, ready to accept Spaniards at their own valuation; he hated piracy and had no special cause of quarrel with Spain. When, therefore, the Count de Villamediana (Don Juan de Tassis) came to congratulate him upon his accession, he expressed a desire for peace. There was no difficulty about the terms, and in 1604 the Constable of Castile (Velasco) with a splendid train of nobles received in London James's oath that he would "not succour the Hollanders or allow English ships to trade in the Indies." With this the situation of the Netherlands changed. The heroic defence of Ostend had dragged on since 1601, with the aid of gallant Vere inside, and of Elizabeth and Henry IV outside. Life and treasure incalculable were poured out upon the sands by Spain and the Archduke. The brave brothers Spinola, by land and sea, exerted their skill and energy in vain. Ostend still stood firm, impregnable behind its sanddunes. On the other hand Maurice of Nassau captured the Sluys after an obstinate siege (August 1604). But James Stuart's friendship with Spain changed everything. The defenders of Ostend, 4000 men, came to terms with Spinola and marched out with the honours of war to the neighbouring fortress of the Sluys; and the "Archdukes" entered the ruined town, hardly purchased by a siege of three years and a loss of 40,000 men.

The Marquis of Spinola, who had reduced Ostend, now hurried to Spain for reinforcements of men and money. With his ships free from the depredations of the English Philip was somewhat better off now, and Spinola returned to Flanders loaded with honours, and with promise of a strong force of Spaniards, Italians, and mercenary Germans. The promised Spanish contingent was captured at sea by the Dutch, but with his Italians and Germans Spinola pushed the campaign across the Rhine to Maestricht, whence he threatened Friesland (autumn 1605). Again funds ran short, and again Spinola hurried to Spain. He found the resources at a low ebb. The silver fleet had not yet arrived, and there was no money in the treasury. The merchants of Cadiz were appealed to, but on the King's credit they would advance nothing. He had already paid to Genoese bankers 30 per cent. for an advance in the previous year: and upon Spinola's own security some money was now raised. But both sides were tired of the fruitless struggle. Through 1606 the fighting went on around Rhineberg with great gallantry on both sides; but Spinola could get no adequate funds to carry on the war, and negotiations were opened for a truce. A suspension of hostilities of eight months was agreed upon from May 1607, in which, for the first time, the "Archdukes" and Spain declared that they made no claim to the control of the United Provinces.

But in the meanwhile another blow was dealt to Spain. Before the truce was ratified the Spanish fleet was well-nigh destroyed by the Dutch off Gibraltar, and the Dutch fleet then proceeded to the Azores to intercept the silver fleet. To fight Spain with her own money had always been a favourite device, and Maurice was loath to give it up: the demand that the truce should be effective both on sea and land was therefore for a time stubbornly resisted by the Dutch. When this was settled it was found that Philip's ratification was signed in the old haughty form "I the King"—which the Dutchmen would not allow, for said they, Philip is no King of ours. Maurice and the Zeelanders were for recommencing the war. Almost every power in Europe intervened in the interests of peace, but Spanish pride was tenacious, and there was nothing submissive about the attitude of the Hollanders. Nothing short of a recognition of their absolute independence would satisfy them, and this Philip and the Archduke were willing to give if they would renounce their claim to trade freely in the Indies. This they would not do, and the negotiations first at the Hague and afterwards at Antwerp came to a deadlock. France and England proposed a long truce on the Dutch terms, but both Philip and Maurice objected to this. Diplomacy was at last successful. The "Archdukes" were sincerely anxious for peace, and their confessor was sent to Spain to satisfy the King's scruples of conscience. Maurice was won over by the length of the truce, and finally, at a great meeting of the States General at Bergen-op-Zoom (April 1609) the momentous truce of 12 years was signed, giving to the United Provinces the independence for which they had fought so sturdily since Brederode had toasted the "Beggars" at Brussels forty-three years before.

The conclusion of peace with England, France and Holland, and the efforts made to restrain Moorish piracy, unquestionably benefited Spanish commerce, and improved the general condition of the country. But unfortunately the corruption and lavishness introduced by Lerma caused the national resources to be as narrow as ever. The King himself spent nearly the whole of his time in amusements and devotion. His religion had now become an abject superstition, and this and his love of idle pleasure made him the tool of Lerma, who himself conciliated the Church by enormous benefactions and rich religious foundations. Pensions, grants, and monopolies were showered by the favourite on the nobles and courtiers whom he wished to attract. Contarini, the Venetian ambassador (1605), says that the King was master of the world because he had so much to give away, and could buy all men. There were 46 Captain Generalships, over 20 Viceroyalties, 500 Knight Commanderships, some worth 20,000 ducats a year each, and other offices in proportion. Most of them were unblushingly sold by Lerma and his underlings, and there was undisguised peculation in almost every branch of the administration. The Duchy of Milan, for instance, instead of remitting revenue to Spain, now produced 200,000 ducats a year less than its cost, and the kingdom of Naples had a deficit of double that amount. The nominal revenues were enormous, much greater than those of any other civilised country, the people were crushed beneath the weight of taxation largely drawn from industry, commerce and food, and yet such were the lavishness and corruption, that in 1605 every source of revenue had been pledged for years in advance at ruinous interest, and, as we have seen, the King had to beg from door to door for his daily food. The clergy of Castile were supposed to support fifty galleys on the Mediterranean coast, but in fact there were only eight; and they were badly found. Naples paid for thirty galleys, but only sixteen existed, Sicily paid for twenty, but there were only ten; and so on through every branch of the administration[1].

Madrid had bitterly resented the removal of the Court to Valladolid (1601) and had murmured openly against the subjection of the King to Lerma and his satellites, Secretary Franquesa and Don Rodrigo Calderon, but what grumbling and remonstrance failed to effect was attained by bribery. Early in 1606 the town authorities offered that if the court was restored to Madrid, the capital would give to the King 250,000 ducats in ten years, with the sixth part of all house rents during the same period. To the favourite Lerma they offered a fine palace worth 100,000 ducats, and to his son the Duke of Cea, and others of his house, palaces rent-free. Franquesa too was openly bribed with a thousand ducats in money; and by these means Madrid again became the capital of Spain. By this time the Cortes of Castile had lost their importance. Their petitions and remonstrances were left unnoticed for many years, and were mostly refused at the end of the period of delay, for the Cortes had now relaxed hold on the purse-strings and "grievances first" had been forgotten. Nevertheless it was found that the 3,000,000 ducats which were now demanded

---

[1] These particulars are taken from the report sent by the Venetian ambassador Contarini to the Seigniory in 1605. In the same report he gives particulars of the total nominal revenue of the King of Spain at the time, which he estimates at 23,859,787 ducats (i.e. "copper" ducats of 375 maravedis = 2s. 5½d.). The amounts however are evidently much exaggerated, as an average of 3 million ducats is stated to be received from the Indies, and over 3 million from Naples, neither of which agrees with statements from other contemporaries: and indeed Contarini admits that everything is pledged, and that the boasts of Spain's strength is unfounded, the country being exhausted. The King, he says, could not raise over 20,000 or 30,000 men in Spain.

annually from Castile could not be raised by the ordinary modes of taxation. Fresh duties were placed upon meat etc. (1603), but by 1607 it had become evident that the people could not pay the amount, and for several years thereafter the ordinary tribute to the King was reduced to 2,000,000 ducats per annum, and even the clergy had to pay their share by special permission of the Pope. But in exchange an extra 1 per cent. was imposed on all sales, to pay 12,000,000 ducats which the King owed to the bankers.

Although Spanish commerce was now safe from the English, French, and Dutch privateers, the Moors in the Mediterranean still terrorised and preyed upon the Spanish coasts. An attempt made by John Andrea Doria to punish them and capture Algiers had failed in 1601. In 1602 Spain, in union with Persia, declared war against the Sultan of Turkey, and the Neapolitan galleys under Santa Cruz attacked and plundered Crete and other Turkish islands in 1603. Thenceforward for years hostilities continued intermittently in the Mediterranean, and on the north coast of Africa, with but little effect in restraining the boldness of the Turks and Moors, who raided the Spanish coasts and attacked Spanish vessels, almost with impunity. Notwithstanding the expulsion of the Moriscos from Andalucia by Philip II, there was still a large population of Moorish descent in the kingdom of Valencia—as indeed there is to-day, in spite of centuries of attempts to eliminate them. Accusations, true or false, were constantly brought against the Valencian Moriscos of aiding and conniving at the descents of the Barbary Moors on the Spanish coasts. Lerma was a Valencian of pure Christian descent, who like the rest of his class, hated the Moriscos bitterly; and as Valencian Viceroy he had been especially severe upon them. Generally speaking they were—as the Andalucian Moriscos had been—industrious, thrifty, and thriving. They had made of the "huerta" of Valencia one of the most smiling spots in the world, and the silk fabrics they produced in the city vied with the finest products of the East. Their Christian neighbours had always looked upon them with jealousy and hatred[1], and repeatedly represented to the Kings that they were occupying space and eating food which should belong to Spaniards of pure descent. Bigot though he was, Philip II was too wise to drive them out entirely, so long as they were professed Christians and paid his taxes to the full. But Lerma brought with him all the Christian Valencian's prejudices. He was quite lacking in political skill or foresight, and listened only to his own provincial intolerance, and the advice of fanatical churchmen, like the famous Ribera, Archbishop of Valencia, who in 1600 and 1604 violently urged the King to expel all the vile breed of Mahomet from his dominions.

When the peace had been sworn with England (1604), James I sent to Philip some letters he had found amongst Queen Elizabeth's papers, showing that the Valencian Moriscos had been carrying on a correspondence with her and the Swiss Protestants, with the object of planning a rising in Spain against Philip. This discovery caused renewed persecution against the Moriscos, which hardened their hearts against the fanatical preaching of Ribera. Again, and again, the Archbishop urged their expulsion—since they could not all be killed. They were, he said, only pretended Christians, they were the "Sponge of Spanish wealth," since notwithstanding the sterile land upon which they worked, and the heavy burden of taxation they specially bore, they were always well off, whilst Christians were starving. Their industry and frugality were in fact the great reproach against them. Their numbers, moreover, were increasing rapidly, for they married early, and were not diminished by entering monasteries, or by wars and emigration. There were in Valencia 19,000 Morisco families in 1573, and 28,000 in 1599. When it came to expelling the whole of them, however, most of the nobles and landowners protested vigorously

---

[1] See Cervantes ("Coloquio de los Perros") for a strong expression of this.

against depriving them of such good tenants, and some of the prelates, even, had their doubts, and appealed to the Pope to temper the zeal of the Archbishop. The Pontiff ordered a commission to sit in Valencia—a fact which of itself is significant of the changed relations between the Spanish Church and Rome since the time of Philip II. The commission consisted of the Archbishop and the Bishops of his diocese, to whom were added by Philip four lay officials, an inquisitor, and nine priests. The board ostensibly sat to devise means for a real conversion of the Moriscos, but the latter were sulky and suspicious. Communications took place between them and their fellows in Aragon. Lerma took fright at their attitude, and in the summer of 1609 persuaded Philip that the only way to obtain peace and unity in his country was to expel all those of known Moorish blood from the kingdom of Valencia. Secret though the preparations were, they soon became known, and fruitless appeals both from the Moriscos, and those who made a profit on them, came in plenty to Lerma.

At length on the 22nd September, 1609, the Marquis of Caracena, the Viceroy, issued the terrible edict of expulsion. With the exception of six of the "oldest and most Christian" Moriscos in each village of a hundred souls, who were to remain and teach their successors their modes of cultivation, every man and woman of them were to be shipped within three days for Barbary on pain of death, carrying with them only such portable property as they themselves could bear. Galleys from all parts of the Mediterranean had been brought to the ports, and into them the poor people were driven. Very many were plundered and murdered on their way to the ports, or on board the ships which they themselves freighted. The greed of the Christians knew no limit. Soon it was whispered that the Moriscos were selling some of their property, in order to carry away money. This was at once prohibited and the poor plundered people were sent away penniless. During the winter some resistance took place in the mountains, and atrocities as terrible as those of the Morisco war of Granada were perpetrated, but by March 1610, the kingdom of Valencia was declared free of its best and most useful citizens. During the six months over 150,000 Moriscos were hounded out of the land which for centuries their forefathers had possessed. This great crime, and greater blunder, was seen even by contemporaries to be a catastrophe for Spain, but its effects were more disastrous and far-reaching even than anyone imagined at the time. During the winter of 1609-10 similar expulsions were effected of the Moriscos of Aragon, Murcia, Andalucia and Catalonia; but worst of all was the expulsion of those of Castile, La Mancha, and Estremadura, where they had become so akin to the "old Christians" as to be hardly distinguishable from them. Various estimates were made at the time of the total number of Moriscos expelled from Spain, varying from 300,000 to a million. The most probable number is perhaps that given by Father Bleda, in his *Defensio fidei*, of 500,000, but to this must be added vast numbers who fled before the publication of the edict, and those who were sacrificed by the Inquisition, or were murdered. With the expelled Moriscos went most of their arts and industries; and Spain has never recovered the blow to her prosperity dealt by the showy, empty-headed Lerma, the idle, narrow-minded King, and the fanatical bigot Ribera. The only political excuse for the measure was the supposed plots between the Moriscos and the national enemy, but it is evident now that the communications, such as they were, had their origin in the ceaseless persecution to which the Moriscos were exposed from the Church and the Inquisition. All they desired was to be allowed to live and labour in quiet, and when this was foolishly denied them through a long series of years, unrest and discontent were the natural results.

The neglect and abandonment of public business by Philip III continued to be scandalous. Jousts, cane-tourneys, religious processions, and bull-fights took up the whole of

the monarch's attention. Neither he nor Lerma could be
approached on business without incredible difficulty and
delay. In the meanwhile the accumulation of wealth by the
favourite's family went on, and the expenditure on the royal
household continued to increase, notwithstanding the constant prayers of the Cortes that a limit should be put upon
the scandalous waste. Philip II had spent upon his household
400,000 ducats a year, whilst the cost of his son's establishment
was 1,300,000 ducats. All this naturally caused murmurs in
the capital. The fashion set by Lerma of grabbing the public
money with both hands had spread down to the humblest
servants of the State, and all citizens outside the pale of office
found themselves simply the prey of the public servants.
Although the expression of public opinion was difficult and
dangerous, yet Spain possessed at the time some of the
brightest literary geniuses of any age, and their mordant jibes
and satires upon the favourite and his imitators passed swiftly
from mouth to mouth on Liars' Parade (the arcade of the Church
of St Philip el Real in the Calle Mayor) or, in the form of
pasquins, mysteriously appeared in the public places of the
capital. Lerma began to take alarm as the attacks increased
in number and bitterness, notwithstanding the severity of his
espionage; and he was forced to throw over some of the
plundering crew as a sacrifice to public discontent. Amongst
others was apprehended one of the councillors of finance,
Alonso Ramirez del Prado, in whose house was found property
worth 800,000 ducats; besides which he possessed nearly
600,000 ducats worth of house property. But the unpopular
Pedro Franquesa, Secretary and Councillor of Finance, was
found to have appropriated a still greater plunder. He was
seized whilst seated at Lerma's side at a tourney and carried
to a fortress. His house was found to be literally crammed
with riches, the mere removal of which to the palace occupied
all the King's fourgons for three days. In the monastery of
the Merced, also, he had hidden vast sums; and a string of

mules bearing 300,000 ducats in money, sent on the road to
Valencia by his wife for safety, were stopped and captured. It
was asserted at the time that he had defrauded the King of a
million of ducats in the arrangement of a loan from the
Portuguese Jews, and that the citizens of Madrid had given
him, not 1000 ducats only, to influence the transfer of the Court
thither, but 100,000 ducats. The sentence pronounced upon
him (December 1609) was a fine or restitution of 1,406,000
ducats, the loss of all titles and offices, and perpetual imprisonment. There was however no abatement in the splendour
of Lerma or his favourite Calderon, although ostentatious
attempts were made, by the issue of severe sumptuary edicts,
to restrain extravagance in others.

Whilst Spanish resources were being thus pilfered and
squandered, Henry IV in France, with the aid of Sully, had
consolidated the French nation and reorganised its finances,
and he was but little disposed to brook the inflated claims of
superiority, and right of interference, still advanced by Spain.
The nation was seen to be decadent, but its pride remained a
danger to Europe. The Spanish territories in Italy, especially
Milan, were disgusted with the misgovernment and malversation
which afflicted them. The ambitious Duke of Savoy, who had
fought on the side of Spain, was bitterly resentful at the way in
which he had been treated when peace was made with France.
It is true that the subsequent peace of Lyons had given him
Saluzzo, but he had lost some of his finest provinces, and the
Spaniards had not raised a finger to help him. He dreamed of
a new alliance which should free him from both France and
Spain, based on a confederacy of the Italian States, England,
and the Swiss; but Henry IV had a greater plan in view,
which should, once for all, humble the house of Austria.
France, the Italian States, England, and the Protestant princes,
were all drawn into the league. The French party in England,
led by Winwood, was still strong. Charles Emmanuel of Savoy
had his eyes on Lombardy, Milan, and Genoa, and was at last

persuaded to join. When all was ready for Lesdiguières to cross with Henry's army into Italy and attack Lombardy, the great Béarnais was struck down by the dagger of Ravaillac (15 May, 1610), and the whole position was changed in favour of Spain.

The only effect produced by the great anti-Spanish league was to prevent the Emperor Rudolph from making good his claim to the Duchy of Cleves. The Regent of France, Marie di Medici, with her Italian and papal traditions, at once broke with the Huguenot connections of her husband. Wise Sully was dismissed for Concini, and Iñigo de Cardenas, the Spanish ambassador, became the right hand of the French Queen-Regent, whose adhesion to Spanish interests once more gave some reality to the arrogant claims of Philip to universal superiority. Margaret of Austria, the Queen Consort of Spain, died in 1611, leaving amongst other children an Infanta Ana, her eldest born, and Philip, Prince of Asturias, heir to the crown (born April 1605). Even before the death of Henry IV Marie de Medici had advocated a marriage between the Dauphin (Louis XIII) and the Infanta; and after her accession to the regency a double match was easily arranged; Louis XIII being betrothed to the Infanta Ana, and Philip, prince of Asturias, to Elizabeth of Bourbon, the daughter of Henry IV. The treaty was signed with extravagant rejoicings and splendour, simultaneously in Paris and Madrid (20 August, 1612), the Duke of Mayenne, and Ruy Gomez's son, the Duke of Pastrana, being respectively the proxies of the sovereigns. The King of Spain was to give a dowry of 500,000 gold crowns, and an adequate yearly allowance to his daughter, but the important clause in the case of both brides was that in which they absolutely renounced, for themselves and their descendants, all claim to succeed to the crowns of their respective countries. The Infanta was to have been delivered to the French on attaining the age of 12 years (1613) but she was a backward child, and notwithstanding the reclamations of the French government, it was October 1615 before the marriage was celebrated by proxy in Burgos, the wedding of the prince of Asturias and his French bride being performed at the same time. The two brides were then exchanged (9 November) on the frontier, the banks of the little river Bidasoa, with a lavish magnificence which had never been equalled, even there, where so many international ceremonies had been enacted.

Thus Spain and France for a short period were once more moved by the same impulse; and Charles Emmanuel of Savoy could hardly have chosen a worse time for pushing his ambitious views. He suddenly seized Mantua and Monferrat, the duke of which had died recently (1613), and announced himself the enemy of Spain, and the liberator of Italy. He tore off his Chain of the Golden Fleece and insultingly cast it at the feet of the Spanish ambassador who had gone to conciliate him, and invaded Lombardy, wasting the country as he went. The reply of Spain was characteristic. By an edict Savoy was declared forfeited and attached to the duchy of Milan. Charles Emmanuel with 17,000 men was beaten by the Viceroy of Milan, the Marquis of Hinojosa, with 30,000. The Duke however took refuge in Asti, where he was clever enough to avail himself of the mediation of Venice and England to make favourable terms with Hinojosa. The latter was at once withdrawn, and the treaty repudiated in Spain. Don Pedro de Toledo was sent in his stead and again defeated Savoy; but old Lesdiguières, whose position, almost independent in Dauphiné, enabled him to indulge his anti-Spanish leanings in spite of Marie de Medici, renounced the bribes of the Catholic party in France and Spain, and went to the assistance of Savoy. Thenceforward for nearly two years the war desolated Piedmont and Savoy, till in 1617 a peace was made (at Pavia) in which the conquests on both sides were surrendered.

But the peace satisfied neither party. The Italians were

restive at the domination of their country by a power so effete as Spain. The Venetian republic, the old-time rival of Spain in the Mediterranean, sided with Italian discontent and Savoy's ambition. The Madrid government was now so weak and confused that the Spanish Viceroys in Italy were to a large extent able to adopt their personal policy. The warlike Duke of Osuna, Viceroy of Naples, attacked and vanquished the Venetian fleet at Gravosa; and in union with the Viceroy of Milan (Toledo) repudiated the peace of Pavia, and turned the whole of the Spanish force in Italy against the republic. They were well seconded by the Spanish ambassador in Venice (Alfonso de la Cueva, Marquis of Bedmar); and the Council of Ten accused them of a treacherous design of destroying the city, and especially Osuna of an intention of proclaiming himself King of Naples. The proofs of these accusations are not forthcoming, and although much superstructure has been raised upon them, they cannot be accepted without grave doubt. In any case the turbulent Osuna was suddenly recalled (1620), to the unconcealed joy of all Neapolitans, and most Italians.

Spain indeed was anxious to be free from wars in Italy, where she had nothing to gain. She was face to face with a larger struggle in which the re-establishment of Catholic predominance in Europe was involved. The Thirty Years' War had already commenced, and the Protestants of Bohemia had conferred upon the Elector Palatine one of the crowns belonging to the house of Austria. The Emperor Ferdinand II was overpowered, and appealed to Philip, his kinsman, for aid (1620). Spain no longer had any interest but a sentimental one in the Empire. Happy circumstances had freed her from the burden that had caused her ruin, and with good government she might now have become prosperous and happy. Yet with incredible folly, bankrupt as she was, she consented to re-enter the vortex of central European politics, and fight for the Empire and for its Catholicism. An army of 8000 men was sent from Flanders to join the Emperor in Bohemia, whilst

Spinola with 30,000 troops crossed the Rhine and invaded the Palatinate. Protestant Germany flew to arms again, as it had done against the great Emperor Charles. The sanguinary battle of Prague (November 1620) completely ruined the cause of Protestant Bohemia, thanks mainly to the money and men contributed to the Emperor's cause by Spain. The sacrifices uselessly made by the latter country, in a matter with which she had no direct concern, were however only now beginning, and for years to come imposed disastrous burdens upon the misgoverned people.

Successive Cortes weakly protested in vain against the penury and misery caused by over-taxation. The people themselves, comparing their own unhappy state with the insolent greed of the public officers, the injustice of the system of taxation, and above all the corruption with which the quotas to be paid by each town or district were fixed, had looked upon the punishment of Franquesa and others as only an instalment of justice and reparation. The unprecedented avarice of Lerma marked him as the man finally to be dragged from his eminence, notwithstanding his ingratiating manners, the affection of the King and his liberal benefactions; but he was too high and far away to attack directly. He had to be approached by sap and parallel. What Lerma was to the King, Rodrigo Calderon, Marquis of Siete Iglesias, was to Lerma. An upstart of no rank, he had become more insolent, if not more splendid, than the favourite himself, and against him first was public fury unchained. The friars who surrounded the King were jealous at the unchecked predominance of laymen, and began to whisper remonstrance in the monarch's ear. The Queen, who during all her married life had urged the King to act for himself, and had only been kept quiet by lavish gifts from Lerma, seconded the prayer of the friars, and suddenly Calderon was dismissed, just before Margaret's death (1611). Whispers were rife that his agents had hastened her death, but she died in childbed from unskilful attention, so that the accusation is probably untrue. The churchmen and nuns were ceaseless in their attacks upon Calderon; and especially Aliaga, the King's confessor—a former creature of Lerma,—who cautiously began to undermine even the influence of the favourite himself, evidently now on the decline, though he was more splendid than ever, in favour of the Duke of Uceda, Lerma's own son, who joined in the cabal against his father. But a more able and ambitious man than either was enlisted against the favourite; a young gentleman in waiting, not a grandee, but a noble of Castile, Gaspar de Guzman, Count de Olivares. Lerma soon discovered the plot, and endeavoured to counteract it by placing near the King his son-in-law, the Count de Lemos, upon whom he could rely. But Uceda and the friars soon drove him away, and thenceforth Lerma was openly insulted and flouted by his son even in the King's presence. The falling favourite adopted a curious device. He sought and obtained a Cardinal's hat, and renounced his lay dignities, but to no purpose, for he was soon driven from Court by Uceda's cabal (October 1618); and with him fell all those who had not joined the new party. Calderon met with a harder fate—imprisonment for many years and confiscation of his every ducat first, and then torture, and a long trial for abuses in his office, for witchcraft, for murder, and a host of other charges. He was finally condemned to death upon the scaffold for one only of the many accusations brought against him; namely the assassination of an obscure man named Juara years before. Whilst he was waiting for his sentence to be carried out or commuted, of which latter event he had great hopes, the bells outside his prison tolled for the death of the sovereign (21 March, 1621). "The King is dead," he exclaimed; "and I am dead too." He knew full well now that Uceda himself would be as powerless as his disgraced father, and that a favourite, stronger and more haughty than either, would make a clean sweep of the whole family of Sandoval and all its associates.

During the latter years of the reign the state of the country had gone from bad to worse. Even the Cortes of Castile to some extent succeeded in reasserting control over the expenditure of the money they voted, in order to prevent its continued waste. The growth of luxury had crowded the larger towns, where most of the nobles lived, and the total population of the country now probably reached 9,000,000, but the agricultural population was fearfully diminished. Davila says that in 1600 there were in the province of Salamanca 8345 agriculturists with 11745 yokes of oxen, whereas in 1619 there were only 4135 workers on the land, with 4822 yokes of oxen. On the other hand there were no less than 32,000 Dominican and Franciscan monks in Spain, and in the two dioceses of Calahorra and Pamplona alone there were 24,000 priests. When in 1618 the financial abuses had aroused general attention, the King ordered the Council of Castile to enquire into and report frankly upon the causes of the distress, and to propose remedies. They went about their work thoroughly, and without hesitation pointed out the real reasons for Spain's poverty. Their report was worthy of more attention than it received. First, they reported, the taxes were insupportable. "The depopulation and lack of people," they said, "are greater than ever before have been seen or heard of...and the realm is being totally ruined and exhausted. The cause of this is the heavy burdens which weigh upon your vassals, and drive them abroad to escape starvation." They recommend that, at any cost, the taxes should be reduced and the abuses in their collection remedied. Secondly, they blamed the lavishness with which the King had granted pensions and concessions, and recommended that they should be withdrawn and abolished. Thirdly, they urged the King to send the nobles and ecclesiastics to live on their lands, instead of idling about the towns; by which means the crowds of importunate suitors in the cities would be brought back to useful work, and agriculture would revive. Fourthly, they were bold enough to tell the King that the scandalous extravagance of dress and living must be reduced; but that for this purpose edicts and pragmatics were useless. He must set the example himself, and first cut down his own expenses. Fifthly, they advocated the abolition of all trammels and obstacles to the sale and circulation of agricultural produce; and the limitation of the religious orders, and of the number of priests, friars, and nuns.

No notice was taken of these wise recommendations. The King soon afterwards started on his pompous voyage to Portugal, still showering pensions and grants on the favourite's favourites, and on his return he was too busy with the palace intrigues about him, and the war in Germany, to think of the woes of his wretched people. In February 1621 he fell ill of fever, and felt that the hand of death was upon him. All that his Church could do to save his life was done. The Virgin of Atocha was brought out from her church, the body of St Isidore carried to the King's bedside, and all the realm was prostrated in prayer for the monarch, who, idle and pleasure-loving though he was, enjoyed, personally, the love of his subjects. Like that of his father, his death-bed was one of rigid devotion, regret for lost opportunities, and faith in divine forgiveness. That he saw now how disastrous his government had been is certain. During his last hours he referred to it more than once. "A fine account we shall give to God of our government," he said on one occasion: and on another, "O! if Heaven would please to prolong my life, how different should my conduct be!" Too late, too late, like most of his house. On the 31st March, 1621, he breathed his last, grasping firmly in his hand the coarse crucifix which had been held in the dying grip, and had lain upon the dead breasts of his father and grandfather. In the twenty-three years of his reign he had missed the splendid opportunity of resuscitating Spain. The burden which had weighed down his predecessors was raised from his shoulders. He had no world-wide ambitions to which he needed to sacrifice his country. What was wanted was honest administration, patience, economy, industry and restraint; and all might have been well. These were the very qualities which Philip III lacked. Inoffensive, devout and well-meaning, his indolence, extravagance and carelessness handed over his suffering country to incompetent favourites who well-nigh bled it to death.

CHAPTER VII.

PHILIP IV, 1621—1640.

AMONGST the many anxieties which had surrounded the remorseful death-bed of Philip III was the tormenting thought that his destined successor had already started on the downward path of idleness and self-indulgence that had led to his own wasted record. When the Prince's household had been formed on his betrothal Lerma had incautiously appointed to an office therein Gaspar de Guzman, son of that overbearing Count de Olivares who, as ambassador in Rome at the time of the Armada, had pushed the interests of Spain so insolently. Lerma and his son Uceda had soon seen their mistake, and had tried to persuade Guzman (who had succeeded to his father's title) to accept the embassy in Rome. He had, however, wider views for himself, and declined it unless he was allowed to keep his appointment in the palace as well. Thenceforward he was known to be working for the succession to the favouriteship, and all the Lerma interest was against him. Several unsuccessful attempts were made to assassinate him, and the young prince as a boy was taught to dislike him. His claim to the grandeeship in right of his wife (a Zuñiga) was unsuccessful, and spies were set about him to counteract any attempt he might make to gain influence over the young prince. Keen, artful, watchful, he worked and waited. Over a boy of eleven or twelve he could gain no control: but when young Philip reached sixteen, and was already married and associated with his father in state affairs, then came Olivares' opportunity. He gained influence over the lad by ministering to his pleasures and passions, and before the King died the nocturnal excursions of the young heir and his favourite were causing scandal.

Whilst Philip III was on his death-bed Olivares obtained from the prince an order forbidding Lerma to come to Court as he intended to do; and as soon as the breath was out of the King's body false Uceda and the whole of the Sandoval party were sent about their business, Uceda himself being arrested, and dying in prison (1624). The greatest Spaniard of them all, Pedro Tellez de Giron, Duke of Osuna, fell first. He had been that strong, ambitious Viceroy of Sicily and Naples who had carried things with so high a hand, conquering Turks and Moors at sea, and the Venetians in Italy. He was imprisoned almost immediately after Philip III's death, and he too ultimately died in prison. Before many months had passed Rodrigo Calderon, Marquis de Siete Iglesias, showy and brilliant as ever, popular and beloved in his misfortune as he had been hated in prosperity, lost his head on the Plaza Mayor of Madrid. Blind to the miserable example of his father, young Philip threw himself into the hands of Olivares as completely as his father had done with Lerma. There is in the British Museum (Egerton MSS. 329) a letter from the Archbishop of Granada (Alvanel, the King's former tutor) to Olivares, written soon after the accession, remonstrating with him for taking the boy-King out in the streets at night. The example, he says, of the King and his minister scouring the streets at undue hours in search of adventure is a bad one, and people already are talking of it. The reply of haughty Olivares is clear enough. He tells the prelate, in effect, that he is an impertinent meddler, and that if he does not mind his own business worse will befall him. If this was the treatment extended to an archbishop, it may well be imagined what sort of reception the remonstrance of less important personages would meet with. Nothing stood in the way of Olivares. Not only was the desired right to cover his head as a grandee given him, but a dukedom (of San Lucar) as well, and almost as many offices as had been taken by greedy Lerma. Then Spain started on a fresh era of favouritism and lavishness, amidst public rejoicing and sanguine hopes.

The condition of the country was truly deplorable; and the fact could not be concealed by Court splendours or a change of favourites. The Cortes of Castile were called together a few months after the death of Philip III (1621), and good fortune has preserved for us the discourses and proposals made in it, and to the King, by the representative for Granada (Don Mateo Lison y Biedma), whose book was privately printed shortly afterwards (1624)). The picture presented is a really terrible one; and although some of the remedies proposed seem shortsighted and inadequate enough to us, yet they show that the wiser heads clearly understood the direction in which improvement might be expected. First the enormous number of public servants should be reduced, and the administration simplified. Titular honours should be given instead of pensions, pluralities abolished, churchmen compelled to bear their full share of the cost of armaments, and economy in the public service rigidly enforced. Again the desolate condition of the provinces is deplored. "The people are now turned adrift wandering on the roads, living on herbs and roots, or else travelling to countries and provinces," where they have not to pay the hateful food tax of the "millions," and the blighting *alcabala*, and so those that remain have to pay the more. Send the prelates, nobles and landowners back to their estates, prays Don Mateo, and, above all, fix a composition or quota of *alcabala* for every town and district. The places where no quota had been appointed are impossible to live in, as the tax farmers or officers exact from the inhabitants daily returns of all transactions. The least mistake or infraction causes a law-suit, where the costs are crushing and ruinous, and the poor people are sold up without mercy and driven to starvation on the most trifling pretext. Give all places quotas, begs the representative of Granada, bring the people back to their villages by granting them privileges for a time, until they can get the land into cultivation again. The most crying grievance seems to have been the costly and oppressive way in which the taxes were collected, the expenses of collection frequently far exceeding the amount received, especially where the taxes or monopolies were farmed. Every separate monopoly, such as playing-cards, quicksilver, pepper, corrosive-sublimate, and a host of others, had its own courts, judges, officers and procedure, so that the farmers of monopolies and taxes were practically judges and plaintiffs as well, and the poor people stood no chance. If they were unable to pay ever so small an amount and were sued for it they knew it meant ruin to them, and in most cases they simply abandoned all their property in despair and became vagrants.

The new ministers made some attempts to grapple with the evils, but their efforts were mainly directed towards the prevention of peculation by high officers, who were now compelled to make a precise disclosure of all their property before and after entering office. Some reduction also was made in the number of useless paid officials, while stricter pragmatics than ever were issued against extravagance in dress and living, horses, coaches, lacqueys and the like, the King himself setting an example by reducing the absurd expenditure on the royal establishment. These reforms were doubtless well meant--for it must have been obvious to Olivares that things could not continue as they were—but, as will now be readily understood, they did not touch the root of the evil, which was a system of taxation that hampered industry and traffic to the extent of killing them, and raised the cost of production to a point which rendered Spanish competition with foreign goods out of the question, except at first hand in the place of origin.

The moment Spanish produce or goods had to pass from hand to hand, or from one place to another, *alcabalas*, tolls, inland custom-houses, octrois etc. made them impossible. The constant attempts of the government to limit the prices at which they might be sold, in the supposed interest of the consumer, further handicapped the producer, and made it not worth his while to produce them at all, excepting in a small way for immediate home consumption. Olivares' new measures at first inspired hopes that something would be done really to ameliorate the condition of the country; but the hope faded almost as soon as it was born. When the Cortes of 1623 had voted the usual subsidies, which had now become a tribute, Olivares astounded them with the demand for 70,000,000 ducats to be spread over a number of years, for the purpose of freeing the royal patrimony from debt. Such a sum in one vote had never been dreamt of in Spain before, and the representatives asserted that it would be impossible to raise it. They had moreover no authority from their constituents to vote such a supply. The opposition came mainly from the cities of Andalucia; and Olivares took the King on a splendid progress thither, in order to influence the town councils personally. By bribery and persuasion Seville was at first induced to consent, but when it was seen that every other city held out Seville itself found pretexts to withdraw its acquiescence, and the project had to be abandoned. But Philip was at war with the Hollanders again now, for the truce of 12 years had expired (1621); the war in Germany continued to make demands upon him; the Moors still harried his territories and commerce in the Mediterranean, and money had to be found somehow. The way adopted, as usual, was to increase again the vicious taxation that was killing the productive power of the country.

The pro-Spanish policy suddenly favoured by Marie de Medici on the death of Henry IV had naturally aroused considerable misgiving in England, as well as in France itself. In the Court of James I there were two distinct parties, each of which sought to solve the difficulty in its own way. Winwood, Edmunds, Carew, and the Elizabethan Protestants were in favour of attracting France back to the alliance which had existed in the time of Henry IV; whilst those of Catholic leanings, Buckingham, the Scots courtiers, and, above all, the weak King, were for currying favour with Spain. Diego Sarmiento de Acuña, Count de Gondomar, the Spanish ambassador, had taken the measure of James Stuart, and by working on his vanity and timidity had entirely dominated him. When the overthrow of Marie de Medici, the murder of Concini (1617), and the renewed disputes between Spain and France about the Grisons and the Valtellina had caused bitterness between the two countries, it seemed a master-stroke to the King of England to join his country in close union with Spain. He was ready to grovel and abase himself to the utmost, if only he could marry his heir Charles to the Infanta Maria. With this end he sacrificed Raleigh at the bidding of Gondomar, and with this end he was ready to acknowledge the most arrogant claims of the Spanish King. But when the husband of his daughter Elizabeth, the titular King of Bohemia, was cast out of his new capital and of his old principality mainly by Spanish arms, James, who thought he was a divinely gifted diplomatist, was more anxious than ever to make terms with a nation which at the same time could restore his son-in-law to his kingdom, and provide his own heir with a wife whose connection would in future allow Great Britain to disregard so unstable a power as France still was.

Cottington and Digby, as well as less official English envoys, had been fooled to the top of their bent by Lerma. Vague hopes, flattering attentions and half promises, kept England in a yielding mood, and prevented a nearer approach to France. Digby (Earl of Bristol) continued after Philip III's death the endless advance-and-retire policy, in order to pledge the Spaniards to something definite. But at last even

James lost patience. He wrote to Bristol that, notwithstanding all the fine Spanish promises to intercede with the Emperor, "the only fruits England had received were dishonour and scorn." "Whilst we are treating, the town and castle of Heidelburg have been taken by force, our garrison put to the sword, Mannheim besieged, and all the hostility used that is within the power of the enemy." Bristol then is instructed to demand an immediate cessation of arms in the Palatinate, and the restoration of Heidelburg etc.; or else that the Spanish forces shall join the English, "for the recovery of our children's honour and patrimony"; or, at least that the English troops should be allowed free passage through Flanders to restore the Palatine. This letter was sent to Spain by Endymion Porter, who was half a Spaniard and had been a page of Olivares. Whilst Bristol was following the wearisome Spanish diplomatic road, Porter saw Olivares (November 1622) and bluntly asked him point-blank to allow a Spanish army to support Vere in the Palatinate, as a condition of the proposed marriage. Olivares haughtily told him he did not understand what he was talking about. "As for this marriage I know not what it means." The next day, however, he smoothed matters over with Bristol, and the long-drawn negotiations still dragged on. There was probably never any intention on the part of Spain to make them real—for Philip III on his death-bed had solemnly enjoined his son to make the Infanta an Empress—but if England could be cajoled into a Catholic course, toleration established, and perhaps even Charles converted, it would all make for Spain and alienate England from the dominant party of reform in France. But such slow methods did not commend themselves to Buckingham, who had long ago been bought by Gondomar and hoped to benefit greatly by the match. To the King's despair, he and the young Prince suddenly started on their foolish trip to Madrid, accompanied only by Cottington and Porter, hoping to carry the position by storm. They suddenly appeared disguised on the night of March 7, 1622, at Bristol's house in the then new street of Alcalá, and thenceforward secrecy was out of the question.

Olivares and Philip made the best of a bad business. Economy was thrown to the winds. Pragmatics forbidding extravagance were all suspended, and whilst the Prince stayed in Madrid a perfect tempest of prodigality reigned. The streets were new paved, the houses new painted, nobles summoned from all Spain to make a show, banquets, tourneys, processions, bull-fights and balls, succeeded each other with haste that left no interval for serious negotiation. But with all the splendour the Englishmen were frozen with the glacial etiquette of the Spanish Court. The Infanta herself was unapproachable: she had no wish for the match, and was probably quite aware that the whole affair was sham. Buckingham shocked the Spanish Court with his easy familiarity, and soon came to loggerheads with Olivares, who looked upon his offhandedness as highly indecorous. Presents of fabulous value were lavished on both sides, professions of eternal love and amity were liberally exchanged by Philip and Charles; but the latter could not afford to appear openly Catholic, and Olivares made it plain that all the concession was to be on one side, and all the advantage on the other. A conditional treaty of matrimony and alliance was signed and sworn to by the King of Spain and Charles, and the most elaborate pretence was made on both sides to cover appearances, but when the Prince took his pompous farewell of Philip (12 September, 1623) it was evident to most people that England had been outwitted, and that cunning James Stuart had allowed his country to be placed in an inferior position, and had been cheated out of the price for doing so.

The bad faith on both sides which had rendered abortive no less than three treaties between France and Spain for the restoration by the latter power of the Valtellina to the Grisons, had in the meanwhile further embittered the relations between Philip and his brother-in-law Louis XIII. Richelieu did not believe in playing unless he had all the cards in his hand, and delayed an open declaration of war until he had joined to him the United Provinces, and the Duke of Savoy, always greedy to seize Lombardy and Genoa. It was time indeed for Richelieu to act. Once more the ambitious projects of Philip II were being revived by Olivares. The Emperor was daily growing more powerful. Bohemia had been suppressed, the Spaniards under Spinola had reduced the Lower Palatinate, and were now threatening the United Provinces. England for the time was befooled with the hopes of the Spanish match, and would not, as in old times, help to withstand Spanish aggression. Unless France struck boldly and strongly she was once more in danger of finding herself shut in by the house of Austria. Spain still held in defiance of France the Valtellina, which connected Lombardy with Tyrol. This was Richelieu's first objective. With French and Swiss troops he invaded the valley, and soon afterwards attracted England to his side by negotiations for the marriage of Charles with Henrietta Maria, Buckingham now being violently against Spain. But again England was outwitted, for after extorting many promises of toleration for English Catholics, Richelieu avoided complying with England's main object, namely the recovery of the Palatinate, and drew her into open and unfortunate hostility to Spain with Lord Wimbledon's ignominious naval attack upon Cadiz (October 1625).

The fever of glory and conquest had seized Spain. The union of France and Savoy with the Protestant powers and England once again divided Europe in the old way. The principalities of Italy, Parma, Modena, and Tuscany, and the republics of Genoa and Lucca, joined the Spaniards; the nobles of Spain contributed a million ducats. Poor and exhausted as the country was, prodigious efforts were made, the Queen and Princesses offering their jewels, and even the clergy promising to maintain a force of 20,000 troops. The property of all French subjects in Spain was confiscated (April 1625), and the war was carried on with immense energy. The French and Savoyards at first overran Montferrat, the Valtellina and the territory of Genoa; but Feria on land and Spinola at sea soon forced them to give up their conquests. But Richelieu was a Cardinal of the Church, and could not go too far in a war on the side of Protestants. Soon the remonstrances of the Pope and the Catholic party in France led to a treaty (January 1626) which gave liberty to the Catholics of Valtellina, on payment of a tribute to the Grisons. But in Germany the war continued, favourable to the Emperor, thanks to the military genius of Tilly and the material assistance of Spain. Spanish men and money in plenty had to be sent to the Archduke, still fighting with the sturdy Dutchmen, who were again upheld as of old by Protestant aid from England and France. Once more the privateers of the republic harried Spanish commerce on every sea, as before the twelve years' truce, and once more all commerce was prohibited between the United Provinces and the Spanish dominions. Energy and boldness here again favoured Spanish arms. Don Farique de Toledo destroyed the Dutch fleet off Gibraltar; and, more important still, Spinola, after a siege of ten months, captured Breda. The Dutch were conquered in South America and expelled from Guayaquil and Puerto Rico; and at the same time the Moorish pirates were almost swept from the Mediterranean.

These great victories once more raised Spanish pride to its highest pitch, and 'Philip the Great' was already the title given to the youthful monarch in whose name they were effected. But there was another side to the medal. We have seen the utter state of exhaustion in which the country was. The wars, however gratifying to national pride, had to be paid for in national blood and money; and although the Cortes of Castile was now effete, and only ventured on fruitless remonstrance, the more independent parliaments of the other provinces made their voices heard with greater effect. The three Cortes of Aragon, Cataluña, and Valencia, were convened for January 1626; and the King promised to be present at each and take the oath as sovereign to respect their rights. The Valencians, however, resented the summoning of their Cortes at Monzon, a place outside of the kingdom of Valencia, and were ready to take offence before the meeting. Philip was popular with the Aragonese, but on this occasion he had considerable difficulty even with them; when, however, the King asked the Valencians at Monzon to give him 2,000 paid troops to be used as he pleased, as well as a money vote, they refused. It would, they said, be the same as the conscription in Castile, and that was against their liberties. The expulsion of Moriscos, too, had ruined the kingdom, particularly the landowners, and they could make no more sacrifices. Olivares alternately threatened and bribed, and the King himself tried persuasion. At last he formally told the Cortes that they must vote the supplies without further ado. But the noble or military members still held out—the Cortes of Valencia consisted of three orders, Military or nobles, Ecclesiastical, and popular—though the King and Olivares threatened and stormed. At last he called them traitors, and gave them one day to do as he bade them. It was necessary that the vote should be unanimous, and under this pressure all the members gave way but one—Don Francisco Millan. When, however, a hint was given that the garotte would be the reward for his obstinacy he too acquiesced in the vote. But even then the difficulties were not at an end. The nobles cavilled about the amount of their quota, and only after much deliberation it was settled that the vote of money should be reduced to 1,080,000 livres in 15 years, half the sum paid by Aragon, and should be paid, not in coin, but in kind. The King was forced to accept, but still the Cortes were discontented and would not formally ratify the vote. At length the King sent to say that he gave them but one half-hour by the watch to vote the supply, as he was leaving at once. Such a violent course threw the Cortes into consternation. All that night they sat in deliberation, and at six in the morning the King sent to say that he had determined to abolish their privilege of "*nemine discrepante*," or unanimity. The angry and indignant Cortes could not believe their ears, and at first protested. But the boldness of Olivares cowed them, and their opposition collapsed. Then came the complete triumph of the King. He ordered them under pain of treason to vote at once and unconditionally all he asked for originally, and then to go about their business. This they did meekly, and the independence of the Cortes of Valencia was thenceforward almost as effete as that of Castile. The King then met the Catalonian Cortes at Lerida, where he sought to dazzle them with feasts and splendour. The rough Catalans however were even more fractious than the Aragonese and Valencians, and insisted upon repayment of their former loans to the King before they voted a ducat. Again fair words and bribes were powerless to move them, and they were equally unyielding to threats. Three days were given to them to decide, but still they held out. Olivares, fearing mischief, suddenly and without notice carried the King and Court away to Castile. In vain the Catalans then voted all that was asked of them to bring the Sovereign back. The only answer they got was a threat of vengeance for their undutifulness; and the seed was sown of a trouble which embittered most of the rest of Philip's life. As if to counteract to some extent the discontent of the Catalans and Valencians, Philip from Madrid voluntarily reduced the contingent voted by the Aragonese (July 1626) to 2,300 men instead of 3,333.

Christian of Denmark had been crushed by Tilly, Mansfield had been defeated by the Imperial troops under Wallenstein, and France was now (1627) at war with England about the unfulfilled conditions of Henrietta Maria's marriage contract. An English fleet was before Rochelle, cooperating with the Huguenots. Richelieu's energy was equal to the occasion, and his and Marshal Schomberg's presence before Rochelle paralysed the Huguenots, and relieved the besieged forts on Oleron and Rhé. Buckingham and his fleet had to return to England (October 1627) disgraced and defeated, with the loss of two-thirds of the force. Richelieu was then able to turn his arms against the Spaniards, who had once more deserted him and had assumed an aggressive attitude on the eternal question of the Duchy of Mantua, which by the death of the Duke had again become vacant and was claimed by the son of the Duke de Nevers and by the Prince of Guastalla. Olivares thought in any case to retain for Spain the strong place of Casale in Montferrat, which he had ordered the Spanish Governor of Milan to seize. The Duke of Savoy also coveted this place, and joined the Spaniards this time, in hope of a share in the spoils. Together they overran Mantua and Montferrat; but when Richelieu was free (late in 1628) from the terrible siege of Rochelle he sent his victorious army to meet the invaders.

Olivares, finding himself thus pledged to a national war with France, recalled Spinola from Flanders to meet the enemy in Italy. He had already made advances to England. In the spring of 1628 he sent an Irish Dominican friar to England to make unofficial overtures to Charles I for peace. The one idea of the English King was to restore his brother-in-law to the Palatinate, and he gladly accepted the overtures of Olivares. Endymion Porter was again sent to Spain by way of Genoa to settle the treaty; and in the meanwhile hasty Buckingham, determined to be avenged for his defeat by the French in the previous year at Oleron, raised his fleet in Portsmouth to relieve Rochelle. He was assassinated by Felton (23 August, 1628) and the relieving fleet was commanded by the Earl of Lindsay. It arrived too late. The heroic Rochelle was in the firm grip of Richelieu and fell (October 1628). In due time the peace between Spain and England was arranged (January 1629), and was ratified by Rubens as special envoy to England in 1630. Thenceforward during the reign of Charles I England counted for little in continental politics. The Palatine Frederick died in 1632, and the main object of Charles's foreign policy—a policy futilely pursued for the next ten years—was the restoration of his nephew Charles Louis to the dominions of his forefathers.

The ancient rivals, France and Spain, were thus face to face in Northern Italy. The ground was cleared by a settlement of the differences between France and England—which was easy now that Buckingham was dead—and the signing of a treaty between France, the Pope, Venice, and the Duke of Mantua (Nevers) to defend the territory of the latter against the Spaniards. Richelieu was victorious nearly everywhere over the Spaniards, Germans and Savoyards. Soon Savoy was in the hands of the French, and after the battle of Javennes, in which Montmorenci and La Force routed his son, the unquiet Carlo Emanuele died broken-hearted (July 1630).

The war continued with varying fortunes. The imperialists captured Mantua, but plague decimated their armies. Slaughter and desolation were wearing out all the combatants. Spinola died of grief in front of Casale (September 1630) on learning of the defeat of his son Philip. His successor Santa Cruz lacked the experience necessary for land warfare, and was surprised and overpowered, apparently at the hour when his victory was assured. The treaty which followed (October 1630), to the indignation of the Spaniards, gave to the French nominee the duchies in dispute, subject to the suzerainty of the Emperor. The French retained the fortress of Pignerol, and the Spaniards received nothing for their heavy sacrifice of men and money.

But the treaty of Casale brought no real peace between France and Spain. The house of Austria must be crushed if Richelieu were to succeed in raising France to the first rank amongst the nations; while Olivares, unfortunately for Spain, could not shake off the imperial traditions which had been the ruin of his country and still supported the emperor. On his side Richelieu had the great Gustavus Adolphus and the Protestants. The Spanish infantry fought, as usual, with desperate bravery, but for a time the Swede carried all before him; for the German imperial troops were many of them Protestant or indifferent, and their hearts were not in their work. The best of the Emperor's generals, Tilly, was killed at Ingolstadt (1632), and all through that terrible winter the Spaniards and men of the south died in multitudes of hardship, wounds, and pestilence. Wallenstein, who succeeded Tilly, was beaten in the hard-fought battle of Lützen, in which Gustavus Adolphus was killed. Twelve thousand imperialists fell in this one fight, and the victorious Swedes, but without their royal leader, captured Leipzig. Jealous Ferdinand II, fearing Wallenstein's popularity and ambition, caused him to be murdered (1634); but the new general (the King of Hungary, the Emperor's heir) was hopeless of being able to overcome the Swedes without more effective aid from Spain. The old Infanta Isabel, sovereign of Flanders, had died childless (1633), and her dominion had unfortunately once more fallen to the King of Spain. The Cardinal Infante Ferdinand had been sent by Philip IV, his brother, as governor, and to him whilst on his way the Emperor appealed for help. The Infante was able, popular and ambitious, and with an army of 18,000 Spaniards marched to the aid of his cousin and brother-in-law. He arrived before Nordlingen at the hour when the imperialists had summoned it to surrender, and a relieving force of Swedes was approaching. The battle that ensued, which lasted for two days, was one of the most terrible of the Thirty Years' War. The imperialists had on their side not only the Infante, but the Dukes of Bavaria and Lorraine; and the Swedes and Protestants were outnumbered. The latter were completely routed, leaving 8000 dead on the field and 4000 prisoners in the hands of the enemy.

The blow to the projects of Richelieu was a heavy one.

He met it by subsidising and encouraging the Hollanders to continue the war with Spain, in order that the Infante might be forced to confine himself to his dominion. Not content with this, he again openly declared war against Spain, as well as against the Emperor. The French under Châtillon and De Brézé met the Infante's troops commanded by Prince Thomas of Savoy at Avenne (May 1635) and completely routed the Spaniards: then, joining the Prince of Orange, they fell upon Tirlemont. But the Infante was stout-hearted, the Spanish infantry was the best in the world, and the tide soon turned. With varying fortunes the war dragged on in Flanders, Germany, and northern Italy. In the spring of 1636 Richelieu decided to make a supreme effort to attack the Spaniards and imperialists at the same time in Germany, Alsace, Franche-Comté, the Milanese and the isles of Lerin, which had been captured by Spain. It was a duel to the death now, in which one of the nations must be humbled. Heavy as were the burdens imposed both upon France and Spain, Richelieu and Olivares respectively contrived, somehow, to raise the necessary resources. Private property in Spain was seized without hesitation, the taxes on food were increased, a rebate was taken on all assignments on public revenues, the Church was squeezed to the utmost, the revenues of Toledo appropriated, and salaries and pensions left unpaid. In France almost every man was forced to take arms, and coach-horses were embargoed for cavalry. For a time the Spanish forces on the Oise threatened Paris itself, until the advance of the Prince of Orange with 30,000 men in their rear caused them to retire with the exception of a small garrison left in Corbie (autumn 1636). This was promptly surrounded and besieged by 40,000 Frenchmen, till it marched out with all the honours of war, a heroic handful against an army. But in a war of material resources Spain was bound to be beaten. With a system of taxation like hers, and with a public administration so corrupt, she could no more cope permanently with France than Olivares could stand against

Richelieu. The blighting system of centralisation introduced by Philip II discouraged the making of great captains; and although there was talent in plenty, and bravery to spare, she had largely to depend upon foreigners like Spinola and Thomas of Savoy to take supreme command of her armies. The young Infante Ferdinand found himself therefore at a critical period (1636), after the death of the Marquis of Aytona, short of resources and without a single Spanish adviser of standing. So great too was the penury in Spain, that Philip wrote to his brother begging him to compel his own household to dress in plain cloth and live frugally on beef and mutton, "with an occasional fowl or partridge."

The dominion of Spain over Flanders was again trembling in the balance. In the last days of the Infanta it had nearly been lost by the treason of Count de Bergues (1632): Holland was at the apogee of its prosperity, victorious at sea over Spanish ships wherever she could find them; and now that Nassau had the declared support of France, and Spain was pledged to war in several parts of Europe at once, only supreme good fortune could preserve to Philip the unhappy Flemish inheritance of his Burgundian forefathers. Some attempt was made by the Pope to bring about a peaceful settlement, but Spain refused to allow the attendance at the conference of the representatives of Holland and the Protestants of Germany, and no results were attained, although Richelieu at this time was desirous of peace. Early in 1637 the war, so far as it regarded northern Italy, was to a great extent limited by an arrangement between the Grisons, Parma and Spain; and this allowed Richelieu to concentrate his forces at other points. Count de Harcourt with a fleet of 40 sail and 20 galleys promptly expelled the Spaniards from the islands of St Marguerite and St Honoré, whilst Cardinal de La Valette reduced Landrecy (July 1637) and La Chapelle; and Orange, who was besieging Breda, was reinforced by an army of Frenchmen. Marshal Châtillon, also, with another

French force, carried all before him in Luxembourg, as did the Duke of Longueville in the Franche-Comté, and the Duke of Weimar in Alsace. In the south of France, which the Spaniards had invaded, they were more unfortunate still. Their army of 13,000 men under the Duke of Carmona was practically destroyed, and all their baggage taken.

The next year, 1638, the tables were to a slight extent turned, and the Spaniards regained some of their lost ground, the siege of St Omer being abandoned with great loss by Chatillon, and the Marquis of Leganes gaining several victories in Lombardy; in one of which (Bremo, July 1638) Marshal de Crequi fell on the French side and all Lombardy was cleared of French. Whilst the armies of Spain were thus dispersed in all parts of Europe, and the Infante with the utmost difficulty was holding Flanders, Richelieu sought to deliver a master-stroke by invading with a powerful force the territory of Spain itself. Crossing the Bidasoa from St Jean de Luz the French rapidly captured Irun, and the beautiful harbour of Pasages, and laid siege to Fuenterrabia both by sea and by land (July 1638).

Condé and the Duke de La Valette (Épernon's eldest son) were in command on land, and the Bishop of Bordeaux at sea. An attempt was made to storm the fortress; but a dashing charge of 6000 Spaniards of the relief force under the Admiral of Castile carried panic into the French camp, and the besiegers fled headlong to the boats (September 1638), La Valette flying to England to escape from Richelieu's accusation of treason. Through the next year, 1639, the various campaigns dragged on with but small permanent result on either side, though the French generally maintained their advantage, except in Italy, where the Marquis of Leganes and Thomas of Savoy almost completely subjugated Piedmont and Savoy—now governed by the widowed duchess, sister of the French King, who had scornfully refused the Spanish offer of peace. In the spring of 1639 the French under Condé again invaded Spain:

this time by Roussillon—which was then a Spanish possession attached to Cataluña. The Spaniards fled before them into Perpignan. There was, as we have seen, no love lost between Olivares and the Catalans; and the latter were left to defend their own principality. This they did worthily. An army of 10,000 men was rapidly improvised; but there was no leader worthy of the name, and they fought for a time in vain. Badly led, kept inactive when they were burning to advance, discouragement seized them. 8000 of them died of the plague before Salcés, but when Condé returned from Narbonne with a fresh French army which he had gathered, of 20,000 foot and 4000 horse, the rest of the Spaniards plucked up spirit and resolved to stay and fight him where they lay. Full of confidence the French stormed the Spanish trenches (1 November, 1639). Regiment after regiment rushed to the charge only to fall dead or dying in the overswollen ditches. Panic at last seized them, and they fled, leaving the Catalans masters of the field, and the fortress of Salcés fell by famine on the 6th January, 1640; the attempt of Richelieu to invade Spain thus failing for a second time. Nor did the maritime attacks on the Spanish coast by the Bishop of Bordeaux produce much more effect, for after some depredations and temporary occupations of Spanish ports, his fleet was scattered by a storm and he returned disabled to France. On the other hand a powerful Spanish fleet of 70 ships and 10,000 men was almost destroyed by the Dutch (21 October, 1639). Four-fifths of the Spaniards were lost, and only seven of their ships escaped into Dunkirk. The Spaniards had taken refuge in the Downs, to escape from Tromp; and simultaneously the Spanish agents and the Dutch addressed Charles I on the subject. He pointed out to the former that they could not remain in English waters for ever; and began to bargain as to what Spain would do for the Palatine if shelter were afforded to her fleet. But before an arrangement could be made Tromp took the matter into his own hands and boldly attacked the Spaniards whilst their ships lay on the Kentish coast. The Spaniards asserted that the English themselves lent him what help they could; and Admiral Pennington was imprisoned for not protecting them. This blow ended prematurely Spain's renewed attempt to become a great naval power. Every nerve had been strained by Olivares to strengthen the Spanish navy, and not without success. The loss now sustained was never completely recovered, and Spain's hold upon the sceptre of the sea was loosened for ever.

CHAPTER VIII.

PHILIP IV, 1638—1643.

WHILST the national resources were being wasted abroad the trade and industry of Spain were languishing. The coasts of Brazil and the commerce of the West were a prey to the depredations of the Hollanders. The silver fleet was regularly intercepted off the Azores, and generally some of its rich cargo went to defray the cost of war against its legitimate owners. Edicts had been published in Spain (1628 and 1630) prohibiting, under pain of forfeiture, all commerce whatever with the enemies of the country; and no manufactured goods of any description were permitted to be imported directly or indirectly from the principal manufacturing countries of Europe. This measure entailed a costly and harassing system of examination, which for a time paralysed commerce altogether. As we have seen, the unwise system of taxation in Spain had driven vast tracts of land out of cultivation; and, together with the expulsion of the Moriscos, sumptuary pragmatics, and other causes, had already almost destroyed manufactures. These new obstacles to trade had the natural result of immensely increasing the cost of living, and still further handicapping Spanish production. Already most of the needs of the country were supplied from abroad. By the middle of the 17th century no less than seventeen formerly prosperous industries had been driven out of Spain, especially those connected with metal working, cordage, and ship-building, whilst the national industries of weaving silks, fine fabrics, and linens, and the manufacture of gloves, in which Spain had always been pre-eminent, were now merely a shadow of what they had been in the time of the Emperor and in the earlier years of Philip II.

To combat the natural rise of prices resulting from the hampering of traffic, Olivares, perhaps with the best of intentions, again began at the wrong end. The value of copper money was once more reduced to the half of its present nominal value—which, as it only reversed the former shortsighted edict, was perhaps a move in the right direction—but persistent, as usual, in regarding the interest of the consumer, and disregarding that of the producer, Olivares caused an edict to be issued again fixing the prices at which all food stuffs had to be sold.

When Philip met the Castilian Cortes in 1638 he had but a sorry story to tell, notwithstanding the bravery with which his troops had fought in all parts of Europe. He had, he told them, borrowed since the Cortes of 1632 the sum of 72,650,000 ducats at eight per cent. interest, secured on the various national revenues; this sum had been spent entirely on the military and naval operations outside the realms of Castile and Aragon, the armed forces at home and the cost of civil government having been defrayed from current revenue. Up to this time all attempts to increase the *alcabala* had been resisted. The "millions" tax on stated articles of food had been augmented, and imposed on fresh articles frequently, but the 10 per cent. on all sales had remained nominally unchanged; although in most cases the system of fixed quotas for towns and districts, and the pledging of the quotas to contractors for advances, had in effect caused the demand for the full tax to be unnecessary, as well as impossible of recovery. In the Cortes of 1639 an additional 1 per cent. on the *alcabala* was voted; but when it was found that the sum produced by the increase was smaller than had been estimated, and a further increase was demanded, the Cortes flatly refused.

They had (they said) voted 9,000,000 silver ducats payable over three years, and they declined to alter the taxation until the three years had expired, although they did vote an increase of the tax upon wine to help the "millions."

It will be well understood that this oppressive taxation, weighing especially on food and industry, was rapidly reducing the provinces to a condition of desolation. Madrid however continued to grow in dirty splendour and squalid luxury. The roadways of the capital were ancle deep in filth or dust, according to the time of year; decent people, especially ladies, were compelled to go in litters or carriages, until it became a perfect craze to promenade in coaches up and down the Calle Mayor. Severe pragmatics were issued against this excessive use of coaches, especially by men, but luxury was never permanently restrained by pragmatics, and there were always loopholes and exceptions by which the edicts might be evaded. The Spanish theatre, which set the fashion and fixed a standard for all the rest of Europe, was now in its prime, and provided intellectual pleasure for the citizens of which they never tired. The two theatres in the capital were always thronged—poor as the people were—the seats costing in all 15 sous each; of which $1\frac{1}{2}$ went to the players, 2 to the town council, $1\frac{1}{2}$ to the hospital, and the rest to the dramatist, the impresario and the government. Neither the severe edicts of Philip II against the education of Spanish youth abroad, and against the introduction of foreign science, nor the rigid control of the Inquisition over literature in the three reigns, had dwarfed the intellectual growth, which even on such uncongenial soil flourished spontaneously and luxuriantly, in obedience to the impulse which in various manifestations was making itself felt throughout the civilized world. Physical science was discouraged, but the southern imagination—the eastern romanticism joined to Celtic keenness of thought and eloquence of word—produced in Spain generations of novelists and dramatists such as the world has rarely seen in any country. The Inquisition was not anxious to suppress works of pure imagination, and most of the successful writers of the literary golden age of Spain were either servants of the Holy Office or ecclesiastics; Lope de Vega, Moreto, Montalvan, Tirso de Molina, Calderon, and many others, amongst them, and even the greatest of them all, "the maimed one of Lepanto," the great Cervantes, died a Franciscan monk. Historical writing, as distinct from chronicling, reached an elegance and vigour in the reigns of the three consecutive Philips of which many examples are still admired. Sandoval, the historian of Charles V, Diego Hurtado de Mendoza, the authority on the Moorish wars of Philip II, Bernardino de Mendoza, the soldier-ambassador, who told so well the story of the wars in Flanders, Perez de Hita who described the civil wars of Granada, Cabrera de Cordoba the historian of Philip II, Florian de Ocampo, Zurita, Mariana, and a host of others, are read by scholars of to day with as much zest as they were in their own times; the poets Fernando de Herrera, Ercilla, Barahona de Soto, and Balbuena, produced odes and lyrics full of vigour and inspiration. But the special directions taken by Spanish intellectual progress in the time of the three Philips were the novel of adventure and the episodical drama. Don Quixote, Lazarillo de Tormes, Guzman de Alfarache, El Gran Tacaño, El Diablo Cojuelo, and even Gil Blas de Santillana, almost certainly a Spanish work, are the direct ancestors of the modern novel. It is easy to trace the descent of the Spanish picaresque romancers through Tom Jones, Roderick Random and Pickwick to our own day; as it is to follow the influence of the famous Philippian playwrights, Lope de Vega, Lope de Rueda and Calderon, upon Beaumont and Fletcher, Dryden, Congreve, Shadwell, and Wycherley; and so through the Georgian dramatic writers to the comedy of imbroglio which still delights English playgoers.

By the time of Philip IV, if Spanish commerce was almost at its last gasp, Spanish agriculture crushed, and the Spanish proletariat mainly kept alive by doles, Spanish wit had become a dominant fashion; and the ragged poet, novelist, or playwright, real or pretended, became one of the most characteristic and conspicuous objects of the capital—then by far the most idle and dissolute in Europe; a byeword for vice and filth with the rest of civilization. Philip IV, himself a poet of some pretensions, and the providence of the literary men who crowded his court, found unfailing relief from his other pleasures in the "Academies," or "floral games," which were constantly being organised in the gloomy old Alcazar of Madrid, or in his own favourite new palace of the Buen Retiro in the suburbs. The bitter satires of Quevedo and his imitators delighted no one more than the stony, reserved man with his dull, bagging eyes, his great mumbling underhung mouth, and his lank yellow hair; whose heart was so human and whose passions so strong, though the traditions of his house bade him show to his subjects only the corpse-like mask which will exist for ever by the genius of Velasquez.

The Inquisition was almost as busy as ever, although there was little Lutheran heresy in Spain left. But the Jews, who had been so numerous in Portugal, were finding their way throughout Spain, and *autos-de-fé* for their benefit were frequently considered necessary. There was however a vile sect, which his enemies said had been invented by Olivares, to drag the King into deeper licentiousness. They were called "Alumbrados," or enlightened ones, and their teaching was that sacrilegious amours of the most blasphemous description might be indulged in without sin, even in the sacred precincts of the convent and the church. With this sect the Inquisition had more than one struggle. Thus, with dissipation, spectacles, and pleasures, the King and his people were kept amused by the all-powerful favourite, who, working upon the monarch's indolence, undertook practically the whole work of the state. The system so laboriously planted by Philip II concentrated the power in the monarch, with the Councils, which have already been described as consultative and executive bodies. But it was found in practice that when the monarch transferred his power to a favourite, the Councils were apt to press their own opinions in opposition to his. This did not suit Olivares, and he destroyed the efficacy of the Councils by causing each member to hand his opinion and arguments in a sealed paper to the King, instead of publicly discussing and voting in the Council chamber as before. As the papers were handed to Olivares, generally unread, he could, and did, take the course he pleased on each question. Many subjects, moreover, were not referred to the Councils at all, but were submitted to special boards nominated and convoked by Olivares *ad hoc*. There were no less than thirteen of these boards, in addition to the Councils; the result being that the cost of administration was greatly increased, and the executive power centred almost unchecked in the hands of the Count-Duke.

Whilst Philip's first wife (Elizabeth of France) lived, she did her best to arouse her husband to a sense of his duty and his position, but the licentiousness of his life continued, and their relations were embittered by mutual jealousy. The atmosphere of the court and capital was, indeed, so vicious that the young Queen herself did not escape scandal. At the first bull-fight in the Plaza Mayor after Philip's accession (1621) the splendid young Count de Villa Mediana (Tassis) had the audacity to appear with a device of silver reals on his breast, with the words over them "*Son mis amores.*" This might possibly have been explained as meaning that he loved money, but he had already been foolish enough to cast admiring eyes on the Queen, and the multitude at once interpreted the device as "My loves are royal." Matters were made worse by a remark of the Queen to her husband referring to the spectacle, that "Villa Mediana aimed well." "Ah!" gloomily replied the King, "but he aims too high." A few months afterwards (August 1622) the Count was shot dead, at the door of his own house (now called the Oñate palace in the Calle Mayor), by one of the royal guards; and in hushed whispers all Madrid asserted that the hand that shot the bolt received its impetus from the King.

In 1639 the war had been carried by the Marquis of Leganes from Lombardy into Savoy. The widowed Duchess, a French princess, being deaf to Olivares' approaches, an intrigue had been raised to oust her from the regency in favour of Cardinal Maurice and Prince Thomas, the uncles of the child-duke and both adherents of Spain. The people themselves sided with the native princes, and the French were beaten everywhere; the duchess was deposed and the city of Turin occupied by the Spaniards. Dissensions however occurred between the Marquis of Leganes and Prince Thomas, and a truce was signed with the French leaving the army of the latter still afoot and the citadel of Turin in their hands. Early in 1640, Cardinal La Valette having died, the new French commander Harcourt reversed the position, re-established the duchess, occupied the principal fortresses and towns and relieved Casale. Thenceforward for a time the war in Savoy flickered on intermittently without interest or permanent effect, the duchess and the French remaining paramount. The long-continued wars with France had so far produced no adequate or decisive results on either side; but under the wise administration of Richelieu his country could far better afford the drain of men and money than could Spain; and the heavy sacrifices demanded of the latter country had aroused deep resentment, especially in the two divisions where the racial and historical circumstances of the people were most distinct from those of Castile—namely Cataluña in the north-east, and Portugal in the west.

There had always existed considerable dislike and jealousy between the Portuguese and Spaniards. On the conquest of the country in 1580 Philip II had earnestly done his best to conciliate his new subjects. He had sworn to preserve all their national privileges, to respect their autonomy, and not to burden them with Castilian taxation; and he kept his word in the letter, even if to some extent he disregarded it in the spirit. The governmental posts were filled entirely by Portuguese who were known to be faithful to him, and Portuguese nobles were welcomed and honoured at the Court of Castile. But with the growth of favouritism, especially under Olivares, all these wise attempts at conciliation were abandoned. Greedy hangers-on had to be provided for. The viceroyalties, the governorships, the bishoprics, the secretaryships and the like, in Spain, Italy, and the Indies, were not enough to go round the greedy crew; and Portugal had to be tapped. In a material sense, already, the Portuguese had suffered much from their change of masters. Their possessions in Brazil, Africa and the East, had been raided and devastated for years by the enemies of Spain, with whom Portugal had no quarrel; Cadiz had taken away from Lisbon much of its commerce, and Portuguese shipping, formerly safe from molestation, was now at the scant mercy of the Dutch privateers. But Olivares, with characteristic disregard of everything but the needs of the moment, imposed upon them in 1636 the Castilian tax of 5 per cent. on all property, moveable and immoveable, and this, together with the insolence of his principal instrument Vasconcellos, had caused a rising. This was suppressed, mainly by the prudence of the regent Margaret, the widowed Duchess of Mantua, a daughter of Catharine, Duchess of Savoy, the younger daughter of Philip II, and consequently first cousin of Philip IV. Olivares, with incredible folly, chose this period to fix a fresh special tax on the Portuguese as a punishment, and, above all, announced a plan for abolishing the Portuguese Cortes, and bringing the representatives of the country to sit in the parliament of Castile, of which in future it would only be a province.

The various branches of the royal house which had a claim to the Portuguese throne have been mentioned in a former chapter. Don Antonio's sons had sunk into obscurity, the Duke of Parma had as much as he could do to hold his own States; Catharine de Medici with her shadowy claim was dead, but the greatest noble in Portugal, the Duke of Braganza, whose grandmother had unquestionably been the true heiress, was wealthy, genial, and popular, and—crowning virtue of all—Portuguese. He had married a Spanish lady of great vigour and ability, a grand-daughter of the Duke of Medina Sidonia—the Armada duke to whose house Olivares belonged— and a great-grand-daughter of the Princess of Eboli. Her strength and ambition stiffened the duke's gentler character, and Olivares began to look upon the pair with suspicion. He tried hard to lure them from their estates at Villa Viçosa, but they were wary. First the Viceroyalty of Milan was offered to the duke; then a flattering invitation was sent to him to come to Madrid, but Braganza, surrounded by his vassals, knew he was safe at home, and decided to stay there. Finding he would not come willingly, Olivares formed a plan to kidnap him on board a Spanish fleet whilst he was inspecting some harbour defences; and this also was frustrated.

The project of Olivares to assimilate Portugal with Spain, although ill-timed, was not unpatriotic or unwise. France had become unified and strong; and Olivares to oppose it had a bundle of more or less disunited realms and dominions, with divergent constitutions and systems of taxation, springing, in at least three cases, from separate races, and held together but lightly by Philip's crown. If Spain had been freed from the unfortunate complications which the imperial and Burgundian connection had brought upon her, and had bent the whole of her powers to the unification of her own institutions and territories, there is a probability that the plan of Olivares might have in the end been successful, at least so far as regarded Portugal. But Philip II had from the first declined to treat the country as a conquest, and instead of banishing the Braganzas, as prudence might have dictated, loaded them with fresh benefits; until, at the time of the separation, the duke owned a third of Portugal, and in personal resources was far more powerful than any royal personage in the Peninsula. When, therefore, discontent at the sacrifices demanded of them had aroused even the servile Portuguese populace to a condition of revolt, it was natural that they should turn their eyes to the Duke of Braganza, whom they had always considered their rightful native sovereign. The Archbishop of Lisbon, Antonio de Almeida, and a few other Portuguese nobles, without difficulty persuaded a large number of their friends to form a society pledged to secure the separation of their country from Spain, and to place the crown on the head of the Duke of Braganza.

Olivares was certainly informed by Vasconcellos, the secretary of the regent, that evil was brewing: but either to lull Braganza's suspicions, or in the hope of gaining him, he wrote kindly to him, gave him authority over the whole of the ports of the country, and sent him 40,000 ducats to raise troops for national defence. The money was used in paying men pledged to the revolt, and the fortresses were packed with soldiers in Braganza's interest, for nearly all the Spanish troops had been withdrawn for the wars. The duke himself remained at Villa Viçosa timid and irresolute until all was ready, his steward Pinto Ribeiro being the head of the conspiracy in Lisbon. Once the duke visited the regent in the capital with a train of unusual number and magnificence. Crowds greeted him in the streets, for revolution was in the air, and the regent sounded a warning note to Olivares. A peremptory summons was sent to Braganza to come to Madrid to inform the King of the defensive state of the country. Feigned acquiescence, pretended illness, and questions of etiquette were resorted to by Braganza to delay his departure. A second urgent command was sent to him with 10,000 ducats to pay for his immediate journey. He sent his household in advance and pretended to start himself. Mendoza, the agent of the conspirators, sought him at his castle of Tapada, and urged him to throw aside his timidity and accept the leadership of the revolt. The duchess added her influence and the duke consented. The chief conspirators were comparatively few— 150 gentlemen and 200 citizens—but the people outside were famine-stricken and discontented, ready to join if the leaders were bold. On the 1st December, 1640, the conspirators in four divisions approached the palace, on what is now the Praça do Commercio, from different quarters, in carriages. The Spanish and German guards were easily overpowered. The hated Vasconcellos, already dumb with terror, was stabbed to death; the regent made but a verbal resistance, but when she talked of rebellion—though she said she was glad Vasconcellos was killed—she was told that King John IV was now the sovereign of Portugal. The populace frantic with joy acclaimed their native monarch, who was still timidly lurking at Villa Viçosa, and the Archbishop of Lisbon assumed supreme power pending his arrival. The regent and all her officers were placed under arrest, and she was coerced into signing an order for the surrender of the citadel to the new government. The command was obeyed with alacrity, and the Spanish rule of Portugal was a thing of the past. Every town in the realm followed the example of the capital. The hated Spaniards were expelled or fled, fortresses fell without a blow, and the only resistance was in the castle of San Gian (Julian) at the mouth of the Tagus. This was soon reduced, and John IV became unquestioned King of Portugal in a three hours' revolt, in which he himself had done nothing. The cause was won, not by Portuguese vigour but by Spanish exhaustion. The news arrived at Madrid at a time of feasting and entertainments for the reception of a Danish ambassador, and cast Olivares into the lowest depth of despondency. All Madrid heard the tidings but the King, and him Olivares knew not how to tell, certain that the monarch, like his people, would naturally place upon the favourite's shoulders the blame of the disgraceful loss. At length it could be hidden no longer, and the Count-Duke entered the King's room with a smiling countenance, whilst the monarch was at play. "Good news! Good news! your Majesty. You have gained a fresh duchy and great estates," he cried. "How so?" asked Philip. "The Duke of Braganza, Sir, has lost his reason and has proclaimed himself King of Portugal, so that your Majesty may possess the 12 million ducats' worth of property he owns." The King was careless and idle, but he was no fool, and he saw how serious the blow was. His rigid face was darkened, as he said, "Well, a remedy must be found."

An attempt at a counter-plot to kill the new King and fire the city was made by the Archbishop of Braga and some Spanish sympathisers, with the connivance of Olivares, but it was discovered by the Queen of Portugal's relative the Marquis of Ayamonte, and four Portuguese nobles of high rank lost their heads, whilst others of humbler station were hanged, drawn and quartered.

A more dangerous conspiracy than this for Philip IV arose out of the separation of Portugal. The brother of the Queen of Portugal, the Duke of Medina Sidonia, was the greatest noble in Spain, nearly all Andalucia acknowledging him as its chief, including the rich city of Cadiz. The success of his brother-in-law, and the persuasions of the new queen, and of his kinsman Ayamonte, induced him to consent to a plot for proclaiming himself independent sovereign of Andalucia, with the aid of the King of Portugal. He was head of Olivares' family (the Guzmans), and when the favourite learnt from his spies of the treason intended, he shielded the duke as much as he might. The duke was summoned in a friendly way to Madrid, whilst an army of 5,000 royal troops was thrown into Cadiz. The duke—a poor creature like his ancestor of the Armada—came and made a clean breast of it, throwing himself with tears and self-reproaches at the King's feet. He was pardoned, for the King was gentle and clement, and Olivares stood by him, but he was never allowed to go to Andalucia again, or to come near the court, and much of his vast wealth was confiscated. Ayamonte was not so fortunate. He confessed that he was the moving spirit in the plot, and lost his life upon the scaffold, Guzman though he was.

To complete the story of treachery arising out of the revolt of Portugal, Lucena, the enlightened secretary of John IV, was convicted of treason and beheaded, on the strength of a forged correspondence concocted by Olivares, his master discovering too late that he had sacrificed an innocent man. More shameful still was the kidnapping and selling to Spain of Prince Edward, brother of the new King. The prince was serving in the imperial army, and was seized with the consent of the Emperor, who kept him a prisoner at Gratz until an offer of 40,000 ducats from Spain induced him to surrender him. He was carried to the fortress of Milan, where in close confinement, treated as a criminal, he expiated by his death the offence of being a Braganza.

But a much greater trouble than the loss of Portugal befell Philip at the same time. Of all the peninsular peoples the Catalans were—and are—most unlike the Castilians. A population of almost pure Romance origin, sharing with their neighbours in the south of France the language, traditions, and literature of their race—a series of accidents rather than obvious fate had brought them under the rule of a Castilian King, instead of their forming the nucleus of the great Romance empire projected by James the Conqueror their sovereign in the thirteenth century. Their character is rough and independent; they are tenacious, industrious, and thrifty, without any of the Portuguese peasant's servility or the Castilian's haughty contempt of manual labour; fully conscious of their superiority over their neighbours in many respects, they repay their disdain with disdain still deeper. It was not to be expected that such a people as this would willingly forget the conduct of the King and Olivares towards them and their institutions in the Cortes of 1626, related above (pp. 230—232), or the similar treatment to which they were subjected by Olivares when he accompanied the King to the Cortes of Barcelona in 1632, on the occasion of the installation of the Cardinal Infante Fernando as Viceroy. Nor was the Count-Duke a man likely to dissemble his dislike to a people who so roughly withstood his probably well-meant attempts to unify and assimilate the institutions of the monarchy.

We have seen how, mainly by Catalan energy, the French invasion had been driven from Roussillon and Salcés been recaptured. The Catalans were ready to make sacrifices willingly, but Santa Coloma, the Viceroy, in his letters to Olivares chose this very opportunity of advising a policy of harsh severity towards them. "Do not allow a single man in the province capable of work to absent himself from the field, and no woman capable of carrying a bundle of fodder on her back....This is no time to beseech, but to command. The Catalans are naturally fickle—sometimes they will and at others will not. Make them understand that the welfare of the people and the army must go before all their laws and privileges....Seize all their beds, even from the highest people in the province, if necessary, and let them sleep on the ground rather than the soldiers shall be badly lodged....If pioneers be wanted and the peasants refuse to go to work, force them; even, if it be necessary, carry them bound. Do not spare force, no matter how they cry out against you. I will bear all the blame." With this feeling, both in the Viceroy and Olivares, it is not surprising that, when the troops returned from the victorious campaign in Roussillon, the province was in a state of sullen revolt. Against the laws of the principality the contingent of Castilian troops under the Marquis of Balbeses (the son of the great Spinola) were lodged in the province, instead of being sent back to Castile. They were, as usual, unpaid, and according to their custom in other countries—Flanders and Italy for instance—they plundered and insulted right and left.

Instead of bending their heads to the yoke the Catalans retaliated without hesitation. The result of the disturbances was an order from the King, violating the privileges of the principality, that each village in Cataluña should support a certain number of soldiers. The Catalans remonstrated in vain. Santa Coloma, though a Catalan himself, passed from severity to severity. Fighting in the streets of Barcelona became frequent and Olivares urged still further rigour. The pulpits resounded with denunciations of the cruelty and oppression of the soldiery, particularly of the famous "Naples" regiment. "Either," wrote Santa Coloma, "relieve the province from the burden, or send me an army strong enough to put down disorder by force." But Olivares did neither. The Viceroy tried to terrorise the people by imprisoning the most influential men, lay and clerical, and at last the revolution flamed out.

On the 7th June, 1640, when the city was full of the harvesters who come down from the mountains when their work is done, a cry of "Vengeance! Liberty! Down with Philip's bad government! Long live the King!" was raised. Like an irresistible avalanche the revolt swept all before it. Every soldier of Castile who could be caught, even in sanctuary, was murdered. In vain Santa Coloma, an old, unwieldy man, sought safety in flight. With fear and grief he fell by the way-side, and was cut to pieces by the infuriated peasants. The flame spread from the county of Barcelona all over the principality of Cataluña. Philip and Olivares had their hands full when the news reached them. At first they attempted to tranquillise the people by the appointment of a popular Viceroy, the Duke of Cardona, but they would not give way on the main point of quartering Castilian troops in the principality and disapproved of the punishment of some soldiers by Cardona, who soon after died. They then tried the aged bishop of Barcelona as Viceroy, but under his nerveless sway the province was soon entirely a prey to anarchy. Severity was then inevitable if Cataluña were to remain attached to Castile. "The revolt," said Cardinal de Borgia in the council at Madrid, "can only be drowned in rivers of blood." Olivares went about the work thoroughly. Every soldier that could be raised in the rest of Spain and Portugal was called to the standard, and the Marquis de los Velez was appointed to the command. The plan was to attack Cataluña through Aragon, Zaragoza being the *point d'appui*, where a large reserve was to be kept to hold in terror the Aragonese; for if they joined the Catalans, as was feared, then indeed would Spain be dismembered. The Spanish commander in Perpignan (Garay) was ordered to attack the Catalans on that side. He urged that the forces should form a junction first and enter the province together, but was overruled. In September 1640 Garay attempted to punish a Catalan village whose inhabitants were negotiating with the French. The peasants were entirely successful, and twice were the Spanish troops and Garay routed. In the meanwhile Barcelona was busy arming, drilling and fortifying, but the great army gathering in Aragon, and the talk of vengeance from Olivares, convinced the Catalans that alone they could ill withstand the national forces. They accordingly sent one of their chiefs, Francisco Vilaplana, to Richelieu at Amiens, to beg for French aid. With some delay and a decent appearance of reluctance, a promise was made of 6,000 foot and 2,000 horse, to be paid by Cataluña. But in the meanwhile los Velez with his army of revenge advanced upon the Ebro, which he crossed at Tortosa (October 1640). The Catalans by this time were discouraged, for no French aid had come. los Velez came promising peace and order, and swore as viceroy, that the privileges of Cataluña should be respected. Town after town submitted, or was taken with but slight resistance, and the march of los Velez almost to the walls of Tarragona was a triumphal progress; even the supposed impregnable fortresses of Coll and Hospitalet fell almost without a blow.

But the Barcelonese had induced the French General d'Epernon in the meantime with three regiments to cross the frontier and occupy Tarragona, in order to stay the advance of the royal army. In the village of Cambrils near Tarragona the Catalans made a sturdy stand, and after their capitulation —it was said by mistake,—700 of them were slain by the soldiery; the chief authorities of the place were hanged by los Velez without trial. It was another matter when Tarragona was reached. Here the French force were strongly placed: los Velez was hampered by contrary orders from Madrid, his artillery had not come up, his stores were short, the galleys had not arrived, and the Aragonese in his army were deserting. The Catalan chiefs, San Pol and Capons, with their troops, had crossed into Aragon, and were devastating the country. Los Velez, at first, was in despair, but he had to deal with an opponent even weaker than himself. d'Epernon came to terms without difficulty, agreeing to return to France, and to persuade the Barcelonese to abandon their resistance (23 December, 1640).

This betrayal only aroused still further the rage of Barcelona, and its brave regiment of volunteers of Santa Eulalia under Rosell; and when los Velez arrived he found the capital prepared for him. Before the attack was delivered the inhabitants formally cast off their allegiance to Spain, and declared Louis XIII Count of Barcelona, surrendering the strong castle of Monjuich to a French officer, M. d'Aubigny, who with 300 French veterans was in the city. On the 26th January, 1641, an attempt was made to storm the outworks by simultaneous attacks at various points. At the first attack the Earl of Tyrone (John O'Neil), leading the Irish regiment, was killed. The Catalans and their few French auxiliaries fought like heroes. The Spanish infantry also fought well, and the Duke of San Jorge (C. M. Carraciolo) with his heavy cuirassiers was always in the hottest of the struggle till he fell dead from his horse. The fort of Montjuich, on its eminence, was closely attacked by the Spaniards under the Marquis of Torrecusa (C. Carraciolo), a Neapolitan, and already the stormers were crying victory under the very walls, when a sudden panic seized them. They had forgotten their scaling-ladders, and whilst they were fighting, the barefooted Catalan sailors from the beach below had swarmed up and taken them in the rear. In the *sauve qui peut* which followed the Castilians were killed like sheep, and down the rocky sides of Montjuich ran rivulets of blood. Torrecusa temporarily lost his reason with rage and shame, and Barcelona with its citizen volunteers held its own against all the military power of Spain.

Los Velez retired defeated to Tarragona; and soon all Cataluña was aflame again. The French King had accepted the sovereignty, and French troops were pouring into his new principality under the Count de la Motte; whilst the warlike Archbishop of Bordeaux with his fleet was on the coast. Los Velez had been succeeded in the command by Fadrique Colonna, Prince of Butera, in Naples, who in April found himself shut up with his army of 14,000 men in Tarragona, surrounded by land and sea by the French and Catalans. Olivares tried to relieve him by sea, with a fleet under the Marquis of Leganes, but the Archbishop of Bordeaux burnt the ships, and the beleaguered force was reduced to greater misery than ever. With a supreme effort Olivares collected every ship he could seize carrying the Spanish flag, to break through the blockade and release the army; and in this he succeeded in August 1641, the Archbishop of Bordeaux retiring before the largely superior Spanish fleet. The resources of Cataluña now began to run short. Richelieu insisted upon the Frenchmen being properly paid, and the costs of the war being borne by the province. Louis XIII was personally appealed to by the Catalans. The principal leader of the revolution, Tamarit, carried to him the conditions under which the Catalans accepted his sovereignty, and begged him in person to visit them. The conditions were accepted but

Louis was busy in the Netherlands, and deputed his Viceroy Marshal de Brézé to take the oath of conformity in Barcelona. The French relieving army under de Brézé met with a check from the Spanish garrison of Perpignan under Mortara, aided by a small force of sailors landed at Rosas by the gallant Torrecusa, now again in the field (December 1641), and Perpignan still continued in Spanish hands. By the spring of 1642 the Spanish forces had been somewhat reorganised. Colonna was dead, and the Marquis of Hinojosa commanded in Tarragona, whilst two independent bodies under the two sons of the former viceroy, the Duke of Cardona, were sent, one to reinforce Tarragona, and the other to operate in Roussillon. Olivares insisted on the latter, consisting of 6000 foot and 2500 horse, going by land, instead of by sea, from Valencia. As a result the whole force was surprised and captured by De la Motte (April 1642).

French armies were crowding now into Roussillon and Cataluña. Schomberg, Meilleraie and De la Motte, with Richelieu behind them, were more than a match for the distracted and inept Spanish commanders, backed only by Olivares and the indolent Philip. Madrid was panic-stricken. Overburdened already, the people could find now neither money nor men to cope with the French upon Spanish soil. Perpignan fell after a desperate resistance, and the province of Roussillon became French for evermore (September 1642). Only one thing more could be done, and that was for the King of Spain himself to conduct the campaign, and arouse the lost loyalty of his people. Olivares had always opposed this; but at last he was overborne. Louis XIII had been personally present at Perpignan, and it was decided that his brother-in-law should take the field on his own side. Philip had from the first been eager to go, and Olivares in vain talked of the danger he would run. Olivares insisted: the King for the first time in his life stood firm. Olivares demurred about the cost of the journey, but at last gave way and with an ill grace accompanied his master on his journey to Aragon. Every device was adopted by him to delay the King's progress. By the time they arrived at Zaragoza, Aragon itself was half over-run by the French, the ancient capital Monzon was in their hands and Philip saw with his own eyes how low his monarchy had fallen. Failing other means, Olivares conspired with Cinq Mars to overthrow the government of Louis. This was discovered and still further embittered relations. The complete loss of Roussillon, the ruin and misery around him, the complaints of his people, at last opened Philip's eyes. He was moody with Olivares, who felt his position slipping from him, and begged leave to retire. The Queen—a sister of Louis XIII—ceaselessly urged his disgrace, and the King was gradually alienated from him. Without consulting him the King appointed Leganes, also a Guzman, to the chief command of all that was left of the army. He was defeated by De la Motte before Lerida; his army melted away, unfed and unpaid as it was, with the generals all quarrelling amongst themselves; and it seemed as if the last hope of Philip was gone, for heart-broken he turned his back on Aragon, and returned to Madrid the end of 1642, almost simultaneously with the death of Richelieu.

With Portugal and Roussillon lost, Cataluña occupied by the French, Italy in open revolt, and disaster on all sides, the easy-going King could not help turning to those who for years past had warned him of the rule of his favourite. They spoke more loudly now. The Queen's tears and entreaties added force to the mordant satires of the pamphleteers, and at last Olivares fell. The King went out hunting and left a note for him (17 January, 1643) telling him politely—almost kindly—that he might go. The fallen favourite in vain tried to justify his rule. There was no hope for him now, and though the King was still considerate and polite, Olivares swayed his sovereign no more. Once, indeed, it seemed as if he would be sacrificed to his enemies. The King wrote, "In short,

Count, I must reign, and my son must be crowned in Aragon. This will not be easy unless I deliver your head to my subjects, who demand it with one voice." This letter sent the Count-Duke mad, and he died in July 1645.

The unmeasured blame usually lavished upon Olivares appears hardly just notwithstanding the disastrous results of his rule. He was a far abler man than Lerma, but entirely wanting in the suavity which made the latter popular amongst the nobles. Philip, who indolently handed his kingship and responsibilities to another, escapes with but light censure, whilst Olivares is condemned for not succeeding under circumstances which made success almost impossible. Spaniards of all ranks were still puffed up with the vain tradition that their country dictated laws to the world, and that their monarch far surpassed any other in wealth and magnificence. Any minister who had dared to tell them that this was not the fact and that the only salvation of the country was for it to attend entirely to its own affairs, to avoid all vain interference in other countries, to acknowledge its secondary rank, from which the Emperor had only temporarily raised it, and for its citizens once more to take to hard manual labour—any such truth-telling minister as this could not have retained power for a week, and Olivares, like others before and after him, was obliged to swim with the tide. It was evident that Castile, effete as its parliaments had become, was not capable of bearing all the expense of an adventurous foreign policy; and it was necessary that the other members of the monarchy should bear their share of the expense, as they had their share of the glory. They appealed, as we have seen, to their privileges, and the only possible policy for Olivares was that of the unification of institutions, by fair means or by foul. Local feeling was too strong for him in some cases, and he failed; but the policy itself, however ill-timed, was not in itself unwise, for the lack of unity between the provinces of Spain has produced a plentiful crop of troubles lasting to the present day. In short, Spanish pride wanted the glory of empire without paying for it. Olivares was no wiser than his contemporaries in economic science, and could only raise money by hampering industry which provided money. As the State took all the resources, the aim of every citizen was to prey upon the State in some form or another. The result was the fatal bureaucracy which still ruins Spain. It is lamentable and pathetic enough, but it is unjust to saddle the blame upon Olivares, who found the system already at work, and whose great sin was that he tried to insist upon all Spaniards making equal sacrifices to pay for the barren pride which all Spaniards shared.

CHAPTER IX.

PHILIP IV, 1643—1665.

ALTHOUGH Philip had announced when Olivares fell that in future he would be his own minister, he was too indolent to persevere in such an arrangement, and soon appointed to succeed the fallen favourite Don Luis de Haro, the nephew and former rival of Olivares. He was a dull, slow, amiable and fairly honest man, already extremely rich, and not unpopular. The unofficial boards established by Olivares were abolished, and the Councils again obtained their influence, the King frequently listening to their deliberations unseen behind jalousies: official reports being presented to him by the secretaries every Friday. In a very short time, however, the sovereign's indolence led to the whole of the affairs being dispatched by Haro, as they had been by his uncle. The death of Richelieu, shortly afterwards followed by that of Louis XIII (May 1643), somewhat changed the relations between France and Spain. The new regent, Anne of Austria, was the sister of Philip IV, her son Louis XIV being only five years of age. France was distracted and divided, but generally desired peace. Spanish pride once more stopped the way, and the fatal resolution was taken of attacking France on her eastern frontier before accepting negotiations. The Infante Don Fernando had done well in the Netherlands, and had more than held his own whilst the wars in Cataluña and the revolt of Portugal had been going on. But unfortunately the young prince had died in Brussels (November 1641) and he was replaced by Don Francisco de Mello, a Portuguese noble faithful to Spain. He also had been successful in capturing Lens, and inflicting a crushing defeat upon the French under Harcourt and Grammont at Honnecourt (1642), for which he had been rewarded by the grandeeship and the title of Marquis of Torrelaguna.

Mello's army consisted of over 20,000 men, 18,000 of them being the veteran Spanish infantry, which was acknowledged to be without rival in the world. A French army somewhat inferior in strength had been organised to threaten the Flemish frontier. It was commanded by the great Condé (Duke of Enghien), then a youth of twenty-one, with Marshal L'Hôpital as his mentor. Mello after a feint on Picardy suddenly entered Champagne through the Ardennes, and besieged the frontier place of Rocroy. Condé at once marched to the relief of the place, and against L'Hôpital's advice, determined to give battle to the Spaniards. Mello, full of confidence in his veteran troops, had left the defiles and approaches behind him almost unguarded. On the approach of the French (18 May, 1643) he posted most of his cavalry in front of the city whilst the enemy drew up as if to attack it. Some slight skirmishing took place during the night, and if Mello had delivered a general attack at this time in all probability the French would have been beaten. But the Spanish general was anxiously awaiting the arrival of Baron de Beck, with some German auxiliaries, and the night was passed by both armies face to face without decisive aggression on either side. At dawn it was seen that the French force which had threatened the cavalry before the city gate had been withdrawn, and Mello sent to recall his horsemen. This was seen by the French and without loss of a moment Condé ordered the attack before the Spanish force was united or Beck could arrive. The lines extended to about half a league in length, and the French advanced simultaneously their left and right wings, the centre remaining in reserve. Condé had arranged his fighting lines somewhat unusually, alternating squadrons of cavalry with companies of infantry, his horse thus being flanked by musketeers. The French left wing under L'Hôpital was twice repulsed by the Spaniards commanded by Mello personally; on the second occasion the Spanish cavalry from before the town came up, and spread complete confusion amongst the enemy, L'Hôpital himself being wounded. The French right was led by Condé in person. Charging with an impetuosity which nothing could withstand he routed the Spanish cavalry under the Duke of Alburquerque, and then promptly rallying his left wing he threw himself upon the victorious Spanish right. Over and over again the main body of veteran Spanish infantry in the centre repulsed his men. With varying fortune the fight continued for six hours; but at last panic seized those that were left of the Spaniards, and they were utterly routed. Mello was captured but escaped. Count de Fuentes was killed on the field; the Spaniards lost 7,000 killed and wounded and 5,000 prisoners, with all baggage, artillery, stores, and standards. Beck with his Germans came up at the moment of defeat, and the auxiliaries shared in the *sauve qui peut*. The battle of Rocroy dealt a deathblow to the prestige of the Spanish infantry, which they never recovered. It was to the Spanish army what the defeat of the Armada was to its navy. In neither case did the disaster arise from want of personal bravery on the part of the men, but from their opponents adopting new methods and tactics, which the Spanish commanders had not skill or adaptability enough to counteract. Condé lost no time in entering Hainault, and pushed his scouts almost as far as Brussels; then suddenly turning he reduced Thionville (22 August, 1643), and infused utter dismay in the Spanish governors of Flanders, who still however with some success made efforts to withstand the French in Alsace by sending an important reinforcement to the imperialists and thus enabling them to win the battle of Tuttlinghen.

Philip, the while, was with his little army in Aragon, for once in his life acting with energy. He recaptured Monzon, and then the Spanish forces under Felipe de Silva routed the French before Lerida, and in the presence of the King Lerida itself shortly afterwards surrendered. The Cortes (June 1643) had voted a supply of 24 millions of ducats in six years from the following year 1644; the silver fleet fortunately arrived rich and intact, and the money was taken as a forced loan. Naples, Sardinia and Spain itself made great efforts to send men, full of enthusiasm now that the King himself was at the head of his army, and with a strong force Philip began to win back some of his principality of Cataluña. In October 1644 he was recalled to Madrid by the death of his Queen, who left him with only two children, the Infante Don Baltasar Carlos, who died two years afterwards aged seventeen, and who is so well known by the pictures of Velasquez, and Maria Theresa, afterwards wife of Louis XIV.

The campaign of the following year under the King was less successful. Discouragement again seized him, and at a congress called by the Pope (Urban VIII) he offered the Catalans a truce for thirty years, which the French refused, except under impossible conditions, and so the exhausting war dragged on. The death of his only son Baltasar in October 1646, so soon following that of his wife, threw Philip into his old dissolute habits, to escape from the religious melancholy which seized upon him as it had done at a similar age upon his ancestors for three generations. In 1647 he appointed his natural son Don Juan José of Austria to be the General-in-chief of the fleet and armies. Don Juan, whom his father had already recognised, was the son of a famous actress in Madrid—Maria Calderon, usually known by the name of the Calderona. He was very brilliant and able. His education had been carefully conducted, his ambition was boundless, and his handsome face and popular manners made him the idol of his father's subjects. Thenceforward until he died the second Don Juan of Austria was a powerful factor in Spanish politics.

In the meanwhile the King was without a male heir. So long as Baltasar had lived he resisted all suggestions of another legitimate marriage. But when his son died, and his excesses shocked the churchmen and nuns around him, he gave way to their persuasions and married his niece Mariana of Austria. She was a bright-faced young girl with all the Austrian characteristics strongly developed. At first the gloomy etiquette with which she was surrounded shocked and overcame her: she was told that it was unbecoming to laugh, however funny the buffoons might be, that a Queen of Spain must be considered to have no legs, since it was not dignified for her to walk, and so forth; but her youth and vitality conquered the depression, and after her stately reception in Madrid (1648) she also became popular with the people, and was a rival of Don Juan for their favour.

The war dragged on for years both on the Portuguese frontier and in Cataluña, where Lerida and Tarragona were stubbornly held by the Spaniards, in spite of Condé and the French, and the struggle in Flanders against the Dutch and French continued without intermission, generally to the disadvantage of the Spaniards. In 1646, Cassel, Mardyck, Link, Bourbourg, Armentières, and other places fell into the hands of the enemy, and Charles of Lorraine with the Spanish troops suffered a crushing defeat at the hands of the French under the Duke of Orleans at Courtrai. In 1647 the Archduke Leopold of Austria was appointed governor of Flanders, and the imperial troops were again sent to bolster up the Spanish domination. Some success attended the Archduke at first, but at length he was utterly defeated by Condé before Lens, after having apparently won the victory. This disaster was a crowning one; and it was evident now to the meanest understanding that Spain must have peace, for she could fight effectively no more.

As we have seen, it had become an old truism to say that the country was exhausted. The working and middle classes had become so long before. Corruption was more rampant than ever: the King told the Cortes (1654) that out of 10,000,000 ducats of the revenue of Castile which he possessed on paper, he could not collect more than 3,000,000, while the revenues of Aragon and Navarre did not reach 2,000,000. The nobles, great and small, were ruined, for the third part of their revenues had to be paid direct to the State: the frequent seizure of the money on the silver fleet belonging to Spaniards had caused the remittances of bullion now to be mostly the property of foreigners, and the silver did not get beyond Seville. The Spanish merchants, thus handicapped, had lost courage. Their ships were a prey to the Dutch, and in a great measure their commerce had been destroyed, almost as thoroughly as industry, trade and agriculture. The raw material, wool particularly, which was still raised, mostly went abroad, to be bought back again as cloth, and paid for in Indian silver. The oppressive forms of taxation, especially the "millions," which now amounted to one-eighth of the value of meat, oil, wine etc., made smuggling universal and led to its being openly connived at by the excise officers. Every device appears to have been adopted for raising money in ways which would ruin industry. The first-floor of every new house was supposed to be at the disposal of the King, and had to be redeemed by a money payment representing its value. This had the effect of checking building, and caused one storey houses to be generally constructed. There was, indeed, hardly an interest or an industry in the country that had not been crushed, except bureaucracy and the Church. Commerce was prohibited with most of the countries of Europe, even with Portugal (1644), with the consequence that the people had to be mainly supplied by contraband goods, which paid the Government nothing. The crushing *alcabala* before Philip's death had been permanently increased to 14 per cent. on the value of all sales, and even the church vessels of silver and gold were ordered to be utilised for the public needs, greatly to the scandal of the faithful, but with hardly any benefit to the treasury. Headed by the Queen (Elizabeth of Bourbon) noble ladies had given up their personal jewelry to be coined. Titles of nobility were openly sold, the value of the national coinage was tampered with, to the complete confusion and despair of the trading classes; and yet, withal, the people were literally dying of starvation, the soldiers in Flanders, Cataluña, and on the Portuguese frontier were unpaid, and still fighting famished and in rags, whilst the King and Court continued in a blaze of splendour, enjoying their tourneys, their bull-fights, and their "Academies," as if their wealth were unbounded.

Philip's troubles seemed to be endless. Whilst his armies were struggling for Cataluña and Portugal, the Kingdom of Naples, long simmering, at last broke into open revolt. The constitution of Naples rendered it illegal for any fresh taxes to be imposed without the prior consent of the Pope, but the vast sums needed by the Philips for the wars had caused constant violations of this condition. Harassed by the Turks and Moors on their coasts, by the rapacity of the Spanish officers sent to govern them—most of whom had bought their offices,—ruined by the illegal drain of men and money from their country, to fight for interests in which they had not the remotest concern, the Neapolitans had made more than one attempt to expel the Spaniards, usually, as we have seen in a former chapter, with the connivance of the French and the Holy See. With the appointment of the Duke of Arcos (1646) to the viceroyalty matters entered an acute stage. The French made a descent upon the island of Elba, whence they fitted out squadrons to attack the Neapolitan ports. The country had already been denuded of men to send to Flanders and elsewhere, and Arcos applied to the city of Naples for a forced loan of a million ducats, in order to raise a new force to recapture the French position in Elba. The only thing remaining to be taxed was fruit, the principal food of the poor, and the new loan was raised by an impost upon that. By the spring of 1647 the people were starving, but clamour as they might they could get nothing but false promises of redress from Arcos. Similar oppression was being exercised by the Marquis of los Velez, viceroy of Sicily, and the people of Palermo broke into revolt and compelled los Velez to abolish the obnoxious tax.

Thus encouraged, the Neapolitans also rose. It was purely a plebeian revolt: the feudal nobility of Naples had with the full connivance of the Spaniards oppressed their vassals to an extent unknown elsewhere since the dark ages, and the people were at length driven by sheer misery and despair to rebel against the cruel tyranny they suffered. They chose for their leader the fisherman of Amalfi, Masaniello, a young man of 24, who had suffered, like his fellows, at the hands of the Spaniards. The flame burst forth on the 7th July, 1647, and the populace in ever-increasing numbers swept from the Market-place, burning the stands of the excisemen, until they came to the Palace, into which they swarmed and invaded the study of the Viceroy. Arcos lost all courage. With trembling lips and pallid face he promised the rioters all they asked, and then tried to escape. He was stopped, and was forced, but without insult, to remain in Naples. He then took refuge in the monastery of San Francesco, and thence fled to the fortress of Castelnuovo. The mob were now the masters. Prisons were opened, armouries emptied, the tax collectors' houses burnt, and some specially obnoxious officers beheaded; but generally speaking the mob of 120,000 men at first were moderate. They discountenanced robbery, and professed personal loyalty to the King. Arcos surrendered everything they demanded, including the abolition of all taxes imposed since the time of Charles V, and went to the length of publicly embracing Masaniello. Soon the lawlessness of the people, restrained before, broke loose. Pillage, arson and rapine stalked through the city unchecked. 'Kill! Kill!' was the only cry, and the lust of slaughter sated itself. The humble Masaniello lost his good sense. Aping the great gentleman, dressed in silver and gold, he insulted the people whose leader he had been. He was surprised and murdered, some said by men in the pay of Arcos, and then the next day, after dragging his body with insults through the streets, the populace worshipped it as that of a saint.

Thenceforward anarchy and murder were supreme in Naples. At one time the Prince of Massa headed the revolt, but he was soon sacrificed by the mob he was supposed to lead, and his place was occupied by various men of low rank. Suddenly a powerful auxiliary of the revolution appeared in Naples. The Duke of Guise was descended in the female line from René of Anjou, and claimed the Crown of Naples. The populace received this prince of romance, who mysteriously dropped as if from the clouds, with unbounded enthusiasm, and proclaimed Naples a republic like the United Provinces, in which Guise was to occupy a similar place to that enjoyed by the Prince of Orange. When a great French fleet under the Duke of Richelieu appeared in the bay soon afterwards it looked as if Spanish domination in Naples was at last at an end. But Mazarin had no wish to aggrandise the house of Lorraine, and the fleet by his orders sailed away again without effectively helping the French pretender, after a brush with the Spanish fleet hastily gathered under Don Juan (October 1647). Arcos was deposed, and Don Juan, co-operating with the Neapolitan nobles and the Spanish garrisons, began to make head against the revolt. By clever diplomacy, as much as by force of arms, he spread disaffection and discouragement amongst the Neapolitans. Guise had become unpopular. By a feint, he and 5,000 of his best men were drawn away to Posilippo, and during his absence Don Juan and the new viceroy Oñate captured the city by a *coup-de-main*. The fickle populace threw down their arms, and cried "Long live the King of Spain!" (February 1648), and thus Naples was preserved to the Spanish dominion.

Spain was not the only country for which peace was a necessity. The Thirty Years' War had exhausted all Europe, and since 1644 negotiations for a general settlement had been slowly progressing at Osnabrück and Münster, amidst much bad faith and sharp practice on all sides. At length (October 1648) the famous treaty of Münster was concluded, which settled the religious question in Germany, gave Alsace to France, and Pomerania to Sweden, and, above all, secured the recognition of the independence of the United Provinces by Spain, after a struggle of eighty years, and opened to the Dutch the ports of the Indies—east and west. The arrangement between Holland and Spain was a blow to Mazarin, for it stifled the French hope of grasping Flanders, but it proved to the world that Spanish pride was at last resigned to the inevitable, and that its humiliation was complete.

The peace of Münster had drawn the Emperor away from the side of Spain, which had sacrificed so much for him, and Philip and France now remained face to face to fight out their quarrel alone. Attempts were made early in 1649 to open peace negotiations, but the Spanish claim that the French should surrender all their conquests was scouted as ridiculous. Mazarin was in the midst of his struggle with the Parliament of Paris. As a foreigner he was extremely unpopular, and persistent attempts were made by the Spaniards to promote the cabal against him. The civil war of the Fronde was preparing, and Mazarin was unable to carry on the campaign in Flanders with the same vigour as before. The Spaniards were therefore successful in recovering some of the places which had been taken from them, and more important still, were joined temporarily by Marshal Turenne and other French malcontents against their own countrymen, Charles Duke of Lorraine joining now one side and now another, to be finally arrested by the Spaniards and confined in Toledo (1564) until the peace of the Pyrenees (1659). The Spaniards had done their best to inflame Mazarin's enemies against him, and at various times had been joined by the "Princes" of the Fronde; but at length a more important recruit than all came to their aid. The Prince of Condé, the victor of Rocroy, who had recently resigned his French Viceroyalty of Cataluña, crossed the Flemish frontier with a considerable army, and was appointed by Philip commander of the Spanish forces in Flanders. At the same time a Spanish fleet was sent to Bordeaux to aid the Fronde there, but Santa Cruz who commanded it was tardy, the ships were badly found, the men unpaid. They returned to San Sebastian without doing anything (1654) and Bordeaux submitted to Mazarin. A traveller of the time tells a story illustrating the waste and corruption in naval matters, as in all else in Spain: "On the beach at San Sebastian I saw a great ship building, but no progress has been made in it for a long time. More millions have been spent on it than would build a dozen such; but only those who have had the spending of it have derived any benefit from the expenditure."

By the aid of the great Condé the Spaniards for a time prospered in Flanders. Rocroy was recaptured, Gravelines and Dunkirk surrendered, and all looked bright, until jealousy broke out between the French and Spanish allied commanders. Turenne had turned his coat again, and in 1655 before Arras scattered the forces under Condé and the Archduke. Quesnay, Landrecy, Chatelet and San Guillain all fell into Turenne's hands; and the Archduke, disgusted with his equivocal position and the instability of his French auxiliaries, resigned the viceroyalty. Don Juan of Austria was sent from Cataluña to succeed him (1656). He signalised his arrival by defeating, in union with Condé, Turenne's army which was besieging Valenciennes, 30,000 strong (16 July, 1656). The French lost 7000 killed and wounded, Marshal la Ferté amongst them, and 4000 prisoners; but their moral loss was greater still. Before the winter closed in, Mazarin, beset on all sides, made another attempt to come to terms with Spain. Many approaches had been made on either side since 1649, mostly with the intervention of the Pope, but the territorial pretensions of both parties had rendered them all fruitless. Matters had, however, now somewhat changed, and circumstances had occurred which rendered both countries more amenable to reason. On the fall of Charles I Philip had somewhat ostentatiously demonstrated his sympathy with the English Commonwealth. His ambassador in England, Don Alonso de Cardenas, had entered into friendly relations with Cromwell, and it was no doubt considered that Spain would be more likely to gain his sympathy than the country of Henrietta Maria. But Cromwell was too clever for Cardenas. When the latter pressed for information as to the destination of the fleet being dispatched to America, he got but a vague assurance that it was not intended to attack Spanish interests, whilst care was taken to spread the idea in Spain that the intention was to oust the French from New France. Suddenly Blake, who had been in the Mediterranean for months, sailed to meet and capture some of the Spanish homeward-bound silver fleet; and Penn and Venables with a strong force of English ships sailed to attack Mexico, Santo Domingo and Jamaica. From the first two places they were diverted, but the third they captured (May 1655), and Jamaica has remained an English possession ever since.

The news fell upon Philip's government like a thunderbolt. Panic reigned amongst the merchants in Seville and Cadiz; swift cruisers were sent scouring the Atlantic to warn the silver fleet, and ruined, bankrupt Spain felt that she had another enemy to meet. When Cardenas had made proposals for an alliance with Cromwell, the latter had demanded the right for the English to trade with the West Indies, the limitation of the power of the Inquisition, the establishment of equal duties in Spain upon English and Spanish goods, and permission for English merchants to buy wool in Spain. The two first demands were scornfully rejected by Spain. Then followed the capture of Jamaica, and Cromwell subsequently signed a treaty of alliance with France (November 1655). This was the combination that frightened Philip into a yielding mood when Lionne was sent to Madrid as French envoy in the summer of 1656. There was an infinite number of knotty points to settle. Territory on both sides was in the possession of the opponents, the position of the Prince of Condé, of the Duke of Lorraine, had to be regulated, the hundred and one points of etiquette and procedure agreed upon, the proposed marriage between the young King Louis XIV and the King of Spain's daughter Maria Theresa negotiated; and for two years the discussion of the preliminaries continued. In the meanwhile the war was being prosecuted vigorously in Flanders on both sides, 6000 English troops cooperating with the French royal army under Turenne, whilst the Prince of Condé and his troops were still on the side of the Spaniards under Don Juan.

Montmédy surrendered to the French in August 1657; Bourbourg, St Venant and Mardyck, followed its fate during the autumn. In the spring of 1658 Dunkirk was blockaded by an English fleet, and besieged on the land side by Turenne, the young King himself being present; the Spanish army of 15,000 men, under Don Juan and Condé, with the Duke of York (James II), whom Philip had appointed to the nominal post of Admiral of the fleet, being about two miles in the rear of the French. The Spaniards were outflanked at low tide and taken in the rear on the Dunes by the French, whilst the English attacked them in front. Panic overtook them and a shameful flight ensued, in which the Spaniards left 3000 dead on the field, and Dunkirk capitulated nine days afterwards (23 June, 1658). Link, Berghes, Dixmunde, Furnés, Oudenarde and Gravelines afterwards fell into the hands of the English and of the French royalists. Don Juan was recalled to take command in the war which still lingered on the

Portuguese frontier; and the Archduke Sigismund came from Germany with 12,000 Germans to replace him and to make a supreme effort to hold Flanders. The effort had not to be made, for first a suspension of hostilities, and afterwards the famous Treaty of the Pyrenees, was signed (autumn 1659), which put an end to the bitter struggle that had completed the exhaustion of Spain.

The war in Cataluña had never ceased; but the Catalans by this time were heartily tired of their French masters, whose conduct towards them, as compared with that of the Spanish Government, was as that of King Stork to King Log. Mortara, the Spanish commander, who was a man of energy and resource, lost no opportunity. He captured Tortosa (November 1650), and then besieged Barcelona, whilst Don Juan blockaded the front by sea. After fifteen months of siege, and incredible suffering from famine, the place capitulated (October 1652) and a general amnesty was granted. The war, so far as the Catalans were concerned, was then practically at an end; but it was important for the French to retain Roussillon and to keep the Spaniards busy, and they captured Figueras and besieged Gerona, which, with the most heroic bravery, held out for seventy days, until relieved by Don Juan. Thenceforward the French made no great attempt to dominate Cataluña, and Mortara gradually gained the upper hand. The Spanish attempt also to regain Portugal had continued uninterruptedly, but with little result. Engagements on the frontier were frequent; plots for the murder or deposition of one or other of the sovereigns were more than once attempted. John IV of Portugal died at the end of 1656; and under his son Alfonso VI, a boy of thirteen, the energetic Spanish Queen of Portugal carried on the war with greater vigour. One frontier place after another fell to the Portuguese, until, in June 1658, the news came to Madrid that the Queen of Portugal had beleaguered the Spanish city Badajoz. Grief, rage, and shame resounded throughout the capital that the despised rebel Portuguese had brought proud Spain to this. A hasty force of 8000 Spaniards were with difficulty collected, and under Luis de Haro himself started for the frontier; but before he arrived the Portuguese had recrossed the border. Haro followed them and met with a crushing reverse near Elvas (14 January, 1658), the King's favourite flying like a coward from the field. Thenceforward all hope of regaining Portugal by force of arms must have vanished, although the pompous boasting and the oblivion to plain facts continued in Madrid.

On the little Island of Pheasants in the delta of the Bidasoa the difficult articles of the Treaty of the Pyrenees were laboriously discussed (August to November 1659). Many times it seemed as if agreement was not possible, but at last all was arranged. Louis XIV was to marry Maria Theresa, her renunciation of the Spanish succession being conditional upon the payment to her of a dowry of 500,000 crowns by Spain. The pregnant results of this article are still an active force in European politics. Condé was replaced in the governorship of Burgundy; Spain surrendered Roussillon to France, and also all Artois, except St Omer and Aire. Gravelines, Bourbourg, St Venant, the Sluys, Landrecy, Quesnoy, Thionville, Montmédy, Damvilliers, Ivry, Marienburg, Philippeville, Rocroy, Chatelet and Limchamp, remained in the hands of the French; whilst the English kept Dunkirk. The fortresses in Burgundy were returned to Spain, with Oudenarde and Dixmunde in Flanders; and Cataluña again became Spanish. Both Charles II of England and the King of Portugal were excluded from participation in the treaty. The Spanish Court tried to make the best of this hard bargain, and Haro was made Prince of the Peace; but it was a bitter blow, and once more proclaimed to the world the decadence of Spain—the result, as we have seen, of the fatal inheritance of the house of Burgundy, of the personal concentration of power by Philip II, and the indolent ineptitude of his two successors. In April

1660 Philip IV accompanied his daughter to the frontier for her marriage with Louis XIV. Once more all the splendour and pomp that the world could provide was lavished on both sides, and the fateful marriage took place in May 1660.

Relieved now of the foreign wars that had borne him down, Philip seriously set about reconquering Portugal. Early in 1661 two Spanish armies entered Portugal, one of 20,000 troops under Don Juan, which crossed the frontier from Estremadura, while the other of 15,000 men, commanded by the Duke of Osuna, invaded the north from Galicia. The Portuguese could at most muster 13,000 men, but the marriage of Charles II of England with the Infanta of Portugal brought an auxiliary force under Schomberg to help them, in return for her dowry of Tangier and Bombay. Thanks to this support the Portuguese more than held their own. Don Juan clamoured in vain for reinforcements, and complained bitterly of Haro, who however died at the end of the year. Civil divisions in Portugal soon gave to Don Juan an opportunity for more effective action. The young King Alfonso VI was a vicious lunatic, and his mother endeavoured to keep him in tutelage. By a *coup d'État* the young King, or rather his favourite Count de Castel-melhor, seized the reins of power. During the confusion caused by the change Don Juan overran the Alem-Tejo and threatened Lisbon. But as usual victory demoralised his troops, who fell to pillage and were wasted by sickness, excesses, and desertion. Castel-melhor was a man of energy and lost no time. Promptly reorganising the government and army of Portugal, he sent the forces to meet Don Juan. Marshal Schomberg was practically in command of the Portuguese, with a considerable force of English auxiliaries. The Portuguese met Don Juan near Evora, which place he had recently captured. Worsted in a first encounter, he tried to retreat to Spain, but was overtaken at Amegial an hour before sunset (8 June, 1663). By nightfall the Spanish army was utterly routed, mainly by the gallantry of the English contingent. Don Juan fought desperately, dismounted and pike in hand, but all to no purpose. 8000 Spaniards were lost, with baggage, standards, and guns; and the prince with difficulty escaped to Badajoz.

But Philip would not accept defeat. Through 1664 the struggle dragged on. In the following year 1665 every soldier that could be spared from Italy and Flanders was collected, and another army sent to the Portuguese frontier. Don Juan was superseded, sulky and disgusted at the intrigues of the Queen Mariana against him; and Count Caracena was sent to command the new army of 15,000 men. He set siege to Villa Viçosa, and on the approach of Schomberg and Marialva imprudently advanced to fight them. The armies met at Montesclaros, and a fierce hand-to-hand struggle ensued. After eight hours of carnage Caracena was forced to retire, leaving 4000 of his men on the field and 4000 more prisoners, with all his guns. On the 20th June, 1665, the news came to Madrid, and it broke Philip's heart. The marble mask was for once dropped. The man who in his life had never allowed his features to betray emotion, but had bared his suffering soul only in those terrible secret letters to the nun Maria de Agreda, lost his self-control. Casting himself in anguish on to the ground he could only sob out "God's will be done"; almost the same words as those with which his grandfather had received the news of the catastrophe of the Armada.

Bitter, cruel disappointment had dogged him through life. The pleasures for which he had surrendered his Kingship had turned to ashes in his mouth; the stately splendour that surrounded him was that of the whitened sepulchre all rotten within. The dreadful sin-steeped face, full of pride still, upon which the great genius Velasquez stamped the inner soul of the King, the lurid letters to the nun, of which his contemporaries knew nothing, compel us profoundly to pity a man so weak of will, so potent of passion, upon whom the curse of such a thorny crown had fallen. There was no favourite, even, now to take some of the burden from him. The intrigues of his young Austrian wife and her second-self the Jesuit Father Nithard had drawn him again into the vortex of the Empire, and he had undertaken to maintain an army to help the Emperor against the Turks; while the English ambassador (Fanshawe) was haughtily reminding him that his power on the sea was gone, and that England insisted upon the free right to trade with all of his dominions. France was again planning fresh aggression upon his Flemish states. His only legitimate son was a sickly infant, his wife was already plotting for a time when he should be dead, and seeking to supplant Don Juan. Whichever way he looked there was no light or hope either for himself or for Spain. Humbled and in despair at the age of 60, on the 17th September, 1665, Philip the Great, "the Planet King," poet, dilettante, and man of pleasure, ended his wasted life. Like his father before him he learnt when it was too late that great positions call for great sacrifices, and his death-bed was embittered with the knowledge that his self-indulgence had reduced the country he loved to utter ruin and degradation.

CHAPTER X.

CHARLES II, 1665—1678.

PHILIP IV on his death-bed left his wife Mariana of Austria regent during the minority of the new King, Charles II, who was but four years old. To assist her he also nominated a Council, consisting of the Archbishop of Toledo, the Inquisitor-General, the President of the Council of Castile (Count de Castrillo), the Vice-Chancellor of Aragon, the Marquis de Aytona and Count de Peñaranda.

We have seen that the roots of the calamities which afflicted Spain were the traditions which bound it to the imperial house of Austria. All that the country needed, even now, was peace, rest, and freedom from foreign entanglements, in which the Peninsula itself had no concern whatever. Boldness, patriotism and common-sense might still have saved the prosperity and happiness of the citizens, though illusive national and dynastic claims would have to be abandoned. But an evil fate at this crucial moment condemned Spain to the rule of a princess, who, though possessed of considerable ability, was absolutely dominated by those very traditions which had been the origin of so many disasters. Ambitious, intriguing and imprudent, she cared nothing for Spain and everything for the Empire. An Austrian to the finger tips, she had been for years before Philip's death plotting for the predominance of the influence of her kinsmen, and weakening the bonds of friendship with France which had been cemented by the marriage of Louis XIV and Maria Theresa. Her very first act of government was to bring into the Council nominated by the King to assist her Father Nithard, whom she appointed Inquisitor-General, in violation of the constitution which excluded foreigners from the Council. Nithard and the Queen were both unpopular. Don Juan had made no secret of his belief that his failure in Portugal had arisen from their machinations in withholding resources from him; and he retired in disgust from Court soon after Father Nithard entered the Council.

In the meanwhile Portugal was a prey to civil dissensions between the unworthy King and his brother Don Pedro, and peace was as needful to that country as to Spain. By the intervention of Charles II of England, at length (February 1668) terms were arranged by which the independence of Portugal was acknowledged, all places held by the enemy on each side being given up, except Ceuta, which continued in the hands of Spain. It was time that the fratricidal strife should be ended, for the resources of Spain were quite inadequate to meet the demands upon them. The whole of the evils noted in a previous chapter existed still, but in a more acute form than ever. Office-seeking and the Church were still the only flourishing interests. Corruption of public officers at home and abroad continued to keep the national treasury bankrupt, however crushing was the weight of taxes upon the people. Manufacture, except that of a few coarse articles for immediate home consumption, was dead: idlers and discharged soldiers, vagabonds and rogues of all sorts, swarmed in the cities and about the Court, but the working hands were so few that even the poor harvests still raised in North and Central Spain were gathered by French labourers who returned to their country again with their wages in their pockets. The trade and industry of Madrid, such as they were, were almost exclusively carried on by Frenchmen, of whom it was said there were 40,000 in the capital, mostly calling themselves Flemings and

Burgundians to escape the differential taxation imposed upon Frenchmen. The total revenues of the Crown of Castile on the accession of Charles II are given officially by a contemporary writer[1] as follows:

	Ducats
The Millions (excise on meat, wine, oil, etc.) ...	2,500,000
Forfeitures	1,300,000
Ordinary and Extraordinary fixed Supply	400,000
Stamped paper	250,000
Customs dues, Wool dues, playing-cards, etc....	2,600,000
Monopolies: Tobacco paper, sugar, chocolate, etc.	400,000
Extra excises on meat, wine, etc.	1,600,000
Militia subsidy	300,000
Special grant for 8,000 soldiers	200,000
First-fruits of offices (half year's emoluments)...	200,000
Ecclesiastical subsidies (Cruzada, Escusado, etc.)	1,600,000
Alcabalas, not assigned	2,500,000
Salt monopoly	700,000
Additional 2 per cent. on Alcabala	1,200,000
Ducats	15,750,000

Of this sum eight and a half million ducats are stated by the writer to be pledged. In any case certainly not more than a third would reach the Treasury. The average amount received from Aragon, Valencia, etc., appears to have been two million ducats, and the annual revenue from the Indies, derived from a royalty of one-fifth of the precious metals mined and other tributes, is set down by Bonnecasse[2] at about one million and a half of ducats. We shall therefore probably be not far wrong if we estimate the national income—apart from the royal patrimony, which was now mostly pledged or alienated—

---

[1] *Solo Madrid es Corte*, por Don Alonso Nuñez de Castro. Cronista del Rey. Madrid, 1669.

[2] *Relation de l'État et Gouvernement d'Espagne* (1665), par R. A. Bonnecasse. Cologne, 1767.

at about 9 millions of ducats[1] actually encashed. The cost of the royal establishments is stated at the same time to have reached the sum of 1,700,000 ducats a year—approaching a fifth of the whole amount received into the national exchequer. The ecclesiastical revenues of the kingdoms of Castile alone amounted to 12 millions of ducats; and the entire annual revenues of the same kingdoms, clerical and lay, are stated at 113 million ducats. If this really was the case the taxation would not seem to have been so onerous as the complaints would lead us to believe; but, as much of the land was now out of cultivation, and the country depopulated, it is certain that the income was vastly inferior to that stated as the nominal value. It will be seen by the above statement that Spain was not in a position to undertake an adventurous foreign policy. The ambition of Louis XIV, however, with a rich and powerful France behind him, soon found a pretext in the Queen-Mother's unconcealed Austrian leanings, for still further aggrandising himself at the expense of his wife's country. It will be remembered that the French diplomatists at the Treaty of the Pyrenees had insisted that Maria Theresa's renunciation of all rights to succeed to the Spanish dominions should be conditional upon the payment of her dowry. The dowry had not been paid, and Louis set up a claim on her behalf to the Spanish Netherlands[2]. The claim, for which there seems to have been no legal ground whatever, was of course resisted, and Louis invaded Flanders (May 1667) with 50,000 men. The Governor, the Marquis of Castel Rodrigo, had only at his command a small, disorganised and unpaid force, and the French without effective opposition captured Charleroy, Courtrai, Oudenarde, Tournai, Lille, Alost, and other Flemish towns. Holland, England and Sweden, against whose interests it had always been that France should dominate

---

[1] This was the nominal copper ducat of 375 maravedis, equal to 2s. 5½d.
[2] The claim was based upon the precedent of the elder daughter of Philip II, the Infanta Isabel, succeeding to Flanders.

Belgium, successively intervened, and Louis offered terms of peace. But his claims to the surrender of Franche-Comté and other provinces were indignantly rejected by Spain, and the war continued. By the middle of February 1668, the Franche-Comté was in the hands of the French, and once more Spain had to be bled to win back a part of the deadly inheritance that had dragged her down. The nobles and the Church subscribed largely, 15 per cent. more was deducted from the assigned revenues, a tax on mules and coaches—the favourite indulgence of the Spaniards—was imposed; and somehow a fresh army was collected. Don Juan was destined to command, in order chiefly to get him out of the way of the Queen and Nithard; but he pleaded ill-health and avoided the trap. Before anything could be done England, Holland and Sweden had arranged with the French and Spanish plenipotentiaries the famous peace of Aix-la-Chapelle (2 May, 1668) by which France gave up the Franche-Comté, but retained all the places she had conquered in Flanders—a most unfortunate and unwise arrangement for Spain, as England and Holland would, as a last resource, have fought her battle for her in Flanders, whereas no power would help her to retain the Franche-Comté; which, moreover, was of no value to her and which she was certain to lose sooner or later.

The dissensions in Madrid between Nithard and Don Juan now deepened; and already a party was forming around each of the contending interests. Matters suddenly came to a head with the arrest of one of Don Juan's closest friends, Malladas, who was garrotted in prison by written order of the Queen two hours afterwards without trial or accusation. Don Juan was indignant, and said so. He was ordered to retire to his castle of Consuegra[1]. Others of his friends were arrested; a plot, real or pretended, was discovered; and Don Juan's own arrest

---

[1] He held Consuegra as a fief in virtue of his office as Grand Prior of Castile.

was ordered. But on the arrival of the officers at Consuegra he had fled, leaving behind him a letter for the Queen, violently denouncing Father Nithard, and protesting his own loyalty. Madrid began to murmur and take sides. Showers of pamphlets and manifestoes were issued by both parties, but the great mass of the people were unquestionably on the side of Don Juan. He had fled to Barcelona, where the German Nithard was especially hated; and there nobles and people received him with open arms. Messages of support came to Don Juan from all parts of Spain, and matters looked dangerous. The Queen took fright and tried conciliation, but Don Juan became the more imperious, and peremptorily demanded the dismissal of Nithard. With a powerful train Don Juan rode through Cataluña and Aragon, as on a triumphal progress, and with 200 horse and 300 foot-soldiers approached Madrid (February 1669). The Queen was all amiability now, and begged him to lay down his arms. Don Juan replied with equal politeness that he intended to do so when the hated German Jesuit had been sent away. The Nuncio exhorted him to obedience, with the same result. "If Father Nithard does not leave by the door," said Don Juan, "within two days from now I will go myself and throw him out of the window." Nearly all Madrid was against the Court, and disturbance seemed inevitable unless the Jesuit departed, when the Council of Castile decided to recommend the Queen to dismiss him. With tears of rage she was obliged to give way, and Nithard was sent off with all the honour she could pay him, and the full enjoyment of his revenues and offices, but with a surging populace around his coach thirsting for his blood.

Don Juan, however, was not allowed this time to carry his triumph further. Having gained his first point, his demands became more exacting, but the people were now inclined to resent fresh pressure upon the Queen as disloyal. Long negotiations were conducted between him and the Queen's emissaries at Guadalajara, and promises of financial and administrative reforms solemnly made to him. But in the meanwhile the Queen's friends were raising an armed force, particularly a body-guard, which afterwards became famous under the name of Chambergos, because they were dressed in French uniforms similar to those worn by the troops of Marshal Schomberg. The formation of this guard was bitterly resented by the town of Madrid, and aroused new sympathy with Don Juan. At last a reconciliation was arranged. Don Juan was appointed Viceroy of Aragon, and made submission to the Queen (June 1669).

The ambition of Louis XIV in Flanders had been whetted by his easy victories, but before he could venture to satisfy it the triple alliance of England, Holland and Sweden must be broken up, and Spain alienated from them. His intrigues to this end had been active ever since the peace of Aix-la-Chapelle. Loving and reassuring messages were sent by various ambassadors to Mariana, warning her of the greedy Hollanders and Swedes and the false Englishmen. On one occasion the French envoy Bonsy proposed that Flanders should be surrendered to Louis in exchange for Portugal, which he would conquer and cede to Spain; and the dethroned and exiled Alfonso VI of Portugal also tried to draw Mariana into a renewal of the war against his country. The designs of Louis, however, were too clearly the conquest of Holland, which would of course have been fatal to the Spanish dominion in Flanders; and Mariana was well advised in refusing to be diverted from the Netherlands. England and Sweden were at length drawn away from Holland by Louis, and the republic then stood alone. Mariana promised aid if Holland were attacked, but the help she could send was but slight, when compared to the overwhelming strength of the French king. Disasters, moreover, still continued to fall upon Spain. Morgan and the buccaneers were carrying rapine and desolation into the Spanish possessions in America. The accumulated hoard of silver, upon which to a large extent the Queen depended, was stolen at Porto Bello on the Isthmus of Panama, while shipping and stores were burnt and cities pillaged with impunity. In the same year (1671) a fearful hurricane destroyed 70 ships in the bay of Cadiz; and the suicidal system of raising the national revenue by overtaxing industry continued unreformed.

When, therefore, Louis XIV invaded Holland (April 1672), in union this time with the impolitic Charles II of England, he at first carried all before him. Both the independence of the United Provinces and the Spanish domination in Flanders seemed trembling in the balance, for Spain was all unready. With a fine, organised army, such as no other monarch could gather, with generals like Condé, Turenne and Vauban, it was easy for Louis to cross the Meuse, and capture, as he did, all the cities he passed. The Rhine was as easily crossed, and Holland lay almost at his mercy. The conditions offered by Louis to the Dutch were such as the doughty burghers could never accept, notwithstanding their disasters on land and sea: but the position was dangerous for others as well as Holland. With France dominating the western seaboard of Europe, Germany would be shut in, and English trade ruined. Spain and the Empire sent all the troops they could collect, and by their aid the Prince of Orange drove back Louis to the French frontier again (September 1673). But, on the other hand, the French established themselves in Franche-Comté, which they have possessed ever since, and the troops of Louis XIV threatened Cataluña. At length (Feb. 1674) the English Parliament, wiser than the King, compelled Charles to withdraw from the French alliance. Some attempts at peace negotiations were made in 1674 at Cologne, but were unsuccessful, and thenceforward the war raged unchecked; the Emperor ravaging Alsace, the French overran Burgundy, whilst the Prince of Orange with an army of allies 70,000 strong held Holland. This army was met by Condé's force, 40,000 strong (11 August, 1674), near Charleroi, and one of the most sanguinary battles of the campaign was fought with but small permanent result, although 25,000 men were killed. At the same time an attempt was made by the Spaniards to recover Roussillon, where the French were commanded by Schomberg. But brave as the Catalans were, the resources they received from Madrid were not sufficient for success to crown their efforts, and the Spanish troops in the principality had to be hurried off to stifle another revolt which had broken out in Sicily. Schomberg even invaded Cataluña, captured Figueras, and attacked, but unsuccessfully, Gerona (1675). In the meanwhile the war was raging fiercely in Flanders, where Orange and the Spaniards under the Duke of Villa-hermosa faced Crequi and Condé, and in Germany, where the French were commanded by Turenne.

At length, principally by the intervention of England, peace negotiations were opened, and the plenipotentiaries of all the powers met at Nimeguen (December 1675). The diplomatic delay was utilised by Louis in reorganising four considerable armies, with which, in 1676, he reopened the campaigns. Louis himself, with 50,000 men, operated in Spanish Flanders, and the Duke de Noailles commanded the French forces attacking Cataluña. During the whole of the year fighting went on, almost without interruption, in Flanders, Germany, and on the Catalan frontier; whilst French money and ships supported the Sicilians in their revolt against the Spanish dominion. The French defeated the Spanish and Dutch fleets in the Mediterranean three times, the great De Ruyter being killed in the second engagement (21 April, 1576). As usual in wars in which Spain joined other powers she was the principal sufferer. Roussillon and Cataluña had been the theatre of a war in which Spanish blood and money had been poured out like water, the Spanish Netherlands had been the field upon which most of the struggle between Louis and the Hollanders had been fought out.

It now became evident that with such a combination as the

King of France had against him, he would not be able to conquer and hold Holland, especially since the English troops had been withdrawn from his service, and a new treaty had been signed (16 January, 1678) between England and Holland, by which the former undertook, if France would not come to terms, to aid the allies with a fleet of 80 ships and 30,000 men. Louis' policy therefore was to draw Holland away from Spain. Orange was principally interested in the independence of the United Provinces, and was persuaded to abandon Spain and the Empire, and make a separate peace. When this was done Spain was obliged to accept almost any terms that Louis would grant her. The *pourparlers* for peace had continued for over two years at Nimeguen. Each party tried to make the best terms for itself, failing which the principal aim of the allies was to prolong the war until England should be obliged to take an active part against France, while Louis sought to break up the confederacy, and kept Charles of England quiet by heavy bribes of money. But when it suited Louis to talk of peace Charles was allowed to intervene with that object, and the long delayed peace of Nimeguen was the result; the conclusion being largely due to the arrangement between Holland and England already mentioned, and the marriage of the Prince of Orange with the Princess Mary, daughter of the Duke of York (James II). The conduct of Charles II of England both during the war and in the peace negotiations was disgraceful in the extreme. He simply put his influence up for sale, and changed sides according to the amount of the bribe offered to him, although the interests of England were exclusively concerned in preventing a French domination of the Netherlands. This both the British people and Parliament well understood, and to their influence, and not the good faith of Charles, was it mainly owing that Louis XIV did not succeed in holding the Flemish seaboard. After the signature of the separate peace with Holland (10 August, 1678), which took place without the knowledge of the Spanish envoys (although it surrendered cities in Spanish Flanders to the French), Louis could exact almost his own terms from Spain. By the treaty of Nimeguen (September 1678), the French restored to Spain the fortresses of Charleroy, Ath, Oudenarde, Courtrai, Binche, Limburg, Ghent, Rodenhuys, St Ghislain and Weres, with the place of Puigcerdá in Cataluña: whilst the King of France retained the whole of the Franche-Comté, and (in Flanders) **Valenciennes,** Bouchain, Condé, Cambrai, Aire, St Omer, Ypres, Cassel, and a few less important places. The Emperor shortly afterwards also accepted hard terms from France. It seemed impossible that Spain could fall lower than this. Utterly beggared now, scornfully taken up and betrayed, as it suited them, by Holland and England; obliged to accept, almost without question, the terms dictated by its enemies; with its young rival Louis XIV growing daily in power, riches, and splendour, Spain had not even yet fully learnt the bitter lesson taught by so many cruel calamities. The tradition of pride and universal superiority was still persevered in. The questions of precedence and etiquette were not by any means the least difficult points in the conclusion of peace, whilst in Spain itself the overwhelming grandeur and wealth of its own monarch continued to be an article of national faith; and his clemency in letting his enemies off so easily a matter for admiring congratulation upon his magnanimity.

CHAPTER XI.

CHARLES II, 1675—1700.

THE canker of favouritism had eaten too deeply into the political system of Spain to be eliminated, except by a monarch of far greater genius and force than Mariana. Soon after the disappearance of Father Nithard from the scene a young hidalgo, who had served in the household of the Duke of Infantado and had joined the party of the Queen, was seen to be advancing with unusual rapidity. Fernando de Valenzuela was one of those facile, plausible Andaluces, who figured so prominently in the court of Philip IV, where the accomplishment of deftly turning an amorous verse, writing a dramatic interlude, or capping a bitter gibe, often opened the way to fortune. After Nithard had introduced him into the palace he married a favourite attendant of the Queen, Doña Maria Eugenia de Uceda, and was appointed the Queen's equerry. During the troubles with Don Juan Valenzuela was invaluable. Quick, bold and ready, he served his mistress well, both inside the palace and in the streets of the capital. Every whisper in "Liars' Parade" was carried to the Queen, and the gossips began to wonder who was the "fairy of the palace." Jealous, watchful eyes surrounded the Queen, and it soon became evident that Valenzuela was not only Mariana's political right hand, but her lover as well. The new favourite rapidly advanced from office to office. He was made a marquis, and soon afterwards "valido," or universal confidant. The nobles who had stood by the Queen against Don Juan were scandalised and indignant; but there was hardly even an affectation of concealment. Valenzuela, like most favourites, began to form a party of his own, by lavishing offices, pensions, honours, and grants, upon his friends; whilst the idlers of the capital were kept amused by continual festivals and by lavish expenditure in beautifying the town.

But freely as Valenzuela might scatter his bribes, the actual resources of the country did not admit of all the greedy crew being satisfied; and the discontented ones—by far the greater number—rallied to Don Juan, who was sulking and intriguing against the Queen in his capital of Zaragoza. When the dangerous rising in Sicily took place (1675) the Queen tried to get rid of her rival by sending him thither in De Ruyter's fleet as Viceroy; but one of Don Juan's friends had persuaded the boy King, unknown to his mother, to sign a letter recalling his base brother to the capital, and Don Juan was already on his way thither. The *coup d'état* had been carefully planned. By the will of Philip IV the King came of age at 15, and on the morning of his birthday (6 November, 1675) Don Juan secretly entered the palace of the Buen Retiro, Madrid. The decree appointing him first minister was ready awaiting the King's signature when Mariana took the matter in her own hands. The boy had naturally been brought up under her influence: he was nearly an idiot, ignorant and weak beyond conception, and his mother, by tears and entreaties, easily induced him to sign an order for Don Juan to return to Aragon. The plan of Don Juan was to rule through the King, and not in spite of the King, for the tradition of the personal power of the monarch was still supreme in the country. He could not disobey the King's order and he returned defeated to Aragon, leaving Mariana and Valenzuela triumphant. All the courtiers who had aided the plot were banished, and more titles and honours were heaped upon the favourite. He was made governor of the Andalucian coast, Master of the Horse to the King, a grandee of Spain of the first class, and finally, prime minister (November, 1676), with a residence in the palace usually occupied by the heir to the Crown.

In the meanwhile Don Juan was plotting in Aragon, where he was popular, and the jealous grandees were aiding him in Madrid. All around him, fool as he was, the young King could not fail to see misery and poverty almost beyond belief. The letters of Madame D'Aulnoy, of Madame de Villars, and other residents in Madrid at the time, testify that, even in the capital, it was quite a common thing for people to die of starvation in the streets, and that famine reigned even in the King's palace, where Madame de Villars says that the ladies of the household had had no food served out to them for a long while, and that even the horses in the King's stable were starving; whilst Madame D'Aulnoy assures us that so great was the penury, even in the houses of the grandees, that although silver and gold plate was in abundance, food was only to be obtained scantily and from hand to mouth. The farmers in the outskirts of Madrid were forced by threats of the hangman to sell the foodstuffs they raised to supply the capital, at the risk of themselves being starved. The population even of the capitals had diminished terribly. At the death of Philip II Madrid was supposed to possess a population of 400,000 souls, but at the period of which we are writing (1677-80) it did not exceed 200,000; and a still greater falling off was seen in Burgos and other provincial capitals. The crushing of agriculture and the corruption of government had at first driven the population into the towns, but by the end of the 17th century the food raised in the country was quite insufficient to maintain them, and the only resource was emigration or starvation.

Either the sufferings of his people or his own feebleness at length prevailed upon Charles II to escape from the tutelage of his mother and her paramour, to whom all the evils which afflicted Spain were unjustly ascribed. Most of the great nobles were in the plot. Valenzuela, seeing they were too strong for him, suddenly fled, and, on the night of 14th January, 1677, the King escaped from the Alcazar to the Buen Retiro, and sent an order for his mother not to leave the palace. The nobles took care this time that her personal influence should not be used on the King, and her voluminous letters probably never reached his hands. Don Juan, as he approached the capital, dictated the terms upon which he would take the direction of affairs. The Queen must leave Madrid, Valenzuela must be arrested, and the hated Chambergo regiment of guards disbanded. Everything was conceded to him, for anarchy, pillage and robbery had invaded even the capital, and a saviour of society was needed. The Chambergos were shipped to Sicily, the Queen was hurried off to Toledo, and Valenzuela was captured in his refuge at the Escorial, where, by order of the King, the monks were secretly entertaining him. After a short confinement in the castle of Consuegra, Valenzuela, stripped of all his honours, was spirited away to the Philippine Islands, and afterwards to Mexico, where he died in obscurity.

But a bitter disappointment awaited those who believed that Don Juan would turn Spain again from a desert to a garden. The same evil systems were continued. Instead of the prudence and restraint that had been expected of him, the Prince displayed neither capacity nor application. He was idle, vain and vindictive, and all those who had not aided him in his plots felt the weight of his displeasure, while his spies never left the Queen Mother, night or day. Whilst he was issuing pragmatics for the adoption of French fashions in dress, or trifling with questions of ceremony and etiquette for the purpose of enforcing his position as a prince of the blood, the Spanish troops were being beaten in Cataluña by the French, for want of support, Puigcerdá was lost, the French were taking Spanish towns in Flanders for the same reason, and Sicily was in the hands of King Louis, until he finally left it of his own accord (March 1678).

The distress in Madrid was worse than ever. All law and order were at an end, and troops of robbers pillaged with impunity the houses in which any valuables could be found. The police and officers of justice were unpaid, there was no armed force to restrain disorder: and soon the townspeople began to clamour for Mariana again. But none could get ear of the King but his brother, and the Queen-Mother was closely guarded in her convent at Toledo. In vain plots were formed against Don Juan, in vain the satires and pasquins were scattered by the thousand: Don Juan stood firm because he had control of the King's signature. The peace of Nimeguen, disastrous as it was to Spain, was received with rejoicing, and for a time distracted the people with renewed hopes of prosperity. The truce thus allowed to Don Juan was utilised in dealing another blow at the Queen-Mother and the Austrian faction. It had been her intention to marry the King to one of her own family, though the person of Charles himself might have been a warning against the repetition of consanguineous marriages. The constant intermarriage of members of the Austrian family, of which Charles was the ultimate result, had reproduced in him the peculiarities of the race to an extent which made him a monstrosity. His chin was so enormous, and stood out to such an extent, that he could masticate nothing; and his speech was almost unintelligible from the abnormal size of his tongue. What had been religious gloom and mysticism in his forefathers, in him had degenerated into childish superstition. Up to the age of ten years he had been treated as an infant in arms; in order not to endanger his feeble health he had been taught nothing, so that he could barely read; and he died of senile decay when most men are hardly in their prime.

This was the unfortunate creature upon whom rested the responsibility of continuing the race of the Spanish house of Austria. If Mariana had remained at his side he would have married the Emperor's daughter, but under Don Juan that was out of the question, and negotiations were opened for a match with Princess Marie Louise of Orleans, the daughter of the brother of Louis XIV by Henrietta of England, daughter of Charles I. Favourable portraits of her were shown to the King, who promptly fell in love with her; no difficulties occurred on either side, and the preliminaries were soon settled. The match was popular in Madrid, and the Queen-Mother determined to make the best of it, foreseeing that after the marriage the influence of Don Juan would decrease, and probably her own be in the ascendant again. The intrigues and events which accompanied and followed this marriage are more fully related than usual in such cases, owing to the then fashion in France of writing letters and memoirs for publication. The French ambassador de Villars, in his *Mémoires de la Cour d'Espagne*, and his wife and Madame D'Aulnoy, in their letters, present an almost microscopic picture of Spain at the period; and to those works readers are referred for more minute details than can be included in a general history like the present. With all the pomp and splendour which the court of *le roi soleil* could produce, the young French princess was married by proxy at Fontainebleau (31 August, 1679), and slowly and with infinite etiquette travelled, followed by a great train through France and Spain, to meet her new husband. She was a light-hearted creature, extremely beautiful, frankly pagan in her animal enjoyment, as befitted a girl brought up amidst the cynical dissoluteness of her uncle's court, but she lacked the common-sense needed to carry out the task for which she was sent, namely, to work upon the King, and influence him for French political aims. Before she arrived at Madrid, Don Juan, whose star was already on the wane, notwithstanding the success of his scheme, died—of fever and ague, it was publicly said, but the Queen-Mother's enemies whispered of poison (September 1679). The breath was hardly out of his body before the King hurried off to embrace and release his mother, who entered Madrid by his side, cheered to the echo by the fickle populace.

On the 3rd November Marie Louise was delivered to her
Spanish court on the banks of the Bidasoa. The household
appointments had been made by Don Juan, but his death had
thrown everything into confusion, and the courtiers were all
quarrelling amongst themselves about their duties and precedence. The Mistress of the Robes to the new Queen was a
harsh, imperious old woman of Don Juan's party, named the
Duchess of Terranova, who began tyrannising over the girl as
soon as she entered Spanish territory, and never ceased to
reproach her for allowing her youth and gaiety to overrule
gloomy Spanish etiquette. The poor princess had wept and
prayed on her knees to her father and uncle up to the last hour
to be saved from the sacrifice; but when she saw that she was
doomed to be Queen of Spain in spite of all, she determined
to please herself in everything and to disregard all other
considerations. This made her position impossible from the
first. The King was frantically in love with the beautiful
creature and could not restrain his impatience, but went to
meet her on the road in spite of all remonstrance. The ways
were deep in mire, the rain fell in torrents, most of the King's
court had dropped behind when Charles met his bride at the
poverty-stricken village of Quintanapalla, near Burgos, where he
married her (19 November, 1679). Amidst the blighting gloom
of the palace of Madrid—"so thick," says Madame D'Aulnoy,
"that it can be seen, smelt, touched"—the toils were woven
around the young Queen. The Queen-Mother was amiable
and diplomatic, but determined that her daughter-in-law should
be influenced by her, or be left to her fate. Marie Louise was
never happy but when she was chatting with her French ladies
or to Madame Villars; but the Austrian faction soon aroused
jealousy against them, and threw all sorts of obstacles in the
way of their seeing her. Instead of making the best of things,
like the former French Queens of Spain, and gradually asserting
her influence over her husband, she cast all prudence to the winds.
Her idiot husband alternated childish rage with maudlin caresses,

but she paid no attention to either. In defiance of etiquette she insisted upon constant violent horse exercise, ate and drank foolishly, to the injury of her health, slept 12 hours a day, committed the dreadful sin of laughing heartily in public, acted in comedies, chatted and smiled from her balcony to French people in the street, and generally scandalised the rigid Court. Over and over again her hope of progeny was disappointed, and by 1685 it was seen that in every sense of the word she was a failure, and that her influence for the furtherance of French aims or the welfare of Spain was past praying for.

The King himself, under the control of a sensible wife, might have turned out better, but, as it was, he went from bad to worse. His only pleasures were hunting and puerile trifles—"such as," wrote a courtier, "running through the rooms from balcony to balcony like a child of six years old; and his conversation corresponds." He only worked a quarter of an hour a day signing the papers placed before him, and the rest of the time was passed in absolute frivolity. The Queen-Mother's Austrian faction, with Mansfeld, the imperial ambassador, were unceasing in their determination to ruin the foolish, unhappy young Queen, although Mariana herself kept ostensibly on good terms with her daughter-in-law. The Queen's favourite companion was a Frenchwoman, a widow, named Quintin, who in April 1685 married one of the French equerries (Viremont). Both were deep in the Queen's confidence, and an attempt was made in April to persuade the King, on some accusation of immorality against them, to order their expulsion. The Queen wept and stormed until the King, greatly to the annoyance of the opposite faction, gave way, and the French favourites were made more of than ever, the Prime Minister Medina-Celi retiring in disgust. But in August a more successful course was tried: Quintin and her husband, and other French people, were accused of a plot to poison the King, who was frightened out of his small wits, and every French person near the Queen was banished. Tears and threats from Marie Louise brought one French girl back to her—the niece of Quintin, to whom the Queen left money in her will—but that was all. Courtiers and populace made no secret of their belief, absurd as it may seem, that the Queen herself was at the bottom of the plot, and all hope for her now was gone. The Austrians had conquered all along the line, and Marie Louise was doomed. Charles from his infancy had been taught to hate the French; he now looked upon them with horror and fear, including even his wife. Surrounded by enemies on all sides, with such a husband as this, the wretched Queen in despair gave herself to her caprices, and ceased to be taken into account. Louis XIV himself tried to arouse her to action, and urged her to take advantage of the King's ineptitude to obtain influence, and in the case of no child being born to her, to forward the succession of a French prince to the Spanish throne. But it was of no avail, for until her death (February 1689)—it was said of poison—she was a cipher in the political intrigues which were thickening around her.

Charles II was too weak and silly to be ruled by a favourite, in the usual acceptance of the word; and here was the crowning failure of the laboriously constructed system of personal concentration of power which Philip II had perfected. We have seen its decadence through the indolence of the monarch shifting his responsibility on to a favourite; but a point had now been reached when the monarch had no sense of responsibility at all, and there was no point upon which to concentrate power. It thus happens that we have in the reign of the last Spanish King of the house of Austria the phenomenon of power seeking for a centre. Prime ministers were appointed who transferred their responsibility to the Councils, and these again shifted it upon their secretaries or subordinate officers, for the representative control had been practically abolished when the personal power of the monarch was established; so that the public discontent, acute as it was, had no object upon which it could cast the responsibility of the sufferings endured. The Duke of Medina-Celi, who was prime minister from the death of Don Juan until April 1685, had to face tumults in the capital aroused by the absolute absence of food (1680) caused by the traditional policy of fixing a low price in the interest of the consumer, oblivious of the conditions which made it impossible for the producer to sell at the price without starving; but the Duke himself was not made a scapegoat, for the responsibility of government was now scattered. Hand in hand with the confusion and semi-anarchy which prevailed, the blackest superstition existed amongst the King, nobles, and people. It was no longer a fervid determination, as it had been in Philip II's time, to establish Spanish domination by stamping out heresy; for the heretic Dutch and Englishmen had fought by the side of the Spaniards against the Catholic King of France, and dreams of European domination had ceased to haunt the slumber of feeble Spain. The Inquisition was no longer a political instrument in the King's hands, but a means of fastening upon the country the thraldom of the churchmen, ignorant, idle, bigoted and tyrannical, who alone had thriven amongst the general ruin. In May 1680, the greatest *auto de fé* ever seen was enacted in the Plaza Mayor of Madrid with a pomp and magnificence unapproached before or since. In the presence of the King and Queen 105 poor wretches from the dungeons of the Inquisition were arraigned; 85 nobles were enlisted as "familiars," and the criminals were either burnt to death, or first garrotted and then burnt, in a great bonfire sixty feet square and seven feet high outside the gate of Fuencarral, the Inquisition, as usual, hypocritically handing them over to the civil authorities for execution.

Spain never reached a lower depth than during the wretched reign of the last Austrian King. "The country," writes Villars to his government, "is reduced to a state of misery difficult to realise without seeing it. The expulsion of the Moriscos, the emigration and constant wars had depopulated the country," and, continues the French Ambassador, "the excessive taxation has rendered the few people that remain incapable of cultivating the land. During the last 40 years these taxes, the officers to collect them, and the tribunals to enforce them have been increased infinitely. Notwithstanding the prodigious sums raised the King gets hardly anything....Commerce is in no better state. With the exception of Castilian wool, which foreigners buy, there is no merchandise or manufacture to attract money. The King has no ships now to protect trade, and his subjects none to trade with, so that all commerce is done by strangers, and two-thirds of the money from the Indies goes direct abroad, and the other third gradually follows it in payment for goods." There was no trade in Madrid but such as depended upon the State service and the Church for its support. The nominal value of the copper coinage (almost the only currency remaining) had been gradually increased to six times its face value. One of Medina-Celi's first acts was suddenly to reduce it to its real value again. This might have been wise if prudently and cautiously carried out, but, as it was, it completed the ruin, for it enormously increased the price of commodities and utterly disorganised trade. So effete had the nation grown that Louis XIV hardly made a pretence of keeping his engagements with it. He occupied Strasbourg, a city of the Empire, laid siege to Luxembourg (which was Spanish), and at last, after centuries of struggle, forced the Spaniards to acknowledge the precedence of France in all things, and made Charles surrender his hereditary title of Duke of Burgundy. But the more Charles ceded the more exacting became Louis. The laboriously arranged peace of Nimeguen became waste-paper when the cupidity of the King of France had to be satisfied; and when the latter claimed the county of Alost in Flanders and other territories adjoining Holland and the Empire, a league was projected between Spain and the two latter powers to uphold the treaty. But the strength of France bore all before it. Notwithstanding a gallant defence by the Spaniards, Humières captured Courtrai and Dixmunde (November 1683). Louis had proposed the arbitration of the King of England, but laid down his own terms. He must, he said, either have Luxembourg or Courtrai and Dixmunde, or else a slice of Cataluña or Navarre, demanding in each case the strongest fortresses. But exhausted as Spain was she could not accept the position of a subject-power whilst she had life at all, and again she had to fight. Louis diverted the Hollanders from aiding Spain and thus had his enemy alone.

Threatening Navarre with one army, he rapidly marched upon Gerona in Cataluña with another. The Spanish troops were as yet unmustered, but the armed Catalan peasants fought with perfect fury, and Marshal de Bellefonds raised the siege (May 1684). At the same time a desperate attempt was made by the French under Crequi and Vauban to reduce the well-nigh impregnable fortress of Luxembourg, defended by Spaniards and Walloons under the Prince of Chimay. After 24 days of unceasing battery the garrison capitulated with all the honours of war (June 1684). Having such pledges as these in his hands Louis could dictate peace to Spain and the Empire. He kept Luxembourg, the city of Strasbourg, Bovines, Chimay, and Beaumont, but restored to Spain Courtrai and Dixmunde after destroying the fortifications. Louis also had defeated the Spaniards in a pitched battle at Ter in Cataluña, and had bombarded Genoa, which was under the protection of Spain; so that the government of Charles was rejoiced to escape even with the hard terms dictated by the treaty of Ratisbon (June 1684). Other smaller potentates, like the Elector of Brandenburg and the Prince Regent of Portugal, followed the example of the great Louis and hectored Spain into humiliating concessions; whilst pestilence swept through Andalucia (1684), floods ruined Spanish Flanders (1683), hurricanes sank the silver fleets

(1682) or corsairs captured them, corruption stalked unchecked through Spain, earthquakes shook Naples to bits and desolated the Indies (1687), and the wretched King, growing more decrepit in mind and body, mumbled his prayers or wandered through his great, grim palace searching for pins in the matting. The palace itself was a hot-bed of intrigue, mostly carried on by priests and women, the Queen-Mother and the Austrian ambassador being pitted against the French ambassador and Marie Louise. In complete disgust Medina-Celi abandoned the sinking ship, after having in vain sought to stem the tide of ruin, and was succeeded by the Count de Oropesa (April 1685).

The new minister began well; he suspended all pensions, abolished crowds of useless offices, civil and military, made a clean sweep of some of the worst abuses of the royal household, and, as a consequence, drew upon him the hate of all those whose interests he touched. But he managed to relieve some of the most pressing needs, and spent most of the money he had saved in maintaining a Spanish force of 12,000 men to aid the Emperor in his great struggle against the Turk. His energy, too, infused some virility into Spanish foreign policy. Largely by the efforts of Ronquillo, the ambassador in London, a secret understanding, usually called the league of Augsburg, was arranged between England, Spain, the Empire, and Sweden, to withstand the encroachments of France, which were a danger to them all (June 1686). To counteract this Louis invaded the territories of the Empire and captured Phalsburg, Mannheim, Spires, Worms, Treves, and other places (1688), and Spain once more prepared for war both on the French frontier of Cataluña and in Flanders. Marie Louise had died (1689) and Charles was the last of his race. He had been deeply in love with his first wife, but he was past illusions now and had no desire to marry again; but Mariana and the Austrian party were as active as ever, and were determined, if they could help it, to prevent a French King from ruling over the crumbling Empire of Spain. The Prince of Orange had surprised Europe by becoming King of England, and that fact had to a great extent altered the political balance of the world. It was no longer a shifty Stuart with an itching palm for Louis's bribes who ruled England, but a prince whose very existence was bound up in Protestantism and the exclusion of France from Flanders; a prince, moreover, under whom England and Holland were really united. Nearly all Europe was interested in keeping Spain and Flanders out of the hands of Louis, and Madrid became more than ever the centre of political intrigue. Generally speaking the Spaniards themselves were in favour of a French prince, a descendant of Anne of Austria and of Maria Theresa, but courtiers, confessors, and ministers were bought, almost to a man, by one side or the other. Badgered and pestered by those who urged upon the poor creature the duty of marrying again, the King at last referred to his uncle the Emperor the choice of a second wife for him. The lady chosen was Princess Mary Anne of Neuburg, a sister of the Empress and daughter of the Elector Palatine, to whom Charles was married in 1689. This was a check to the French interests which could only be met by war against Spain and her allies. Humières operated in Flanders against the Dutch and Spanish forces all the summer of 1689, with but little result; but in the following year (1st June, 1690) the Duke of Luxembourg defeated the allies under the Prince of Waldeck at Fleurus, where 6000 of the vanquished were killed, and 8000 made prisoners, although the Spanish rank and file covered themselves with glory in their defeat, even as they had done at Rocroy. Louis was not so fortunate in his support given to James II in his attempt to recover his English crown, and the battle of the Boyne established William of Orange firmly in his seat. He, therefore, was able to withstand the vengeance of the victorious King of France. Not so unfortunate Spain and its other allies. Mons in Hainault fell in the presence of Louis XIV himself (April 1691), and Hal in June. Savoy was completely overrun before the end of the year, whilst the armies of France on the Rhine oppressed the people and country with a tyranny of the most revolting description. The Duke of Noailles had been beaten in Cataluña (1689) by the Catalans and the Castilian soldiers sent to their aid, but the old quarrels between the people of the principality and the King's troops continued. This paralysed the opposition to the French, who in 1691 captured Ripoll and other places, and in 1692 took Urgel, whilst a strong French fleet threatened Barcelona and the coast towns, and a revolt of the Catalans themselves took place in protest against the wars entailed by the Austrian connection. The French also ceaselessly harried the Spanish possessions on the north coast of Africa and in America, either directly or by subsidising the Moors or the buccaneers. With these constant wars the funds saved by Oropesa's financial reforms were soon swallowed, whilst the enmity towards the minister still remained. The traditions of governmental corruption were not easily forgotten, and although Oropesa himself may have been—probably was— honest, his subordinates and relatives were certainly not so, and especially his wife, whose unscrupulous greed was proverbial. The German Queen too was greedy, rapacious and a virago, and in order to fulfil her mission it was necessary for her to form a party. She did so by heading Oropesa's enemies, who were the strongest influence at Court and in the country, and she was powerfully aided by Father Matilla, the King's confessor, and by the Queen-Mother, whose influence was still great. The poor King assailed on all sides by intrigue, infirm of mind and will, in wretched bodily health, had allowed himself to be persuaded that a curse of witchcraft rested upon him. But he hated change. Oropesa was kind and gentle to him, and for a time he held out. The Queen and the ambassador left him no peace, night or day, and at last he dismissed Oropesa (1691) with tears and lamentations at his helplessness.

Around the King, his German wife and her friend the baroness Berlips were now supreme, and the nominal ministers of the crown were merely ciphers. There was no limit to the greed of Mary Anne of Neuburg. The revenues again began to fall off, for many of Oropesa's reforms were revoked, and the most absolute confusion of administration resulted. There was no first minister now, and no responsibility anywhere; the King consulted the Councils direct, or indeed anyone who happened to be near him.

In 1693 the King was thought to be dying, and on his recovery he was persuaded to divide the kingdom into three governments, to be administered respectively by the Duke of Montalto, the Constable of Castile, and the Admiral of Castile, as the King's Lieutenants. This was a complete violation of the constitutions and traditions of the various States, and nearly all Spain was against it. It was for a government such as this to wring from ruined Spain resources for carrying on the war with the most powerful monarch in Christendom. The taxes could not be increased, and the only means which occurred to the ministers were to extort contributions from every person who was thought to be able to afford them, and to compel every town and village in the land to provide one soldier for each ten inhabitants. Dismay and terror were the natural result. Those chosen, and even those capable of bearing arms, fled by the thousand, and a still greater dislocation of ordinary life was produced (1695). Confusion grew daily. In 1696 it was acknowledged that no more money could be obtained from the country, and all payments were suspended.

This being the condition of things under the German faction, the French party, aided by general discontent and the money of King Louis, had now a promising prospect of bringing about a change. The King was growing more and more infirm, and had frequent fits of illness which seemed to threaten his life. The party which had the control of him in his last hours would in all probability have their way with

Spain, and the struggle now was on both sides to be in at the King's death. In the meanwhile the wars continued without cessation, and with varying fortunes. In 1693 the allies under the King of England were routed at Neerwinden, and soon after the Spanish garrison surrendered Charleroi after a 27 days' siege, whilst in the following year Noailles and Vendôme were victorious everywhere in Cataluña over the Catalan guerrilleros, and over the Germans under Hesse-Darmstadt. Then the tide changed somewhat. Luxembourg died, the French lost Dixmunde and Huy, and most important of all, Namur was captured by the King of England (September 1695). The gigantic armaments needed to face all Europe victoriously, together with the lavish expenditure of the *roi soleil*, had thrown even the finances of France into confusion, and Louis again began negotiation. First he seduced the Duke of Savoy away from the confederation, and secured peace so far as Italy was concerned (1696), and then cast all his available strength against Barcelona. There were 12,000 fighting men in the city under Hesse-Darmstadt, and the warlike Catalans struggled bravely. But the Madrid government was poverty-stricken and unready: a force was hastily organised under Don Francisco de Velasco to relieve the Catalan capital, but Vendôme made short work of them, and after 52 days' siege Barcelona fell, to be followed shortly by most of the principality. There seemed to be no end to the calamities which beset Spain all over the world. Marshal Catinat in Flanders had captured important Spanish places. The coasts of South America were devastated by buccaneers, Cataluna was in the hands of the French, the Emperor was again in a death-struggle with the Turk in Hungary, and though with a bad grace, the Madrid government were forced to join in the peace negotiations at Ryswick opened between the French and the allies. The terms agreed upon were not unfavourable to Spain. Louis restored Cataluña, Luxembourg, Mons, Ath and Courtrai to Spain, recognised William III as King of England, and gave up to the German princes all the territory he had taken from them.

This apparently lame ending to a great war, in which France had been victorious at enormous cost, was the result of the dynastic intrigues which with the failing health of Charles II were now approaching a crisis. It did not suit Louis to appear as an enemy to Spain at a time when he was plotting to obtain the succession to the crown for himself or one of his house. Both Louis and the Emperor Leopold were grandsons of Philip III, and both of them had married daughters of Philip IV. As we have seen, both the mother (Anne of Austria) and the wife (Maria Theresa) of Louis had renounced for themselves and their successors any claim to the Spanish throne. The renunciation had been most precise and solemn, but in the case of Maria Theresa had been made conditional on the payment of the dowry, which had never been paid. The claims of her descendants would seem therefore to have been preferable to those of the Archduke Charles, the Emperor's second son, who claimed as representative of Charles V in the male line.

The respective claims divided Europe into two camps. For centuries England and Germany had struggled to keep the French out of Flanders. It now looked as if the prize would fall to Louis from the mere force of circumstances. The Queen-Mother had died (May 1696), but the English ambassador Stanhope, the imperial ambassador Harrach, the Queen and her courtiers were ceaseless in their intrigues to keep possession of the King and to forward the succession of the Austrian; whilst the French party, headed by Cardinal Portocarrero, a former friend and minister of Mariana, and advised by Harcourt the French ambassador, sought to counteract them before the King finally succumbed. Soon after the death of Mariana, Oropesa had been recalled by the King (September 1696), but warned by his past experience his reforming zeal had abated. The Queen and her *camarilla* were all-powerful inside the palace, though cordially hated by the people outside; and no person suspected of sympathy with the French party was allowed to approach the King. Poor Charles, sick nearly to death, in hourly fear of poison, with a dread of his violent wife and her German bloodsuckers, and with the terror of witchcraft upon him, could only weep and mourn the happy days with his beautiful French wife. Whenever he was well enough to stand, the Queen dragged him out and made him totter and stagger in religious processions, or go through the ceremonial forms of his position, nodding and babbling incoherently to the ministers or ambassadors whom he was obliged to receive. "The King is so weak" (writes Stanhope, 14 March, 1698) "that he can scarcely lift his hand to his head to feed himself, and so extremely melancholy that neither his buffoons, dwarfs, nor puppet-shows...can in the least divert him from fancying everything that is said or done to be a temptation of the devil, and never thinking himself safe without his confessor and two friars by his side, whom he makes lie in his chamber every night." The confessor was an autocratic priest, called Father Matilla, a creature of the Queen, but there was a great noble also, Count Benavente, whose office of Gentleman of the Bedchamber gave him access to the King. He was gained by the French faction, and when the King complained of the misery he was in he advised him to consult the Cardinal Archbishop Portocarrero. One night, when the Queen had retired, the Cardinal was introduced secretly to the King's chamber. It was late at night when the Cardinal returned home, but late as it was he summoned his friends to devise a plan for rescuing the King. Monterey, Leganes, the Ronquillos, Urraca, some of the ablest and most popular of Spanish nobles, came to his summons. The first thing to do was to change the confessor, and in a few days the Court and Queen were thunderstruck to find that the King had signed an order banishing Matilla, and appointing a new confessor, Froilan

Diaz. Matilla died of poison or a broken heart within the week, and Father Diaz kept the conscience of the King in favour of the French faction. The Queen bravely stood her ground for a time, and tried to win over the priest, but without success. When she began to pester the King he plucked up courage to tell her that she wanted to kill him, and bade her leave him in peace; and at length she saw that the French faction was popular and strong and endeavoured to keep friendly with both sides.

The succession was claimed not only by the French candidate, the young Duke of Anjou, second son of the Dauphin, and the Austrian, Charles, second son of the Emperor, but also by the Electoral Prince of Bavaria as grandson, through his mother, of the Empress Margaret, younger daughter of Philip IV and first wife of the Emperor Leopold; and this candidature was the most favoured by the Spanish lawyers. Oropesa considered it good policy for him to embrace it, and this for a time introduced a third party into the palace intrigue. Louis XIV, who knew that he could not obtain Spain for his grandson without fighting for it, endeavoured as a preliminary measure to divide his opponents, and proposed the dismemberment of the Spanish monarchy; Spain, Flanders and the Indies to go to the Prince of Bavaria; Naples, Sicily, the Tuscan ports, and Guipuzcoa falling to the share of the Dauphin, whilst Milan was to be taken by the Archduke. On the plea of maintaining the balance of power he concluded a secret treaty with England and Holland to enforce this solution. Spain and Austria were indignant, and Oropesa under this impression persuaded the King to appoint the Prince Joseph Leopold of Bavaria his heir. Against this the Emperor protested so violently as to offend the Spaniards and still further injure the chances of his son; whilst Louis looked on, well satisfied with the result of his diplomacy, especially when the young Prince of Bavaria died at the age of six, under the grave suspicion of poison (February 1699).

Much now depended upon the transfer of Oropesa's influence to one side or the other. The chances were in favour of his siding with the Austrian. Famine reigned in Madrid: poverty and misery had reduced the population to the last depth of despair. There was no government worthy of the name; no one had seen the King for a long time past, and it was easy to raise a tumult under such circumstances. Suddenly in April 1699 a riot broke out. "Death to Oropesa! give us bread," cried the multitude, as they surged towards the palace. "Let us see the King!" shouted they, as they stood in front of the great balcony of the Alcazar. The Queen told them that he was asleep. "He has slept too long: wake him," was the answer, and the dying King was brought tottering out on to the balcony. Benevente told the crowd in his name that the King would pardon them for the tumult, but he could not reduce the price of bread, for it was Oropesa who had the supplies, they must ask him. The hint was enough, and Oropesa became the scapegoat, and to the sorrow of the King the minister was forced to retire. With him went into exile all the friends of the Austrian cause; and Portocarrero, the popular brothers Ronquillo, and the Frenchmen were supreme. But the Queen and a few churchmen who stood by her made one more effort to recover the ground. Ever since the advent of the new confessor Diaz she had caused him to be watched. His proceedings were secret, but it was at last reported by the spies and even chattered in the capital that strange exorcisms and ghastly incantations were being practised on the King. The full details cannot be given here[1], but the results of the exorcisms had been to reduce the King to the last extreme of bodily and mental feebleness. The Queen was furious, and tried to move the Inquisition to take action, but the Inquisition was no longer what it had been. Only three years before

[1] For particulars see essay entitled, "The Exorcism of Charles the Bewitched," in *The Year after the Armada etc.*, by Martin A. S. Hume. London, 1896.

a royal commission had been appointed to report to the King on the complaints against the Holy Office, and in a vigorous and scathing denunciation the commission condemned the Inquisition as a national danger. Thenceforward the Inquisition walked warily and for a time refused to be used as a tool of the Queen's intrigue. On the death of the Inquisitor-General she procured the appointment for a nominee of her own, who promptly laid hands on the King's confessor. But to the Queen's dismay the Council of the Inquisition refused to confirm the action of its chief. Then followed a dispute which lasted for years, to the final triumph of Diaz and the Council of the Inquisition, many of whose members were on the French side. Again the Queen saw that the French party were too strong for her and she had to make the best of it.

By the beginning of 1700 it was seen that the King's end was near. Another attempt to arrange a partition was made from London in February of that year by a treaty between France, England and Holland, the Archduke Charles being given Spain, Flanders and the Indies, the Dauphin receiving the Two Sicilies, the Milanese, the Tuscan ports and Guipuzcoa; but the Emperor would have none of it, and protested against the proposed dismemberment. The anger of the Spaniards was unbounded, especially against England, and William III dismissed the Spanish ambassador for his violent language, whilst Stanhope was forced to leave Madrid. In the meanwhile the dying King shifted from side to side as those near him at the moment swayed him. Sometimes he broke out in childish fury at his inheritance being wrangled about before his own eyes, and even husbands proposed for his wife before he was dead. Usually his sympathy was more on the Austrian side than the French, through the influence of the Queen and the excessive zeal of the French party; but Portocarrero was a host in himself. The Pope was on the side of the French prince, and Louis XIV now openly threatened to oppose by force the attempt to establish the

Archduke on the throne. Torn with conflicting emotions Charles the Bewitched lay on his death-bed at the end of September 1700. All the images and relics of special sanctity in Madrid were brought to his bedside, until the room became too full to hold any more. Portocarrero never left him, and the churchmen urged that his conscience would not be free until he had by will left his kingdom to his rightful heir. "Only God," he sighed, "can give kingdoms, I am nothing now." But by the 3rd October he gave way and signed a will leaving the whole of his vast dominions to Philip of Anjou. Once after that he wavered under the Queen's persuasion, and promised at last to make the Archduke his heir. But it was never done. On the 29th October he signed a decree appointing the Queen, Portocarrero, Arias, the Duke of Montalto, the Inquisitor-General Mendoza, Counts Frigiliana and Benavente a committee of government pending the arrival of the new King in Spain. From that day till the afternoon of the 1st November, 1700, Charles the Bewitched lay dying. Violent fevers and deadly lethargy alternately shook or paralysed his decrepit frame—39 years of age, but looking 80—until it could resist no longer, and like the last flickering ember of what once was a great furnace, the degenerate worn-out race of the Spanish Habsburgs sank to its inglorious ending, after nearly two centuries of sustained calamity unexampled in the history of the world. From the greatest Charles to the smallest one disaster and decay had uninterruptedly pursued their unfortunate people. The inheritance of the Empire, and especially the possession of Flanders, had imposed untold misery upon millions of innocent Spaniards; unwise fiscal laws had brought to ruin a prosperous country; favouritism, sloth and bigotry had emasculated a vigorous and hardy race; and as a crowning legacy of woe, the last King of the house of Austria left Spain exhausted and bankrupt, a prey to the vultures who flocked to fight over its remains.

CHAPTER XII.

PHILIP V, 1700—1714.

IMMEDIATELY following the death of Charles a hurried meeting of the regents was held in the palace, and soon afterwards the saloons and antechambers were crowded with an anxious gathering of grandees, bishops, courtiers and foreign ambassadors, to hear the contents of the momentous will which was to decide the future of Spain. The dying King had changed his mind so often that there was still considerable doubt about his final disposition, at least among the Austrian party, who hoped against hope that the Queen had gained her point at last. But all uncertainty was soon removed by the jubilant announcement that the young Duke of Anjou, Philip de Bourbon, was the new King of Spain. Louis XIV himself was doubtless well prepared for the news, but the decision imposed upon him was of vast importance. It was clear that he would have to fight for it in either case, but if the partition of Spain according to his own proposal was persevered in the territory of France itself would be greatly increased, whereas if he accepted for his grandson the whole inheritance it would be the house of Bourbon, and not France, which would permanently benefit. In such case his reported boast, that the Pyrenees had disappeared with the accession of Anjou, only meant that for a generation or two family ties would unite the policy of the two nations. Not without some hesitation he decided to prefer the aggrandisement of his family to that of his country, and introduced his young grandson to his Court as the new King of Spain. Philip V was a bright-faced handsome lad of 17—as his portrait at Versailles testifies—and Spain was full of hope that the spell of evil was broken at last. As soon as swift couriers could carry to Madrid the news of his acceptance of the inheritance, Philip V was proclaimed in his capital as King of Spain and the Indies, with all the pomp and ceremonial of old times, and almost simultaneously the first Bourbon was acclaimed in Flanders, Naples, Sicily, and Milan. Even Cataluña, where the German Prince of Hesse-Darmstadt was viceroy, accepted with rejoicing the new sovereign whose first act of kingship was to dismiss Hesse-Darmstadt and replace him by Portocarrero's nephew the Count de Palma.

Philip bade farewell to France on the 28th January, 1701, and his progress to his capital was a triumphal march. Hopes beat high. Surely now, thought the people, the past of starvation and oppression was gone for ever. This smiling young prince would bring them peace and plenty—aye and glory too—with the help of the all-powerful King of France, henceforward for ever their friend against all the world. But the evils of Spain were too deeply rooted to be smiled away by a pleasure-loving boy.

The Duke of Harcourt, the clever French Ambassador who knew Spain well, took his seat in the Council—which, said Louis XIV, in future all French ambassadors must do. The friends of the Austrians were banished to a man, and even the Queen was sent away to Toledo. Portocarrero had nothing to do now but carry out the orders of the Frenchmen, and he did it with alacrity. Unwarned by the fate of Oropesa, the first reforms he adopted were a wholesale abolition of offices, concessions, grants and pensions conferred by previous monarchs, a measure which, it is true, diminished the waste of the treasury, but caused the deepest discontent in a capital whose main industry was the public service. Frenchmen and foreigners had for many years done most of the work and trading in Madrid and the north, and many of these men with the advent of a French monarch also threw themselves into government places, which redoubled the discontent of Spaniards. The disorganisation in the finances was so complete that those who lived on the confusion, a wealthy and powerful class, were able successfully to obstruct all attempts at real reform.

In his instruction to the new French ambassador Marsin, sent to Spain to replace Harcourt, Louis XIV writes: "Extreme confusion reigns in all affairs; it would appear as if the monarchs of Spain had tried by their bad conduct to destroy their realm rather than to preserve it. This disorder has grown so much in the last reign that it may be said that there is now in Spain no government at all. The rights of the crown in the West Indies have been sacrificed to the greed of the viceroys and subordinate officials, who have ruined commerce, which is now monopolised by the foreign enemies of Spain. The incapacity and self-seeking of ministers have prevented the reform of the financial disorder; *for it is sufficient in Spain that an abuse be old-established for it to be scrupulously maintained without any care being taken to consider whether a thing which perhaps may have been good in the past is bad for the present.*" In these last words Louis expressed tersely the principal difficulty which always stood in the way of the introduction of reforms into Spain; and it was this conservative feeling, and its kindred hatred to foreigners as such, that rendered almost barren even the efforts of enlightened ministers and financial experts sent by Louis. The young King himself soon lost heart and gave himself up to idleness and dissipation, which frequently called for the angry reproofs of his grandfather, whose formal advice to him when he left for Spain, full of wisdom as it was, especially cautioned him against self-indulgence in every form. But Philip was young and thoughtless. "Never forget that you are a Frenchman," wrote his grandfather to him, and in this he obeyed him. The two men who swayed most of the administrative power, Portocarrero and Arias, Archbishop of Seville, vied with each other in truckling to France in order to keep supreme. French peers were given the same rights in Spain as Spanish grandees. French servants crowded the palace, French adventurers swarmed and swaggered in the streets, and Portocarrero and his Council became more and more unpopular. Anyone who dared to gainsay the French faction was branded as an "Austrian," and jealousy and discontent soon pervaded the capital. During all the reign of Charles II no new Cortes of Castille had been called, the permanent deputation of the previous Cortes continuing from time to time, as a mere formality, the supplies formerly voted. It now became necessary for the Cortes to recognise the new King and receive his oath to maintain the privileges of Castile. The members of the old Cortes collected for this ceremonial as usual in the church of San Geronimo (April 1701); but when some of the nobles, undesirous of leaving the reorganisation of the finances in the hands of the Frenchman Orry, and anxious to reassert the old constitution of Castile, clamoured for a new Cortes to be convoked to discuss ways and means, Portocarrero and his Council refused, and the extinction of the parliamentary rights of the Kingdom was complete.

The young King was betrothed to Marie Louise, daughter of Victor Amadeo of Savoy, and in September 1701 he went to meet his bride at Barcelona, receiving the oath of allegiance of the Cortes of Aragon at Zaragoza on his way thither. The Aragonese received him with tumultuous joy, although when it came to voting supplies they were less expansive, and afterwards in Barcelona where the Catalan Cortes were assembled, the same warm welcome was extended to him. The Cortes of Cataluña also were not effete yet. They were liberal in their offers of money, but they bargained for full return in the form of privileges. Philip wanted money badly and gave the

Catalans, but with a bad grace, almost all they wanted before they voted the supplies. He was indeed already faced by the coalition of Europe against him. The Emperor had protested against his accession from the first: the Queen-Dowager and her friend the Inquisitor-General swore that Charles II in his last hours had verbally revoked his will and had left the kingdom to the Archduke. William III of England was furious at the way he and others had been hoodwinked by the talk of partition, and still more at the recognition by Louis of the Pretender as King of England on the death of James II (September 1701). Thus, although England and Holland had consented formally to recognise Philip, the elements of a strife in which all Europe was to join were already let loose. The Emperor was only just free of his struggle with the Turk, but when the French troops occupied Mantua by permission of the duke he at once declared war against Louis for the violation of the treaty of Ryswick, and sent Prince Eugene in command of the Imperial troops to Italy. A more direct blow was struck at Philip V by the promotion of revolts in Naples, and even before the young King had met his bride on the frontier at Figueras he saw the embarcation of all the troops he could muster in Cataluña for his Italian kingdom (December 1701). But he showed thus early that he was made of different stuff from the later Austrians by insisting, against the advice of all his ministers, upon himself going to Naples and Sicily and meeting his Italian subjects face to face. Philip II, he said, had lost Holland because he had not gone thither in person. "If I lose territories it shall not be for that reason."

The new child-Queen (she was only fourteen), when she crossed the frontier, dismissed her Piedmontese attendants, but Louis XIV and Mme de Maintenon had placed by her side one of the cleverest old women in Europe, Anne Marie de la Tremouille, the widow of the Duke of Bracciano (Flavio Orsini) whom the French called Princess des Ursins and the

Spaniards Ursinos. She was an epitome of political knowledge and court-procedure, and soon obtained complete dominion over the Queen and her young husband. Philip left his bride behind him, to his grief and hers—for they were already deeply in love with each other—and sailed from Barcelona for Naples in April 1702, whilst the Queen slowly journeyed through Cataluña and Aragon to Madrid. Nothing could exceed the diligence and ability with which this girl of fourteen superintended the government in Madrid during the absence of her husband. Instead of the round of dull devotion and idle entertainments with which other Queen-Consorts had filled their lives, she, with the wise old Princess of Ursinos at her side, was untiring in her application to work. She would sign nothing until she understood it. She insisted upon all complaints being investigated and reports made to her. Supplies of men and money for the war in which Philip was engaged were collected and remitted with a regularity unequalled for years past. The manners of the Court were reformed; immorality, so long rampant in Madrid, was frowned at, and instead of the news of the wars in which Spain was engaged slowly filtering from the gossips of the palace to the streets, the Queen herself read from the balcony to the people below the despatches she received from her absent husband. She did more in the way of administrative reform than any of her predecessors, but as yet she could only administer things as she found them, and, as we have seen, the root of the governmental system itself was vicious. Portocarrero and his Council were extremely unpopular, and the Austrian party was busy intriguing, so that the brave young Queen was heavily handicapped and was necessarily guided by the Princess of Ursinos, whose task it was to bend Spain to the will and interest of Louis XIV. But the Spaniards were suspicious and hated foreigners. During Philip's absence from Madrid Louis instructed his ambassador Marsin cautiously to broach the cession of Flanders to France. Spain had no money, he said, to pay for the war in Italy, and as a last resource he had to meet all the expense. It was not just that he should do so without some return. The King was easily persuaded, but the proposal got wind and a perfect storm of protest from the country caused it to be shelved for the present.

Meanwhile Prince Eugene had been operating against the French in Northern Italy, besieging Mantua and Cremona, but with indefinite results except the capture of Marshal Villeroy; while the rebellion in Naples in favour of the Archduke, which had broken out and been partly suppressed in September 1701, still smouldered. Philip V arrived at Naples with a fleet of 28 French vessels on the 16th April, 1702, and found the city seething with revolutionary excitement, which his ardent attempts to conciliate the Neapolitans were insufficient entirely to allay. Thence the King travelled to his dukedom of Milan (June 1702) and with an army of 30,000 men, assisted by the Duke of Vendôme and Count Aguilar, he crossed the Po in July, defeating on its banks an imperial force collected to oppose him. On the 15th August the two armies met in a great battle near Luzzara, where Prince Eugene unsuccessfully attempted to surprise the French. The losses on both sides were great, but the advantage was unquestionably in favour of the Bourbon army. Philip in this and other subsequent engagements bore himself with great gallantry, and by the end of the campaign he had the satisfaction of seeing the imperialists cut off from communication with the north although Prince Eugene himself left for Vienna to be made Minister of War. Philip V was back in Milan on his way to Spain by the end of September 1702, a prey already, young as he was, to the hypochondriacal melancholy which subsequently engulphed him. He was a brave and ardent lad, but the task imposed upon him was far beyond his capability and he eventually sank beneath it. The evil traditions which were ruining Spain had, indeed, now struck so deep that no one man however gifted could have remedied them, much less a young foreigner of no great ability. Troubles were thickening around Spain on all sides. The league between England, Holland, Denmark, Austria, and the new kingdom of Prussia was now complete: England was to furnish two-thirds of the naval force, and one-third of the troops required by the allies, and in the case of victory, the Archduke Charles was to have Spain and the Indies, most of Flanders was to have been annexed to Holland, whilst England was to enjoy free commerce with America, and retain any coast places she might capture.

A contingent of 10,000 men under Marlborough was sent to the Rhine (1702), and King William was himself preparing to follow when he suddenly died. Marlborough, however, was instructed to assure Holland and the Empire that Anne would respect the engagements entered into by her predecessor. In Spain the enemies of the Bourbons were busy. The Admiral of Castile (Melgar[1]), one of the prime advisers of the two former German Queens, and many grandees of the highest rank were in close communication with the allies; the dismissed Hesse-Darmstadt—now a grandee of Spain—was plotting in Lisbon, and between them they proposed that the English and Dutch fleets should surprise Cadiz. In July 1702, fifty ships under Sir George Rooke, with 12,000 men commanded by the Duke of Ormond, suddenly sailed into the bay and summoned the city to submit to King Charles III. As had happened in 1587 and 1596, the place, and indeed all the coast of Andalucia, were practically defenceless: 300 men only were in the garrison and the walls were crumbling beneath the rusty guns. There were no munitions of war and no naval force, and the whole south of Spain was apparently at the mercy of the enemy. But fortunately for the Spaniards there was no Drake, or Howard, or Ralegh, on the English fleet this time. Whilst the commanders

[1] Juan Tomas Enriquez de Cabrera, Count de Melgar, and after his father's death, seventh Duke of Medina de Rio Seco, in whose family the Admiralty of Castile was hereditary. Melgar died in Portugal in 1705 and the hereditary post of admiral then became extinct.

were wrangling over the plan of attack and sacking coast villages, the brave heart of the little "Savoyarde" in Madrid was shaming the slothful Spaniards into action. Unless they moved more quickly she told them she herself would start on the morrow and arouse Andalucia. Her jewels and valuables were offered for the national defence, and her eloquence spurred Portocarrero and others to make similar sacrifices. Archbishops gave their revenues, nobles their lands, the people their poor savings, and soon Andalucia was in arms. A great silver fleet of 13 galleons with a convoy of 23 Spanish and French ships on its way to Spain heard that Cadiz was threatened by enemies and took refuge in Vigo. Whilst Andalucia was arming the English before Cadiz learnt the news and sailed away to Vigo. There they forced the harbour, and Chateau Renaud, the French admiral, was overpowered. Nine of the galleons were captured and the rest sunk, and all the convoy captured or destroyed. A part of the treasure had already been landed and was seized by the government, but most of it fell into the hands of the English, and the loss crippled Philip sadly.

When the young King arrived in Madrid from Italy (January 1703), the nobles who sided with the Austrians had cast off the mask and had fled, and the forces for and against him were ranged at home and abroad. He acted with spirit and decision beyond his years, taking into his own hands the whole management of affairs, to the exclusion even of Portocarrero, and daring moreover to resent and check the haughty interference of the new French ambassador Cardinal d'Estrées, who had replaced Marsin. The Cardinal thought that he had been sent to govern Spain and began by offending Portocarrero and the rest of the Spanish ministers. He then objected to the influence of the Princess of Ursinos and managed to set Louis XIV against her. Louis wrote an angry letter to his grandson, directing him to depend entirely upon D'Estrées and Portocarrero, and to abandon the management of affairs himself. But the Princess outwitted the diplomatists and the old King; placed herself in the position of the injured party, and instead of being driven out of Spain, as was intended, had to be prayed by Louis as a favour to stay where she was.

Thenceforward for a time she was almost supreme, and independent of Louis XIV. Portocarrero and Archbishop Arias retired; d'Estrées returned to France, and the ministers who surrounded the King, Count Montellano and the Marquis de Canales, were deep in the confidence of the Princess. Very gradually, and amidst constant jealousy and intrigues between French and Spanish, some sort of order was introduced into the financial management of the country. The lavish traditions of favouritism which had grown up under the later Habsburgs were superseded, old irrecoverable arrears of taxes which kept land out of cultivation were remitted. The administration of justice was simplified, a large number of special tribunals abolished; the monastic orders were regulated, and limited in numbers; and many small measures of interior reform were introduced, not on the recommendation of the Cortes—for they were not called—but by edict of the King after enquiry into petitions laid before him by men of standing or knowledge. But Spain was now fighting the allies nearly all over Europe, in union with the Empire; and most of Philip's time and thoughts were taken up in the difficult task of raising men and money from his exhausted country. He completely re-organised the army; introduced the French system and tactics, armed his infantry with bayonets on their muskets, abolished the golilla or stiff curved collar, formed squadrons of dragoons to act as mounted infantry, and companies of grenadiers. Poor as the country was, the example of the King and his wife infused some spirit into the people; and in an incredibly short space of time, Philip had a good force of 30,000 infantry and 10,000 cavalry on the frontier of Portugal, the King of which country had joined the great alliance against him.

Considerable forces were also sent to Flanders and Italy, and once more Spain showed that, though misgovernment had brought her down, her spirit had not been entirely crushed. Some of Philip's success must in fairness be given to Orry, the French financier who was bringing into order, with infinite patience and skill, the monetary affairs of the country. There were no lavish favourites to squander pensions to adherents, no bombastic and inflated corruption to intercept funds before they reached the treasury, and the only people who complained were those whose pay, pensions and emoluments, had been stopped. These formed a large and powerful class in Madrid and the chief cities, and from them the supporters of the Austrian were principally drawn.

Meanwhile the war had been going on with varying success elsewhere. In 1702 Marlborough had driven Boufflers as far south as Cologne on the Rhine, and Liege on the Meuse, and in the following year he completed the conquest of the Electorate of Cologne by taking Bonn, Huy, and Limburg, whilst, on the other hand, the French under Villars and the Elector of Bavaria had beaten the allies at Hochstädt (September 1703). The unstable Duke of Savoy had been drawn away from the side of the French King and his son-in-law Philip, and joined the allies against them, receiving the investiture of Montferrat as the reward of his apostasy. But the main result of the fighting in the two years had been to reduce the Emperor to a condition almost as abject as that of his late Spanish kinsmen. The Hungarian rebels were at the gates of Vienna, and the victory gained by Marshal Tallard over the Prince of Hesse laid open the road to the French on the other. It was then that the genius of Prince Eugene and Marlborough shone brightest, and plucked victory out of defeat. The story is told vividly by Eugene himself in his memoirs, and cannot be repeated here, but it will suffice to say that Marlborough, acting in concert with Eugene, followed the course of the Rhine and Necker, reached the Danube near

Ulm, where he joined Prince Louis of Baden (22 June, 1704), and stormed the heights of Schellenberg on the 2nd July. Thus he mastered the course of the Danube, with the exception of Ulm and Ingoldstadt. On the 11th August Marlborough and Eugene joined, and together (13 August, 1704) attacked the Bavarians and French under the Elector and Marshal Tallard, at Blenheim. Marlborough with the English and Dutch commanded the left wing, and Eugene with the Austrians the right. The result, mainly owing to the skill of Eugene and Marlborough, was the utter rout of the French. Tallard was taken prisoner, and 40,000 men out of the 60,000 French and Bavarians were captured or disabled. This drove the French out of Germany, cowed the Hungarians, and placed Bavaria at the Emperor's mercy.

But in Spain matters of even greater direct interest were taking place. The Archduke had visited Holland and England, and had been received in both countries as Charles III of Spain. An English and Dutch squadron under Sir George Rooke, with 14,000 men, conveyed Charles to Lisbon, where he disembarked with royal honours (4 May, 1704) surrounded by the Spanish grandees who had espoused his cause. The intention was to invade Spain rapidly in union with the Portuguese army of 28,000 men, in the hope that discontented Spaniards would join them. But Portugal was unready, and in the meanwhile, with an activity new to Spain, troops from Flanders, Milan, and elsewhere had been concentrated on the Portuguese frontier to the number of 40,000 men, under the Duke of Berwick, natural son of James II. Philip V joined him from Madrid, and invaded Portugal from Alcantara (May 1704) simultaneously with movements on the north under the Marquis de las Minas, and on the south under Tilly. Place after place fell almost without a blow. With hardly a check the Spanish force overran the greater part of Portugal, until the heat became too great for the continuance of the campaign, when (July 1704) Philip returned to Madrid after demolishing the fortresses of Portalegre, Castel Davide and Montalvan, whilst Berwick joined the force operating in the northern province of Beira. An English fleet commanded by Rooke sailed from Lisbon with Hesse-Darmstadt and 4,000 men on board, and attacked Barcelona, but without success, as the Catalans, for the moment, were loyal; a similar result attended another squadron which threatened the coasts of Andalucia. But Rooke's fleet on its way back called in at Gibraltar. The fortress was neglected, and there were only 100 men in garrison. The place capitulated with but little difficulty (July 23, 1704), and the gate of the Mediterranean became an English possession.

A powerful French fleet of 52 vessels had been concentrating at Toulon to oppose the English in the Mediterranean, and on receiving news of the capture of Gibraltar sailed under the Count de Toulouse, natural son of Louis XIV, but after an indecisive engagement before Malaga (24 August, 1704) were driven back to port by Cloudesley Shovell, and thenceforward during the war the English and Dutch remained masters of the sea. A desperate attempt of the Spaniards under Villadarias and the French under Tessé to recover Gibraltar also failed (February 1705), and Tessé was recalled. In the absence of Philip on the Portuguese frontier the Princess of Ursinos had at last succumbed to French intrigue against her (1704) and had retired to Toulouse on the threat of Louis XIV that if she did not do so immediately he would abandon Spain and his grandson to their fate. The instructions of the Duke de Grammont, the new French ambassador to Spain, were that he was to make a clean sweep of all the friends of the Princess and obtain control of the government. But Louis had underrated the power and ability of Marie Louise, who deeply deplored the banishment of the Princess. Marshal Berwick resented Grammont's interference and retired. Orry, the finance minister, was sent back to France, the Spanish ministers were dismissed, and the obedient servants of France, the

Duke of Montalto, Counts Monterey and Mancera, Archbishop Arias, and their like, were restored to office. But the young Queen took no pains to hide her opposition to the change. Louis sent scolding letters to her upon her presumption in wishing, "at the age of 18 to govern a vast disorganised monarchy," against the advice of those so much older and wiser than herself; but, at last recognising the uselessness of openly opposing the wishes of Marie Louise, he took the wiser course of conciliating and re-enlisting the offended Princess of Ursinos. In vain his representatives in Madrid warned him that she could not be trusted to serve French interests blindly. She was too clever and strong to be ignored, and was invited to Versailles, given *carte blanche*, and returned in triumph to Madrid (August 1705). Orry was sent back to Spain, Grammont was recalled to France, and once more the triumphant Mistress of the Robes governed the Queen, the Queen governed the King, and the King was supposed to govern the country, whilst the Spanish nobles, in jealous gloom or fuming discontent, looked on at the foreign intrigues which were juggling with the destinies of Spain.

During the year 1705 the English and Portuguese had been carrying the war over the border into Spain, but with no permanent result. In the autumn they besieged Badajoz with a strong force under General Lord Galway, but Marshal Tessé came up just in time to relieve the place and the allies retired, Galway being wounded in the fight (15th October, 1705. The Earl of Peterborough also arrived in Lisbon with 12,000 men, and with a considerable fleet reduced a number of places on the Spanish coast. Hesse-Darmstadt joined them at Gibraltar, and in August 1705 they landed a strong force at Denia on the Valencian coast. Already the kingdom of Valencia was ready for revolt, and Charles III was proclaimed King of Spain amidst the plaudits of the people. Brushing aside the attempt to restrain them the forces of the allies marched to Valencia, largely reinforced by disaffected

Spaniards, and were received throughout the kingdom with enthusiasm. In the meanwhile the fleet had pushed on to Barcelona, where the Austrian King Charles III landed with Peterborough and Hesse-Darmstadt. The Catalans were "Austrians" now almost to a man; the Viceroy Velasco in the city was short of men and material, and was soon surrounded by land and sea. On the 14th September, 1705, an attempt was made to storm Monjuich by Hesse-Darmstadt and Peterborough simultaneously, in which the former commander was killed. The bombardment was kept up on the following days, and on the 17th a bomb exploded the magazine of Monjuich, which fortress then fell into the hands of the allies. From this point of vantage the attack upon the devoted city was redoubled and for a fortnight the terrible destruction continued unabated. On the 3rd October, Peterborough gave Velasco five hours in which to surrender the place, which it was seen could hold out no longer. Whilst Peterborough was arranging with the Viceroy the terms of the capitulation, the Catalan citizens rose against the Neapolitan and Spanish soldiers, and a terrible massacre occurred. The country people in the suburbs joined the citizens, and the German troops under the Archduke entered the walls at the same time. Peterborough, indignant at the action of his allies, whilst he— the commander-in-chief—was negotiating, offered to restore order and save the lives of the Viceroy and the Bourbon troops. He chivalrously kept his word, restoring the plunder taken by his German allies, and escorting the Spaniards in safety to the boats. When all was over, and the English troops had mastered disorder, Charles III of Spain, the Austrian Archduke, entered the Catalan capital in state, and received the oath of allegiance as sovereign Count of Barcelona (5 November, 1705). By the end of the year all Valencia and Cataluña and part of Aragon had thrown off the yoke of the Bourbon King, and rapine and anarchy reigned supreme over the war-swept provinces. Whilst this was happening in Spain the Bourbon cause had prospered for the moment in Northern Italy, Prince Eugene having been forced back by Vendôme into the Tyrol after the battles of Cassano and Cassinato; whilst Villars succeeded in preventing Marlborough from penetrating into Lorraine, the English general being confined to Flanders, where he endeavoured to raise the siege of Liege, which place was invested by Villeroy. In the following year 1706 (23 May) Marlborough vanquished Villeroy at the great battle of Ramillies, driving the French to Brussels with a loss of 13,000 killed. This led to the occupation of Brabant and most of Spanish Flanders by the allies, Ostend itself falling after only ten days' siege. The Bourbon cause was now (1706) as unfortunate in Italy, where Prince Eugene at length succeeded in effecting a junction with Savoy, and at Turin (Sept. 7) completely routed the French under Marsin and the Duke of Orleans, the French and Bourbon troops thereupon retiring from Northern Italy by an arrangement with the Emperor.

The great interest in the struggle was thus centered in Spain. Philip and his Queen were well-nigh at their wits' end. The discontent of the Spanish nobles in the capital had come to a head, and they had, through the Duke of Medina-Celi, remonstrated against the exclusively French influence which surrounded the King, demanding that the French ambassador should not sit at the Council, and that affairs should be despatched as formerly by a Spanish Secretary of State. But when the complaining nobles themselves were invited to take charge of affairs they refused. Most of their order in Valencia, Aragon and Cataluña, had declared for the Austrian, and those who still stood by the Bourbons were sulky at the complete loss of the pay, pensions, and plunder which they had enjoyed under the former Austrian régime. The struggle for Philip's crown had reached its acute stage. All the east of Spain had thrown off his allegiance; and the south was almost ready to do so. To whom could he turn but to the France that had sent him on his difficult errand? He and his young wife had tried their best to be Spanish first and French afterwards, but if Spaniards stood aloof in suspicion of them, then upon Louis XIV they must lean. And they did so. "To your Majesty," wrote Philip, "after God I owe my crown. You will not let the sceptre be torn from the hands in which you have placed it, nor will you allow me to be sent back to France a discrowned King." He would, he said, himself head his army to recover Cataluña, and begged his grandfather to advise and help him in this supreme crisis of his fortunes. Marie Louise, too, humbled herself before the French King, and promised to be guided in her regency only by the French ambassador Amelot. All the French troops that could be spared from the Portuguese frontier were withdrawn, Marshal Berwick remaining there on the defensive with such fresh Spanish levies as could be raised; and Philip, with immense difficulty, at last found himself at the head of a force sufficiently strong to march on Cataluña, under the guidance of Marshal Tessé. He left Madrid in February 1706 with 20,000 men and marched through disaffected Aragon towards rebel Cataluña. The plan agreed upon was for the King's army to attack Barcelona direct from Aragon, whilst at the same time the Duke de Noailles with a French force advanced upon the city from the north, and the Count de Toulouse blockaded it by sea. The Austrian King retired behind the walls of Barcelona, and the bombardment began in April, the King himself remaining in the midst of the operations. The Archduke inside had but a small garrison, but the whole province was in his favour, and the savage Catalan guerilleros left the Bourbon besiegers no peace, while even the women and boys in the city made frequent determined sallies against the French army. At length on the 7th May, when Philip had gained the outworks, and was about to capture the city, the English fleet appeared and Toulouse fled. Eight thousand fresh troops were landed for the Archduke, and as a crowning disaster news came to Philip that the allies had beaten the Spaniards on the

Portuguese frontier and were marching on Madrid. Escape was the only alternative. But how? All Aragon behind the King was in semi-revolt; and Philip had the humiliation of stealing away into France, leaving behind him all his baggage, guns and stores. From Perpignan Philip travelled rapidly by Narbonne, Toulouse, and Pau, into Navarre, and so to Madrid, where he arrived heartbroken and well-nigh despairing on the 6th June. But even there no repose was vouchsafed to him. Marshal Berwick was in full retreat before the allies under the Earl of Galway, and the Marquis de las Minas and the King and his Court fled to Burgos (20 June). With marvellous rapidity the allies marched from Salamanca, and a few days after Philip V had disappeared. Charles III was proclaimed with all pomp King of Spain in the capital of the realm, amidst the gloomy silence of the Madrileños. The rest of the cities of Castile which were occupied by the allied troops followed the example of Madrid, offering only a tacit opposition to the new King, but all Castile outside the reach of the English muskets stood faithful to Philip.

But Berwick in the meanwhile was not idle. He had already made Galway's communications difficult; and now with considerable reinforcements from Navarre he advanced to attack the allies in Madrid. Philip shook himself out of the melancholy which had prompted him to listen to suggestions for his embarcation for America, and again became energetic. The allies evacuated Madrid, and fled on Berwick's approach to Alcalá, where they were joined by Charles III and Peterborough. But disorganization had seized them, and they made no stand at Alcalá, but retreated into the kingdom of Valencia; and Philip entered his capital again amidst the joy of his people (October 1706). In Valencia Charles III was still supreme. The Marquis of Santa Cruz, admiral of the Spanish galleys, joined Charles and delivered to him the arsenal of Cartagena; and more important still, Aragon at last decided to break with the Bourbons, and the Austrian King was proclaimed in Zaragoza (July 1706). Thenceforward the war raged with varying fortunes. Cartagena was recaptured by Count Mahony, but the allies took the Balearic Isles for Charles. Alcantara was again taken by the Bourbon troops, but Naples declared in favour of Charles (May 1707). Alicante, which had held out so long for Philip, now fell into the hands of the allies, and through the whole of the kingdom of Valencia the war was pursued with vigour, particularly by Berwick, who commanded Philip's forces. It may be said generally that, so far as Spain was concerned, the beginning of 1707 marked a great change in favour of Philip's cause. The two Castiles, Navarre, the Basque provinces, most of Andalucia and Estremadura, had now definitely and vigorously espoused the cause of the Bourbon, and had spared no sacrifice to help it. Whatever may have been Philip's failings, his name of "El animoso" (The Spirited) was well deserved, and his bravery and activity in the excitement of war had touched a sympathetic chord in the hearts of his people. Money that had been hoarded for years was brought out for him. Men who might well have avoided the hardships and dangers of war eagerly joined his standard, and almost the last ducat to be obtained in the towns of Castile was cheerfully lavished in his service. Philip knew now who were his friends and who were his enemies. The sulky nobles in Madrid who had welcomed the Austrian were banished or had fled, the Queen-Dowager was packed off to Bayonne, and the struggle had become localised. It was all Spain against the East and North-East: the Gothic-Celt-Iberians against the men of Romance blood.

Spain had lost the Milanese by the retirement of the Bourbon troops from North Italy. But bitter as had been the blow to her, the armies withdrawn were welcome as reinforcements for the defence of Spain itself. In the spring of 1707 it was seen that the critical battle was approaching. Berwick with the Bourbon army was at Almansa, endeavouring to avoid an engagement until the new French army from Italy under the Duke of Orleans should approach; whilst Galway and Las Minas were trying to force a battle. Berwick's force was weak, especially in infantry, but the Spanish officers under him were chafing at his necessary inaction, and murmuring that his English blood was stronger than his Spanish loyalty. Suddenly, on the 25th April 1707, Galway attacked Berwick's army. Everything was in favour of the allies, but the gallantry of the Spanish cavalry and Berwick's dash turned the tide when the victory of the allies seemed assured, and the English and German troops were routed with great slaughter. The victory was complete: 12,000 prisoners were taken by Berwick and 5,000 of the allies were killed, whilst the Spanish loss only amounted to 2,000 men. The battle of Almansa gave Spain to the Bourbons. Berwick was made a grandee of Spain, with the dukedom now borne by his lineal descendant the Duke of Alba, and was decorated with the Golden Fleece: it was evident that the greater part of Spain preferred the Frenchman, and this battle practically confined the Austrian to the principality of Cataluña. Zaragoza and the rest of Aragon did not long resist the combined armies of Berwick and Orleans.

The autonomy of the Aragonese, so stubbornly held in the past, those privileges which even Philip II, with all his power, dared only sap stealthily, were abolished by a stroke of the pen by Philip V, thanks to the victorious armies of Frenchmen which crushed the ancient kingdom under their iron heels. The French cause in Germany also prospered under Villars. Marshal Tessé forced Prince Eugene to raise the siege of Toulon and retire beyond the Alps into Italy again; but Marlborough in the Netherlands held Vendôme on the defensive. Early in the following year 1708 Admiral Leake with a British squadron reduced the island of Sardinia—a Spanish possession—and the Moors captured the fortress of Oran, which for centuries had been held by Spanish arms. But in the Netherlands the Bourbons received a crushing blow in 1708. Vendôme had been joined by a French force, nominally led by the Duke of Burgundy, the eldest son of the Dauphin; and Ghent and Bruges opened their gates to him. Marlborough, who was waiting for Prince Eugene, placed himself between them and Brussels, to protect the capital, but perceiving that Vendôme was about to besiege Oudenarde, he determined to attack him at once. By a rapid march he crossed the Dender and secured Lessines, and forced the French across the Scheldt. Cadogan held the passage of the Scheldt at Oudenarde, and, thanks to dissensions between Vendôme and Burgundy, was able to surprise and destroy the French advance. The superior generalship of Marlborough completely routed the main body, 9,000 Frenchmen escaping to France, and the rest of the survivors taking refuge in Ghent (11 July 1708). Marlborough followed up the victory by capturing Lille (22 October 1708), Ghent, and Bruges (December), and practically driving the Bourbon force out of what had been Spanish Flanders. The winter was a terrible one, and the resources of France were well-nigh exhausted. There was no adequate force between the victorious troops of Marlborough and Eugene, and the gates of Paris. By a great effort the Emperor Joseph had sent a fresh army under Staremberg to aid his brother in Cataluña, and the English parliament had voted a million sterling to carry on the war vigorously. Louis had in 1706 made overtures of peace, on terms which would secure Spain and the Indies to the Austrian, Flanders to the Dutch, whilst Philip was to receive Milan, Naples and Sicily. This would have suited the Dutch; but neither the Emperor nor the English would agree to it. After the disastrous campaign of Oudenarde, Louis was again forced to sue for peace (spring, 1709). This time he offered to surrender the whole Spanish succession, but as Philip had just caused his infant son Luis to receive the oath of allegiance from the Cortes as heir to the Spanish Crown, the allies, not unnaturally, demanded some guarantee that Louis XIV would insist upon his grandson's renunciation of the Spanish Crown. This he refused—indeed it is almost certain that the proposal itself was only a feint to gain time, and divide the allies—and the war consequently re-commenced.

Marlborough and Eugene held most of Flanders, but Mons in Hainault was still in the hands of the French, closely beleaguered by the allies. Villars advanced from Valenciennes to relieve the place. He had to cross a wooded ridge by an open gap between two forests. Here Marlborough met him (11 September 1709), and the superior generalship of the Englishman enabled him, though repeatedly repulsed, completely to rout Villars, the only French marshal he had not already vanquished. This battle of Malplaquet was the most deadly in the 18th century, no less than 40,000 men being returned as killed and wounded, and Mons and the rest of Hainault fell into the hands of the allies. In Spain itself the war was almost at a standstill. The jealousy between the French and Spanish troops had reached such a point that, in the autumn of 1709, they were nearly attacking each other, and the important fortress of Balaguer in Cataluña had been lost in consequence. Bézons, the French marshal, was even accused of plotting to come to terms with the allies and place the Duke of Orleans, Philip's cousin, on the throne of Aragon. This feeling, added to the critical condition of France, decided Louis to adopt a fresh policy, in union with Philip. The latter affected to free himself entirely from French tutelage, and to depend upon Spanish support alone. The capital was already in revolt against the interference of French ministers in the government and even against the Princess of Ursinos. Amelot, the French ambassador, was driven out of Spain, and barely escaped with his life, whilst the Princess faithfully promised to abstain in future from all political action. In September 1709 Philip hurriedly left Madrid to join the army in Cataluña, and, in pursuance of his new policy, sent most of the Frenchmen with Marshal Bézons back to France, the Spanish Count de Aguilar remaining in supreme command. The patriotic pro-Spanish nobles Medina Celi, Ronquillo and Bedmar were entrusted with the government, on the advice of Portocarrero, who died shortly afterwards, and for a time all went smoothly. But it soon became evident that in secret Philip was as much swayed by French influence as ever, and that the Spanish ministers were merely figure-heads to beguile the public, and had no power over the government. The improvement in finance and administration introduced by the French, which alone had rendered a continuance of the war possible, soon began to fall away when left to the hands of Spanish administrators, whose traditions and instincts were opposed to the new system; and but for the secret help of the Princess, and Philip's Italian favourite the Marquis of Grimaldo, the government of the State would have broken down completely.

Affairs had indeed reached a condition in the spring of 1710, that made it vital, both for France and Spain, that a cessation of the war should be arranged, on almost any terms. The characteristic course adopted by Louis was again to try to convince the allies that a complete separation had taken place between France and Spain, whilst secretly assuring Philip that he should not be abandoned. Most of the remaining French regiments were withdrawn from Spain, their places being filled by Walloons and Frenchmen enlisted independently under the Spanish flag. Louis began by approaching the Elector of Bavaria and the Dutch, to the latter of whom he offered the four strong places in the Netherlands still held for Philip, namely Luxembourg, Namur, Charleroi, and Nieuport. When Philip himself was informed of the proposal he violently protested against it in the name of Spain; but Holland was diverted from the separate treaty by the rest of the allies, who offered better terms. Louis, however, begged for peace so earnestly, that a conference was finally held at Gertruydenberg (March 1710), where he offered to recognise Charles as King of Spain and the Indies, leaving to Philip only Sicily and

Sardinia. He consented also to withdraw all aid from his grandson, to allow the troops of the allies to march through France for the subjugation of Spain, and even to contribute a million livres a month to the cost of their campaign. But nobody believed in Louis XIV now; and the conference came to nothing, Philip loudly protesting during the whole course of the proceedings that, under no circumstances, would he surrender any part of his dominions—except Jamaica to the English in exchange for Minorca, and Sardinia to the Duke of Savoy in exchange for Lombardy.

When peace was found to be impossible, both Louis and Philip made another vigorous effort to carry on the war. The pride of the Spaniards, especially, was aroused. The whole of Philip's forces for the first time were placed under the command of a Spaniard (Aguilar) and the youth of Spain once more flocked to the standards. Louis XIV and his family sacrificed even their household plate and jewels, and, by the summer of 1710, five fresh French armies were in the field. Villars was again in Flanders, Harcourt on the Rhine, the Duke of Berwick in Dauphiné, Bézons in Cataluña, and Noailles in Roussillon.

Philip had in Cataluña a larger and more homogeneous force than at any previous time. The bellicose loyalty of Spain had been touched by the King's patriotic appeal. The harvest had been an abundant one, the silver fleet from New Spain had arrived intact and unusually rich, and when Philip took the field in May 1710 he assumed the personal command of his troops, full of hope and determined to hold his crown in despite of all. His perplexities nevertheless were many. His best general Aguilar had deserted him in consequence of some dispute with the Queen, and the Prime Minister Medina Celi had been discovered in communication with the enemy for the recognition of the Archduke, and had been imprisoned in the fortress of Pamplona where he shortly afterwards died.

Unfortunately Philip selected as his military adviser Villadarias, who had been beaten in his attempt to recover Gibraltar; a man quite incompetent to conduct military operations on a large scale, especially against generals like Stanhope, Staremberg, and Belcastel. The armies first met at Almansa, on the 13th June, and Philip was forced to retire with considerable loss, owing to a dashing charge of the English cavalry. His next stand was at Lerida, but the unskilfulness of Villadarias allowed that place to be turned, and the King himself had to escape by flight. The armies ultimately met on the heights of Almenara where the Spaniards were completely routed. The King and his army fell back into Aragon, and, on the 20th August, made another stand before Zaragoza, where, notwithstanding the partial success of his right wing, Philip's army was again beaten, and driven in full flight upon Madrid. The Archduke entered Zaragoza in triumph, but on the advice of Stanhope foolishly neglected to take advantage of his opportunity and seize Pamplona, by which means he could have kept the French out of Spain. He preferred to advance on Madrid, which capital he again entered as a conqueror (28th September), the Madrileños, as before, turning upon him but frowning faces, whilst Philip was vigorously re-organising his army at Casa Tejada. The administration of Charles during his stay in Madrid was extremely oppressive, and increased the hatred of the people to his cause; but what aroused the fury of the city most was the sacrilegious attacks upon churches made by the Protestant English and Dutch troops. Soon up to the very gates of the capital Castilian guerrilleros in great numbers harassed the invaders, night and day: there was no safety for the "Austrians," even in their quarters, for the stealthy knife or the shot out of the darkness told—even as they did in the Peninsular War a hundred years afterwards—that when Spaniards were too weak to fight they were strong enough to murder.

In the meanwhile, prayers and entreaties went for help

from Valladolid, the seat of government, to Versailles. Marie Louise was as brave and determined as ever, and when the King's melancholy threatened to overcome him, she and the Princess of Ursinos aroused him again to his duty as a king. Aguilar nobly rallied to his sovereign again; and soon Vendôme crossed the frontier from France with a fine force of cavalry. With 30,000 men, mostly Spanish recruits, he at once marched upon Madrid, where the allies were growing more and more uncomfortable; for news had reached them that de Noailles was again busy in Cataluña. Their communications, moreover, were threatened; and on the approach of Philip, Charles once more evacuated the capital and retreated to Barcelona; whilst Stanhope took the road to the Portuguese frontier with 5,000 Englishmen. He was followed and overtaken by Vendôme at Brihuega, and forced to surrender before Staremberg's help could reach him; and Staremberg himself was met at Villa-Viciosa by Vendôme and completely defeated. He fought well and his retreat was masterly, but Villa-Viciosa practically sealed the fate of Spain. Vendôme and Philip, with immense activity and all the prestige of victory, pursued Staremberg and the remnants of his force. Aragon submitted to Philip, Gerona fell before the attacks of de Noailles, Tortosa was relieved, and the Portuguese frontier harried by the victorious Spaniards under the Marquis de Bay. The campaign of Vendôme in Spain in the winter of 1710—11 proved that the Austrian Archduke would never be acknowledged King of Spain. But an unexpected event provided a solution and changed the whole aspect of affairs. The Emperor Joseph I died in the prime of life, and the Archduke became Emperor. It was as much opposed to the interests of England and Holland that the Emperor should possess the whole Spanish monarchy as that it should fall under the dominion of France. A change of government in England and the defeat of the French in their campaign on the Flemish frontiers in 1710 facilitated the opening of negotiations for a general peace. The first overtures were between England and France alone, and in the autumn of 1711 the bases of agreement were settled. 1. The Crowns of France and Spain were never to be united, and to this Philip himself agreed. 2. Gibraltar, Minorca, St Kitts, Hudson's Bay and Newfoundland were to be held by England. 3. The fortifications of Dunkirk were to be demolished. 4. A treaty of peace and commerce was to be made. 5. The English were to have a monopoly of the slave trade with America, and 6. Louis was to recognise Queen Anne and the Protestant succession in England.

In the meanwhile Marlborough, who had captured Bouchain in September 1711, was accused by the Tories of peculation and replaced by the Jacobite Ormond, who merely stood on the defensive and left the fighting to Eugene. After infinite difficulty, particularly with regard to the cession of fatal Flanders by Philip to the Elector of Bavaria, the treaties of Utrecht were finally signed by all the powers but the Empire (14 April 1713). The terms agreed upon were to set their mark upon the map of Europe for a century at least and to solve most of the questions which had made Europe a vast camp for the greater part of two hundred years. The Emperor held out until the following year 1714, when, owing to the defeat of Eugene by Villars at Freiburg and Landau, he was forced to accept the terms agreed upon, and to make the separate treaty of Rastadt in March 1714; whereby the Austrians acquired the Spanish Netherlands, with the exception of the frontier towns, which were to be occupied by the Dutch in accordance with the Barrier Treaty of the previous year, and Gueldres, which had been ceded to Prussia. Austria was also to retain Naples, Milan and Sardinia, Sicily having been ceded to Savoy. All the places on the right bank of the Rhine were returned to the Empire, and Landau was ceded to France. The electors of Bavaria and Cologne were restored to their dominions.

It will be observed that these terms are infinitely less favourable for the allies, and especially for the Emperor, than the offers previously made by Louis; but the desertion of the confederation by England in consequence of Charles' accession to the Empire, and the fall of the Whig Government in England had changed the position. England's conduct towards the Catalans is exceptionally open to criticism, as the whole of their ancient privileges were abolished as a matter of course when they came again under the sway of Philip, although from the first their resistance against him had been exerted on the understanding that in any case the allies should protect them. The whole of Europe, however, was weary of war, Louis XIV was old and failing, and the obstinate adherence of most of Spain to Philip proved that it would be impossible for an Austrian archduke to conquer and hold the country by force. And thus it happened that after an obstinate struggle of eleven years in which all Europe took part, the last will of Charles the Bewitched made a Bourbon King of Spain.

CHAPTER XIII.

PHILIP V, 1714—1731.

During the long continued conferences of Utrecht, Baden and Rastadt, Barcelona held out obstinately against the Duke of Berwick. The Catalans would die, they said, in the breach, but they would never accept the Bourbon for their King. In vain Queen Anne of England urged them to accept Philip's pardon, and enjoy in future *the same liberties as the Castilians*. This was pouring oil upon the flame, for above all things the stubborn Catalans claimed their almost independent rights. At last (11 September 1714) the place was stormed by Berwick's troops amidst scenes of hellish carnage. "Kill and burn," was the watchword. Every street corner was a shambles with its great heap of slain, cannon-shot ploughed the streets, and foot by foot the city had to be won. The Catalans sought no quarter but fell where they fought, until at length Berwick gave the command for the city to be burnt. Then the place surrendered, and after 13 years of struggle, the most obstinate and deadly in the modern history of Europe, Cataluña was brought back to the fold, shorn of all her privileges, and assimilated to contemned Castile.

Philip was now really King of Spain for the first time, and at peace with all the world, except nominally with the Emperor. The inheritance of Flanders, which had dragged the dominant country down to ruin, was fortunately gone. The King's energy in the wars and his determined adherence to Spain had made him popular with most of his subjects; many of the bad traditions of the house of Austria had disappeared in the years of stress, since Charles the Bewitched had died; and at this juncture a really able sovereign might have raised Spain gradually to happiness and prosperity. But Philip was not the man. We have seen how, when he was a mere lad, his first temporary separation from his wife had thrown him into a despairing lethargy resembling insanity. As years had gone on he had become more and more uxorious, and the Queen and the clever old Princess of Ursinos had the most complete dominion over him. Unfortunately the brave little Savoyarde, who had long been ailing, sank at last under the anxieties and fatigues of her position, and died (February 1714); and Philip was cast on his own resources. The first result was to increase greatly the influence of the Princess. She was the only person allowed to see him, and when he retired to mourn at the palace of Medina Celi, the monks were turned out of a neighbouring monastery to accommodate the Princess, and a passage was made between the two houses. The gossips very soon began to say that the King was about to marry her, though she was old enough to be his grandmother. It was seen at once that Philip must marry someone without loss of time, or he would lose what wits were left to him, and the marriage-mongers of Europe were promptly on the alert. During his retirement the Princess persuaded him to dismiss Cardinal Giudice, whom he had just made Inquisitor General, and to entrust the principal management of affairs to Orry, the Frenchman who had done so much to reorganise the finances.

The Princess and Orry immediately set about completely revolutionising the administration. Ronquillo, who, like many of the Spanish nobles, had opposed Philip's recent edict—confirmed by the Cortes May 1713—introducing the Salic law into Spain, retired from the presidency of the Council of Castile, and his duties were divided amongst five presidents of Councils. Grimaldo remained minister of war and the Indies, but all the others were changed, Orry with the Princess at his back being practically supreme. The result was a still further advance in the administration and collection of the revenues, but there was no reform in the system and incidence of taxation. Almost immediately after the death of the Queen, Philip's confessor Father Robinet and other courtiers began intriguing for the choice of her successor. Louis XIV proposed several princesses, but in the meanwhile the Princess of Ursinos, who was nearer the King than any other person, was settling the matter in her own way. There was in Madrid at the time an Italian priest named Alberoni, who represented the Duke of Parma at Philip's court, and had managed to persuade the King that Parma had espoused the cause of the Emperor in the late wars, not from sympathy but from compulsion. Alberoni had come to Spain as a sort of clerical buffoon to the coarse-minded Duke of Vendôme, and on his patron's death he was sufficiently established to remain. The man was artful, cunning, and absolutely without finer feelings of any sort. The day after the Queen's death he suggested to the Princess of Ursinos the Duke of Parma's niece and stepdaughter, Elizabeth Farnese, as the future Queen of Spain. The young princess was the daughter of Dorothea sister of the Queen Dowager of Spain, widow of Charles II; and there was no male heir to the Parmese throne. The proposition commended itself to the Princess of Ursinos. This was a chance, she thought, of re-establishing the Spanish footing in Italy, and at the same time obtaining a consort for Philip who would act under her influence. Louis had had other views for his widowed grandson, and did not take kindly to the match, but was grudgingly won over by Chalais the Princess' nephew. Philip himself was as wax in the hands of the Princess, and willingly accepted Elizabeth of Parma as his wife. No time was lost, and, on the 16th September 1714, Philip was married by proxy in Parma. The connection was welcomed by the bride's family and by the Pope as a protection against the imperial claims to the suzerainty over Parma and Piacenza, whilst for the reasons already stated it was flattering to Spanish pride. Its principal recommendation, however, in the eyes of the Princess of Ursinos was Alberoni's assurance that Elizabeth was a simple tractable young maiden brought up humbly, who would be a facile instrument in the hands of the masterful old woman who had vicariously ruled Spain since the accession of Philip.

Alberoni's part was a difficult one to play. He had to keep up an appearance of adhesion to the Princess whilst making plans for her sudden and complete overthrow. He went to Alicante to meet the new Queen though he was suffering from fever, but only to learn there that Elizabeth had changed her plans and travelled overland. On her way she stayed for some days with her aunt the Queen Dowager at Bayonne. Marie Anne had her own score to settle with Ursinos, and doubtless instructed her niece accordingly—not that Elizabeth Farnese needed much instruction in imperious self-assertion. The new Queen was in no hurry to meet her husband, and from the first showed an intention of doing as she liked, refusing to dismiss her Italian suite at the frontier as had been arranged. When Alberoni first met her at Pamplona she was inclined to look askance at him as a friend of Ursinos, but she soon understood the position, and when the old princess advanced to meet her at Jadraque, a short distance from Guadalajara where the King awaited her, she was fully armed for the fray. The Princess herself was also quite aware by this time of the impending struggle before her. It is asserted that the Princess made some remark about the tardiness of the Queen's journey; but be that as it may, hardly had the two women met than the young termagant called loudly, "Take this old fool away who dares to insult me": and then without an hour's warning the Ursinos was pushed into a coach and hurried through the snowy winter's night over the bleakest uplands in Europe. Dressed in her court dress, with no change of clothes or proper protection against the weather, without respect, consideration or decency, the old princess who had done so much for Philip and for Spain was hustled out of the country she had served. She saw now for certain, what she had feared for some time past, that the wily Italian clerical-clown had tricked her, and that her day was past. The dominion of the new Queen over the spirit of Philip was soon more complete even than had been that of the Princess, and a letter of cold compliment from him was all the consolation or thanks that the Ursinos got for her protracted labours in Spain. So long as Philip had a masterful woman always by him to keep him in leading-strings, it did not matter to him very much who the woman was. The Queen was imperious, ambitious, and intriguing. Alberoni, whose craft had raised her to the throne, was her principal adviser, and almost the first exercise of power on their part was to reverse all the arrangements made by the Princess of Ursinos. Cardinal Giudice was recalled and made principal minister. Orry and his coadjutor, the enlightened Spaniard Macanaz, were obliged to fly to France; and the reforms which they had so laboriously introduced were for the most part abolished. The friends of the absent Princess were persecuted without truce or mercy; the complaints against the proceedings of the Inquisition, which had been a feature of the more enlightened French party, were rigidly suppressed, and Spaniards were flattered with the idea that they were no longer ruled by French influence. Even the King's confessor was forced to retire, and within a few months of the arrival of Elizabeth the ideas which ruled Spain were those of the sly churchmen from the petty Italian States.

Louis XIV died on the 1st September 1715, and his five-year old great-grandson succeeded under the regency of Orleans. There was no love lost between Philip and his cousin, who more than once during the war had plotted to supplant him on the Spanish throne. Philip himself had indeed some thought of claiming the regency of France. All this had the effect of pushing still further into the background French influence in Spain. During the war and the prevalence of French ideas the old fabric of government had practically disappeared. The grandees, who in the later Austrian period had obtained so much power and profit, had lost their foot-hold: many had espoused the cause of Charles, and most of the rest were too effete for service in circumstances where action and not bombastic pretence was needed. The Cortes as an initiator of legislation was practically effete; and the Councils, which, in the plan of Philip II, had been the hands and brains of the monarch, had under the long rule of favourites now lost effective power. All that remained was the absolute power of the monarch, advised by an informal camarilla arbitrarily chosen and dismissed by him and the four Secretaries of State. Aragon and Cataluña had lost the privileges so stubbornly upheld for centuries. The old order had gone: it was the task of Philip to establish the new. It has already been pointed out that the reforms introduced by the French ministers in Spain during the long war had been mainly administrative, and with the object that the revenues gathered might really find their way into the exchequer, instead of sticking to the hands of the collectors as previously; but little or no attempt was made to reform the system of taxation itself. Spanish industry was now almost dead, in consequence of the "alcabalas" and "millions" raising the cost of production to a point which rendered competition with foreign manufactures impossible. Almost the only exports were food and raw material, whilst Spanish hands were idle, and Spanish stomachs starved. Already new ideas, in religion, politics and economics, were rife throughout the rest of Europe; but Spain, for many reasons which will have been seen in the earlier pages of this book, had been isolated from the general march of opinion, and could hardly look for reform of its institutions, unless it came in a foreign garb which Spaniards regarded with distrust.

The task, therefore, which faced Philip's new wife and her Italian advisers, was a difficult one. The first step was for Elizabeth to gain absolute mastery over her husband, and this she did. Sacrificing her own ease-loving habits, she devoted herself to his passion for hunting, and, knowing his uxorious nature, she used all her woman's wiles to render herself necessary to his hourly existence. She succeeded completely. Alberoni was watchful, and kept the Queen up to the mark, spurring her ambition, checking her extravagance, and counteracting her hankering after the young Italian chaplain Maggiali, with whom she had enjoyed a girlish flirtation. Elizabeth was fractious at times, but her uncle, the Duke of Parma, could usually bring her to reason; and at last the battle was won. Philip had no will of his own, and Elizabeth Farnese was absolute mistress of Spain. Thenceforward for many years the country was ruled not by Spanish or by French methods, but as an Italian State, and in a large measure to serve Italian ends. These ends were the eventual succession of Elizabeth's issue to the States of Parma and Tuscany, under Spanish influence; the recovery of Spanish territories in Italy occupied by the Emperor; and the consequent establishment of Spanish instead of Austrian supremacy over most of the Italian peninsula.

The first step was to draw the maritime powers to the side of Spain. A treaty of commerce was concluded with England, by which the latter power gained great advantage (December 1715) and the implied recognition of George I as King of England against the Pretender. The Dutch were also conciliated, thanks to Ripperdá, the Dutch ambassador in Madrid, and the Pope was won over by the sending of six Spanish galleys to aid the Venetians against the Turks in the Adriatic (July 1716). Alberoni soon supplanted Giudice as principal adviser, and, in spite of great opposition in Rome, was made a Cardinal in July 1717. The Emperor was in the midst of a renewed struggle with the Turk on the Danube, and most of his allies had been drawn away from him. Alberoni was busy winning the northern powers, either to sympathy or neutrality, and at length a pretext was taken, ostensibly against Alberoni's wish, but really by his contrivance, to attack the imperial occupation of Sardinia.

The Emperor in the meanwhile had again managed to draw England into a defensive alliance with him; but by Alberoni's clever diplomacy it was rendered for some time ineffective. The regent Orleans had remained cold to the blandishments of the Cardinal, who tried to persuade him to join Philip in his attack upon imperial interests, and equally unmoved at the Breton plot against him fomented by Alberoni: but England, France and Holland together endeavoured to mediate between the Empire and Spain, on the basis of the recognition of the right of presumptive succession of Elizabeth's infant son Charles (born January 1716) to the Duchies of Parma, Piacenza and Tuscany. The overtures were haughtily rejected by Spain; and Sardinia was taken by a Spanish force in November 1717. Alberoni had from the first pretended that he was against the war, but when the Emperor showed that he intended, if possible, to enforce the terms of the treaty of Utrecht, the Cardinal displayed a vigour and energy that surprised Europe. Economies had been introduced everywhere in the finances of Spain, silver from the Indies came safely now, and money was forthcoming in abundance. Once more Spanish patriotism was appealed to, and again it responded splendidly. The Catalan irregulars, so lately fighting on the other side, joined in bands; the youth of south and central Spain flocked to the standards, and even the smugglers of the Sierra Morena deserted their trade of cheating the State in order to serve it. France and England—especially the latter—protested vigorously, and threatened war, if the terms of the treaties of Utrecht guaranteed by the powers were broken, and the Pope, deeply offended, withdrew the ecclesiastical subsidies collected in Spain, a fruitless step, for Alberoni disregarded the withdrawal and collected them still. The threads of Alberoni's diplomacy were so numerous and cunningly contrived that none of the Courts of Europe was free from his intrigues. Jacobite plots in England, conspiracies against the regent in France, plans for arousing the suspicions of the Emperor against the new King of Sicily (the Duke of Savoy), attempts to bribe the King of Sweden to aggression against the Empire; these and many others were resorted to, until all Christendom was set by the ears, whilst Spanish armaments were completed. At length, one of the finest forces that had ever left Spain was ready in Barcelona (June 1718). There were 30,000 choice, well-armed troops, with full supplies of every sort, 22 ships of the line, 10 other ships of war, and 320 sail of transports. The expedition was under the command of Don José Patiño, and landed its freight of armed men in Sicily under the Marquis of Lede in July. The Sicilian nobility and militia, who hated the Austrian and the Savoyard, joined the invaders almost to a man, and in a few days the whole island was in the hands of the Spaniards. Suddenly Admiral Byng with the English fleet appeared, and landed 3,000 Germans at Messina, whereupon the Spaniards retreated to the south of the island. On the 11th August 1718 the English and Spanish fleets met off Syracuse. There had been no declaration of war, and the Spanish admiral, Gastañeta, lay to until the stronger English fleet assumed a hostile attitude. The Spaniards were divided and taken at a disadvantage; they could not compare in seamanship with the English, and though they fought bravely the whole fleet was destroyed or captured, with the exception of four ships and six frigates. The allies, Austria, France, and England, had already offered as an ultimatum to Philip that Sicily should become Austrian, Sardinia go in exchange to the Duke of Savoy, and Parma and Tuscany be secured in reversion to the Infante Charles; but Alberoni had violently refused such terms, and dismissed the English ambassador Stanhope with the most haughty insolence. The Spanish ambassador retired from England, and war was declared in December 1718; and a few weeks afterwards the regent Orleans, against whom Alberoni had plotted a vast but abortive conspiracy, also declared war against Spain. The reply of Alberoni to this was the arming of an expedition in Spain, to aid the Pretender in Scotland. Six sail of the line, with 6,000 men and a great store of arms, left Corunna in March, but only two ships with 1,000 Irishmen arrived in Scotland, the rest being driven back to Spain.

Alberoni worked like a giant to organise a great naval expedition to attack and raise Brittany against the Regent, but in this respect the force and readiness of the allies frustrated him. In April 1719, 30,000 Frenchmen under Berwick crossed the Bidasoa, and overran the Basque provinces. Philip, with his wife, his eldest son Luis, and Alberoni, with difficulty raised a fresh force of 15,000 men in Navarre, to relieve Fuenterrabia, but he was too late, for the whole of the provinces offered to submit to France, an offer which Berwick refused. He was not, he said, fighting against Philip, but only to free him from an odious foreign minister; whilst the King of Spain was just as careful to assert everywhere that he was not in arms against his nephew but against Orleans. Without apparent reason Berwick suddenly abandoned the Basque provinces, and advanced on to the Catalan frontier from Roussillon, capturing Urgel and attacking Rosas. But tempest and pestilence decimated his army, and he again retired into France (November 1719). In the meanwhile an English squadron had captured Vigo and Pontevedra (October 1719) and had devastated the north-west coast of Spain. After hard and constant fighting all the summer in Sicily, Messina had finally capitulated to the Austrians in October; and to make matters worse for Philip, the Dutch had at last been drawn into the confederation against him. This was not at all what the Queen had been led to expect from Alberoni's artful intrigues, and she began to listen to the private approaches made by the allies through the Duke of Parma and others, for the dismissal of a minister who, it was believed, had brought so much trouble to Spain. The

King had sunk into a condition of hypochondria, but when he could be aroused, he too was anxious for the cessation of a war which he personally had never sought. His Jesuit Confessor, Daubenton, had turned against Alberoni, and used his influence to ruin the Cardinal. On the 5th December 1719 Philip and the Queen left Madrid for the suburban palace of the Pardo, leaving behind them a decree of expulsion for Alberoni. He was not allowed to see the King or Queen again, but was hurried off to France through Cataluña, where, in dire danger of being torn to pieces by the Catalans who hated him, he bade farewell to Spain, thunderstruck and indignant at the blow that had been dealt to him. Alberoni always insisted that he had been opposed to the war, but was over-ruled by the Queen, the Duke of Parma, and the King. Whether this be true or not, he had no sooner disappeared from the scene than the whole of the responsibility for the war, and all the other troubles of the country, was placed upon his shoulders. No accusations against him were too gross or calumnious to be welcomed at Court, and the Queen professed herself grateful even to the allies for opening her eyes to the real character of such a monster. Alberoni was a convenient scapegoat, for his enemies were many and bitter, and his fiscal reforms—the reduction of the value of the coinage, and the abolition of interior provincial custom houses—had injured many interests, but there is no denying that he showed immense energy and ability in raising and employing the resources needed for the carrying on of the war, and that his political combinations, however treacherous and dishonest, were masterly in their extent and aims. In his later period he was unquestionably hampered, and perhaps frustrated, by the wilfulness of the Queen and the secret attacks of his enemies at Court, but for all his faults, he was the first minister who succeeded in raising Spain again from the slough of ignorant impotent pride into which she had fallen, to be an active force in the councils of Europe.

As soon as Alberoni had left, talk of peace began to prevail, the initiative being taken by the United Provinces. But Philip was in no yielding mood, especially on the much debated question of the surrender of Gibraltar and Minorca by the English. The powers, however, sent envoys to Madrid and negotiations were continued, the principal aim of the English being to arouse the fears of Philip against Orleans, and to separate Spain from France in the coming peace. At length (26 January 1720) Philip adhered to the agreement of the Triple Alliance, persuaded thereto to a great extent by his new prime minister, a slow-witted Parmese called the Marquis Scotti. Philip by this instrument surrendered Sardinia to Savoy, repeated his renunciation of the crown of France in exchange for the Emperor's abandonment of his claim to Spain, renounced for ever any claim of Spain to Flanders, or to the territories in Italy occupied by the Empire, including Sicily; and by the same agreement the presumptive succession of the issue of Elizabeth Farnese to Tuscany and Parma was acknowledged. No sooner was the treaty signed and Philip free from war in Europe than a great force sailed from Cadiz, and with admirable gallantry relieved Ceuta, which Spanish fortress had for many years been intermittently besieged by the Moors.

Philip was now himself really at peace for the first time since his accession twenty years before. Spain had sacrificed much, but her position was stronger and more stable for the sacrifice, coupled with the improved administration which Philip's foreign ministers had successively introduced. But the Emperor, though he had adhered to the agreement, was still sulky, and delayed a final settlement; whilst the regent of France also delayed the surrender of Fuenterrabia in the hope of getting better terms from Spain separately. England, with similar views, sent Stanhope to Madrid to make a separate alliance for the purpose of forcing the Emperor to comply with the terms of his agreement. The result was a diplomatic scramble in Madrid, each of the powers trying to outwit the other, and to turn Spanish policy in the direction of its own interests. At length the treaty of peace and mutual restitution between Spain and England was signed (13 June 1721), in which England certainly obtained the advantage; and on the same day a league of England, Spain and France was formed for maintaining the articles which had been agreed upon. Repeated promises were made by George I that Gibraltar should be restored, but the question of compliance was always left open on some pretext, and the promise was never kept.

In order to cement the new alliance between Spain and France it was arranged that the Prince of Asturias, the Infante Luis, Philip's heir, should marry Louise Elizabeth, the daughter of the regent Orleans, and that the infant daughter of Philip and his second wife should in due time be wedded to the young King of France, Louis XV, the two princesses being exchanged on the frontier in January 1722, and Louise Elizabeth married to Luis, whose age was 17, at the end of the same month. This was followed by an engagement between the Infante Carlos and the younger daughter of the regent, by which stroke of policy Elizabeth Farnese appeared to secure her son's safety when he should succeed to his Italian dominions. French influence thus again became paramount in Madrid; England was thrown into the background, and the carefully planned combinations of Stanhope and his instruments, including the Duke of Parma, were disappointed. The congress of the powers for the final settlement of peace still continued at Cambrai, and thither to a great extent the intrigues were now transferred. The Emperor was delaying the fulfilment of the terms with regard to the Italian succession of Carlos, whilst preparations were openly made in Spain for an expedition to enforce the Infante's claims, and England, which had now sided with the Emperor as against the regent and Spain, was threatened by the help given by the Spanish government to James Stuart the Pretender. But again death stepped in and altered the situation. The Marquis Scotti had never been much more than a figurehead of the government, the real power behind the throne being the Confessor Daubenton, whose advancement to the post of first minister had been imminent when suddenly, in August 1723, he died; and almost simultaneously Cardinal Dubois, the prime minister of France, also died, to be followed to the grave very shortly afterwards by the regent Orleans himself and the Duke of Tuscany. The first three deaths took away the principal promoters of the intrigue, the object of which was the subjection of Spain to French interests; but their plot had already been carried too far for their death entirely to frustrate it.

The King had fallen into a condition of melancholy religious mania, and for long periods together he would retire from the sight of the world to a hunting-box in the wood of Balsain. In 1721 he had commenced to build near to this place, at immense expense, a sumptuous palace called St Ildefonso de la Granja, which should remind him of the beloved Versailles of his youth. Here he moped, fretted and prayed, passing his monotonous life without change from year to year in constant *tête-à-tête* with his wife, who never left his side night or day. The Council of State was practically dead, and affairs were conducted by the nominal chief minister and an informal camarilla. In these years, however, after the strong Alberoni had gone, and only Scotti or the King's favourite friend Grimaldo remained, the Queen had to depend in a great measure upon herself. Her task was a difficult one, for she dared not let her influence appear openly. Her every thought was the promotion of the interests of her own children by the King, but the Spanish people were already resentful and jealous at the thought of being dragged into war again for the purpose of making the sons of the King's second wife Italian sovereigns, and she knew that if she lost her popularity entirely she could do nothing. Daubenton and the French ambassador Chavigny, therefore, had exercised more power than they otherwise would have done, and in the King's lethargic frame of mind easily persuaded him of the vanity of all human grandeur and of the advisability of abdication in favour of his heir Luis, who had married the regent's daughter. In January 1724, the world was startled with the news that the King of Spain was tired of the world and had laid down his crown, intending henceforward to live privately with his wife in his favourite abode of St Ildefonso, high up on the mountains of Segovia looking towards France. "Having," says Philip in his decree, "considered maturely for the last four years the miseries of this life, owing to the infirmities, wars and turmoil which God has sent me during the twenty-three years of my reign; and seeing that my eldest son Luis...is married and of sufficient age, judgment and ability to govern with justice...I have determined to abdicate all my States...to my said eldest son Luis."

The instructions given to the new king by his father were more like those of a monk than a monarch, and Philip II himself was not more devout on his deathbed than was his descendant at a time when the ideas which produced the French revolution were already throbbing in men's minds.

Some of the more old-fashioned Spaniards were in favour of convoking Cortes to confirm the abdication, but the ideas of Louis XIV had by this time thoroughly permeated the councils of the Spanish monarch, and the once powerful Cortes of Castile was now but a shadow. Luis was still a mere youth, but as he had been born in Spain and was of frank, pleasant manner and affable address, his accession was extremely popular with the Spanish people, who promptly dubbed him "the well-beloved." Philip had appointed a council of nobles to advise him, all Spaniards, with Don Juan Orendain as principal Secretary of State, in place of Grimaldo, who remained near his old master, with very good reason, as we shall presently see. The Queen had done her best to prevent the abdication; and, although she at last consented to bury herself in St Ildefonso, it was with no intention of becoming a cipher. On the contrary, it soon became evident that the young king and his advisers did nothing without orders from the Granja, and that Grimaldo was still in reality principal Secretary of State. The matter which principally concerned the government was the succession of Elizabeth's eldest son Charles to the grand duchy of Tuscany. The Emperor's long-delayed recognition of his right was at last grudgingly given, but when Elizabeth endeavoured to send her son to Florence with the title of Grand Prince, almost everyone in Europe objected. The Spaniards were determined not to be dragged into war; the Emperor, of course, opposed the premature assertion of Spanish power in Italy; the reigning Grand Duke and his people objected to be ruled from Spain, and the King of England protested. Again the congress of Cambrai was called upon to settle the vexed question, and once more the intrigues were woven both in Spain and all over Europe, either for or against the extension of Spanish power in Italy. We have seen in the earlier pages of this book that nearly the whole of Spain's calamities had their origin in her foreign possessions in Europe. Now that she was free of Flanders and might have had peace, an evil fate had decreed that an intriguing and ambitious queen-consort should keep all Europe in a turmoil for years after the peace of Utrecht, in order that her sons might become petty Italian sovereigns under the ægis of Spain rather than that of the Empire. The Spanish party, who objected to see their country dragged at the tail of the Queen's maternal ambition, tried again and again to withdraw the young king from the tutelage of St Ildefonso; but the Queen and Grimaldo were always too clever for them. The vast sums taken from the treasury by Philip to build his new palace in the last years of his reign were made a pretext for sowing dissension between father and son; the light and imprudent behaviour of Elizabeth of Orleans, the young wife of the boy king, was seized upon for the promotion of a plot for the separation of the young couple that set both palaces by the ears. Confusion was paramount, with, as Marshal Tessé wrote, a king who was no king, when an attack of malignant smallpox cut short the already troubled life of Luis the Well-beloved after a reign of only seven months (August 1724).

The position of Philip was extremely difficult. He had solemnly renounced the crown and public affairs for ever: but his next son, Fernando, was only 11 years old, the peace of Europe was still trembling in the balance at Cambrai, and above all the busy brain of Elizabeth Farnese was plotting and planning for the aggrandisement of her own children. Prompted by her, the Council of Castile met and begged Philip once more to take the reins of government, but the feeling of the country was strongly against it, especially amongst the nobles, whose political power had now almost disappeared. The next heir however, being a child, could hardly be acclaimed without a Council of Regency, to which there were many powerful objections. Philip himself was, as usual, torn by agonies of doubt between devotion to his oath and his own, and his wife's, ambition. Churchmen met in solemn conclaves, and decided the point—according to the political party to which they belonged. Elizabeth Farnese eventually triumphed. Philip's scruples were overcome, and he again accepted the crown which he had a few months before sworn to abandon for ever. The Spaniards were bitterly disappointed at the return of the gloomy, uxorious, semi-lunatic to govern them, for they knew that the Italian clique would be paramount, and Spain's welfare sacrificed to the interests of Elizabeth Farnese's sons. But, as frequently happens in politics, events which could not have been foreseen again shifted the kaleidoscope and all the combinations were changed in the course of a few weeks.

Louis XV was a sickly, backward boy of 15, and the death of Orleans had brought his enemy the Duke of Bourbon to the head of affairs in France. He was determined that, if he could help it, none of the house of Orleans should succeed in the expected event of the King's death. Marshal Tessé had accordingly been sent during the short reign of Luis to Spain for the purpose of urging upon Philip the assumption of the heirship to the crown of France on his nephew's death, notwithstanding the renunciation made before, at, and after, the peace of Utrecht. Philip refused, although it has often been asserted that his abdication of the crown of Spain was effected with a view of claiming that of France, and on his refusal Tessé had more than hinted that Bourbon, in order to prevent the succession of an Orleans, would at once marry Louis XV to a Princess capable of bearing an heir to the French crown, and break off the marriage with Philip's six-year-old daughter, who had been brought up from infancy in France with the object of being married to the King. Philip seems to have shown no resentment at the time; but when Luis died, and his French widow, whose behaviour had shocked everyone, was sent back to France, it must have been evident to Elizabeth Farnese that the French connections were weakening, and if the little Spanish Princess were returned unwed, relations would become strained indeed.

For over twenty years an insuperable gulf had yawned between the Austrian and Bourbon descendants of the Emperor Charles V; but cunning brains had for some time past been thinking of the possibility of union. Alberoni had always played off Austria against France, and one of his many schemes was the re-establishment of a community of interests between the two countries. He was in Rome, in good favour, and on Philip's re-accession the gossips of Madrid talked about his recall. But a craftier head, even than his, was working secretly in the same direction, and the new policy was carried out by a new man. Baron Ripperdá, one of the most extraordinary adventurers in history, was a Dutch nobleman of some wealth, who had represented the United Provinces in Spain after the treaty of Utrecht. Facile, plausible, and ambitious, he had managed to ingratiate himself with the Spanish Court and Alberoni: his ostentatious conversion to Catholicism aiding his popularity. On his resignation of the Dutch ministry at the end of 1716, he decided to settle in Spain, and was full of great projects for reviving the cloth industry in his adopted country, for which purpose valuable monopolies were granted to him; Dutch spinners, weavers and machinery, were imported, and a flourishing manufacture was successfully established at Segovia. He was still about the Court, and had the Queen's ear: on several occasions he had hinted that a close alliance with the Empire might force England to surrender Gibraltar; and now on the return of Philip to the throne, and the impending rupture of the marriage contract between the little Infanta and Louis XV, his project assumed practical form. His activity in restoring Spanish industries by the introduction of foreign workmen, enabled him to travel without remark, and he undertook a secret mission to Vienna to lay his plans before the Emperor (November 1724). His mission coincided in point of time with the rupture of the two marriage contracts between France and Spain, namely that of Louis XV with the Infanta, and Don Carlos with Mdlle de Beaujolais, younger daughter of the late Duke of Orleans. Elizabeth Farnese, and of course her husband also, were furious at the insult offered to them; and Ripperdá was ordered to accede to almost any terms to bring about an alliance with Austria. He succeeded beyond expectations, and the treaty of Vienna resulted; with which he returned to Madrid in the late autumn of 1725.

Concurrently with this, an intrigue had been conducted in Rome by Cardinals Alberoni and Cienfuegos, with a similar object; namely the humiliation of England, the ruin of the house of Hanover, the restoration of the Stuarts, the spoliation of France, and the re-establishment of Catholic supremacy in Europe. By the treaty of Vienna Elizabeth Farnese's son Charles was to be acknowledged in his Italian succession: but at what a cost! In addition to vast sums of money, commercial privileges were granted to the Emperor such as no treaty had ever given before. All Spanish ports in Europe and the Indies were thrown open to Austrian commerce: the trading companies established by the Emperor at Trieste and Ostend were to conduct the trade of the east and west through his dominions, to the ruin of England and Holland. Ripperdá was voluble and boastful, and his mission leaked out long before it was concluded. It was soon answered by a counter-combination of the other powers: England, France and Prussia, who signed the treaty of Hanover in September. In Spain honours were showered upon Ripperdá without stint. He was made a Spanish duke, director-general of commerce and shipping, and eventually prime minister. His ministry was a thorny one, for he had deceived the Queen into the belief that the Emperor would send his eldest daughter, Maria Theresa, to be married to the Infante Charles, and his idle boasting rendered easy of defeat his persistent intrigues to separate France and England. His restless activity in the introduction of reforms into Spain, and the importation of foreign workmen and ideas, rendered him intensely unpopular, whilst the Catalans and Aragonese, disappointed that the Emperor had made no stipulation in the treaty for the restoration to them of their provincial privileges, raised a revolutionary outbreak in the north-east. Ripperdá's fall was rapid and complete. In May 1726 he learnt that a warrant was drafted for his arrest and seclusion. He fled to the shelter of the English embassy, where he endeavoured to make terms with the King. After much discussion he was taken from the embassy and removed to the castle of Segovia, whence he escaped. His subsequent extraordinary adventures in England, and in Morocco, where he became a Mahometan and prime minister of the Sultan, although of great interest, do not belong to the history of Spain.

Though Ripperdá had fallen, the one object of the Queen's life, namely the aggrandisement of her own children, at the expense of Spain if necessary, remained. In Spain itself this was now well understood, and resented: the Austrian connection was extremely unpopular, especially amongst the nobles; and even the King's ministers were divided, Orendain (Marquis de la Paz) being in favour of it, whilst Grimaldo, Bermudez the King's confessor, Patiño and others, were desirous of an alliance with England and France. The scale was turned by the Queen's new favourite, the Austrian ambassador Marshal Königsegg, who became, all but in name, prime minister of Spain. All those who had opposed the Austrian alliance were sent about their business. Bermudez, the King's confessor, was replaced by Father Clarke, a rabid Jacobite, Stanhope the English ambassador (Lord Harrington) was treated with studied insult, and Cardinal Fleury's attempts to restore good relations between England and France were frustrated. Through the winter of 1726, the Spanish coasts rang with naval preparations for the coming war with England: and in February 1727 the Spaniards laid siege to Gibraltar, and Stanhope left Madrid. Admiral Hozier ineffectually tried to blockade Porto Bello, and seize the silver fleet, but the home government would not allow him to attack the place, and pestilence swept his crews from his rotting ships, he himself dying broken-hearted. After four months of fruitless siege of Gibraltar, under Count de las Torres, against the advice of the more experienced Spanish Generals, who saw that whilst England held the sea they were powerless, Philip grew disgusted at the failure. The Emperor sent him no help; his own resources were giving out, and the dangerous illness of Louis XV once more seemed to bring near the possibility of

Philip, or one of his sons, becoming King of France. In these circumstances, therefore, he listened willingly to the advances made to him by the Abbé Montgon, the Duke of Bourbon's secret agent, for a reconciliation; Elizabeth Farnese, indeed, at once began to plot for the purpose of obtaining the crown of France for her son Charles, whilst Ferdinand, the King's eldest son, should inherit Spain. But Cardinal Fleury had other views, and Louis XV lived on, so the dynastic intrigue came to nothing, but the ultimate result was negotiations for a general peace. The negotiations dragged for a long time, for the contending interests were many, but finally, thanks to Fleury's loyalty to the English alliance and Patiño's efforts, the Congress of Soissons met in order to arrive at an agreement for peace. The Emperor's principal object was to secure the succession of his daughter Maria Theresa; and for this he was willing to sacrifice the Ostend Company of the Indies. England was determined to keep Gibraltar, and this was the main difficulty with Spain; whilst Elizabeth Farnese's desire was to establish her son in the Italian duchies, and to revenge herself upon the Emperor for cheating her twice in the matter of the marriage of his daughter with the Infante Charles. In order to compass this object she practically gave to England all it demanded. Gibraltar was passed over in silence, English trade to the Indies and the slave monopoly were restored, and the separate treaty of Seville was signed in November 1729 between England, France, Holland and Spain, leaving the Emperor isolated, and providing for the sending of Spanish garrisons to the Italian duchies to support the claims of the Infante Charles, when he should succeed.

This meant another change in the influences that surrounded the Queen. The Austrian party, Königsegg, Orendain (Paz) and the rest of them gave way to the first really capable statesman that Spain had produced for a long time, Patiño, a financier and organiser of all but the first rank, and to others of the modern school of politicians, who had from the first opposed the alliance with Austria. The Emperor protested against the Italian agreement, but fruitlessly. A large Spanish force was collected in Barcelona; and Elizabeth called upon France and England to send their contingents, as stipulated by the treaty of Seville. They were in no hurry to do so; and when Antonio Farnese, Duke of Parma, died (January 1731) the Emperor at once seized the duchy: nominally in the interest of the Infante Charles, but really to assert his own suzerainty. The divergence of English and French interests, and the complaints reciprocally made by Spain and England of depredations at sea, Gibraltar being again threatened by the Spaniards, had already caused a coolness between the signatories of the treaty of Seville. The entrance of the imperial troops into Parma, however, brought matters to a crisis. Patiño, wisely, was for peace with all the world, especially with England. The adventurous foreign policy which a close French alliance had always forced upon Spain was distasteful to him: the aid of England under the circumstances was vital, and had none of the objections which the introduction of French forces into Italy would have offered. English influence was invoked, George II exerted himself, and without Fleury's knowledge, a separate treaty was agreed to in Vienna (March 1731), between Spain, England, Austria and Holland. The "pragmatic sanction" of the Emperor establishing his daughter's succession was guaranteed by the maritime powers, on the condition that she should not marry a Bourbon; the Ostend Indian Company was abandoned, and the Infante Charles peacefully recognised as Duke of Parma and heir of Tuscany. Philip and his wife were still at Seville, whither they had gone nearly two years before for the translation of the body of St Ferdinand, when the glad news came to them (July 1731). In October the 6000 Spanish troops to occupy the duchies sailed from Barcelona, escorted by the English fleet, commanded by Sir Charles Wager. The young Infante was enthusiastically

welcomed by his present and future Italian subjects; and so at
last after years of constant plotting, and secret treaties innumerable, Elizabeth Farnese had triumphed in the great object
of her life: all Europe accepted the sovereignty of her son
over the Italian dominions of her forefathers. She had kept
Europe in effervescence for years, but she had her way; and
the persistence of one woman had re-established Spanish influence in Italy and raised Spain once more to a leading place
in the councils of the world.

CHAPTER XIV.

PHILIP V—FERDINAND VI, 1732—1759.

THE questions which had for so long divided Europe appeared for the moment to be settled, but before the conditions of the treaties were complied with, new causes of anxiety arose. Spanish naval armaments continued actively: the fleet that had returned from Italy remained in commission, and no adequate explanation could be obtained from Philip's government. By the spring of 1732 a fleet of no less than 600 sail was collected at Alicante with an army of nearly 30,000 men, and half the nobility of Spain. Since the great times of Charles V no such armament had been seen in the Mediterranean. The Emperor and the republic of Genoa, especially, were alarmed, but their fears were set at rest in June, just as the fleet was sailing, by a manifesto of Philip announcing the object to be the re-conquest of Oran, which it will be recollected had been lost in 1708 by reason of the desertion of Santa Cruz to the Archduke with the fleet destined for its relief. On the approach of the Spaniards the Moors of Oran evacuated the place, and the Christian flag again floated over the citadel. The Moors made several unsuccessful attempts to recapture the city; and at the instigation of Ripperdá, now Moorish prime minister, a determined attack was made upon the Spanish garrison at Ceuta, but also without success. The Spanish show of force had, however, other objects than the conquest of Oran. The Pope was offended that the new Duke of Parma had not recognised his suzerainty over the duchy, and the refusal of Spain to regard Tuscany entirely as an imperial fief kept the Emperor sulky. The yoke of the Austrian, too, had galled the Neapolitans and Sicilians more than that of the Spaniard, and they were ready for revolt. Spain and Austria both considered themselves aggrieved on the question of the suzerainty, and both appealed to the King of England to mediate between them. George II was patiently endeavouring to arrange a reconciliation when the death of Augustus II, King of Poland (Elector of Saxony), threw all Europe again into ebullition. France was interested in restoring the dispossessed Stanislaus, Louis XV's father-in-law, to the throne, and this the Emperor would not allow. Austria, Russia and Prussia joined their arms, and France became more friendly with Spain; England and Holland being principally concerned in maintaining peace.

For two years Philip had lived in absolute retirement in the palace at Seville, sunk into lethargy, slovenly and dirty in his habits, repulsive in appearance, and vacant in mind; but by a sudden revulsion, such as occurred to him at intervals, he became interested anew in the great problems which agitated Europe, and once more took charge of his government, which had been carried on entirely by the Queen and Patiño. The Queen's idea was to grab, if possible, the crown of Poland for her son Charles, but Patiño suggested a better idea. Whilst the Emperor was busy about Poland, why not seize Naples and Sicily for Charles? The French would be only too ready to help, the people were eager for the return of Spanish rule, and the plan would be easy. The Queen was delighted, and an alliance with France to carry out the idea was signed in the Escorial in October 1733. Charles declared himself free of the imperial suzerainty, and whilst the war raged in Central Europe and Lombardy a considerable Spanish force sailed from Barcelona to help the young Infante Charles, Duke of Parma, to reconquer Naples. The Pope was in favour of Spain, and sent his aid to Charles; the Austrian garrisons were weak, and the expected reinforcements of 20,000 men had not arrived.

One strong place after another was abandoned by the Austrians. On the 10th May 1734, Charles entered the city of Naples in triumph, and the kingdoms of Naples and the Two Sicilies returned to a Spanish prince after 27 years of Austrian domination; but they were no longer to be provinces governed by greedy viceroys from Spain, but were to have a king of their own, who in time should become a Neapolitan. Gaeta and Capua held out for a time in the kingdom of Naples, and Messina, Syracuse, and Trapani in Sicily, but at last all surrendered and Charles was crowned at Palermo King of the Two Sicilies in July 1735.

All had gone adversely for the Emperor in Italy: the French, Sardinians and Spaniards had beaten him out of Lombardy with immense slaughter. But the siege and fall of Dantzig destroyed the last hope of Stanislaus: Augustus III of Saxony was accepted by the Poles as their king, and the *raison d'être* of the war disappeared. Again, owing to the efforts of George II, peace negotiations were commenced; at first secretly between France and Austria, with the result that in October 1735 it was agreed between them, that Stanislaus should possess for life the duchy of Lorraine, which on his death should pass to France, while the future Dukes of Lorraine should be compensated with the duchy of Tuscany, which in the interim should be garrisoned by Austrians instead of Spaniards. Charles was acknowledged King of Naples and Sicily, on his renunciation of Parma and Tuscany, the former of which duchies should be joined to Milan, and go to the Emperor.

The Spaniards, and particularly the Queen, were violently indignant at this treaty being made over their heads, but they protested in vain. Parma was Elizabeth's own duchy: her son Charles had been popular with the people, who hated the Germans. The Spanish Queen had other sons to provide for and wished to make one of them Duke of Parma and Tuscany in place of his brother; but Spain could not fight all Europe for it, and Elizabeth decided to bide her time till the next scramble gave her another chance, the preliminaries of the second treaty of Vienna being reluctantly accepted by Spain in May 1736.

For a short time Spain tasted the blessings of peace. During the stay of the court at Seville the Queen had taken a fancy to the magnificent pictures by Murillo, which were there seen at their best, and of which, curiously enough, there was no specimen amongst the enormous accumulations of paintings amassed by the successive Spanish monarchs, and no less than twenty-nine of his canvasses were brought back to Madrid for the galleries of St Ildefonso. All Europe was being ransacked in the intervals of war to satisfy the Queen's craving for sculpture, paintings and the like; and the King himself vied with his wife in his eagerness to purchase specimens of the works of the most approved artists of the time. The gloomy old palace of Madrid, which Philip hated, had been destroyed by fire on Christmas Day 1734, and the best artists in Italy and Spain were summoned under the abbé Juvara to erect the present splendid granite edifice on its bluff over the Manzanares. Thenceforward both Philip and his wife were indefatigable in their zeal for collecting beautiful things, according to their lights, to adorn their palaces. No small part of the duties of the Spanish ambassadors was to bargain with artists and dealers for their treasures; and, notwithstanding the fact that many hundreds of splendid canvasses, torn from their frames during the fire at the palace, lay forgotten in the cellars of the Archbishop's palace, vast numbers more were bought of all schools, from the splendid Flemish and Italian masters to the insipid degeneracy of the modern court painters, from Titian, Dürer, Rubens and Vandyck, to Rane and Van Loo. Again and again, during his attacks of despondency, the King had talked of abdicating, but Elizabeth Farnese was always at hand to prevent it.

The vast expenditure of the palace and the drain of constant war had exhausted even the increased resources provided by the wisdom of Patiño and his brother the Marquis of Castelar; all the people desired was peace, but the maternal ambition of Elizabeth was still unsatisfied, and all had to give way to her imperious will. Her duchy of Parma had gone to the Emperor, and until she got it back for her kin Europe could know no durable peace. In August 1737 she contrived to marry her second son Philip to the Princess Marie Louise, eldest daughter of Louis XV, and this was a distinct step in advance; but before another could be taken the storm burst in a new direction.

The treaties of Utrecht had given to England the monopoly of the slave trade, and many trading privileges in Spanish America. British factories existed at Panama, Vera Cruz, Buenos Ayres, Cartagena and elsewhere, and the ships trading with slaves were exempt from examination or duty. This enabled the Jamaica colonists, who were already enriched by the plunder of the Buccaneers, to carry on an active contraband trade to the great loss of the Spaniards. Reprisals and mutual recrimination were the result, and matters at length reached a crisis. Spain did not wish for war, especially with England, and agreed by the convention of the Pardo (January 1739) to pay an indemnity of £95,000, pending a peaceful arrangement of all open questions by a conference at Madrid[1]. In return Spain pressed for the payment by England of certain claims made by her against the South Sea Company. The answer was a commencement of hostilities on the part of England, owing mainly to public clamour and greatly against the will of Walpole. Admiral Vernon suddenly appeared before Porto Bello (Isthmus of Panama) with six ships of the line. The garrisons of the fortresses fled, and the city, which was one of the great depots for the wealth of Central America and the West Indies, was sacked and destroyed (22 November 1739).

---

[1] The main points at issue, beyond the indemnity claims, were the right of search and the delimitation of Georgia.

The news once more awoke Philip from his lethargy. All Spain rang with indignation: their country, said the Spaniards, was no longer impotent, as it had been under the later Austrians, but could resent and revenge attacks upon its honour and welfare. Money had already been collected for another purpose; expenses were cut down to the lowest, pensions and salaries suspended; the interest on debts had been reduced and forced loans resorted to; and just in time the Indian silver fleet fortunately arrived safely. Spanish corsairs soon scoured the sea in search of English merchantmen, and in a few months prey to the value of £234,000 had fallen into their hands. This was a new Spain which England had to face, no longer the helpless victim of the previous century. All Englishmen were expelled from Spain and trade with them strictly prohibited; Gibraltar was threatened by an army under the Duke de Montemar, another Spanish force threatened the English in the Balearic Isles, whilst the Duke of Ormond collected a squadron in Galicia to invade Ireland in the interests of the Pretender. A French fleet also hovered on the English coast. England, on the other hand, was not idle. A squadron of English ships attempted to blockade Ferrol, but the Spanish fleet gave them the slip and sailed to South America to reinforce the Spaniards there. Anson, though he had lost most of his ships, plundered and ravaged on the Pacific coasts of South America; and Admiral Vernon, after his exploit at Porto Bello, determined to attack Cartagena on the Spanish Main. The city was rich and populous, defended by the citadel of St Lazaro on a hill commanding the port. The loss of the place would have ruined the Spanish power in America; and at first it seemed as if its loss was inevitable. General Wentworth with 10,000 men landed under the guns of the fleet, and carried all before him in the harbour. The splendid courage of Eslava the Viceroy, however, saved the place. The English attack on the citadel failed, the deadly climate thinned their ranks, and Vernon was forced to abandon his attempt, a similar evil fortune attending his attack upon Santiago de Cuba shortly afterwards. The great Patiño had not lived to see the triumph of his enlightened colonial and naval policy—he had died in 1736—but the vigour he had introduced into all branches of the administration had borne rich fruit, and England found, as Walpole had predicted, that a new Spain had been called into existence, capable of defending herself even upon England's own element.

Patiño's scheme had been to revive Spain by imitating the policy of England and Holland; the fostering of trade by subsidised companies, by bounties, and by the exclusion of foreign goods from the colonies. During the fourteen years that had elapsed since he had first guided the administration this great change had occurred. Spain was able to hold her own in America, as well as in Europe, and to defend her rights upon the sea. Elizabeth Farnese, however, cared nothing about America or the sea, except so far as concerned the pieces of eight brought by the silver fleets. Her view at present was bounded by the desire of regaining the lost Italian duchies for her second son Philip; the war which had been forced upon her by England could not help her in this, and caused her to spend the money she had scraped together to buy the duchies if possible. But in October 1740 an event occurred which again threw all Europe into the seething cauldron of war, and opened to Elizabeth's unquiet spirit a wider ambition than ever for the aggrandisement of her offspring. The Emperor Charles VI died, and with him the male line of the imperial house of Austria. For years he had struggled to obtain the guarantee of Europe for the succession of his daughter Maria Theresa, and had secured the confirmation of his "pragmatic sanction" by the last treaty of Vienna. But the interests in opposition were many and diverse. The dominions of the Habsburgs were scattered and disunited in race, faith, and language, and though Charles' daughter at first succeeded peacefully, the muttering of the great storm could already be heard approaching. The Austrian monarchy was poor and exhausted with the long struggle against the Turk, and lay an easy prey to ambition. Philip V was made to claim the whole inheritance, as the senior descendant of the Emperor Charles V, whose line it had been arranged in the family compact should succeed in case of the extinction of that of Ferdinand I; but the Spanish claim was only intended as a lever for obtaining the Austrian dominions in Italy—Lombardy and the Milanese—which, joined to Parma and Tuscany, now possessed by Maria Theresa's husband, would make a respectable kingdom for Elizabeth's second son Philip. The new King of Poland, the Elector of Bavaria, the King of Sardinia and the King of Prussia, also claimed the whole or parts of the imperial inheritance, and all Europe was interested in preventing the whole from again falling to one monarch. Whilst diplomatic protests and paper claims were being made, Frederick II of Prussia occupied Silesia with 20,000 men, defeating the Austrians at Mollwitz, and a general war commenced.

The details of the long and terrible struggle for the Austrian succession cannot be related in this work: only the Spanish share in it can be lightly summarised. The English Mediterranean fleet under Admiral Haddock was jealously watching the movements of Spain, and a plan of the Duke of Montemar had been approved by Philip V to take a Spanish army to Italy through the republic of Genoa, whilst a Neapolitan force advanced through Papal territory, and a French army accompanied Don Philip to Milan. At the last moment Campillo, the new minister of war in Madrid, changed the plan, in spite of Montemar's remonstrances, and the Spanish squadron, which in November 1741 left Barcelona with 25 battalions of infantry and a few cavalry, sailed to Orbitello as its rendezvous instead of to Sestri, as Montemar wished. At the same time Montemar himself with another force marched into Italy through France by permission of Fleury. Protected by a French fleet, the Spanish squadron managed to escape Haddock's ships, and 14,000 Spanish troops were landed on Genoese territory. Charles Emmanuel, Duke of Savoy (King of Sardinia), had old ambitions in Lombardy as well as Elizabeth Farnese, and after some hesitation sided with Maria Theresa, in order to check the spread of Spanish influence in Italy. By the time Montemar advanced with the united armies of Spain and Naples, Charles Emmanuel and an Austrian army were ready to receive them. Montemar's army was discouraged with the long delay and many contretemps which had befallen it, and the men deserted by thousands; Cardinal Fleury broke his promise to send a French army with young Philip, the Neapolitans had no stomach for the fight, the English fleet blockaded the French and Spanish ports; and at last, hopeless of effecting any useful purpose, Montemar fell back before Charles Emmanuel and General Traun, and re-entered Neapolitan territory (August 1742). Almost simultaneously (22 August) Commodore Martin with an English squadron appeared in the Bay of Naples, and gave the King one hour in which to agree to withdraw the Neapolitan contingent from the Spanish army. Under the threat of immediate bombardment of the city Charles was forced to comply.

The treaty of Breslau (July 1742), by which the Kings of Prussia and Poland withdrew from the war, placed Spain in a difficult position. Charles Emmanuel could afford to be obstinate now, for he had Austria at his back, and he knew that the old Cardinal Fleury would not involve France in a great war to benefit Elizabeth Farnese's second son. But in January 1743 the timid, temporising Cardinal died, and Louis XV was free from a tutelage which had galled him. A bolder policy was adopted, and soon young Philip on the frontier of Piedmont was joined by 10,000 French troops, whilst Count de Gages, the new Spanish General, unsuccessfully attacked the Austrians at Panaro. Charles Emmanuel now thought the time had arrived for him to receive payment for his efforts and carried on a complicated double set of negotiations with Austria on the one hand, and France on the other, for the possession of Lombardy. With much repugnance Maria Theresa at last partly gave way, and the treaty of Worms was signed (September 1743), by which Charles Emmanuel received Vigevano, with part of Pavia and Piacenza, and abandoned his claim to Milan. This led to an immediate declaration of war by France against Austria and a close alliance between France and Spain. The treaty of Fontainebleau (October 1743) was intended to be a permanent family pact, binding the Bourbons together for offence and defence; Gibraltar and Mahon were to be taken from the English; the portion of Savoy nominally ceded to France by the treaty of Utrecht was to be wrested from Charles Emmanuel; Parma and Piacenza, with Milan, were to be won for young Don Philip; and the two Bourbon sovereigns of France and Spain were to stand shoulder to shoulder against the world. The war in Italy now commenced in earnest. The great naval battle off Hyères, between the Spanish and French fleets and Admiral Matthews, was indecisive (22 February 1744), but at least it relieved the blockade of Toulon; whilst on the other hand the Austrian Lobkowitz drove the Spaniards back along the east coast of Italy to the frontier of Naples. Charles III then abandoned his neutrality and joined the Spaniards, in spite of Lobkowitz's energetic generalship, and the Austrians were obliged to retire on to the Adriatic coast. All through the summer (1744) the struggle went on in the north of Italy. Don Philip and his Frenchmen and Spaniards penetrated into Piedmont, but ineffectually besieged Coni; and in October were forced to retreat to Dauphiné, abandoning their artillery and baggage, and barely escaping capture.

The Bourbon cause was strengthened early in 1745 by the adhesion of the republic of Genoa, where, in May, Gages and Don Philip effected a junction, and, including the Genoese contingent of 10,000 men, marched an army of over 60,000 strong to invade the Milanese. By clever strategy they separated Charles Emmanuel from the Austrian Schulemburg and completely routed the former (September), capturing thereafter in rapid succession the cities of Alessandria, Valenza, Casale and Asti. Don Philip was thus able to enter Milan in triumph in December, the whole country greeting him as its sovereign, except the citadels of Milan, Mantua, Alessandria and Asti. Thus beaten, Charles Emmanuel listened to a talk of separate negociations with France—so weak had the family pact proved already. Preliminaries were agreed to in February 1746, by which Charles Emmanuel was to have Lombardy, and Don Philip to be contented with Parma and Piacenza; but, when Elizabeth Farnese learnt that her affairs were being settled without her consent, the embryo arrangement was soon upset, and the war recommenced more energetically than ever, particularly on the part of Charles Emmanuel, who promptly drove the Spaniards out of Milan. A Spanish force in Parma under Castelar only escaped by the strategy of Gages; and soon Parma shared the fate of Milan. At Piacenza the Franco-Spanish army was literally cut to bits by Lichtenstein (16 July 1746), and the ambitious dreams of Elizabeth Farnese seemed to melt into thin air.

The waste of life and treasure, for the purpose of winning a throne for the Queen's second son, had caused the most bitter discontent in Spain, where peace was recognised as being the first need of the country. Under the fostering care of the modern statesmen of the Patiño school, particularly Ustariz, the Spanish industries were painfully struggling to life again, and at the very time when every man and every ducat were wanted at home, blood and gold were poured out like water for no object but to satisfy an imperious woman's maternal ambition. Louis XV and the French people were still less concerned in Elizabeth's object—notwithstanding the family pact—and urged that peace should be made.

Elizabeth was forced to agree, for without French aid she was powerless against Austria and Savoy. Her only condition was that Charles Emmanuel should not receive Lombardy, whoever else had it. Whilst the negociations were in progress —on the 9th July 1746—Philip V was struck with apoplexy and died. He had for years past at frequent intervals believed himself to be *in articulo mortis*, but the troubles and disasters of the war had at last realised his dream. He was a heavy, dull devotee, frequently quite insane for considerable periods in his later years. For him, his throne had been a constant penance and anguish, and only the command of his imperious wife had kept him in it so long: some great crisis or strong excitement alone shook him out of his lethargy, and enabled him for a brief period to do justice to his original qualities, which were overlaid by indolence and sensuousness. Spain owed little to him personally, but he was a new man, belonging to a fresh family, coming from a more enlightened country than Spain, and his very presence broke the gloomy spell of the house of Austria, which by regular gradations had descended from genius to idiocy, and dragged unhappy Spain to the lowest depths of humiliation and despair. Philip V represented a new era; and modern ideas, though strenuously combatted by ignorance, selfishness and bigotry obtained some small footing under his rule. Saddled with the exhausting wars of succession, and the awful waste of resources caused by Elizabeth Farnese's ambition; bled to death, almost, by the lavish expenditure entailed by a desire to rival in arid Spain the splendours of the Court of Versailles; in intellectual and material progress the country during Philip's reign was nevertheless remarkable. It is true that the evil old system of taxation in Castile was unaltered. The alcabalas of 14 per cent. on all sales were still supposed to be collected, but were mostly paid in quotas, and monopolies and exemptions were granted, and bounties paid to certain industries, which in many instances counteracted the oppressive taxes; the hated food tax of the "millions" still rendered life expensive, and production costly; but the people were to some extent saved from the constant extraordinary demands, oppressive procedure and illegal extortions of the tax-farmers, which had driven land out of cultivation under the Austrian Kings. A beginning of reform had been made in the kingdom of Valencia in 1717. The revenue there had been raised by a tax of 5 per cent. on every retail transaction, a 5 per cent. duty on all merchandise or produce entering or issuing by land or sea from the territory, and an additional 5 per cent. on certain specified goods. These Valencian taxes were all abolished except the coast custom-houses in the year mentioned, and replaced by a single tax upon salt, all tolls, octrois etc. being also cleared away. The result of this was that, although the Valencian textiles could not compete with foreign goods for America, they could now supply the home market; and the looms increased in number from 300 in 1717, to 2,000 in 1722. The decayed industries, moreover, were revived by the introduction of large numbers of artificers from abroad; and especially the trade of ship-building was practically re-introduced by the incessant care of Patiño. The Cortes were now never summoned for financial purposes, and many of the taxes imposed in times of pressure during Philip's constant wars are indefensible from the point of view of the modern economist; but, withal, the tendency was in the right direction, and in such a country as Spain it was impossible to proceed except by very slow stages, as the zealous Frenchman Orry had found to his cost.

In the year of Philip's accession the national revenue of Spain is stated by Canga-Argüelles to have amounted to 142 millions of reals (equal to $2\frac{1}{2}d.$ each), whereas it had grown by 1737 to 211 millions, the expenditure, however, increasing in still greater proportion; namely, in the reign of Charles II, 193 million reals, in 1701, 247 millions, and in 1737, 336 millions of reals. The palace expenditure of Charles II had amounted to about 11 millions of reals annually, but the extravagant tastes of Philip and his wife increased the expenditure of the palaces to three times that amount.

Philip was well-meaning, merciful and magnanimous, but he was overweighted. His mental infirmities and his bodily indulgence made him a mere cipher in the hands of his wife, and although the material renaissance of Spain coincides with his period, it received little impulse from him, except in acquiescence and good intentions—which in the case of a monarch counts for much.

By his first wife Philip had had four children, of whom only his successor Ferdinand VI survived him. By Elizabeth Farnese he had six children, of whom four were living at the time of his death, Charles King of Naples, Don Philip, and the Cardinal Don Luis, with three daughters, one of whom, the Dauphiness, died a few days later. With the accession of Ferdinand VI, whom she hated and had treated badly, the sun of Elizabeth Farnese set, though she did not cease to intrigue in her retirement at St Ildefonso in favour of her sons. She was treated by her step-son with characteristic generosity and kindness. Her ambition of course ceased to be the turning point of Spanish foreign policy, but Ferdinand's filial respect and magnanimity prevented any sudden or violent change in his councils. He maintained his father's principal ministers, the Marquises of Villarias and Ensenada, and continued the *pourparlers* of peace which had been commenced: but the famous Marquis de la Mina was sent to replace Gages and Castelar in command of the defeated Spanish forces in Italy, most of which had taken refuge in Genoa, where they were blockaded by the English fleet and threatened by the Austrians and Savoyards. Mina and Maillebois, the French marshal, decided to escape whilst they could by land, and left Genoa to the far from tender mercy of the Empress-Queen (September 1746). Charles Emmanuel and the Austrians, under Count Brown, with the co-operation of the English fleet, invaded Provence, and were sweeping all before them when (December 1746) a popular rising took place in Genoa. The infuriated people, mad with rage at the humiliation they had suffered, defeated the 10,000 Austrian troops in their neighbourhood. This demoralised the Austrians in Provence, who were driven back again over the Var by the French and Spaniards (February 1747), and finally after much desultory fighting Schulemburg and the English were forced to raise the siege of Genoa (6 July 1747), the former hurrying to the aid of Charles Emmanuel. But before he could arrive the King of Sardinia had inflicted a crushing defeat on the French at Exilles. All through the autumn and winter the hostilities continued without important result; but in the meanwhile the negociations for peace proceeded. Marshal Saxe had carried the French arms successfully through Flanders, which somewhat equalised matters. England was desirous of friendship with Spain; Europe was anxious for peace; and so, above all, was the amiable and popular Ferdinand, whose great ambition was to make Spain happy, prosperous and enlightened. He, too, was married to a woman of stronger will than his own. It was a common saying in Madrid that Ferdinand had not succeeded Philip, but that Queen Barbara (of Braganza) had succeeded Queen Elizabeth (Farnese); and though Elizabeth tried her hardest to cause a continuance of the war, which with French aid should give her son Philip a crown, Barbara had her way; her Portuguese kinsmen succeeded in their mediation, and the treaty of Aix-la-Chapelle, which had already been agreed to by the English and French, was accepted by Ferdinand and Maria Theresa (October 1748). The new treaty, though it did not satisfy Elizabeth Farnese's ambition for her son Philip, made him the sovereign Duke of Parma, Piacenza and Guastalla. Maria Theresa was acknowledged by all Europe; England obtained important commercial concessions, Charles Emmanuel was guaranteed his kingdom of Sardinia, and Europe was at peace once more. An additional separate treaty was made between England and Spain in the following year, October 1749, called the treaty of Aquisgran, by which Spain undertook to pay the South Sea Company £100,000 for the suspension of its slave trade privileges for four years, and confirmed the many commercial advantages granted to England in previous treaties.

Ferdinand was now 36 years of age, and found his country, for the first time for at least a century, in the enjoyment of a durable peace with all the world. We have seen how, in spite of the constant waste of war, the tenacity of the Iberian race had shown itself under the newer régime of the Bourbons. In the midst even of the calamities which Elizabeth Farnese's ambition had brought upon Spain, the arts of peace had still re-blossomed. Philip and Elizabeth were not only the liberal patrons of the arts, but had helped and encouraged Spanish literature as actively, and far more judiciously, than had Philip IV. To them and their advisers is owing the foundation of the noble National Library in Madrid, the Royal Academy of History, the Seminary of Nobles, and a host of learned societies and universities which placed Spanish scholars at no disadvantage with those of other countries. It was this part of his father's character, a love of peace, enlightenment and the gentler arts, that Ferdinand inherited from Philip V, and during his short reign he, and his Queen Barbara, devoted most of their attention to promoting the best interests of their country. The French and Italian influence over Spanish politics was now thrown into the background: Ferdinand and his ministers were Spaniards before all, and inaugurated a truly patriotic policy. On the death of Villarias, he had been succeeded by Don José Carvajal, a descendant of the house of Lancaster, and consequently more inclined to the English than the French connection, but honest, upright and intelligent. With him, and soon to become omnipotent, was a man of immense energy and ability, a banker and commercial man by origin, Somodevilla, Marquis de Ensenada, who practically re-created the Spanish navy, and gave great impulse to Spanish commerce, but whose career was ruined subsequently by his extravagance and lavishness. To these two ministers was left the government of the country. Both the King and Queen loved quietude and family life, and all they asked was that Spain should be peaceful and prosperous, and that they personally should be relieved from harassing cares. Little intrigues of course went on around them. The sweet voice of the Italian singer Carlo Broschi (Farinelli), of which Philip V had never tired, charmed the new monarchs, especially Barbara, still more, and the singer was surrounded by place-hunters and diplomatists; the king's confessor Rábago was head of a palace clique which dreamed of governing Spain; and the envoys of France and England, already at issue again about the delimitation of their American colonies, made of Madrid a focus of intrigue, in which Sir Benjamin Keene was generally victorious.

In the teeth of French opposition a treaty was arranged in 1752 between Spain, Maria Theresa and the Dukes of Tuscany and Parma, with the adherence of Charles Emmanuel, which guaranteed at length the neutrality of Italy, and banished one of the principal pretexts for future wars. Curiously enough, the Infante Charles, King of Naples, was the only one who now sounded a note of discord at the Italian arrangement, which deprived his children of the hope of obtaining the duchy of Tuscany; and Charles consequently made approaches to France against his brother's kingdom. Keene found in this a pretext to try to draw Ferdinand more to the side of England, but Carvajal avoided the pitfall. French intrigue also captured the other Spanish Infante, Philip Duke of Parma, who had married a French princess. Thanks to Keene's sleepless diligence Ferdinand's breach with his half brothers grew wider and wider. Charles, the elder, already gave himself airs as assured successor to the crown of Spain—for Ferdinand had no children—and encouraged Ensenada, who favoured the French faction, to promote the influence of Duras the French ambassador in Madrid. The Spanish ambassador in London, an Irishman named Richard Wall, seconded

Carvajal and Keene in their efforts to unite England and Spain. The French Government demanded his recall on charges of intrigue against French interests. A strict enquiry proved the accusations to be groundless (October 1752), and Wall was raised to the post of minister of State after the death of Carvajal in the following year. The acquittal of Wall and his temporary restoration to his post in London dealt a blow to French interests, and especially to the Marquis of Ensenada, whose foreign policy tended to a close offensive and defensive alliance between the Bourbon kings. Whilst Carvajal lived, he steadily avoided entanglement with either France or England, who were now rapidly drifting towards war, although his sympathy was in favour of the latter power, and his friendship with Sir Benjamin Keene was intimate and sincere. In April 1754 this high-minded minister died; and for a moment it seemed as if Ensenada would become supreme, in which case Spain might once more be dragged into the impending war at the tail of France. But Ferdinand was determined to have peace in his time, and was supported in his determination by his friends the Duke of Alba (Duke of Huesca) and the Count de Valparaiso, who advised him to recall Wall and entrust him with the ministry of State. Ensenada and his friends were not shelved without a struggle, and for a time intrigues on both sides were active, Farinelli on this occasion using his great influence with the Queen in favour of the Marquis.

But the arrival of Wall on the scene completed the triumph of the anti-French party. The new minister, eloquent and ingratiating, with all the vivacity of the Irishman, soon became master of the situation, and a pretext was found for the disgrace of Ensenada. At the instance of the English government a proposal had been made by Portugal to cede to Spain the colony of Sacramento, at the mouth of the river Plate, in exchange for seven provinces belonging to Spain on the north of that river, and the province of Tuy in Galicia. The Jesuits of Paraguay protested and the inhabitants of the seven provinces revolted against the change, and when after Carvajal's death, Ensenada first discovered the negotiation which had been concluded through English influence, he secretly appealed to the King of Naples to interfere. Charles accordingly sent a protest to his brother, to the immense indignation of the latter. The treaty was suspended, and the English and Portuguese interests were for the moment vanquished. Ensenada lost no time in negotiating secretly a close alliance with France, unknown to his colleagues, or even the king; he subsidised opposition to the English in America, and was rapidly dragging Spain into war, when Keene, Wall and the Duke of Alba discovered his proceedings and divulged them to the king. On the night of 20th July 1754, Ensenada was arrested in bed by the king's guard, and hurried off to Granada; and with him fell all his friends of the French party. His wealth and splendour had raised up many enemies, and accusations of all sorts were rife against him, but none were proved, and he was allowed to live in dignified retirement away from the court. He had during his ministry given an enormous impetus to the prosperity of the country, reviving agriculture, promoting irrigation-canals, improving roads, subsidising manufactures, and once more created a Spanish marine. To him was due also the re-opening of Spanish mines. It had been illegal to export any of the precious metals from Spain. Ensenada encouraged silver mining and allowed export of metal, but imposed a royalty for the benefit of the State—$3\frac{1}{2}$ per cent. in Spain, and 6 per cent. in America. But above all he continued in Castile, to a great extent, the financial reforms already adopted in Valencia, abolished tax-farming, and initiated a project for suppressing the hateful tax of the "millions" on meat and other articles of food[1]. Under his auspices, also, the long pending questions

[1] Between 1742 and 1750 the increase of the revenue was 5 millions of ducats annually, the estimated revenue for the latter year being 27 million ducats. The Indian revenues, which—as has already been shown—were about 3 to 4 millions of ducats, rose under Ensenada to 6 millions yearly.

with Rome, respecting the patronage of the Spanish church, were set at rest. The sleepless papacy had never ceased, during the long period of Spain's weakness, to encroach, so far as it could, upon the royal patronage of the church, which we have seen was insisted upon by Charles V and Philip II. Complaints of the encroachments of the clergy had been constant, and convention after convention had been negotiated with the popes for the remedy of the crying abuses, the papacy always seeking in the alleged interests of discipline to exercise some control over the selection of church dignitaries. At last (1753) the famous *Concordat* was signed, by which the King of Spain's right of patronage was unreservedly acknowledged by the Pope (Benedict XIV), with the exception of 52 benefices reserved for the Pope; and for the prelates the patronage of all benefices which might fall vacant in their dioceses during the months of March, June, September and December. Although, unfortunately, Ensenada and Carvajal differed in their foreign policy, it is not too much to say that they, together with their predecessor Campillo, opened a new period of prosperity and power for their country.

Wall wisely followed the same course, and thanks to the determination of the King and Queen, as well as to the wisdom of the minister, the persistent efforts of the English and French governments to drag Spain into their quarrel in America failed. The wounds which Spain had received in her century of constant war, as well as the natural calamities which befell her by the terrible earthquakes, destroying whole cities in Spain (1755), needed, indeed, the prudent, tranquil policy followed

---

The adoption by Ensenada of measures similar to those referred to in a former chapter with regard to Valencia (1717) had the effect of enormously promoting the national industry of silk weaving, the number of looms having increased in 1751 to 14,600 in all Spain, in addition to the royal factory at Talavera. Ensenada's great plan for replacing the alcabalas and millions by a single tax upon salt and the revenues from exterior custom-houses was under consideration when he fell.

by Ferdinand VI. There were, it is stated, still 18,000 square leagues of the best land in Spain entirely out of cultivation, and 2,000,000 of the inhabitants on the verge of starvation. The recovery from such long-standing misery was necessarily very slow, but as much as any human beings could do under the circumstances, was done by Ferdinand and his ministers. It needed all their prudence to keep clear of the war between the two great powers, for part of the struggle was enacted on Spanish land, Minorca being captured from the English by the Duke of Richelieu, while the ill-fated Byng was defeated in Spanish waters (1756). Efforts, indeed, were made to bribe Ferdinand into taking sides against England by an offer of the cession of Minorca, and the crown of Poland for his half brother Philip; but he was firm in his determination. Spain needed all her resources for herself and she should not be drawn into her neighbour's quarrels whilst he lived, though his new fleet was now able to protect Spanish commerce against the depredations of the corsairs of either nation and of the Moorish pirates. In August 1758 Queen Barbara died, to the intense grief of her husband. Like his father before him, he fell into a complete state of lethargy and shut himself off from all communication with the world. Whilst he was thus isolated, and in a condition of intermittent lunacy, the French party formed a conspiracy to raise his brother Philip (Duke of Parma) to the throne, to the detriment of Charles King of Naples; but Pitt divulged the plot, and it fell through. Gradually the King lapsed into entire madness, and eventually died on the 10th August 1759 after a reign of 13 years. He was buried with his beloved wife Barbara in the Church of the immense convent of the Salesas at Madrid—now the lawcourts—which they had founded, leaving his crown to his halfbrother King Charles, and appointing as regent pending the new King's arrival, his mother Elizabeth Farnese.

It is difficult to exaggerate the intellectual advance which Spain had made during the short breathing time of peace under Ferdinand. The foundation of academies and learned bodies went on apace; subsidies and scholarships were granted liberally to men of science, art, and letters, to enable them to pursue their investigations in Spain and abroad; and foreign scholars and artificers were also attracted to Spain. In almost every direction advancement was remarkable. The Inquisition in the reign of Philip V had continued its proceedings with as much vigour as ever, though with less publicity. During the reign of Philip there were no less than 14,000 persons sentenced to various punishments by the Inquisition, 782 *autos-de-fé* being held; but a great change came with Ferdinand. Not only were the causes much less numerous, but the tribunal itself was entirely altered in character. The age of light had dawned, and the Holy Office itself was on its trial. The procedure now was mild, the punishments trifling, and without degradation to the offender. Ferdinand had found Spain, struggling painfully into the light, still ruined, bankrupt, and miserable. He left it enjoying comparative prosperity, with a fleet of fifty ships of war and three millions sterling in the treasury.

CHAPTER XV.

CHARLES III, 1759—1788.

ONLY a very brief summary can be given of the events of the reign of Charles III. He was extremely popular with his Neapolitan subjects, who had prospered exceedingly under his rule. By the treaty of Aquisgran (1749), against which Charles had protested, it was provided that the throne of Naples should pass to the Duke of Parma, his brother, in case Charles succeeded to Spain; Parma, Piacenza and Guastalla being divided between Austria and Sardinia. Both Charles and his subjects were opposed to this arrangement; and by means of diplomacy and a money payment, an arrangement was made by which Naples should pass to Ferdinand, the third son of Charles, then aged 8 years. The eldest son, Philip, was excluded from the succession in consequence of imbecility, and the heirship of the crown of Spain was secured to the second son, Charles Antonio, thenceforward Prince of Asturias. Charles III landed at Barcelona on the 17th October 1759, and it very soon became evident that neither he nor his wife, Amelia of Saxony, intended to allow the Queen Mother to obtain the upper hand again. They were polite and considerate to her, but firm in excluding her from the political influence, for which she yearned in order to obtain the duchy of Tuscany for her youngest son Luis, the cardinal archbishop of Toledo. On his slow progress through Cataluña and Aragon, the new King won all hearts by remitting arrears of taxes, and restoring some of the privileges which the provinces had lost under Philip V. In Madrid he adopted a similar policy, and the rejoicings of the people at his state-entry (13 July 1760) were such as had not been seen since the palmy days of the house of Austria.

Up to this time, Madrid had remained one of the most backward and filthy capitals of Europe; the people even, of the lower class, still swaggered about armed to the teeth; and in defiance of pragmatics, the big slouch hats of the men were pulled over the eyes, and the corner of the long cloaks thrown over the lower part of the face, until they looked, as Charles' favourite the Marquis of Squillaci (Esquilache) said, more like conspirators than the subjects of an enlightened monarch. Charles was entirely surrounded by ministers and friends belonging to the new "philosophical" French school, who looked upon religion as a relic of the dark ages, and exalted the secular power of the monarchy in order to oppose the priest. The first acts of the new king were therefore to endeavour to turn Spaniards into as close an imitation of Frenchmen as possible, and to make Madrid a bright, clean European city of the modern type, rather than the gloomy capital it was. Streets were to be paved and swept, pipes and gutters were to carry off the drainage, and the warning cry of "*agua va*" was to be heard no more. An urban police was established, men were to go "unmuzzled" and unarmed, and lanterns were to illuminate the streets at night. Wall had still remained at the head of affairs, the only change in the ministry being the appointment of Squillaci as minister of finance. All the new-fangled changes which the Spaniards hated were laid to the charge of the Italian minister. Broadbrims and long cloaks had been good enough for their fathers: why said the Madrileños, should they be forbidden to wear them? Lanterns might be wanted in some cities, but Spaniards could be trusted, as well by night as by day. Personally the King did not run counter to the religious convictions of his people, and his first act after the ceremony of taking the oath to the united Cortes of the nation, was to proclaim the Virgin of the Immaculate Conception the official patron of Spain; but the men he had brought from Naples with him made no secret of their contempt for the fat priests and monks that crowded the capital, and with their ecclesiastical pretensions trenched upon the royal prerogative.

Only a few months after his accession the King, at the age of 43, lost his wife (September 1760): he remained a widower for the rest of his life. Thenceforward Charles allowed himself to be drawn more and more to the side of France. Negotiations for peace were opened between Austria and France early in 1761, but the conferences of Augsburg hung fire, and later in the year the new Spanish ambassador in Paris, Grimaldo, opened negotiations for a treaty, in which France and Spain mutually agreed to defend each other's territories—a most one-sided arrangement for Spain. When, therefore, the French ambassador in London (Bussy) presented to Pitt the terms of France for peace, he also made claims on account of Spain, with whom England was at peace. The English government indignantly refused to consider such demands, and in answer to Lord Bristol's remonstrances, Charles informed him that he had signed a new "family compact" with the French King (August 1761), Naples and Parma being included in the arrangement. Bristol left Madrid in December. In two years, therefore, Charles had allowed himself to be caught in the snare which his less able half-brother had avoided for 13 years, and Spain was once more at war with England, for no quarrel of her own. English subjects were expelled from Spain, English ships in Spanish ports captured, and on the refusal of the King of Portugal to join in the "family compact" (May 1762) his country was invaded by Spanish and French troops. An English army of 10,000 men under Count Lippe, with large stores of arms for the Portuguese, was promptly sent to Portugal. Through the summer the campaign on the frontier continued, some partial successes of the Spaniards under O'Reilly and Ricla being more than counterbalanced by the victories of Lippe and Burgoyne; the Spanish commander-in-chief, Count de Aranda, being compelled to retire into Spain on the approach of winter. In the West Indies the English carried all before them, capturing Martinique from the French, and Granada, St Vincent, St Lucia and Tobago from the Spaniards. Finally, in June 1762, Admiral Pocock with a powerful English fleet appeared before Habana, and landed 8000 men under the Earl of Albemarle. The place was well prepared for attack, with a strong garrison and 16 ships of war in the harbour, and the defence was both gallant and sanguinary; but after a month of siege the English stormed the fortress of Morro, capturing it only after immense carnage. At last, to the great indignation of his countrymen, the governor, Pardo, surrendered the place with 15 million dollars of treasure, an enormous quantity of arms and stores, and 12 ships of war (13 August 1762). In October Manila surrendered to another English fleet, with a promised ransom of 4 million dollars, which was never paid. Although the Spaniards had captured the Portuguese province of Sarmiento on the river Plate, it was clear to Charles that, at this rate, Spain would soon sink into its former position of penury again; and he willingly listened now to Lord Bute's suggestions for peace. The Duke de Nivernais and Grimaldo were sent to London, and a treaty was concluded in February 1763, by which the French ceded to England various territories in Asia, America and Africa, and again surrendered Minorca; whilst Spain gave up Florida, the exclusive claim to cut logwood on the coast of Campeachy and the right to fish on the banks of Newfoundland, and England returned Habana and Manila.

Wall had done his duty to Spain, but the family pact with France and the war with England were distasteful to him, and he earnestly sought permission to retire, now that the war was ended. For a time the King absolutely refused to part with so able a minister, and it was not until Wall feigned semi-blindness that he was allowed to resign upon a handsome pension, and with every mark of honour; living beloved and respected on his estate near Granada until 1778. He was succeeded by Grimaldo, the negotiator of the "family compact"; "more of a Frenchman," wrote Lord Rochford, "than the French ambassador." With such a minister, Spanish relations with Great Britain soon became strained again, and for a time war seemed almost inevitable on the question of the expulsion of the English settlers from Honduras, and the recriminatory claims of both powers with regard to the non-fulfilment of the clause relative to the logwood question in the last treaty of peace. Finally, however, concessions on both sides were made, and by the end of 1764 the imminent war was avoided; but the discussions on the subject, following a war in which the Spanish American colonies were principally interested, had attracted the attention of Spaniards to that part of the world. During the constant wars in the mother country the colonies had been allowed to go on in their own way, Spanish Governors and officials, clerical and lay, plundering right and left, with little or no thought of the benefit of the people over whom they ruled. The one object was to get rich quickly and return to Spain; and all the evils of the mother country were magnified in the colonies. Out of the 4 to 6 millions of dollars which were sent from America annually for the royal treasury, it is stated that less than a fifth actually reached its destination; whilst one Archbishop Viceroy of Mexico sent no less than a million dollars to Spain on his own account.

A vigorous attempt was now made (1765) to reform and modernise the colonial governments. Inspectors with large discretionary powers were sent out, and the administrations were entirely reorganised, not without some resistance, but to the immense benefit both of Spain and the colonies. The reforming zeal continued also in Spain itself, under the two Italian ministers Grimaldo and Squillaci. The Madrileños had looked sourly from the first upon the introduction of foreign ideas in the capital, and particularly upon the attempt by sumptuary laws to compel Spaniards to wear cocked hats, bag-wigs and coats, instead of "chambergos" (wide brimmed hats), "guedejas" (sidelocks) and long cloaks; and their discontent had been artfully kept alive by the priests and by grandees of the old Spanish school. Squillaci was the principal scapegoat. The King had from the first made the Inquisition and the Clergy understand that in future he, and not they, should be master, and though the monarch himself was too high to be attacked, his foreign advisers were fair game. In March 1766 a strict pragmatic was issued forbidding the wearing of cloaks beyond a certain length, and wide brimmed hats, on pain of imprisonment; and public officers were posted in the streets with shears, to clip the offending garments to the required dimensions. This order, coming after several similar attempts to interfere with the personal habits of the people, aroused popular fury. Some hidden hands organised a revolt. On the 23rd March 1766, Palm Sunday, some men ostentatiously paraded in the Plaza of Anton Martin in the forbidden garb. They were challenged and resisted, and an infuriated mob collected, as if by magic, in cloaks and broad brims. The officers were overpowered, and the tumult swept in irresistible numbers into the Great Square before the palace. "Death to Esquilache" was the cry, and "Viva España." The minister had fled to hiding, but his house (the famous house with the seven chimneys) was sacked. The crowd at first was induced to disperse on the promise from the King that all their demands should be conceded, but encouraged by their success, they returned to the palace. A small picquet of the King's Walloon guards fired upon the mob. This was enough; for the Walloons were foreigners too. Henceforward every Walloon guard to be discovered was murdered; the corpses were dragged through the streets, and the heads, crowned with broad brimmed hats, were carried aloft on the tops of poles. For the next two days slaughter and pillage raged supreme, and those who raised the storm were powerless to stay it.

They demanded that only Spaniards should rule them, and that the Walloon guard should be suppressed; that Spaniards should dress as they pleased; that municipal monopolies should be abolished, that the price of bread should be lowered, and that the King himself should personally promise compliance. Some attempts at temporising only further aroused their fury, and at last Charles had to give way and do as he was bidden. But during the night the King was ill-advised enough to fly to Aranjuez, and the mob, feeling that they were betrayed, again took possession of the capital. The King saw now that they were not to be trifled with, and was persuaded to return in a few days, whilst Squillaci went disguised to Cartagena, and thence to Naples, where he died.

The revolt of Esquilache, as the Spaniards call it, struck a death blow to two long standing institutions in Spain, the domination of foreign ministers, and the right of the Sovereign to interfere in the dress and personal habits of his people; but if, as was alleged, the priests were behind it and thought that it would re-establish the power of the Inquisition and the Church they were mistaken. The new Spanish ministers were Musquiz for Finance, General Muniain for War; the presidency of the Council was given to Count de Aranda, a man of great intelligence, but greater vanity, who cared nothing for the Church; a zealous, but not too prudent, reformer. The revolutionary agitation still continued and a plot was discovered to kill the King; the most arbitrary and revolting punishments were inflicted upon the supposed offenders. The Jesuits on the one hand, and the Voltairians on the other, were accused of being at the bottom of the unrest; and all over Spain the feeling became more and more bitter between the erstwhile omnipotent Church, and the free thought which stood at the back of the coming French revolution. Bread riots, and demands for the fixing of lower prices for food, continued all through the spring and summer of 1766; and Aranda, when he took in hand the reins of government, was face to face with a state of affairs which could only be dealt with by vigorous measures. The new minister was full of liberal ideas. The monopoly of wealth and consideration held for so many years in Spain by the clergy, whilst the country was backward in material progress, compared with the rest of Europe, galled his patriotism and common sense. He had lived abroad for years, and saw how enlightenment had spread in other countries, which had shaken off the yoke of priestcraft; and his one idea was to bring Spain abreast of Europe, let the cost be what it might. In his zeal he forgot that the people for whom he desired to legislate were conservative in thought, bound to old prejudices and traditions, with a history of three centuries in which the Church and the priest had been the main instruments of secular policy; and, although he perseveringly sought for popularity, by almost undignified means, his severity against the rioters, and his hurry in reform, made the populace regard him with doubtful eyes. The King's promises to the mob were broken: the Walloon Guard was re-established, the municipal monopolies still flourished, the price of food was still almost prohibitive, and pressure was again put upon the leaders of the people, to persuade them to abandon the Spanish dress. When the change of costume had at last been made, and not till then, did Charles III condescend to re-enter his capital in triumph with the intention of again residing there (December 1766): but though the Madrileños were at last tricked out like Frenchmen to please their monarch, many a grim look, many a muttered curse, followed him in his progress.

Early in April 1767 an order was suddenly given for the expulsion of the Jesuits from Spain, and under circumstances of great hardship the decree was executed; the fathers, with nothing but their personal belongings, being hurried simultaneously from their monasteries to various ports appointed, and shipped for foreign countries, to the number of 6000. Almost at the same time the Spanish colonies were also freed from the presence of the fathers of the Company. Charles III explained the expulsion to the Pope as "simply an indispensable economical measure"; but it fell like a thunderbolt upon Spain and the papacy. "This," wrote the Pontiff, "is the last drop in the cup of our affliction": but neither prayers nor threats could move Aranda, or his King. It had been proved to their satisfaction, that the Jesuits were at the bottom of the revolutionary disturbances, with the real object of re-establishing the supremacy of the clergy in Spain, and the Jesuits must go— not, it was explained, because they were monks, but because they were members of a society disloyal to the government of the country. The society was rich, and had many friends in Spain, and the expulsion threatened for a time to provoke revolt, but the severity of Aranda had cowed the people; none dared to move, and the omnipotence of the Church in Spain, as an instrument of secular government, fell before the new order of ideas which was hurrying Europe to revolution. The Cortes had gone, the Inquisition and the Church were powerless, and the personal despotism of the monarch stood forth, naked and unshamed, unprotected now by the glamour of the faith from the attacks of the legions advancing against it.

In the meanwhile, foreign affairs again grew overcast. The cession of Louisiana by France to Spain, in the treaty of Fontainebleau, had been resisted by the colonists to the extent that the territory had to be conquered forcibly by Spanish troops. Choiseul continued to try his hardest to draw Spain into war with Great Britain, and had prompted Charles to establish a governor on the Falkland Isles, which were claimed by England. A considerable Spanish force sailed from Buenos Ayres and ejected the English from the islands (June 1770), and public opinion in England at once clamoured for war. Spain, backed by Choiseul, refused the demands of Harris, afterwards Lord Malmesbury, the English *chargé d'affaires*, and active preparations on both sides were made for hostilities. But Choiseul fell, thanks to the influence of Mme. Dubarry,

and Louis XV drew back and left Spain to face England alone.
This did not suit Charles III, who had hoped that the "family
compact" would have stood the strain, and he had to apologise
to George III and withdraw his forces from the sterile and
inhospitable Falkland Isles, which were useless to him. The
blow to Spanish pride, however, was none the less great; and the
enemies of Aranda, who were many, succeeded in causing his
dismissal; Figueroa at first, and afterwards the celebrated Count
de Campomanes, succeeding him. In the meantime Clement
XIV, whilst openly pretending to agree with the Bourbon
sovereigns who had demanded the suppression of the Society
of Jesus, had astutely avoided compliance. The Spanish
bishops, with the exception of fourteen, sided with the King, but
the fall of Choiseul in France, and the change of ministers in
Parma, had left Spain almost alone on the question; and by
the end of 1771 the immediate danger to the society appeared
at an end. But Charles himself was as obstinate as the
Pontiff, and the appointment (May 1772) as his ambassador of
Moñino, afterwards the famous Count de Floridablanca, as
zealous a reformer, but a far more tactful diplomatist than
Aranda, turned the scale against the Jesuits. Clement shuffled
as long as he dared, but even Austria, under the enlightened
Joseph II, had deserted him, and in the face of a great
European coalition, which threatened the Catholic supremacy
of the Papacy, he signed (July 1773) the decree suppressing
the Society of Jesus throughout Christendom: but he bitterly
resented the pressure which wrested the brief from him, and
invested it with as little force and authority as he could.
"This suppression will be my death," he said, as he signed the
brief, and though in this his anticipation may not have been
fulfilled, his act condemned to extinction one of the most
powerful organizations ever devised by man, and confiscated
the property of one of the richest corporations in the world,
to please the Bourbon family confederacy.

The civil reforms initiated by Campillo and Ensenada continued uninterruptedly under Aranda and his successors. The vast tracts of land which had been abandoned and left waste were equitably divided amongst the inhabitants of neighbouring villages, the poorer people being first considered: the export and import of grain were allowed, under certain prudent restrictions with regard to the price of food in the home markets. Agriculture revived as if by magic, and the royal revenue benefited to an unprecedented extent. A government registry for titles and mortgages made the transfer of land easy and cheap, the coinage was reformed and unified, prohibitive protective duties were placed upon calicoes, muslins and other foreign textiles, greatly to the loss of the English manufacturers but to the advantage of the home producer; whilst raw material was freed from duties, operatives were brought from abroad in great numbers to teach Spaniards industrial processes in factories subsidised by Government, and an attempt even was made by royal decree to break down Spanish pride by announcing (1773) that it was no degradation for hidalgos to engage in handicrafts. Canals and splendid roads, which are still a just source of pride to Spaniards, were constructed from one end of the country to the other, marshes were drained, irrigation works fertilising great areas were opened, the postal service throughout Spain was organised, diligences ran regularly on the fine new highways, and even the grim deserts of the Sierra Morena, the lurking place of brigands and outlaws, were populated by 6000 Bavarian immigrants planted in thirteen new villages by the reforming ministers of Charles III. The sloth of centuries was at last broken through. This was a new Spain which had arisen out of the ashes of the old. Wiser than his French kinsman, Charles opened his arms to the spirit of reform which was throbbing through the world, and the horrors of the French Revolution spared his country; though the weakness and folly of his son and grandson subsequently exposed it to trials almost as terrible. Financial and administrative reform also progressed apace; the collection of the public revenue was now economical and regular, the cost not exceeding 8 per cent. of the amount collected; and the great plan for the substitution of one single impost for all taxes was still the favourite project of each successive minister. The police regulations for the preservation of decency and order were minute and severe, in accordance with the ideas of the time, but they completely transformed Spanish urban society, suppressing license, discouraging vagabondage, and promoting industry and thrift. Education, taken from the hands of the Jesuits, was nationalised and secularised, the Universities were purged and rendered effective, and the Inquisition was sternly told for once, and for all, that civil offences must be tried by civil tribunals (April 1774). The Holy Office had, indeed, lost its importance, and its last struggle to keep up its ancient power in the face of new ideas was its persecution for alleged Voltairianism of Olavide, the enlightened director of the German colonies in the Sierra Morena, whom it kept in prison for two years, when he escaped to France. The odium and scandal brought upon the Inquisition by this persecution was a death-blow to what remained of its power, thenceforward but a shadow. In 1780 its last victim was burnt alive in Seville, a poor friendless old woman accused of sorcery: for it dared now to grasp no higher prey.

The Spanish army was in the meanwhile reorganised on the Prussian model of the great Frederick, and the navy once more became such as befitted that of a leading maritime power. Charles soon found occasion to employ both services against the Moors, who attacked the Spanish fortresses of Ceuta and Melilla on the coast of Africa (February 1775), and who were defeated and were obliged to sue for peace. The treaty was promptly broken by the Spaniards, who in July 1775 sent a strong expedition of 20,000 men under Count O'Reilly to attack Algiers. It had been intended to take the Moors by surprise, but they had their spies in Spain, and on O'Reilly's arrival he found them fully prepared. The result of the attack was a

hideous rout and carnage of the Spaniards, and O'Reilly for
a time became the best abused man in Spain, Grimaldo the
Italian minister sharing his unpopularity. Most of the ministers
were Aragonese, and friends of Aranda; the heir apparent,
the Prince of Asturias, and his wife (Maria Luisa, Princess of
Parma), were also opposed to Grimaldo; whose great supporter
in France, the Duke of Choiseul, had fallen, on the death of
Louis XV (March 1774); and the author of the "family compact," distrusted by all parties, gladly accepted the embassy to
Rome, in order to be free from his thankless ministry. He was
replaced by Count de Floridablanca (Moñino), a politician of
his own school, but a Spaniard. Spain was however not long
at peace. The great Portuguese minister, the Marquis of
Pombal, always vigilant to extend the frontiers of the Portuguese colonies, in union with England, as against France and
Spain, had attacked the Spanish colony of Buenos Ayres. In
return, a strong Spanish fleet had captured, without resistance,
the island of Santa Catalina on the coast of Brazil, and had
once more taken possession of the colony of Sacramento.
When England and France were about to join in the war,
Joseph I of Portugal died (February 1777), and the new Queen,
a niece of Charles III, promptly dismissed Pombal, who had
plotted to exclude her from the succession. An arrangement
with Spain was thus made easy, and a treaty of peace was
signed in October, by which Sacramento and the navigation of
the rivers Plate, Parana and Paraguay, became Spanish in
exchange for vast disputed territories in the interior of the
continent on the Amazon. But though henceforward Spain
and Portugal were friends, a still greater contest was brewing,
in which the former country had to take part.

The war of independence had broken out in North America
(August 1776). The French Government had eagerly welcomed
the deputies sent by the United States and had recognised
the new republic (March 1778). The result was a declaration of war between England and France, who were soon at

close grip in all four quarters of the globe. Both belligerents sought the aid of Spain, the one pointing out the evil example of aiding colonial revolt and the other invoking the terms of the "family compact" and the desirability of crippling England. Aranda in Paris was for war against England; Floridablanca, more cautious, was in favour of a temporising policy, in pursuance of which the Spanish Government offered to mediate between the disputants (January 1779), a proposal which, as no doubt was foreseen, was indignantly rejected by England, who claimed to deal alone with her revolting colonies. The answer of Spain was a declaration of war against England (June 1779), although the "family compact" was no longer quoted as an excuse for the measure which, as its results proved, was a disastrous precedent for a great colonial power like Spain. Aranda, the Spanish ambassador in France, was full of wild talk of invading England, of capturing Gibraltar, of ousting England from Hindostan and much else; and patriotic fervour was raised to fever pitch in Spain itself against England, whose maritime power was considered a standing danger to the rest of the world. In the summer of 1779 the French fleet of 32 sail of the line joined the Spanish fleet of a similar strength in Cadiz harbour, under Don Luis de Cordoba, whilst another Spanish squadron lay at Ferrol. In all, Spain alone had afloat 68 ships of the line and many smaller vessels, whilst the English squadron in the Channel under Hardy only consisted of 38 ships, the coasts of Great Britain being also in a bad state of defence. But the plans of invasion again came to nothing. Hardy lay in the Downs, and the allies did not like the look of him, though they were the stronger. Autumn came on, bad food and consequent scurvy killed great numbers of French and Spaniards, and the allied fleets were glad to seek shelter in Brest, crippled and disabled, with all hopes of the invasion at an end.

Spain had blockaded Gibraltar by land and sea with a force ten times as large as Lord Elliot had for the defence of the rock; but gallant Rodney, after capturing a Spanish flotilla with supplies for the Cadiz fleet (January 1780), slipped through the Spanish squadrons which had intended to intercept him, and relieved Gibraltar, entirely routing and capturing the Spanish blockading fleet, which however made a brilliant defence under Admiral Langara. Thence the English admiral sailed to attack the Spanish possessions in America. The Spaniards in the meanwhile had expelled the English from Campeachy and had co-operated with the Americans against the English in Florida and on the Mississippi, capturing Mobile in March 1780. The cordiality between the French and Spanish had not survived their joint fiasco in the invasion of England, and negotiations for peace with Spain were commenced at an early stage by Lord North's government on the basis of the cession of Gibraltar. Floridablanca was quite willing to listen to them, but it was soon found that the *quid pro quo* demanded by the English, namely the Island of Porto Rico, the territory of Oran, the fortress of Omoa, with a money indemnity of two million sterling, was too high a one for Spain to pay, and the negotiations were broken off. During the war Floridablanca initiated a policy of what was called "armed neutrality," by which, in union first with Russia and subsequently with most of the other powers of Europe, it was agreed, among other things, that the ships of neutral powers should in future be allowed to enter or leave the ports of belligerents freely, except during a *bona-fide* blockade or when they carried contraband of war. This understanding, as it did not include England, amounted to a universal confederation against her at sea, and threatened to bring into open hostilities against her all the countries of Europe.

In the face of this formidable coalition England stood firm; but, whilst she was struggling in America, her small garrison in Minorca was surprised by a strong French and Spanish fleet with 8000 troops on board, who captured the island. General

Murray and his little band held out in the castle of St Philip for many months against an army, but at length (February 1782), decimated by starvation, scurvy and fire, they surrendered to honourable terms, even the enemy acknowledging their bravery: Minorca thus returning to the crown of Spain after 74 years of English possession. The victorious Spaniards then again besieged Gibraltar, where Elliot's garrison had been increased to 7000 men. The Spanish land forces outside numbered 40,000 soldiers; and, for the first time in modern warfare, "floating batteries," with ironclad decks, were employed by the allies. They were constructions of enormous size, very heavily armed, and great results were expected from such huge machines. For a time their cannonading was damaging, but on the 13th September Elliot's red-hot shot set fire to some of them, and the Spaniards burnt the others. A terrible panic ensued, in which 1500 men were burnt or drowned, whilst the English gunboats captured as many more. On the 10th October the English fleet under Howe approached to relieve the garrison. Although he only had 30 sail against the enemy's 50, he managed to run four ships of munitions into the harbour, and with the rest of his fleet successfully evaded the allies. Every plan which science or experience could suggest was adopted to capture the place, but without success, for the Spanish and French officers were at variance from the first, and effective co-operation was impossible.

On the other side of the Atlantic the struggle still raged. Florida was now in the hands of the Spaniards, and Lord Cornwallis had been beaten at Yorktown: but on the other hand the allied expedition against Jamaica had been scattered by Rodney and Hood. The result of Spain's help to American revolt was soon seen in her own colonies. Revolts against Spanish misrule and oppression gained force from the example of the north. Tumults arose in Peru and Buenos Ayres, where anarchy reigned for months; and as many, it is said, as 100,000 men, mostly Indians, were sacrificed. England, Spain and

France had suffered much, American independence was seen to be inevitable, and terms of peace were at length discussed. Spain's first demands were exaggerated and impossible, and the war was about to recommence when France began to negotiate alone. This brought Floridablanca to his senses, and though at first he roundly rejected the preliminary treaty signed at Paris (January 1783), he had to give way with much reluctance, and made peace in the autumn without the recovery of Gibraltar, though Minorca and Florida remained Spanish.

For the next three years the efforts of the Spanish Government were principally directed against the Algerian and Tunisian pirates, and at length a treaty was made by which (June 1786), for a payment of money by Spain to the Regency of Algiers, an undertaking was given that piracy in the Mediterranean should cease. After many centuries, the Christian and the infidel sheathed their arms. Thousands of Christian captives were liberated, commerce was safe, and the scores of leagues of fine land on the Valencian coast, freed from the raids of the pirates, were again brought under smiling cultivation by a prosperous and happy population. Spain was at peace throughout the world, emerging from the dark past into the light of day: free to continue by the hands of Spaniards the work of regeneration begun by impulse from abroad—or to sink back again into the slough from which foreign enlightenment had partly lifted her.

For the last two years of his life Charles successfully strove to keep the peace of Europe unbroken. The death of Frederick the Great, and the continued dissensions between England and France, together with the revolution in Holland, furnished elements of strife which, but for the prudent intervention of the King of Spain and Floridablanca, would have led to war. The only question remaining for which it was worth while for Spain to fight, was the possession of Gibraltar; and both Whigs and Tories in England made it clear now that the rock would not be surrendered, unless Britain itself was crushed.

This was wisely recognised by Charles and his enlightened minister, and the rest of the monarch's days were given up to the re-organisation and reform of his own country. There was no phase of public welfare that did not receive attention. Hospitals, asylums, poor-houses and free-schools, sprang up all over Spain, thanks to the initiative of the monarch. Savings-banks, benefit societies, and philanthropic institutions, were established, whilst vagrancy and mendicancy were put down with a stern hand. Men of science and learning, skilled organisers of industry[1], and experienced artificers, were brought from abroad in large numbers, and under their guidance new industries were founded and fostered by the Government. The famous glass factory of the Granja, whose products vied with Venice, the porcelains of the Buen Retiro, the cotton velvets of Avila, the fine leathers of Seville and Cordoba, the machinery, watches, optical instruments, and fancy goods of Madrid, all became famous and profitable under the patronage of Charles III. Public credit was raised and funds procured for these reforms, and to pay off old loans, by the establishment of the national Bank of St Carlos, and the issue of interest-bearing government bonds for 800 millions of reals, which were freely circulated at par. The "alcabalas" and "millions," which had killed Spanish industry, were reduced from 14 per cent. to 5 per cent. in Castile, and suspended altogether in the case of goods or produce sold in the place of origin; and the deficit was made up by a 5 per cent. tax on incomes from land, and 2 or 3 per cent. on the rental of holdings. The great project of the

[1] An ancestor of the writer—Andrew Hume—was one of these. He was appointed in 1788 Director-General of the new Royal button factory in Madrid, with a monopoly for all Spain. A large number of other English, Scots and Irishmen, of all ranks, at the same period were similarly established in Madrid and Seville. In the Capital all these families have now died out or have been merged into Spanish families. More curious still is the complete assimilation of the large Bavarian agricultural communities in the south.

single tax was abandoned in favour of this system of graduation, and the "alcabalas" ceased to have the disastrous effect which they had exercised for so long.

During the reign of Charles III, the population of Spain had increased to $10\frac{1}{4}$ millions of souls, a rise of a million and a half in twenty-seven years; and the public revenue, which is stated by Dr Clarke to have been £5,431,899 in 1760, had grown to 616,300,000 reals—over £6,000,000—in 1787, although the reforms and economies in the collection of taxes must have caused the actual increase of the receipts in the Treasury to be much greater than here represented. It will be seen that most of Floridablanca's reforms were directed to the relief of industry and the workers, at the expense of the landowners, the nobles and the Church. These classes were still vigorous, and naturally looked upon the reformer with dislike. Turbulent Aranda too, though a reformer himself, was jealous of Floridablanca, and, with Count O'Reilly, joined the malcontents. Satires, pasquins, and newspaper attacks rained upon the great minister, who unwisely retorted by prosecutions and proscriptions, which increased his unpopularity, and at length, to the grief of the King, he begged permission to retire.

Already (October 1788) the mutterings of the great storm that was to shake the world were heard on the other side of the Pyrenees. Charles had stood firm against all attempts to draw him into the complications which foreboded another great war, and begged his minister not to abandon his post. Whilst the matter was yet pending, the King's health broke down. He was an old man, but his regular, temperate life, passed mostly in the open air, had so far preserved his vigour unimpaired. Trouble, however, had not spared him. His son, the King of Naples, had turned out badly; death had been busy of late in his family, his heir was a poor weak-minded creature with a termagant wife; and the cloud that hung over the Bourbons in France oppressed the King's spirit with ideas of coming calamity. When he came from the Escorial to Madrid in December

1788, it was seen that he was failing; and in a few days he fell ill of fever. His answer to the bishop who asked him on his deathbed, whether he pardoned his enemies, reveals the magnanimity of the man. "How should I wait for this pass before forgiving them?" he said. "They were all forgiven the moment after the offence." He died at dawn on the 14th December, 1788, aged 73, the only good, great and patriotic, King that providence had vouchsafed to Spain in modern times. Enlightened, generous, and just; sleepless in his vigilance for the good of his people, in his 29 years of reign he did much to repair the calamity and misery which the errors of his predecessors had brought upon his country. With a strong and wise successor Spain might have continued happy, prosperous and powerful. But Charles IV was too weak, worthily to wield the sceptre of his great father, and once more the afflicted country became the plaything of a contemptible favourite. The shameful days of the Lermas, the Olivares, and the Valenzuelas, were enacted over again; until at last the generous, sound-hearted people, purified and strengthened by suffering, arose in their might, and claimed the rights of popular self-government, which the Cortes of Castile in the days of darkness had allowed tyrants and favourites to filch from them. But the remedy came too late. The evils from which the country suffered were too deeply seated to be cured by paper Constitutions, unless they were accompanied by restraint and enlightenment on the part both of governors and governed. Betrayed again and again by unworthy rulers, made the plaything of military and political adventurers, unhappy Spain was forced into the revolutionary career which it has followed almost uninterruptedly for the last ninety years.

BIBLIOGRAPHY OF SPANISH HISTORY,
1479—1788.

GENERAL.

Historia General de España. Modesto Lafuente and Juan Valera. 25 vols. Barcelona, 1888. The best modern history of Spain.

Historia General de España. J. de Mariana and J. M. Miniana. 10 vols. Madrid, 1794—5. Miniana's portion is useful.

Reinas Catolicas. Flores. Madrid, 1770. Lives of the Spanish Queens.

Historia eclesiastica de España. V. Lafuente. Madrid, 1874.

History of Religious Intolerance in Spain. A. de Castro. London, 1852. Translated by Parker. Written from the anti-Catholic point of view.

The Spanish Protestants. Same author. London, 1851. Ditto.

Histoire critique de l'Inquisition. Llorente. Paris, 1817.

Historia de la Civilizacion Iberica. J. Oliveira Martins. Madrid, 1893. Translated from the Portuguese by Tajonera.

El Poder Civil en España. M. Danvila y Collado. 6 vols. Madrid, 1885—7. A work of the highest value, giving a full history of all the Cortes held, and the growth and decay of civil power.

Documentos ineditos para la historia de España. In progress. Madrid. 112 volumes published. Containing innumerable documents of the highest value relating to episodes in Spanish history. See General index of the series.

Relazioni degli Ambasciatori Veneti. Alberi, and continuations by Berchet and Barozzi. Florence, 1839—1863.

Restablecimiento de las fabricas y comercio de España. Ulloa. Madrid, 1740. (Exposition of the evils of the financial system.)

History of the Expulsion of the Moriscos. Wars of the Comuneros. Inquisition, etc., etc. Tracts by Geddes. London, 1702—6.

Historia Constitucional de la Monarquia española. Du Hamel. Madrid, 1848.
Fürsten und Völker von Süd-Europa im sechszehnten und siebzehnten Jahrhundert. Vol. I. L. von Ranke. Berlin, 1857.
(*a*) The Ottoman and Spanish Empires in the sixteenth and seventeenth centuries. (English translation from an earlier edition by W. K. Kelly.) London, 1843.
(*b*) L'Espagne sous Charles V, Philippe II et III. (French translation by Haiber.) Paris, 1863.
Gobierno Politico de los Pueblos de España. Santayana. Madrid, 1796.
Civil, Commercial, Political and Literary, History of Spain. Wyndham Beawes. London, 1793. 2 vols. A much slighter work than its title implies.
Historia de la legislatura española. Antequera. Madrid, 1849.
Histoire des Cortès d'Espagne. Sempère. Bordeaux, 1815.
Boletin de la Real Academia de la Historia. 31 vols.
Memorial historico Español. 33 vols. These two periodicals contain many valuable monographs and documents.
Apuntes sobre et bien y et mal de España. Causas de su decadencia. Gandara. Cadiz, 1810.
Biblioteca Española economico-politica. Sempere. Madrid, 1804. 3 vols. (Economic causes of Spain's decay.)

FERDINAND AND ISABELLA, PHILIP I AND CHARLES I (V).

Calendar of State Papers. Foreign and domestic, Henry VIII (to 1539. In progress). Foreign. Edward VI and Mary (to 1558). Spanish (to 1542. In progress). Venetian to 1556.
Crónica de los Reyes Católicos. Hernando del Pulgar (the royal chronicler). Valencia, 1780.
Ælii Antonii Nebrissensis...... Decades II. Ejusdem de Bello Navarrensi libri II. Lucii Marinæi Siculi de Rebus Hispaniæ memorabilibus libri XXII. These three works are printed in Hispaniæ illustratæ...Scriptores varii. A. Schott. Frankfort, 1603.
Anales de la corona de Aragon. J. Zurita (to 1516), continued by B. L. Argensola and D. J. Dormer. Saragossa, 1610—1697.

Opere inedite. F. Guicciardini. Vol. VI (his embassy to Spain, with a description of country and people). Florence, 1864.
Crónica de los Reyes de Castilla. Cayetano Rosell. Biblioteca de autores Españoles. Vol. LXX, 1878.
Ferdinand and Isabella. W. H. Prescott. 3 vols. London, 1838 (and other editions).
Los Reyes Católicos. V. Balaguer. Madrid, 1894 (in progress).
Geschichte von Spanien. F. W. Schirrmacher. Vol. VI. Gotha, 1893 (to 1492 only. In progress).
Elogio de la reina católica Donna Isabel. D. Clemencin. Madrid, 1821. (Valuable for its treatment of social and economic history.)
Histoire de la réunion de la Navarre à la Castille, 1479—1521. P. Boissonnade. Paris, 1893.
Der Kardinal Ximenes. P. Hefele. 1844 (translated by J. Dalton. London, 1860).
Studien und Skizzen zur Geschichte der Reformationszeit. W. Maurenbrecher. Leipsic, 1874 (essays mainly relating to Spanish history).
La reina D. Juana la Loca. A. Rodriguez Villa. Madrid, 1892. (M. Gachard has also in several monographs criticised the theory of Juana's sanity as advanced by Bergenroth in Calendar of State Papers. Spanish.)
Letras de Fernando de Pulgar. Cartas de Gonzalo Ayora. Biblioteca de autores Españoles. Vol. XIII. Madrid, 1856.
Cartas de los secretarios del Cardinal D. Fr. Francisco Jiménez durante su regencia. V. de la Fuente. Madrid, 1885.
Négociations diplomatiques entre la France et l'Autriche, 1500—1530. 2 vols. E. Le Glay. Collection doc. inéd. Paris, 1845.
Opus epistolarum. Petrus Martyr ab Angleria. Amsterdam, 1670. (Monographs on these invaluable letters by J. H. Mariéjol. Paris, 1887. H. Heidenheimer. Berlin, 1881. J. Gerigk. Braunsberg, 1881. J. Bernays. Strassburg, 1891. H. A. Schumacher. New York, 1879.)
Naugerii Opera. Containing a journey of Navagero in Spain.
Historia de la vida y hechos del emperador Carlos V. Prudencio de Sandoval. 2 vols. Pamplona, 1634.
De rebus gestis Caroli V. Juan Ginés Sepúlveda. Madrid, 1780.

Vida y historia de Carlos V. P. Mejia. Biblioteca de autores
Españoles. Vol. XXI. Madrid, 1858.
Collection de voyages des souverains des Pays-Bas. Vol. II.
Itinéraire de Charles-Quint. M. Gachard. Brussels, 1884.
Papiers d'Etat du Cardinal Granvelle. Vols. I to V. C. Weiss.
Collection doc. inéd. Paris, 1845.
Correspondance de Charles-Quint et d'Adrien VI. M. Gachard.
Brussels, 1859.
Korrespondenz des Kaisers Karl V. K. Lanz. 3 vols. (from the
Brussels Archives). Leipsic, 1844—6.
Correspondence of the Emperor Charles V. W. Bradford (from
the Vienna Archives). London, 1850.
Comentario de la guerra de Alemania hecha por Carlos V. L. de
Avila y Zuñiga (giving a Spanish view of the Emperor's
German campaign). Biblioteca de autores Españoles. Vol.
XXI. Madrid, 1858.
History of the reign of Charles V. Robertson. Ed. by W. H.
Prescott. 2 vols. London, 1857.
Geschichte Karls V. H. Baumgarten. 3 vols. Stuttgart, 1885-92.
(The best history of the Emperor, but ends at 1539.)
Historia del Levantamiento de las Comunidades de Castilla.
A. Ferrer del Rio. Madrid, 1850.
Der Aufstand der Castilianischen Städte gegen Kaiser Karl V.
K. von Höfler. Prag, 1876.
Don Antonio de Acuña genannt der Luther Spaniens. K. von
Höfler. Vienna, 1882.
 (This writer has made the reign of Philip I and the early
years of Charles peculiarly his own, but his valuable mono-
graphs are usually buried in the necropolis of scientific
periodicals.)
La Germanía de Valencia. M. Danvila. Madrid, 1884.
 (M. Danvila is engaged upon an exhaustive history of
the revolt of the Communes, based upon the innumerable
documents hitherto only partially utilised in local histories.)
Rivalité de François 1er et de Charles-Quint. F. A. A. Mignet.
2 vols. Paris, 1875. (A useful book becoming rare.)
Storia documentata di Carlo V. in correlazione all' Italia. G. de
Leva. 5 vols. Venice, 1864-1894. (Relates mainly to the
Emperor's Italian policy, but has a wider use.)

Los Españoles en Italia. F. Picatoste. 3 small vols. Madrid, 1887. (Illustrates the demoralisation of Spanish character due to the Italian Wars.)

CONSTITUTIONAL AND ECONOMIC HISTORY OF THE ABOVE REIGNS.

Cortes de los antiguos reinos de León y de Castilla. Vol. IV. Madrid, 1882. (The text of the proceedings to 1537.)
Introduction to the above. 2 vols. M. Colmeiro. Madrid, 1883-6.
L'Espagne sous Ferdinand et Isabelle. J. H. Mariéjol. Paris, 1892. (A concise and very useful description of society and institutions.)
Essais sur l'administration de la Castille au XVI° siècle. M. J. Gounon Loubens. Paris, 1860. (Constitutional subjects admirably treated.)
Die wirthschaftliche Blüte Spaniens im XVI. Jahrhundert und ihr Verfall. K. Häbler. Berlin, 1888. (This original monograph has been more censured than confuted.)
Die Geschichte der Fugger'schen Handlung in Spanien. K. Häbler. Weimar, 1897.
Spaniens Niedergang während der Preisrevolution des XVI. Jahrhunderts. M. J. Bonn. Stuttgart, 1896.
Historia de la Economía política. M. Colmeiro. Madrid, 1863. (Rich in statistics.)
Derecho administrativo Español. M. Colmeiro. Madrid, 1876.

NOTE. The introductory chapters are necessarily so slight that it has been thought useful to add a bibliography extending in some respects beyond their limits.

The relations of the Catholic Kings and of Charles V to Italy, America and North Africa, and of Charles V to the Netherlands and Germany would require separate bibliographical schedules beyond the compass of this work.

The following list is strictly confined to the books actually consulted in writing the main body of the work.

Philip II.

Calendar of Spanish State Papers. Elizabeth. Rolls Series, 1892—8.
History of the Reign of Philip II. Prescott. 3 vols. London, 1855. Valuable only for the early part of the reign to 1568.
Philip II of Spain. Martin Hume. London, 1897.
The Year after the Armada. Same author. London, 1896.
The Rise of the Dutch Republic. Motley. London, 1859.
La Historia de Felipe II. Luis Cabrera de Cordoba. Madrid, 1876—7.
Vida y hechos del Señor Rey Felipe II. Porreño. Valladolid, 1863.
Testimonio autentico y verdadero de las cosas notables que pasaron en la dichosa muerte del Rey Felipe II. Valencia, 1589. (An account of Philip's death by an eye-witness.) Cervero de la Torre.
Nueva Luz y verdad historica sobre Felipe II. Fernandez Montaña. Madrid, 1891. An unrestrained panegyric.
Mas Luz etc. Madrid, 1892. Same author. Ditto.
Estudios historicos del reinado de Felipe II. Fernandez Duro. Madrid, 1890. (Defeat of Los Gelves, Antonio Perez etc.)
Guerra de Granada. Mendoza. Valencia, 1795. (A contemporary account of the Morisco war.)
Historia de la rebelion y castigo de los Moriscos de Granada. Marmol Carbajal. Malaga, 1600.
Historia de los Vandos, etc. and Guerras Civiles de Granada. Perez de Hita. Valencia, 1597 and Cuenca, 1619.
Estudios sobre Felipe II. R. Hinojosa. Madrid, 1887.
La Princesa de Eboli. Muro. Madrid, 1877.
La Armada Invencible. Fernandez Duro. Madrid, 1885.
La gloriosa defensa de Malta. Calderon de la Barca. Madrid, 1796. (Best account of the siege of Malta.)
Correspondance de Granvelle. Piot. Brussels, 1884.
Papiers d'État de Granvelle. Weiss. Paris, 1843.
Histoire de Philippe II. Forneron. Paris, 1882.
Correspondance de Philippe II. Gachard. Brussels, 1848—79. (Mainly on Flemish affairs.)

Correspondance de Philippe II avec ses filles. Gachard. Paris, 1884. (Familiar letters to his children.)
Histoire de la Guerre de Flandres. Strada. Brussels, 1712.
Philippe II Roi d'Espagne. Baumstark (translated by Kurth). Liège, 1877.
Élisabeth de Valois. Du Prat. Paris, 1850. Life of Philip's third wife.
Don Carlos et Philippe II. Gachard. Brussels, 1863.
Antonio Perez et Philippe II. Mignet. Paris, 1881.
Historia de las alteraciones de Aragon. Pidal. Madrid, 1862—3. (Account of the revolt of the Aragonese.)
Obras y relaciones de Antonio Perez. Geneva, 1649.
Histoire de la Réunion de Portugal à...Castille. Conestaggio. (French translation.) Paris, 1680.
Recueil des actions et paroles mémorables de Philippe II. Cologne, 1661.
De Rebus Gestis Philippi II. Sepulveda. Madrid, 1780.
Vita del Catolico Ré Filippo II. Leti. Cologne, 1679.
Vita del Catolico Don Filippo II con le guerre de suoi tempi. Campana. Vicenza, 1605.
L'Espagne au 16me et 17me siècles. Morel Fatio. Paris, 1878.
Ein Ministerium unter Philipp II. Philippson. Berlin, 1895. (An account of Granvelle's Ministry, 1579—86.)
Epochen und Katastrophen: Don Carlos und Philipp II. Schmidt. Berlin, 1864.
Zur Geschichte des Don Carlos. (In the Wiener Jahrbücher, Vol. XLVI.) Ranke. Vienna, 1829.
Calendar of Venetian State Papers. Rolls Series. In progress.
The Defeat of the Armada. (Collection of English documents.) Laughton. London, 1894.
Bosquejo historico de la casa de Austria. Canovas de Castillo. Madrid, 1869.
Historia del Mundo del tiempo de...Felipe II. Herrera. Valladolid and Madrid, 1606—1612.
Relacion del Viage de Felipe II a Zaragoza, Barcelona, etc. (1585). Madrid, 1876.
History of the Progress and Suppression of the Reformation in Spain. McCrie. Edinburgh, 1829.
Don Philipe el Prudente. Vanderhammen. Madrid, 1632.

Philip III.

Vida y hechos del Rey Felipe III. Gonzales Davila, the king's historiographer. Madrid, 1771. (The original MS. is in the possession of the author.)
Dichos y hechos del Sr Don Felipe III. Porreño. Madrid, 1628.
Memorias para la historia de Don Felipe III. Yañez. Madrid, 1723.
Historia de Felipe III. (Usually attributed to his gentleman-in-waiting Vivanco, but now known to have been written by another courtier named Novoa.) A minute record of court life and intrigues. Documentos ineditos LX y LXI. Madrid, 1875.
Relacion de las cosas sucedidas en España desde 1599 hasta 1614. Cabrera de Cordoba. Madrid. (Documentos ineditos.) A very full contemporary chronicle.
Relacion de Simon Contarini a la Republica de Venecia. Madrid. (Documentos ineditos.) A valuable descriptive and statistical account of Spain in 1605.
Viage del Rey (Felipe III) a Valencia. Anon. Valencia, 1599.
Guerre di Fiandra. Bentivoglio. (English translation by the Earl of Monmouth.) London, 1652.
History of the United Netherlands. Motley. London.
Sucesos de Sevilla 1592—1604. Ariño. Sevilla, 1873.
Memorable espulsion...de los Moriscos de España. Guadalajara y Xavier. Pamplona, 1614.
Condicion Social de los Moriscos de España: causas de su espulsion etc. Janer. Madrid, 1857.
Viage de la Catolica Real Majestad Felipe III...a Portugal. Lavaña. Madrid, 1622.
Casamientos de España y Francia y Viage del Duque de Lerma. Mantuano. Madrid, 1618. An account of the marriage of Anne of Austria, etc.
Winwood State papers. London, 1725.
Vita di Don Pietro Giron Duca d'Osuna Vicerè di Napoli. Leti. Amsterdam, 1699.
B. M. Egerton MSS. 347 (Life and death of R. Calderon).

Philip IV.

Estudios del reinado de Felipe IV. Canovas del Castillo. Madrid, 1888—9. Full accounts of the revolt of Portugal and of the battle of Rocroy.

Cartas de Sor Maria de Agreda y de Felipe IV. Madrid, 1885. An extraordinary political and religious correspondence between the king and the nun, extending over several years.

Documentos ineditos, vols. 69, 77, 80 and 86 for histories of Philip's reign; and vols. 96 and 97 for correspondence touching the wars in Catalonia.

Viage del Rey Felipe IV a la frontera de Francia. Castillo. Madrid, 1657. Account of the marriage of Maria Theresa.

Historia de los hechos de...Don Juan de Austria en Cataluña. Bremundan. Zaragoza, 1673.

Epitome de los principios y progresos de las guerras de Cataluña 1640 y 1641. Barcelona, 1641. Written from the Catalan point of view by Sala.

Avisos, 1654—58 and 1660—64. Barrionuevo. Madrid, 1895. 4 vols. Interesting Spanish news letters.

Avisos (1640—44). J. Pellicer. Seminario Erudito, vols. 31 to 33. (News letters.)

Guerra de Cataluña. F. M. de Melo. Madrid, 1808. (Minute account by an eye-witness.)

L'Espagne au XVIme et XVIIme siècles. Morel Fatio. Bonn, 1878.

Memoirs of Spain during the reigns of Philip IV and Charles II. John Dunlop. Edinburgh, 1834.

Memoirs of Lady Fanshawe, with letters. London, 1829. Relating to the last years of Philip IV.

Original letters of Sir Richard Fanshawe (English Ambassador in Spain). London, 1702.

Recueil des Instructions données aux ambassadeurs de France etc. (Espagne). Edited by Morel Fatio. 1st volume, 1649—1700. Paris, 1894.

Tratado de...algunas fiestas que se han hecho etc. MS. G 32. Royal Academy of History, Madrid. (Transcript in possession of author.) Diego de Soto y Aguilar. Very minute account of the visit of Charles Stuart to Madrid, by a Spanish courtier.

Fragmentos historicos de la vida de...Olivares. Unpublished (?) contemporary MS. in possession of author. Full biography and apology of Olivares by Vera y Figueroa, Count de la Roca, one of his strongest partisans; containing also much information about Charles Stuart's visit. See also a similar manuscript, B. M. Add. MSS. 25689 and Egerton 2053.

Discursos y Apuntamientos de Don Mateo de Lison y Biedma. Secretly printed (Madrid, 1623?). A most valuable statement of the condition of affairs on Philip's accession.

Révolutions de Portugal. Vertot. Bruxelles, 1843. The revolt of Portugal.

Voyage d'Espagne (1655). Aersens de Sommerdyk. Amsterdam, 1666. Extremely curious and valuable account of Spain at the period.

Relation de l'état et Gouvernement d'Espagne. Bonnecasse. Cologne, 1667. A few years later.

The Earl of Bristol's defence. Camden Miscellany, vol. 6. Edited by S. R. Gardiner, 1871.

Lettres écrites de Madrid en 1666 et 1667. J. Muret. Ed. Morel Fatio. Paris, 1879.

Epitome de los principios y progresos de la Guerra de Cataluña (1640—41). Sala. Barcelona, 1641.

Historia de la Conjuracion de Portugal. Amsterdam, 1689.

Masaniello ó la sublevacion de Napoles. Rivas. Madrid, 1848.

Historia de Don Felipe IV. Cespedes. Barcelona, 1634. The first years of the reign.

Letters from Spain. J. Howel. London, 1754.

Historia del levantamiento de Portugal. A. Seyner. Zaragoza, 1644.

Prince Charles and the Spanish marriage. S. R. Gardiner. London, 1869. (Dr Gardiner's History of England from the accession of James I contains much information on the relations between England and Spain.) See also Clarendon, "Cabala" and Thurloe State papers; and B. M. Egerton MSS, where there is a large number of Spanish documents relating to this reign and to those of Philip III and Charles II, etc. See Gayangos' Catalogue of Spanish MSS.

Charles II.

Solo Madrid es Corte. Nuñez de Castro. Madrid, 1669. Statistical account of Spain on the accession of Charles.
Dunlop, *op. cit.*
Recueil des instructions, etc., *op. cit.*
Mémoires de la Cour d'Espagne 1679—81. Villars. Edited by Morel Fatio. Very valuable statistical account of Spain by the French Ambassador. Paris, 1893.
Lettres de Madame de Villars. Paris, 1823. Familiar letters about Charles and his first wife.
Relation du voyage d'Espagne. Mme d'Aulnois. La Haye, 1702. Similar letters on same period.
Spain under Charles II. (Correspondence of Stanhope, English Ambassador at the end of the reign.) London, 1860.
Descripcion de las circunstancias, etc. (Description of Charles's first marriage.) Madrid, 1679.
Mémoires touchans le mariage de Charles II. Paris, 1681.
Documentos ineditos, LXXIX. (Letters from the Duke de Montalto to Ronquillo, Spanish ambassador in England.) Accounts of events at court, 1685—88.
The Year after the Armada, etc. Hume. For particulars of the exorcism.
Négotiations relatives à la succession d'Espagne sous Louis XIV. Mignet. Paris, 1835—42.
Letters of Sir William Temple, etc. London, 1700. Relating to the peace of Nimeguen (1665—1672).
Menor edad de Carlos II. Documentos ineditos, vol. 67. An account of the regency of Mariana of Austria.
Relation of the differences in the Court of Spain. (Don Juan and Nithard.) London, 1678.

Philip V and Fernando VI.

Memoirs of the kings of Spain of the house of Bourbon. Coxe. London, 1815.
Elizabeth Farnese. E. Armstrong. London, 1892.
Memoirs of the Duke of Ripperdá. London, 1740.
Lives of Ripperdá and Alberoni. Moore. London, 1819.
Memoirs and Correspondence of the Earl of Peterborough. London, 1853.
The Spanish war of Succession. Parnell. London, 1892.
Mémoires du Duc de St Simon. Paris, 1842.
History of Cardinal Alberoni. London, 1819.
Mémoires du Maréchal de Berwick. Paris, 1778.
Mémoires du Maréchal de Grammont. (Collection Petitot.) Paris, 1826.
Mémoires du Marquis de Louville. Paris, 1818.
Lettres de Mme de Maintenon et de la Princesse des Ursins. Paris, 1826.
Recueil des instructions, *op. cit.*
Comentarios de las Guerras de España é historia de Felipe V. Bacallar y Saña Marques de San Felipe (up to 1711, with continuation to 1725 by Campo Raso). Madrid, 1790.
Mémoires de l'abbé Montgon. Lausanne, 1752.
Recueil des lettres, etc. écrites par M. l'abbé Montgon. Liège, 1732.
Relacion de lo ocurrido desde la batalla de Zaragoza hasta la vuelta de S. M. Zaragoza, 1711.
Relacion diaria desde que el Rey Don Felipe V. salio de esta corte hasta la victoria de Brihuega. Madrid, 1711.
Noticia biografica del Marques de Ensenada. Navarrete. Madrid, 1848.
Correspondence of Sir Benjamin Keene and Colonel Stanhope at the Record Office (Spanish papers), and Lord Essex's papers in the Brit. Museum, Add. MSS. 27731, are of the greatest value in elucidating the relations between England and Spain at this period.
Historia Civil de España. Belando. The valuable portions of this history are the notes and comments by Macanaz on the reign of Philip V, forming a bitter attack on foreign influence in Spain. They were published separately in 1744.

CHARLES III.

Historia del reinado de Carlos III. Danvila y Collado. Madrid, 1893—5. A monumental work of the highest value.
Storia del regno di Carlo III Ré di Spagna. Beccatini. Venezia, 1790.
Historia del reinado de Carlos III en España. Ferrer del Rio. Madrid, 1856.
Gobierno del Señor Rey Don Carlos III. Muriel. Madrid, 1839.
Charles III et les jésuites de ses états. Carayon. Paris, 1868.
Coxe, *op. cit.*
Letters concerning the Spanish nation. Clarke. London, 1763. Interesting statistical account of Spain on the accession of Charles, written by the chaplain of Lord Bristol's embassy (1761).
Travels through Spain in 1775 and 1776. Swinburne. London, 1787.
Modern state of Spain. Bourgoing (English translation). London, 1808. An entertaining and valuable book. 1777—88.
Real detencion con que S. M. Don Carlos III honró la ciudad de Barcelona. Barcelona, 1759. Charles' arrival in Spain.
B. M. Egerton MSS. 368. For contemporary account of the Squillaci riots.
The MS. State Papers of the reign, especially important documents of Aranda and Floridablanca, are in the archives of Alcalá de Henares, where they have been consulted by the author.
There are also numerous Spanish manuscripts of great value relating to this period, and to the wars with England, in the Brit. Museum. See Gayangos' Catalogue of Spanish MSS.

NOTE.—The part of Navarre North of the Pyrenees remained connected with the rest till 1530. Roussillon, recovered by Aragon in 1493, was finally lost to Spain in 1659.

FRANCE
Nimes
Montpellier
Toulouse
Bayonne
Pau
Carcassonne
Narbonne
Gulf of Lions
Perpignan
ROUSSILLON
ANDORRA
Port Vendres
C. Creuse
G. of Rosas
Pamplona
NAVARRA
Huesca
Saragossa
1710
Lerida
CATALONIA
Manresa
Barcelona
1652 1696
1705-6 1714
Reus
Tarragona
1641
Vich
Gerona
1652
Palamos
Mataro
R. Ebro
ARAGON
KINGDOM OF
ARAGON
Tortosa
Vinaroz
Benicarlo
Castellon de la Plana
Segorbe
Valencia
VALENCIA
Alcoy
Alicante 1706
Almansa
1707
Murcia
Carthagena
Lorca
C. de Palos
Mar Menor
Torrevieja
Aguilas
Villaricos
Carboneras
de Gata
BALEARIC ISLES
Minorca
Mahon
1708
MAJORCA
Palma
Cabrera
Iviça
Formentera
C. de la Nao
Columbretes
MEDITERRANEAN SEA
ALGIERS
Blidah
Miliana
Orleansville
ALGERIA
AFRICA

1. Holland, Zealand, &c.—The United Netherlands — Independence recognised by the Treaty of Münster, 1648.
2. Roussillon ceded to France by the Treaty of the Pyrenees, 1659.
3. Artois ceded to France by the Treaty of the Pyrenees, 1659.
4. Portugal — Spanish, 1580-1640— Independence acknowledged 1668.
5. The Franche Comté ceded to France by the Treaty of Nimeguen, 1678.
6. Luxemburg ceded to France by the Treaty of Ratisbon, 1684, and restored by the Treaty of Ryswyk, 1697; finally ceded to Austria by the Treaty of Rastadt, 1714.
7. Flanders, Brabant, &c.—Spanish Netherlands—ceded to Austria by the Treaty of Rastadt, 1714.
8. Duchy of Milan ceded to Austria by the Treaty of Rastadt, 1714.
9. Sardinia ceded to Austria by the Treaty of Rastadt, 1714, recaptured 1717, again ceded 1720.
10. Kingdom of Naples ceded to Austria by the Treaty of Rastadt, 1714, recaptured by the Infante Charles and erected into a separate kingdom, 1734.
11. Sicily ceded to Savoy, 1714, recaptured from Austria and united to Naples, 1735.

NOTE.—Parma, Modena, and Tuscany, although not Spanish possessions, are coloured in consequence of their close connection with Spanish history in the 18th century.

SPANISH POSSESSION

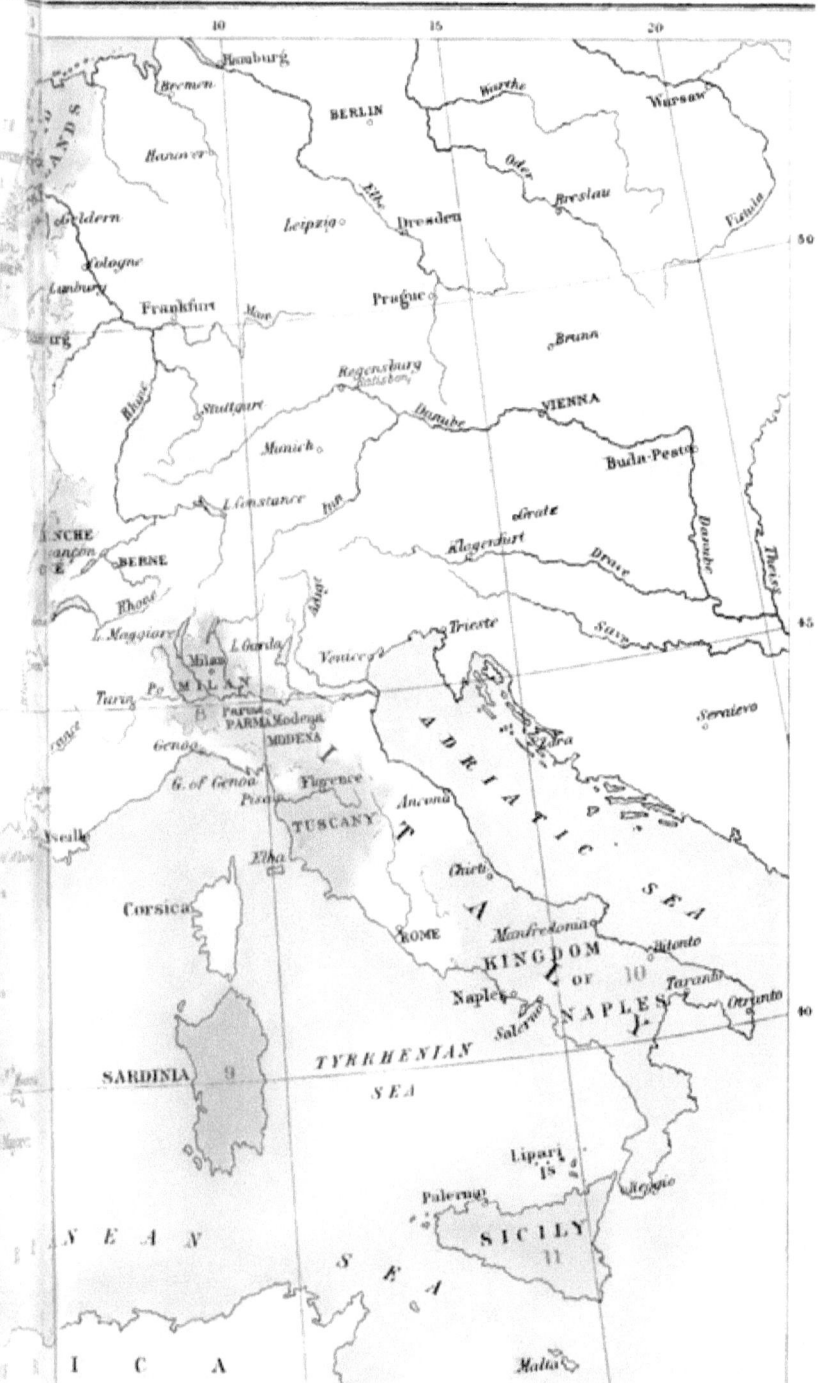

INDEX.

Aben Humeya, 153, 154
Acuña, Antonio de, Bishop of Zamora, leads a revolt, 36, 40; enthroned as Archbishop by the mob, 41; aids Padilla's widow, 42; flees and is captured, *ib.*
Administration under Ferdinand and Isabella, 22-24; division of the Royal Council, 22; *see* Councils
Admiral, Grand, loses all importance, 13
Adrian of Utrecht, tutor to Charles I, 32; coadjutor in the Spanish regency, *ib.*; protests against foreign intruders, 33; appointed regent, 35; attacks Segovia, 36; is deposed, *ib.*; his retirement demanded, 39; sent to Valencia to take the oath for Charles, 43; reviews the armed trades of Valencia, *ib.*; elected Pope, 50; at disaccord with Juan Manuel, *ib.*; will not join the alliance against France, *ib.*; takes the Emperor's side, 51; dies, *ib.*
Africa, Spanish in, 3, 5, 6, 30; Ferdinand's view of, 10; Jiménez's conquests in, *ib.*; Spanish garrisons in, 11; America distracts attention from, *ib.*; Mahometan power in, 67-70; *see* Algiers, Tunis
Agreda, Maria de, 282
Agriculture in Spain, increase of tillage, 84; thriving state of, 85; ruin of, 195, 247, 271, 297
Aguila, Don Juan del, 189; invades Ireland, 204
Aguilar, Count, 324, 339, 341
Aigues-Mortes, meeting of Charles I and Francis I at, 71
Aix-la-Chapelle, Treaties of, in 1688, 288; in 1748, 384
Alba, Duke of, sails against Algiers, 73; defends Perpignan, 74, 103; besieges Metz, 92; at Mühlberg, 93; Neuburg intended for, *ib.*; Charles' character of, 105, 106; sent to Spain, 109; his advice to Philip, 110; sent to Italy by Philip, 121; represents Philip at Cateau-Cambresis, 123; leads the war-party, 124; marries Elizabeth of France for Philip II, 126; furious at the Fleming nobles, 144; hated in the Netherlands, 147; overbears Gomez and the peace-party, *ib.*; leaves Spain, *ib.*; meets Catherine de' Medici at Bayonne, 150; destroys Egmont and Horn, 158; hangs 500 would-be emigrants, 159; defeats Orange at Heiliger Lee, *ib.*; his executions, *ib.*; publishes an amnesty, *ib.*; introduces the *Alcabala*, 135, 159; massacres the Huguenots, 160; crushes Flanders, but not Holland, *ib.*; recalled, *ib.*; disgraced through

Index.

Perez' wiles, 160, 167; conquers Portugal, 167, 168
Alba, Duke of (Duke of Huesca), 387, 388
Albany, Duke of, 47
Albemarle, Earl of, 395
Alberoni, Cardinal, arranges Philip V's second marriage, 348; intrigues against Ursinos, 349; chief adviser of Elizabeth, 350; his policy, 352, 365; plots against George I and Orleans, 354; takes Sicily, *ib.*; dismisses the English ambassador, *ib.*; aids the Pretender, 355; expelled, 356; at Rome, 363
Albert, Archduke, Viceroy of Portugal, 185; defends Lisbon, *ib.*; husband of Isabel and joint sovereign of the Netherlands, 194, 198; arrives in the Netherlands, 202; negotiates with Maurice and Elizabeth, 203; defeated by Maurice, *ib.*
— *see* 'the Archdukes.'
Albret, House of, robbed of its Spanish territories, 7, 45; has a party in Spanish Navarre, 46; abandoned by Francis, 55
Albret, Jeanne d', heiress of Navarre, 2; bride-elect of Philip II, 72, 105; marries the Duke of Cleves, 72; again proposed to Philip, 113
Alburquerque, Duke of, 268
Alcabala, 21, 26, 38, 41, 136, 195, 226, 228, 245, 271, 281, 351, 381, 409; in Flanders, 159
Alcalá, 335
Alcaldes, 18
Alcantara, battle of, 168
Alcántara, Order of, 14
Alcazar, battle of, 167
Alcira, 43, 44
Alençon, Duke of, schemes to rule the Netherlands, 167; crowned, 171; dies, 185
Alessandria, taken by Lautrec, 60; by Don Philip, 380
Alfonso of Aragon, his exploits, 4

Alfonso VI of Portugal: his accession, 279; a vicious lunatic, 281; quarrels with Don Pedro, 285; dethroned and exiled, 290
Algiers, threatened by Spain, 10; Barbarossa ruler of, 67; under Turkish suzerainty, 68; attacked by Charles, 73; by J. A. Doria, 210; by Count O'Reilly, 403; undertakes to suppress piracy, 408
Allen, Dr, 175
Almaden, mines of, 87
Almansa, battles of, 337, 342
Almeida, Antonio de, Archbishop of Lisbon, 253, 254
Almenara, battle of, 342
Alsace, assigned to France at Münster, 275
Alumbrados, the, 248
Amelia of Saxony, wife of Charles III, 392; dies, 394
Amelot, Michel, ambassador at Madrid, 334, 339
America, discovery of, 3, 6, 11
— Spanish Colonies in, 83–85, 88; 90–91, 396, 407
Amiens, League of, 92
d'Ancre, Marshal, 229
Andalusia, revolt in, 35–6; chiefly loyal, 39; Moors expelled from, 155, 195, 213; Philip IV in, 228
Andrew, Archduke, occupies Cleves and Westphalia, 203
Anjou, House of, its claims on Naples, 6
Anna, Infanta, daughter of Philip III, marries Louis XIII, 216, 217; renounces her claim to the Crown, *ib.*, 312
Anne, daughter of Maximilian II, marries Philip II, 168; dies, *ib.*
Anne of Austria, Regent of France, 266
Anne of Brittany, marries Charles VIII, 6
Anne of England, adheres to William III's engagements, 325; recognised by Louis XIV, 344
Anson, ravages South America, 375
Antonio, Don, Prior of Crato, claims

Index. 427

the Portuguese Crown, 167; defeated by Alba, 168; flees to England, *ib.*; favoured by clergy and people, 184; invades Portugal, 185
Antwerp, 'Spanish Fury' at, 164
Aquisgran, treaty of, 384, 392
Arabella Stuart, chosen by English Catholics as Elizabeth's successor, 205
Aragon, united with Castile, 1; its connection with Sicily, Naples etc., 3, 4; its relations with France, 6; resists the Inquisition, 18; Council of, 24; constitution of, 25; independence of, 26; opposition to Charles in, 34; acquires Roussillon, 45; Charles's treatment of, 82; Philip visits, 112; rising in, 192; Philip III beloved by, 199, 321; Moors expelled from, 213; loses its autonomy, 337; submits to Philip, 343; revolts, 365; *see* Cortes
Aranda, Count de, in Portugal, 395; president of the Council, 398; his reforms, 399, 402; secures the expulsion of the Jesuits, 400; dismissed, 401; ambassador in Paris, 405; opposes Floridablanca, 410
'Archdukes, the,' inherit the Netherlands, 194; enter Ostend, 206; make an eight months' truce with Maurice, 207; sign the truce for 12 years, 208
Arcos, Duke of, viceroy of Naples, 272; flees, 273; deposed, 274
Arias, Archbishop of Seville, 317, 321, 327, 331
Armada, the, 177-184
'Armed Neutrality,' 406
Army, Spanish, before the war of Granada, 27, 28; reputation of the infantry, 47, 267; reorganised by Philip V, 327; by Charles III, 403
Arras, battle of, 276
Arthur, Prince of Wales, marries Catherine of Aragon, 9

Artillery, in the Moorish war, 28; in the Anglo-French war of 1415-1453, *ib.*
Artois, ceded by Spain to France, 280
Arundel, Earl of, represents England at Cateau-Cambresis, 123
Asti, county of, 65, 67, 217; citadel of, 380
Athens, claimed by the Kings of Aragon, 4
Aubigny, M. d', 260
Audience, *see* Chancery; at Seville and Galicia, 23
Augsburg, Diet of, 113; League of, 307
Augustus II of Poland, 371
Augustus III accepted as King of Poland, 372
d'Aulnoy, Madame, 297, 300
d'Avalos, *see* Pescara
Avenne, battle of, 239
Aversa, the French capitulate at, 62
Avila, Santa Junta at, 36
Ayamonte, Marquis of, discovers the plot to murder John IV, 255; executed for treason against Philip IV, 256
Aytona, Marquis of, 240

Badajoz, sieges of, 279, 331
Baden, Prince Louis of, 329
Balaguer, Fort, 339
Balearic Isles, conquered by Aragon, 4; raided by Barbarossa, 73
— *see* Minorca, Majorca
Baltasar Carlos, Infante Don, 269
Barbara of Braganza, marries Ferdinand VI, 384; secures peace, *ib.*; dies, 390
Barbarossa, alias Kheir-ed-Din, succeeds his brother in Algiers, 67; accepts the suzerainty of the Porte, 68; takes Bona, Constantine and Tunis, *ib.*; loses 60 ships at Goletta, 69; raids the Balearic Isles, 73; allied with France, *ib.*; Charles' second expedition against, *ib.*; dies, 74

428

Barcelona, revolt in, 258; declares Louis XIII its Count, 260; withstands Los Velez's assault, 261; capitulates, 279; taken by Vendôme, 311; attacked by Rooke, 330; taken by Peterborough, 332; besieged by Philip V, 334; stormed by Berwick, 346
— Treaties of, in 1493, 6; in 1529, 63
Barrier Treaty, 344
Bavaria, Elector of, 328, 329, 344
— Joseph Leopold, Electoral prince of, claims the Spanish crown, 314; dies, ib.
Bay, Marquis de, 343
Bayard, Chevalier, as a general, 47; dies, 50
Beatrice of Portugal, wife of Charles III of Savoy, an admirer of Charles I, 70; daughter of Manoel, 167
Beck, Baron de, 267
Bedmar, Marquis of, ambassador at Venice, 218
Beggars of the Sea, 146, 208
Belcastel, General, 342
Bellefonds, Marshal de, 306
Benedict XIV, concludes a Concordat with Ferdinand VI, 389
Benevente, Count, 313, 315, 317
Bergen-op-Zoom, Truce of, 208
Berghes, Marquis de, Governor of Hainault, prevents persecution, 144; at Madrid, 147; overborne by Alba, ib., 158
Bergues, Count de, 240
Berlips, Baroness, 310
Bermudez, Father, 366
Berwick, Duke of, invades Portugal, 329; resigns, 330; in Spain, 334–336; wins Almansa, 337; conquers Aragon, ib.; in Dauphiné, 341; storms Barcelona, 346; invades Spain, 355
Bézons, Marshal, accused of treachery to Philip V, 339; in Catalonia, 341
Bicocca, battle of, 49
Biserta, ceded to Charles I, 70

Blake, Robert, 277
Blanche, Queen of Navarre, divorced from Henry IV of Castile, 2; bequeaths Navarre to him, ib.
Blavet, seized by the Spanish, 189
Blenheim, battle of, 329
Boleyn, Anne, execution of, 75
Bologna, Charles I crowned at, 64; the Council of Trent transferred to, 94
Bombay, acquired by England, 281
Bona, 68, 70
Bonn, 328
Bonnivet, Guillaume de, outgeneralled by Pescara, 50
Bordeaux, taken by Mazarin, 276
Bothwell, Earl of, 205
Bouchain, 344
Boufflers, Marshal, 328
Bouillon, Principality of, 46
Boulogne, taken by Henry VIII, 75; negotiations at, 203
Bourbon, Cardinal de, proclaimed King as Charles X, 187
Bourbon, Constable, deserts Francis I, 51; Charles' promises to him, ib., 52; invades Provence, 52; quarrels with Pescara, 53; retreats, ib.; at Pavia, 54; loses his promised crown and bride, 55; attacks Rome and dies, 59
Bourbon, Duke of, 363
Boyne, battle of the, 308
Braganza, Barbara of, see Barbara
— Catherine of, see Catherine
— Catherine, Duchess of, granddaughter of Manoel of Portugal, 167
— Prince Edward of, 256
— John, Duke of, see John IV of Portugal
Breda, siege and fall of, 233
Brederode, Admiral, 146, 208
Bremo, battle of, 241
Breslau, treaty of, 378
Brézé, Duc de, wins Avenne, 239; in Spain, 262
Brihuega, battle of, 343
Bristol, G. W. Hervey, Earl of, 394

Bristol, John Digby, Earl of, 229, 230
Brittany, united to France, 6; protected by Henry VII and Maximilian, 8
Brochero, Diego, commands fleet sent to Ireland in 1601, 204
Broschi, Carlo (Farinelli), 386, 387
Brown, Count, 383
Bruges, taken by Marlborough, 338
Brussels, 112, 165
Buckingham, Duke of, leans to Spain, 229; visits Madrid, 230; quarrels with Olivares, 231; turns to France, 232; his expedition to Rochelle, 236; assassinated, *ib.*
Buenos Ayres, factory at, 374; attacked by Portugal, 404; anarchy in, 407
Bugia, acquired by Spain, 10
Burgos revolts, 35
Burgoyne, General, 395
Burgundy, claimed by Charles I, 45, 63; ancient English alliance with, 51, 75, 98; ceded by the treaty of Madrid, 55
Bussy, M. de, 394
Bute, Lord, 395
Byng, Admiral, defeats the Spanish at Syracuse, 354; defeated, 390

Cadiz, factions in, 20; prosperity of, 88; burnt by Essex, 193; attacked by Wimbledon, 232; threatened by Rooke and Ormond, 325
Cadogan, Earl, 338
Calahorra, Bishop of, 172, 173
Calais, captured by Guise, 22; retained by France 124
Calatrava, Order of, 14
Calderon, Maria, 269
— Pedro, 247
— Don Rodrigo, 209, 219, 220, 225
Cambrai, Treaties of, 1508, 7; 1529 ("the Ladies' Peace"), 63
— congress of, 358, 361
Campeachy, 395, 406
Campillo, 377, 389, 401
Campomanes, Count de, 401

Canales, Marquis de, 327
Capua, 372
Caracena, Count, defeated at Montesclaros, 282
— Marquis de, Viceroy of Valencia, 212
Cardenas, Alonso de, Spanish ambassador to Cromwell, 277
— Iñigo de, Spanish ambassador at Paris, 216
Cardona, Duke of, 258
Carew, Lord, 229
Carlos, Don, son of Philip II, 113; betrothed to Elizabeth of Valois, 125; at an *auto da fé*, 130; deformed, 147; plans for his marriage, 147, 148; his lunacy, 148; bent on going to Flanders, 149; plots to murder his father, *ib.*; imprisoned, *ib.*; dies, 150
Carmona, Duke of, 241
Carranza, Bartolomé de, Archbishop of Toledo, 129; imprisoned by the Inquisition, *ib.*; dies, 130
Cartagena (Spain), 336
— (S. America), 375
Carvajal, Don José, 385, 389; dies, 387
Casa de Contratacion, 82, 88
Casale, 380
— Treaty of, 237
Cassano, battle of, 333
Cassinato, battle of, 333
Castelar, Marquis of, 374, 380
Castel Davide, 330
Castel-melhor, Count de, seizes power in Portugal, 281
Castelnovo, 73
Castile, united to Aragon, 1; relations with Portugal, 2; and France, 6; position of the Crown at Isabella's accession, 11; towns of, 18-20, 35, 80, 81; judicial system of, 23, 24; revenue of, 2, 6, 27, 286; Ferdinand regent of, 31, 32; Philip I in, 31; Charles and Juana succeed to, 32; craves a resident king, 33; dissatisfied with Charles I, 33, 34; decline of liberty in, 78,

133, 157, 320; reforms advocated in, 79, 321; under Philip II, 134; Moors expelled from, 213; cleaves to Philip V, 335; *see* Cortes *and* Council

Catalonia, in the 15th century, 2; resists the Inquisition, 18; prosperity of, 27; visited by Philip II, 112; Moors expelled from, 213; repels Condé, 242; character of its people, 256; Santa Colonna on, 257; revolt in, 258—261; occupied by the French, 262, 263; recovered, 279, 280; twice invaded by Louis XIV, 292, 306, 310, 311; restored at Ryswick, 311; welcomes Charles VI (III), 332; conquered by Philip V, 346; loses privileges, *ib.*; revolts, 365; *see* Cortes

Cateau Cambresis, Peace of, 124, 125

Catherine of Aragon, marries Arthur of England, 9; marries Henry VIII, *ib.*; divorce of, 60; dies, 75

Catherine of Austria, sister of Charles I, marries John III of Portugal, 104

Catherine of Braganza, marries Charles II, 281

Catherine de' Medici, Leo X plans a French match for her, 48; marries Henry II, 66; her Italian claims, 70; Dauphiness, 72; political guide of Elizabeth Valois, 132; tries to marry Margaret Valois to Don Carlos, 147; declines to exterminate the Huguenots, 150; covets Flanders for Alençon, 166; Philip's policy towards, *ib.*, 173

Catherine of Navarre, marries Jean d'Albret, 2

Catherine of Spain, daughter of Philip II, marries the Duke of Savoy, 178

Catinat, Marshal, 311

Cerda, Don Martin de la, 203

Cerdagne, mortgaged to Louis XI, 2; united to France by Louis XIV, *ib.*; ceded to Spain by Charles VIII, 6

Ceri, Renzo da, 53, 59

Cerisola, battle of, 74

Cervantes, Miguel, 247

Cervia, held by Venice, 62; restored to the Pope, 64

Ceuta, 285, 357, 370, 403

Chambergos, the, 290, 298

Champigny, joins Orange, 164

Chancellorship, Grand, attached to the See of Toledo, 13, 33, 34

Chanceries or *Audiences*, the, at Valladolid and Granada, 23

Charleroi, battle of, 291; fall of, 311; offered to Holland, 340

Charles I (V) of Spain, his birth, 31; his accession, 32; arrives in Spain and dismisses Jiménez, 33; takes the oath in Aragon, 34; encounters opposition there and in Catalonia, *ib*; elected Emperor, *ib.*; his dealings with the Castilian Cortes, 21, 34, 35; makes Adrian regent, 35; his conduct after the revolt of the Communes, 42; quarrels with the Valencian Cortes, *ib.*; aids the Valencian nobles, 44; causes of the war with Francis I, *ib.*; his resources, *ib.*, 46; his army, 47; courts Henry VIII and the papacy, *ib.*; Mary Tudor promised to, 48; meets Henry VIII, *ib.*; abandons Ferrara, *ib.*; detaches Parma and Piacenza from Milan, 49; crowned at Aix, *ib.*; at the Diet of Worms, *ib.*; drives the French from Lombardy, *ib.*; rules harshly in Italy, 50; his offers to Bourbon, 51; invades Provence, 52, 53; wins Pavia, 54; makes the treaty of Madrid, *ib.*, 55; sends Francis to Spain, 56; his relations with Clement VII, 51, 56, 58; threatened by the League of Cognac, 57; his Italian position, 56—58; takes Milan, 58; disavows Moncada's actions, 59; captures Clement,

60; his difficulties, 60, 61; makes the treaties of Barcelona and Cambrai, 63; lands at Genoa, 64; crowned with the Iron Crown at Bologna, ib.; crowned as Emperor, ib.; makes peace with Venice, ib.; restores the Medici, ib., 96; his treatment of Savoy and Genoa, ib.; change in his circle, 66; his settlement of the succession, 66, 76, 94, 108, 113; leagued with the Italian States, 66; his attitude towards the Turks, 67; takes Goletta and Tunis, 69; restores Muley Hassan, 70; receives Goletta, Bona, and Biserta, ib.; acquires Milan, ib.; invades Provence but retreats, 71; signs a ten years' truce at Nice, ib.; meets Francis at Aigues-Mortes, ib.; quarrels with Francis, 72; invests Philip with Milan, ib.; invades Algiers, 73; his last war with France, 74; at the Diet of Speyer, ib.; crushes the Duke of Cleves, ib.; annexes Guelders, ib.; invades France in concert with Henry VIII, 75; makes peace at Crespy, ib., 91; his policy in Spain, 76; his manners, ib.; marries Isabella of Portugal, 77; his relations with the Cortes of Castile, 78—81; his system of government, 82; encourages agriculture, 85; makes the Ebro canal, ib.; sells the Moluccas to Portugal, 88; his debts, 89; his colonial policy, 91; attacks the Protestant Princes, ib.; wins Mühlberg. 92; publishes the *Interim*, ib., 95; driven from Innsbruck by Maurice of Saxony, 92; recovers South Germany, ib.; fails to take Metz, ib.; his ecclesiastical policy, 93—95; his disputes with Paul III, 95; confers Milan, Siena, and the Vicariate of Italy on Philip, 97; his friendship with England, 98; marries Philip to Mary Tudor,

ib., 115; retires to Yuste, 98, 118; trains Philip, 102, 105, 106, 113; makes him regent, 105; guarantees Maximilian's succession, 108; his policy in the Netherlands, 108, 109; sends Philip to Italy, 110; attends the Diet of Augsburg, 113; confers on Philip Naples and Sicily, Milan, the Netherlands, and Spain, 118; takes farewell of the Flemings, ib.; resigns the imperial crown, ib.; makes the truce of Vaucelles, ib.

Charles II of Spain, his accession, 284; comes of age, 296; escapes his mother's power, 298; his appearance, 299; marries, 301; his habits, 302, 306; government of, 303—305, 310; accepts the treaty of Ratisbon, 306; marries Mary Anne of Neuburg, 308; dismisses Oropesa, 309; illness of, 310, 313; recalls Oropesa, 312; said to be bewitched, 315; leaves his dominions to Philip and dies, 317

Charles III of Spain, his Italian claims, 353, 357; betrothed to Orleans' daughter, 358; the match broken off, 364; recognised as Duke of Parma, 368; welcomed in Italy, 369; repudiates the imperial suzerainty, 371; conquers Sicily and Naples, 372; aids the French faction in Spain, 386; protests against the exchange of Tuy for Sacramento, 388; succeeds to Spain, 392; arranges the succession, ib.; lands in Spain, ib.; signs the 'Family Compact' of 1761, 394; at war with England, ib.; invades Portugal, ib.; makes peace, 395; his regulations of dress, 397, 399; expels the Jesuits, 399; occupies the Falkland Islands, 400; abandons them, 401; his reforms, 402, 409; attacks the Moors, 403; makes a treaty with Portugal, 404; joins France and America

against England, 405; attempts to make peace, 406; signs the treaty of Paris, 408; makes a treaty with Algiers, *ib.*; dies, 411; his character, *ib.*
Charles IV of Spain, 392, 404, 410, 411
Charles I of England, visits Madrid, 230, 231; marries Henrietta Maria, 232; his foreign policy, 235—237; his death, 277
Charles II of England, marries Catherine of Braganza, 281; procures the recognition of Portuguese independence by Spain, 285; in the Triple Alliance, 288, 290; allied with Louis, 291; allied with Holland, 293
Charles VI, Emperor (called III of Spain), his claim to the Spanish Crown, 312; lands at Lisbon, 329; proclaimed in Valencia, 331; enters Barcelona, 332; besieged there, 334; proclaimed in Madrid, 335; accepted by Aragon and Naples, 336; wins Almansa and Almenara, and re-enters Madrid, 342; evacuates it, 343; becomes Emperor, *ib.*; accepts the treaty of Rastadt, 344; allied with England, 353; postpones a final settlement, 357; acknowledges the Italian claims of Charles of Spain, 361, 365; makes the treaty of Vienna in 1725, 364; desires Maria Theresa to succeed, 367, 368, 376; agrees to the treaty of Vienna of 1731, 368; recognises Charles as King of Naples and Sicily, 372; makes the treaty of Vienna of 1736, 373; dies, 376
Charles VIII of France, 6, 7
Charles the Bold, confiscates Guelders, 46
Charles Emmanuel, King of Sardinia, joins Maria Theresa, 378; receives Vigevano, 379; beaten by Don Philip and Gages, 380; treats with Louis XV, *ib.*; defeats the Spanish, *ib.*; invades Provence, 383; wins Exilles, 384
Charles Louis, Elector Palatine, 237
Chatelet, 276
Châtillon, Marshal, wins Avenne, 239, besieges St Omer, 241
Chavigny, persuades Philip V to resign, 360
Chièvres, Guillaume de Croy, Lord of, minister of Charles I, 33; dies, 49, 66
Chili, colonisation of, 88; trade with, *ib.*
Chimay, Prince of, 306
Chinchon, Count de, 169
Choiseul, Duc de, 400, 401, 404
Christian of Denmark, crushed by Tilly, 235
Christine of Denmark, marries Francesco Sforza, 64
Cienfuegos, Cardinal, 364
Cinq Mars, Marquis of, intrigues with Olivares, 263
Clarke, Father, 366
Clement VII, Pope, 51; the centre of the Spanish party under Leo X, *ib.*; aids Francis I, 54; his relations with Charles, 56, 58, 59; flees to Sant' Angelo, 59; escapes from the sack of Rome, *ib.*; in Charles's power, 60; surrenders the keys of the Papal States, 61; his policy, 62; concludes the treaty of Barcelona, 63; veers towards France, 66; meets Francis I, 67; his death, *ib.*
Clement XIV, forced to suppress the Jesuits, 400, 401
Clement, Jacques, murders Henry III, 187
Clergy, Spanish, power and wealth of, 15; taxation of, *ib.*, 135; reformation of, 16, 30, 38; in the revolt of the communes, 40; in the Valencian revolt, 44; refuse a subsidy, 61, 79; supply money for Charles's German war, 93; dependent on the Crown, 119, 128; numbers of, 221

Index. 433

Cleves, Duchy of, occupied by Archduke Andrew and Mendoza, 203
Cleves, Duke of, occupies Guelders, 72; marries the heiress of Navarre, *ib.*; crushed by Charles, 74
Cloth-trade, the, growth of, 83—85, 136; revived by Ripperdá, 364
Cobos, Francisco de los, minister of Charles I, 66, 105, 106
Cognac, League of, 57, 92
Coligny, Admiral, 122
Colonna, Fadrique, Prince of Butera, 261, 262
— Prospero, as a general, 47; defeats Lautrec, 50
— Vittoria, wife of Pescara, 57
Columbus, his voyages, 3
Committee of Thirteen, of Valencia, 43, 44
Communeros, revolt of, 35—42
Concini, Concino (Marshal d'Ancre), murder of, 229
Concordat of 1753, between Ferdinand VI and Benedict XIV, 389
Condé, Henry, Prince of, 241, 242
— Louis, Prince of, wins Rocroy, 267; takes Thionville, 268; wins Lens, 270; joins the Spaniards, 276; governor of Burgundy, 280; his Flemish campaigns, *ib.*, 291, 292
Coni, 379
Constantine, taken by Barbarossa, 68
Contarini, Gaspard, 208, 209
Corbie, siege of, 239
Cordoba, revolts against the Inquisition, 18; forms a loyal union with Seville, 39
— Gonsalvo de, wins Naples for Spain, 7; assumes the protectorate of Pisa, 8; creates the Spanish infantry, 28; aided in Italy by Pedro Navarro, 29; suspected of infidelity, 31
— Don Luis de, 405
Cornwallis, Lord, 407

Corregidores, 19, 20, 37, 81, 133
Corsica, almost conquered by Alfonso of Aragon, 4
Cortés, Fernando, shares in the Algerian expedition, 73; conquers Mexico, 90; honoured by Charles, 91; his expeditions to the North-West, *ib.*; dies in poverty, *ib.*
Cortes of Aragon, Composition and powers of, 25, 104; take the oath of allegiance to Philip II, 103; in 1518, 34; in 1542 (Monzon), 103, 104; in 1551, 114; in 1564, 141; in 1593 (Tarazona), 192; in 1626, 234; in 1701 (Zaragoza), 321
— of Castile, their powers and composition, 20, 110, *note*; frequently summoned by Charles I and Philip II, less often by Ferdinand and Isabella, 21, 78; relations with Charles I, 33, 78; projected reform of, 38; demand reforms, 79, 111; advise an amnesty for the communes, 79; refuse to allow a *sisa*, 80; the nobles cease to be summoned to, *ib.*; deterioration of, *ib.*, 81; their economic standpoint, heresies, and measures, 84–87, 89, 90, 112; their laws abrogated by Charles I and Philip II, 128; a mere machine for legalising exactions, 133; protest against illegal taxation, 156, 157; Philip declares their annual supplies to be obligatory tribute, 157; cease to be summoned afresh, 320; in 1476, 21; in 1480 (Toledo), 15, 21; in 1498, 22; in 1499, *ib.*; in 1501, *ib.*; in 1502, *ib.*; in 1518 (Valladolid), 33; in 1519 (Santiago and Corunna), 34, 35; in 1523, 78; in 1525 (Toledo), 79; in 1527, 61, 79; in 1528 (Madrid), 87, 102; in 1538, 79–80; in 1544 (Toledo), 106, 108; in 1548 (Valladolid), 110–112; in 1551 (Madrid), 114; in 1555, 127, 128; in 1560 (Toledo), 137; in 1563,

H. S. 28

140, 148; in 1566, 155; in 1570, 156; in 1573, 157; in 1576, *ib.*; in 1586, 179; in 1588 (Madrid), *ib.*; in 1593, 198; in 1598, 199; in 1621, 226; in 1623, 228; in 1632, 245; in 1638, *ib.*; in 1639, *ib.*; in 1643, 269; in 1654, 271; in 1701, 321; in 1713, 347

Cortes of Catalonia, in 1519 (Barcelona), 34; in 1542 (Monzon), 103, 104; in 1626 (Lerida), 235, 257; in 1632 (Barcelona), 257; in 1701 (Barcelona), 321
— of Valencia, 25; crushed by Philip IV, 235; in 1520 (Valencia), 43; in 1542 (Monzon), 103; in 1626 (Monzon), 234

Corunna, Cortes removed to, 35, 38
Cottington, Lord, 229
Councils, Administrative, growth of, 82; rendered ineffective by Olivares, 249; rehabilitated, 264; become effete, 351
Council of Aragon, 24, 77, 82
— Royal, of Castile, its legal element increased, 13, 22; its composition and organisation, 22—23; its functions, 23, 134; dislikes the spread of tillage, 84; inquires into the causes of distress, 221
— of the Chamber, detached from the Council of Castile, 82
— of Finance, 24, 134
— of Flanders, 82
— of the Hermandad, 24
— of the Indies, 82
— of Italy, 82
— of the Military Orders, 24
— of Night, the, 169
— of State, the, separated from the Royal Council, 22; its character, *ib.*; its functions consultative and relating specially to foreign affairs, *ib.*, 133, 134; only two Spaniards in, 76; defined, 82
— of War, 134
— of Trent, *see* Trent
Courtenay, Edward, a candidate for Mary Tudor's hand, 115

Courtrai, battle of, 270; taken by Louis XIV, 306; restored at Ryswick, 311
Crequi, Marshal de, 241, 292, 306
Crespy, peace of, 75, 109
Creswell, Father, 205
Cromwell, Oliver, attacks the Spanish Indies, 277; his demands, *ib.*; allied with France, 278
— Thomas, fall of, 75
Cruzada, the Bull of, Council of, 24; nature of, 27; the Santa Junta on, 37; proceeds seized by the Communes, 41; a source of revenue, 135; Pius IV threatens to withdraw the King's right to sell, 142; Pius V renews it, 161
Cuba, 5, 91
Cuenca, See of, 15
Currency, scarcity in Spain, 86, 89, 200; measures regarding, *ib.*, 201, 245, 305
Cyprus, taken from Venice by the Turks, 161

Daubenton, Father, 356, 359, 360
Dauphiné, promised to Bourbon, 52
Denia, Marquis of, confidant of Charles I, 76
Denmark, joins the league against Louis XIV, 325
Desmond, Earl of, rebels, 166; supported by Philip and the Pope, *ib.*
Deza, Cardinal, persecutes the Moriscos, 153, 154
Diaz, Father, 314; accused of bewitching Charles II, 315, 316
Dixmunde, 278, 306, 311
Dominican Friars, the Inquisition in their hands, 16; attack the followers of Erasmus, 61
Doria, Andrea, recovers Genoa for the French, 60; abandons Francis I, 62; Doge of Genoa, 65; shares in the invasion of Tunis, 69; and in Charles' attack on Algiers, 73; meets Philip II in the Bay of Rosas, 112
— John Andrea, in the expedition

to Tripoli, 137; flees, 138; at Lepanto, 162; attacks Algiers, 210
Dragut Reis, 74; ravages Sicily, Naples, and Minorca, and captures Tripoli, 137; defeats the Spanish, 138; besieges Malta, 139
Drake, Sir Francis, harries the Spanish colonies, 170; burns the shipping in Cadiz, 180; attacks the Armada, 182; invades Portugal, 184
Duarte, son of Manoel of Portugal, 167
Dubarry, Madame, 400
Dubois, Cardinal, 359
Dunkirk, taken by Condé, 276; retaken, 278; kept by England, 280; dismantled, 344

Eboli, Princess of, 190, 191, 252
Ebro canal, made by Charles I, 85
Edward VI, his friendly relations with Charles I, 98; dies, ib., 115
Egmont, Count, signs a petition for the withdrawal of Spanish troops, 126; remonstrates against Granvelle's conduct, 144; visits Philip, 146; executed, 158
Elba, seized by France, 272
Eleanor, Queen of Portugal, and France, 51, 55, 113
Elizabeth of Bourbon, daughter of Henry IV, marries Philip IV, 216, 217; renounces her claim to the Crown, ib.; her relations with Philip, 249; desires Olivares' fall, 263; dies, 269
Elizabeth Farnese, marries Philip V, 348; banishes Ursinos, 349; her rule, 350; her policy, 352, 356, 359, 361; aims at the French crown, 367; her success in Italy, 369; her later schemes, 371, 374, 376, 390; opposes the treaty of Vienna, 373; retires, 383; regent on Ferdinand's death, 390
Elizabeth Tudor, her accession, 123; her attitude towards Philip, 124; Philip's policy towards, ib., 166; aids the Flemings, 150, 158;

negotiates for a marriage with Charles IX, ib.; seizes £31,000 from a Spanish fleet, 156; expels the Spanish ambassador, ib.; seizes Spanish shipping, ib.; supports Alençon and the Huguenots, ib.; Scotch, French, and Spanish plots against, 174-176; assists Don Antonio, 184; subsidises Henry IV, 188; sends Essex to France, 189; dies, 205
Elizabeth of Valois, daughter of Henry II, betrothed to Don Carlos, 125; marries Philip II, 126, 131; beloved by the Spaniards, 126; catches smallpox, ib.; object of her marriage, 132, 147-148; dies, 150
Elliot, Lord, defends Gibraltar, 405-407
Elvas, battle of, 280
Emanuel of Portugal, marries the Infanta Isabella, 9
Empire, The, Charles I in, 92; refuses a Spanish Emperor, 94; relations with Milan, 97; succession to, 108-110; Thirty Years' War in, 218, 219, 238, 275; at war with France, 232, 237, 239, 291-294, 305-312, 322-344, 371-372; religious question in, settled at Münster, 275; struggles with the Turks, 63, 66, 283, 307, 311, 352
Enghien, Duc d', defeats Guasto at Cerisola, 74
England, relations with Spain, 4; alliance with Burgundy, 51, 75, 98; relation to the Netherlands, 47, 63, 97; importance of her friendship to the Spanish Crown, 97, 98, 115, 124; dread of Philip's marriage in, ib.; persecution in, 117; unwilling to fight France, ib., 121; loses Calais, 122; loses Guisnes, 123; supplies Philip with money and a fleet, ib.; alleged Catholicism of, 125; Flemish immigrants in, 145; seminary priests in, 174; proposed invasions of,

174-6; prosperity of, 201; Philip III's attempted invasion of, 202; inclines to Spain under James I, 229; dragged into war with Spain by Richelieu, 232; at war with France, 235; unimportant on the Continent, 237; intervenes between Louis XIV and Spain, 287; her conduct at Utrecht, 344; makes a commercial treaty with Spain, 352; allied with the Empire, 353; forces a war on Spain, 374

Englefield, Sir Francis, 175

Ensenada, Marquis of, 383; recreates the navy, reforms the taxation, and encourages commerce, 385, 388, 401; favours France, 386, 389; set aside, 387; secretly negotiates with France, 388; arrested, *ib.*

Epernon, General d', occupies Tarragona, 260; returns to France, *ib.*

Erasmus, his followers defend Charles I, 61

Escobedo, Juan de, sent to be a mentor to Don Juan, 163; accompanies him to Madrid and Flanders, 164; sent to Spain, 165; murdered by Philip's order, 166, 190, 191

Eslava, Viceroy of Cartagena, 379

Espinosa, Cardinal, Don Carlos tries to murder, 148; made Inquisitor-General, 152; persecutes the Moriscos, 153; dies, 160

Essex, Earl of, sent to France, 189; burns Cadiz, 193

d'Estrées, Cardinal, ambassador at Madrid, 326; offends Portocarrero and Ursinos, *ib.*; recalled, 327

Estremadura, Moors expelled from, 213

Eugene, Prince, in North Italy, 322, 324; defeated at Luzzara, *ib.*; wins Blenheim, 329; defeated by Vendôme, 333; wins Turin, *ib.*; raises the siege of Toulon, 337; defeated at Freiburg and Landau, 344

Exilles, battle of, 384

Falkland Isles, seized by Spain, 400; restored to England, 401

Family Compact of 1761, 394

Farinelli, see Broschi

Farnese, Alexander, Duke of Parma, sent to conquer the States, 165; wins Gemblours, 166; sows strife between the Catholics and Protestants, *ib.*; marries, 167; collects 30,000 men for the Armada, 177; advocates peace, *ib.*; refuses to start till the Channel is clear, 181, 183; joins Mayenne and relieves Paris, 188; quarrels with Mayenne, 189; relieves Rouen, but retreats and dies, *ib.*

— Antonio, *see* Parma, Duke of
— Cardinal, elected Pope as Paul III, 67
— Elizabeth, *see* Elizabeth
— Orazio, affianced to the Dauphin's bastard, 96
— Ottavio, marries the Duchess of Parma, 95, 96, 126
— Pier Luigi, son of Paul III, 95; murdered by Gonzaga, 96

Felton, John, 236

Ferdinand of Aragon, 1, 6, 7, 8-10; his domestic policy, 12-15; and the Papacy, 15, 16; jealous of the towns, 20; and the Castilian Cortes, 21; appoints assessors to the Justicia, 25; rarely summons the Cortes of Aragon, 27; studies artillery, 28; regent of Castile, 31; surrenders the regency, *ib.*; regent again, 32; restores order, *ib.*; his intentions as to the succession, *ib.*, 108; encourages foreign settlers, 87; admits Aragon to the American trade, 88

Ferdinand and Isabella, their system of government, 12-15, 19-21

Ferdinand VI of Spain, his accession and policy, 362, 383, 387-390; marries Barbara of Braganza, 384; makes the treaties

Index. 437

of Aix-la-Chapelle and Aquisgran, 384; his character and counsellors, 385, 387; concludes a Concordat with Benedict XIV, 389; a lunatic, 390; dies, *ib.*
Ferdinand I, Emperor, 32, 33; sent out of Spain by Charles, 34; elected King of the Romans, 66, 108; makes a truce with the Turks, 91; negotiates with Charles V as to the succession, 94, 108; Emperor, 118
Ferdinand II, Emperor, attacked by Frederic of Bohemia, 218; aided by Philip III, *ib.*; has Wallenstein murdered, 238
Ferdinand, King of Naples, son of Charles III, 392, 410
Ferdinand, Cardinal Infante, governor of Flanders, 238; at Nordlingen, *ib.*; resists Richelieu, 239; his straits, 240; Viceroy of Catalonia, 257; dies, 266
Feria, Count, Spanish ambassador in England, 123; demands aid for Philip II, *ib.*; propitiates Elizabeth, 124
— Jane Dormer, Duchess of, 175
— Lorenzo, Duke of, ambassador in Paris, 190
— Duke of, recovers the French conquests, 233
Ferrara, claimed by Leo X, 48
— Duke of, holds Modena and Reggio, 62; pardoned by Charles I, 64; dependent on him, 65
Ferté, Marshal la, 276
Fieschi, John Louis, attempts to seize Genoa, 96; is drowned, *ib.*
Figueras, 279, 291
Figueroa, chief minister of Charles III, 401
Flanders, suzerainty ceded to Charles by Francis, 55; Alba in, 159-160; Requesens in, 160; Don Juan in, 164, 165; Farnese in, 165, 166; governed by the Archdukes, 194; claimed and invaded by Louis XIV, 287; ceded by Philip V to the Austrians, 344

Flanders, Council of, 82
Fleurus, battle of, 308
Fleury, Cardinal, 366, 367, 368; gives the Spanish passage to Italy, 377; dies, 378
Florence, controlled by Leo X, 48; ruled by a Medici, 56; opposes Charles I, 58, 63-64, 71, 96; Spanish garrison withdrawn from, 96; *see* Medici
Florida, exploration of, 11; ceded to England, 395; fighting in, 406; retained by Spain, 408
Floridablanca, Moñino, Count de, ambassador at Rome, 401; chief minister, 404; initiates the 'Armed Neutrality' policy, 406; accepts the treaty of Paris, 408; his reforms, 408-410; retires, 410
Foix, House of, marriages of, 2, 7
— Germaine de, marries Ferdinand of Aragon, 7; punishes the Valencian rebels, 44
Fontainebleau, treaty of, 379, 400
France, hostility of Maximilian and Ferdinand to, 45; grounds of quarrel with Spain, *ib.*; position of, 46; Reformers in, 123, 125; Philip proposes to dismember or conquer, 186-189; united by Henry IV, 190; allied with Cromwell, 278; acquires Alsace, Artois, and Roussillon, 280
Franche Comté, proposed union of with the Netherlands, 72; restored to Spain at Aix, 288; finally occupied by France, 291
Francis I, wins Marignano, 8, 45, 47; his rivalry with Charles, 44, 45; saves Ferrara from Leo X, *ib.*; disavows responsibility for attacks on the Netherlands, 49; overruns Spanish Navarre, *ib.*, 53; captured at Pavia, 55; accepts the treaty of Madrid, *ib.*; Eleanor of Portugal betrothed to him, *ib.*; concludes the League of Cognac, *ib.*; unites with Henry VIII to procure Clement's release, 60; invades Italy, *ib.*; alien-

ates Doria, 62; his armies destroyed, *ib.*; accepts the treaty of Cambrai, *ib.*; abandons de la Marck and the Duke of Guelders, *ib.*; meets Clement at Marseilles, 66; intrigues with Pope and Protestants, 67; demands Milan, Genoa and Asti, *ib.*; allied with the Sultan, *ib.*; claims and occupies Savoy, *ib.*; makes a truce with the Netherlands, *ib.*; concludes a ten years' truce at Nice with Charles, *ib.*; meets Charles at Aigues-Mortes, *ib.*; allied with Barbarossa, 73; last war with Charles, 74; allied with the Turk, *ib.*; attacked at home by Henry and Charles, 75; makes peace at Crespy, *ib.*, 91

Franciscans, Quiñones, General of the, 60; attack the Erasmian sect, 61

Franquesa, Secretary, 209-214

Frederic II, occupies Silesia, 377; makes treaty of Breslau, 378

Frederic, Elector Palatine, elected King of Bohemia, 218; ruined at Prague, 219; dies, 237

Fregoso, 74

Freiburg, battle of, 344

Frigiliana, Count, 317

Fronde, the, 275

Frundsberg, at Pavia, 54; crosses the Alps, 58; joins Bourbon, 59
— the younger, shares in the Algerian expedition, 73

Fuenterrabia, occupied by the French, 51; siege of, 241; held by Orleans, 357

Fuentes, Count de, 268

Fuero, or *For*, town charter, 18, 19

Fugger, House of, their dealings with Charles I, 87, 88

Gaeta, 372

Gages, Count de, 378, 379

Galera, 155

Galicia, separate *Audience* of, 23; represented in the Cortes, 81

Galway, Lord, 331, 335-337

Garay, defeated by Catalan rebels, 259

Gardiner, Bishop, imposes hard conditions on Philip II, 116

Gastenata, Admiral, 354

Gattinara, Chancellor, 34, 56

Gavignana, battle of, 64

Gelves, Los, island of, captured by the Spanish, 138; defended by de Sande, *ib.*

Gemblours, battle of, 166

Genoa, attacked by Alfonso of Aragon, 4; French partisans replaced by Imperialists in, 49; recovered by Doria for the French faction, 60, 61; Charles lands at, 64, 65; its fleet, bankers and merchants, *ib.*, 87; aids the attack on Tunis, 69; jealous of Venice, 73; Gonzaga's intentions towards, 96; Fieschi's attempt to betray, *ib.*; Philip II visits, 112; joins Spain against Richelieu, 232; bombarded by Louis XIV, 306; aids the French and Spaniards. 379; blockaded by the English, 383; the populace defeat the Austrians, 384

George I, promises to restore Gibraltar, 358; signs the treaty of Seville, 367

George II, makes the treaty of Vienna, 1731, 368; attempts to reconcile Austria and Spain, 371; arranges the treaty of 1735, 372; espouses Maria Theresa's cause, 378; makes the treaties of Aix-la-Chapelle and Aquisgran, 384

George III, at war with Spain, 394; aids Portugal, *ib.*; makes peace with Spain and France, 395; vindicates his claim to the Falkland Isles, 401; at war with the colonies and France, 404; attacked by Spain, 405; treats for peace, 406; makes the treaty of Paris, 408

Germania de Valencia, the, its origin, etc. 43

Gerona, 279, 292, 306, 343

Gertruydenberg, Conference of, 340

Ghent, rebels, 72; crushed by Charles I, *ib.*; taken by Marlborough, 338

Gibraltar, taken by Rooke, 330; held by England, 341, 344; negotiations concerning, 358, 367, 406; besieged in 1727, 366; besieged by Montemar, 375; blockaded by Spain, in 1779, 405; relieved by Rodney, 406; blockaded in 1782, 407; relieved by Howe, *ib.*

Giron, Pedro de, 35; supersedes Juan de Padilla, 40; is suspected of treason and withdraws, *ib.*

Giudice, Cardinal, 347, 350

Goletta, siege of, 69, 70

Gomez, Ruy, 114; leader of the peace party, 121; desires to get rid of Alba, *ib.*; governor to Don Carlos, 148; his views on Flanders, 149; protests against the oppression of the Moors, 153; his party paramount, 160; dies, 163

Gondomar, D. S. de Acuña, Count de, ambassador to James I, 229; procures Raleigh's execution, *ib.*

Gonzaga, Ferrante, sails in the expedition against Algiers, 73; governor of Milan, 95; his plots and plans, 96

Grammont, Duke de, ambassador at Madrid, 330; recalled, 331

Granada, conquest of, 1-6, 15, 17; represented in the Castilian Cortes, 20; Chancery, 23; mainly loyal in the revolt of the Communes, 39; Charles I visits, 77; the Moors buy exemption from the Inquisition, 78; cloth trade in, 84; revolt in, 153; Don Juan sent to, 154; Moors expelled from, *ib.*; unable to pay taxes, 157

Granada (West Indies) captured by England, 395

Granvelle, Nicholas de, minister of Charles I, 66

Granvelle, Cardinal de, corresponds with Alba, 110; in the Netherlands, 118; represents Philip at Cateau Cambresis, 123; advises moderation, 125; chief adviser to the Duchess of Parma, 127; his recall demanded, 144, 145; viceroy of Naples, 163; recalled to govern Spain, *ib.*; dies, 169

Granvelle, De (Champigny), brother of the Cardinal, at one with Orange, 164

Gravelines, battle of, 123; taken by Condé, 276; by the English, 278

Gregory XIII, and Carranza, 130; urges Philip to invade England, 164; quarrels with him, 172, 173

Grey, Lord, loses Guisnes, 123

Grimaldo, Marquis of, minister of Philip V, 340, 347, 359, 360, 361, 366

— Marquis of, ambassador, negotiates the 'Family Compact,' 394; minister, 396; ambassador at Rome, 404

Guadalajara, revolts, 35

Guadalcanal, mines of, 87

Guastalla, Don Philip, Duke of, 384

Guasto, Marquis del, governor of Milan, 74, 95

Guayaquil, Dutch expelled from, 233

Guelders, Duchy of, confiscated by Charles the Bold, 46; reverts to Charles I, 72; occupied by the Duke of Cleves, *ib.*; annexed by Charles, 74; ceded to Prussia, 344

— Duke of, dispossessed by Charles the Bold, 46; attacks the Netherlands, 49; abandoned by Francis I, 55, 63; makes a convention with Charles, 72

Guevara, Antonio de, sues for pardon, 42

Guicciardini, Francis, his opinion of Ferdinand of Aragon, 10

Guise, House of, paramount in France, 132; its policy, 166, 173, 174

Guise, Francis, Duke of, in Italy, 121; takes Calais, 122
— Henry, Duke of, aims at the crown, 174; in Philip's pay, *ib.*, 175, 186; murdered, 186
— and Lorraine, Henry, Duke of, 192, 274
Guisnes, taken by the French, 123
Gustavus Adolphus, at Lützen, 238

Habana, taken by England, and restored, 395
Haddock, Admiral, 377
Hainault, Calvinism in, 144
Hal, fall of, 308
Hanover, treaty of, 365
Hapsburg, Austrian House of, 7, 9, 198
Harcourt, Count de, 240, 250, 267, 341
— Duke of, ambassador at Madrid, 312, 319
Hardy, Admiral, 405
Haro, Don Luis de, favourite of Philip IV, 266; defeated at Elvas, 280; dies, 281
Harrington, *see* Stanhope
Harris, *see* Malmesbury
Hassan, son of Barbarossa, 74
Heidelberg, League of, 94
Heidelburg, capture of, 230
Heiliger Lee, battle of, 159
Henrietta Maria, marries Charles I, 232
Henry II of France, marries Catherine de' Medici, 66; becomes Dauphin, 72; allied with Maurice of Saxony, 92; seizes the Three Bishoprics, *ib.*; aids Fieschi, 96; overruns Roussillon and besieges Perpignan, 103; makes the Treaty of Vaucelles, 119; breaks it, 120, 121; intrigues against Mary Tudor, 121; at war with England, *ib.*; defeated at St Quentin, 122; acquires Calais and Guisnes, 122, 123; defeated at Gravelines, *ib.*; signs the treaty of Cateau Cambresis, 124; dreads the reformers, 123, 125; killed, 126

Henry III of France, childless, 185; murders the Guises, 186; aided by Navarre and the Huguenots, 187; murdered, *ib.*
Henry IV of France, 185; excommunicated by Sixtus V, 186; aids Henry III, 187; proclaims himself King, *ib.*; defeats Mayenne, wins Ivry, and invests Paris, 188; repulses Farnese, 189; becomes a Catholic, 190; enters Paris and makes peace with Spain, *ib.*; forms an anti-Spanish league, 215; assassinated, 216
Henry IV of Castile, 2
Henry VII of England, 8
Henry VIII of England, marries Catherine of Aragon, 4, 9; attacks France, 8; visited by Charles I, 34, 48; lends him money, 47; his power and wealth, 48, 51; attempts mediation, 51; openly joins Charles, *ib.*; invades Picardy, 51, 75, 97; Protector of the Holy League, 58; his divorce, 60; demands Clement's release, *ib.*; makes peace, 63; excommunicated by Clement VII, 66
Henry, Cardinal, King of Portugal, 167; dies, *ib.*
Hermandad, the, 12, 13, 23, 24, 27
Hesse, Philip, Landgrave of, restores Duke Ulrich to Würtemberg, 67; captured at Mühlberg, 92; imprisoned, 93
Hesse-Darmstadt, Prince of, 311, 319, 325, 328, 330, 331, 332
Hinojosa, Marquis of, Viceroy of Milan, defeats Savoy, 217; in Spain, 262
Hochstädt, battle of, 328
Holland, Lutherans in, 145; resists Alba and Requesens, 160; revolution in, 408; *see* United Provinces
Honnecourt, battle of, 267
Hood, Admiral, 407
l'Hôpital, Marshal, 267, 268
Horn, Count, demands Granvelle's recall, 144; executed, 158

Hospitallers, the Knights, expelled from Rhodes, 68; settled in Tripoli and Malta, *ib.*; at the invasion of Tunis, 69; lose Tripoli, 137; besieged in Malta, 139, 140; repel the Turks, 140
Howard, Lord, defeats Armada, 182
Howe, Lord, relieves Gibraltar, 407
Hozier, Admiral, blockades Porto Bello, 366
Hudson's Bay, 344
Huguenots, under Henry II, 123, 125; hate the Guises, 132; massacred by Alba, 160; support Alençon's Flemish claims, 166; threatened by the treaty of Nemours, 186
Humières, Marshal, 306, 308
Huy, 311, 328
Hyères, battle of, 379

Idiaquez, Juan de, 169
'*In Cœna Domini*,' the Bull, 173
Indulgences, Sale of, 24, 27, 37, 38, 135, 142, 161
Industry in Spain, growth of, 83-6; depressed by taxation, 90; crushed, *ib.*, 244, 271, 351; encouraged, 380-382; revived, 402, 409
Infantry, Spanish, created by Gonsalvo de Cordoba, 28; reputation of, 47, 267; at Ravenna, *ib.*, 54; at Pavia, 55; at Gavignana, 64; at Rocroy, 268
Ingolstadt, battle of, 238
Inquisition, the, its origin and character, 16, 17; its value to the Crown, 18, 119; a source of revenue, 18, 27; extent of its popularity, 18; slighted by Philip I, 32; supported by Charles I in Valencia, 77; Philip II's attitude towards, 119, 128, 142; its treatment of Carranza, 129; resisted in Naples, 139, 140; regulated by the Cortes of Aragon, 141; at the Council of Trent, 142; and Pius V, 161; imprisons Perez, 192; the Aragonese desire its abolition, 199; persecutes Portuguese Jews, 248; attacks the 'Alumbrados,' *ib.*; under Charles II, 304, 315, 316; under Philip V and Ferdinand VI, 391; under Charles III, 403
Interim, the, published, 92, 93
Ireland, invaded with Philip's aid, 166; Spanish commissioners in, 203; del Aguila's invasion of, 204
Irun, fall of, 241
Isabella of Castile, marries Ferdinand of Aragon, 1; aspires to conquer Tlemcen, 10; her accession, 11; her position, 11, 12; her policy, 12-15; her opinion of Aragon, 26; leaves the regency of Castile to Ferdinand, 31; encourages foreign settlers, 87
Isabella of Portugal, marries Charles I, 77; her conduct at Philip's birth, 101; her death, 103
Isabella, daughter of Ferdinand of Aragon, marries John II of Portugal, 9; and on his death his brother Emanuel, *ib.*; dies, *ib.*
Isabella, daughter of Philip II, born, 150; intended for the English Crown, 178; her Breton claims, 186; proclaimed Queen of France, 188; proposed as bride to Guise, 190; wife of Archduke Albert and sovereign of the Netherlands, 194, 198; arrives in Flanders, 202; dies, 238
— *see* 'Archdukes, the'
Italy, Charles VIII invades, 6; Ferdinand of Aragon in, 6-9; Leo X's position in, 48; hostilities of 1521-5 in, 49-54; hatred of the Spanish in, 55, 56; league to secure liberty for, 56-57; French expelled from, 62; Charles in, 64; changed state of, 65; Charles' settlement of, 97, 108, 113; Philip II's position in, 120, 121; Henry IV's schemes in, 215; Philip III's wars in, 217-218; Philip IV's wars in, 233,

237, 241, 250, 272-274; Philip V visits, 324; his wars in, 333; Charles Emmanuel's wars in, 378-381, 384
Ivry, battle of, 188

Jamaica, conquered by England, 277; contraband trade of, 374; expedition against, 407
James IV of Scotland, 8
James I of England, attempts to convert, 175; disinherited by Mary, 179; King of England, 205; makes peace with Spain, 206; exposes the treachery of the Valencian Moors, 211; joins Henry IV's anti-Spanish league, 215; mediates between Savoy and Spain, 217; sacrifices Raleigh, 229; his policy as to the Palatinate, 229-231
James II of England, joins the League of Augsburg, 307; defeated at the Boyne, 308
James Stuart, the Pretender, 322, 355, 359
Jativa, a centre of revolution, 43
Javennes, battle of, 237
Jesuits, expelled from Spain and her colonies, 399-400; suppressed by Clement XIV, 401
Jews in Spain, their power, wealth, and position, 16, 17; persecuted by the Inquisition, *ib.*, 248
Jiménez, Cardinal, undertakes the conquest of North Africa, 10; on the conversion of Granada, 17; hates the Cortes, 21; regent of Spain, 32; proclaims Charles, 33; dismissed, *ib.*; dies, *ib.*
John, Don, of Portugal, marries Juana, sister of Philip II, 127; dies, *ib.*
John, Don, of Austria, *see* Juan
John II of Aragon, 4
John II of Portugal, marries the Infanta Isabella, 9; dies, *ib.*
John III of Portugal, marries Catherine, sister of Charles I, 104; lends Philip II money, 108; negotiates for Philip's marriage with his sister, 114
John IV of Portugal, his marriage, 252, 253; proclaimed King, 254; dies, 279
Joseph I, Emperor, 333, 338, 343
Joseph II, Emperor, 401
Joseph Emmanuel, King of Portugal, 394, 404
Juan, Infante, marries Margaret of Austria, 7, 9; dies, 9; pretended son of, 44
Juan of Austria, Don, brought up in Gomez's tenets, 154; expels the Moors from Granada and Andalucia, *ib.* 155; takes Galera, 155; defeated at Seron, *ib.*; advises a compromise, *ib.*; wins Lepanto, 162, 163; captures Tunis and refuses to dismantle it, 163; wins over Escobedo, *ib.*; visits Madrid, 164; betrayed by Perez, *ib.*, 191; arrives in the Netherlands, 165; sends Escobedo to Spain, *ib.*; breaks with the States and occupies Namur, *ib.*; wins Gemblours, 166; dies, *ib.*
Juan José of Austria, Don, General-in-Chief of Spain, 269; his birth and character, *ib.*; recovers Naples for Spain, 274; governor of Flanders, 276; defeats Turenne, *ib.*; defeated at Dunkirk, 278; blockades Barcelona, 279; invades Portugal, 281; beaten at Amegial, 282; superseded, *ib.*; flees from arrest, 289; secures Nithard's dismissal, *ib.*; Viceroy of Aragon, 290; procures his own recall, 296; defeated by Mariana, *ib.*; plots against her, 297; at the head of affairs, 298; arranges the King's marriage, 299; dies, 300
Juana, daughter of Ferdinand of Aragon, marries Philip I, 9, 31; mentally deranged, 31; lands in Spain, *ib.*; kept in confinement by Philip, *ib.*; succeeds jointly with Charles, 32; refuses

to join the Santa Junta, 36; recovered by the royalists, 40
Juana, sister of Philip II, marries Don John of Portugal, 127; regent of Spain, *ib.*; imprisons the bearers of Papal Bulls, 128
Julius III, Pope, 96
Junta, Santa, at Avila, 36
Junta, Supreme, of the Hermandad, 12; abolished, 13
Jurats, the, in towns, 19, 20
Juros, mortgages on land or taxes, 26
Justice, administration of, in Castile, 23; in Aragon, 25
Justicia, the, of Aragon, his position and functions, 25, 82
Justin of Nassau, 182
Juvara, Abbé, 373

Keene, Sir Benjamin, ambassador at Madrid, 386, 387, 388
Kheir-ed-din, *see* Barbarossa
Kinsale, beleaguered by Mountjoy, 204
Königsegg, Marshal, 366, 367

La Chapelle, captured, 240
'Ladies' Peace, the,' 63
La Force, Marshal, 237
Lake, Admiral, captures Sardinia, 337
Landau, battle of, 344; ceded to France, *ib.*
Landrecy, 240, 276
Landriano, battle of, 62
Langara, Admiral, 406
Lannoy, Viceroy of Naples, 56, 57, 59, 60
Las Casas, Bartolomeo de, 37
Laso, Pedro, 40
Lautrec, Marshal, 50, 60, 62
La Valette, Cardinal de, reduces Landrecy and La Chapelle, 240; dies, 250
— Duke de, 241
— Parisot de, Grand-master of the Knights of St John, 139, 140
League, the Holy, opposes Henry III and Henry IV, 187

Leagues, of Amiens, 92; of Augsburg, 307; of Cognac, 57, 92; of Heidelberg, 94; of Venice, 6, 9
Lede, Marquis of, 354
Leganes, Marquis of, 241, 250, 261, 263, 313
Leghorn, 96
Lemos, Count de, 220
Lennox, Earl of, intrigues with Philip, 174; flees, 175
Leo X, holds the balance in Italy, 48; declares his alliance with Charles I, 49; dies, 50
Leopold I, Emperor, governor of Flanders, 270; defeated at Lens, *ib.*; and at Arras, 276; resigns, *ib.*; joins the League of Augsburg (as Emperor), 307; claims Spain for his son, 312; resents the first Partition Treaty, 314; protests against the second, 316; declares war on Louis XIV on Philip V's accession, 322; joins William III's last league, 325; his difficulties, 328
Lepanto, battle of, 162
Lerida, 269, 270, 342
Lerma, Duke of, favourite of Philip III, 198; his extravagance, 199; transfers the capital to Valladolid and back, 200, 209; his dealings with the currency, 200, 201; promotes the invasion of Ireland, 204; his corruption, 208; persecutes the Moriscos, 210, 211, 212; attacks on, 214, 219; dismissed, 220; promotes Olivares, 224; tries to kill him, *ib.*
Lesdiguières, Constable, commands Henry IV's army, 216; aids Savoy, 217
Leyva, Antonio de, 29, 47; defends Pavia, 54; wins Landriano, 62; dies, 71
Lichtenstein, Prince of, wins Piacenza, 380
Lille, fall of, 338
Limburg, fall of, 328
Lindsay, Earl of, 236

Lionne, Hugues de, 278
Lippe, Count, 394, 395
Lisbon, English expedition against, 184, 185
Literature in Spain, 247, 248
Lobkowitz, in Italy, 379
Lodi, 53
Lombardy, French expelled from, 7, 8, 49; Charles I.'s success in, 51; Imperialist plots in, 96; Charles VI expelled from, 372
Longueville, Duke of, 241
Lorraine, assigned to Stanislaus, with reversion to France, 372
— Cardinal of, represents Henry II at Cateau Cambresis, 123
— Charles, Duke of, defeated at Courtrai, 270; imprisoned at Toledo, 275
Louis XI has a mortgage on Roussillon and Cerdagne, 2; his saying about France, 47
Louis XII, 7-9
Louis XIII, betrothed to the Infanta Anna, 216, 217; quarrels with Philip IV, 232; at war with Charles II, 235; accepts the Crown of Catalonia, 261; sends an army to Spain, 262; dies, 266
Louis XIV, accession of, 266; marries Maria Theresa, 281; claims the Netherlands and invades Flanders, 287; makes the treaty of Aix-la-Chapelle, 288; tries to gain Mariana, 290; allied with Charles II, 291; in Flanders, 292; aids the Sicilian rebels, ib.; makes peace with Orange, 293; makes the Peace of Nimeguen, 294; marries his niece to Charles II of Spain, 300; his advice to her, 303; seizes Strasburg, 305; claims Alost, ib.; invades Catalonia, bombards Genoa, and captures Luxemburg, 306; his gains by the Treaty of Ratisbon, ib.; invades the Empire, 307; supports James II, 308; takes Mons, ib.; captures Spanish towns, 309;
wins Neerwinden, but loses Namur, 311; makes peace with Savoy, ib.; takes Barcelona, ib.; concludes the Treaty of Ryswick, ib.; claims the Spanish Crown, 312; makes the first Partition Treaty, 314; makes the second, 316; accepts Charles II's will, 318; his opinion of Spain, 320; recognises the Old Pretender, 322; makes the Princess of Ursinos adviser to Marie Louise, 323; proposes the cession of Flanders to France, ib.; outwitted by Ursinos, 327; asks for peace, 328; feigns abandonment of Spain, 340; his offers at Gertruydenberg, ib.; makes the Treaties of Utrecht and Rastadt, 344; dies, 350
Louis XV, his accession, 350; betrothed to the Infanta, 358; breaks off the Spanish matches, 364; signs the treaty of Hanover, 365; signs the treaty of Seville, 367; freed from tutelage by Fleury's death, 378; signs the treaty of Fontainebleau, 379; treats with Charles Emmanuel, 381; negotiates with Philip V, 381; makes the treaty of Aix-la-Chapelle, 384; at war with England, 389; takes Minorca, 390; offers Minorca to Ferdinand VI and Poland to Don Philip, ib.; signs the 'Family Compact,' 394; makes peace with England, 395; dies, 404
Louis XVI, recognises the United States, 404; at war with England, 405
Louis, Prince, of Portugal, takes part in the invasion of Tunis, 69
Louise of Savoy, Queen-Mother of France, affects a general peace, 63
Louise Elizabeth of Orleans, marries Luis, Prince of Asturias, 358; her conduct, 362; sent back to France, 363

Louisiana, ceded by France to Spain, 400
Lucca helps Philip IV against France, 232
Lucena, secretary of John IV of Portugal, 256
Luis of Spain, son of Philip V, 355; marries Louise Elizabeth of Orleans, 358; succeeds on Philip's abdication, 360; dies, 362
Luis, Archbishop of Toledo, son of Philip V, 383, 392
Luther, Martin, condemned at Worms, 49
Lützen, battle of, 238
Luxemburg, conquered by Louis XIV, 306; restored at Ryswick, 311; offered to Holland, 340
— Duke of, 308, 311
Luzzara, battle of, 324
Lyons, peace of, 215

Macanaz, 350
Machiavelli, Nicolo, his opinion of Ferdinand of Aragon, 10
Madrid, rising in, 35; capital removed from, 200; capital restored to, 209; state of, under Philip IV, 246; population of, 297; devoted to Philip V, 335–342; Charles III's improvements in, 393; revolts against his regulation of dress, 397
— treaty of, 55
Maggiali, Father, 352
Mahony, Count, 336
Maillebois, Marshal, 383
Maintenon, Madame de, 322
Majorca, war of classes in, 44
Malladas, 288
Malmesbury, Harris, Lord, 401
Malplaquet, battle of, 339
Malta, Hospitallers settled in, 68; siege of, 139, 140
— Knights of, see Hospitallers
Man, Dr, ambassador at Madrid, 156
Mancera, Count, 331
Manifestacion, privilege of, 82
Manila, taken by England, 395

Mannheim, siege of, 230
Manoel, King of Portugal, marries Leonora, sister of Charles I, 113; dies, *ib.*; his descendants, 167
Mansfield, Count, defeated by Wallenstein, 235
Manuel, Juan, ambassador at Rome, 10, 47, 50
Mantua, house of, 96; Philip II in, 112; seized by Charles Emmanuel, 217; disputed succession to, 236; taken by the Imperialists, 237; taken by Don Philip, 380
— Duke of, 65
— Margaret, Duchess of, regent of Portugal, 251; warns Olivares of Braganza's plans, 253; arrested and forced to yield the citadel to Braganza, 254
Marck, Robert de la, threatens Luxemburg and Namur, 46; attacks the Netherlands, 49; abandoned by Francis I, 63
Margaret of Austria, sister of Philip I, marries the Infante Juan, 9; Regent of the Netherlands, 63; converts the truce with England into a general peace, *ib.*; death of, 66
Margaret, bastard daughter of Charles I, marries Alessandro de' Medici, 63; *see also* Parma
Margaret, daughter of Maximilian II, marries Philip III, 198; dies, 216
Margaret Tudor, Duchess of, 8
Margaret Valois, intended by her mother for Don Carlos, 147
Maria, daughter of Charles I, marries Maximilian II, 108; co-regent of Spain, 111
Maria of Portugal, marries Philip II, 104, 106; dies, 108
Maria, Queen of Portugal, 404
Maria Luisa, of Parma, marries Charles IV, 404
Maria Theresa, daughter of Philip IV, 269; marries Louis XIV, 281; renounces her claim to Spain, 280, 287, 312

Maria Theresa, Empress, 365; her succession conditionally guaranteed, 368; her accession, 376; signs the treaty of Worms, 379; accepts the treaty of Aix-la-Chapelle, 384; guarantees Italian neutrality, 386

Mariana of Austria, marries Philip IV, 270; intrigues with Father Nithard against Don Juan, 282, 283; regent of Spain, 284; makes Nithard Inquisitor-General, 285; forced to dismiss him, 289; at war with France, 289-293; accepts the Peace of Nimeguen, 294; her relations with Valenzuela, 295; outwits Don Juan, 296; driven from power, 298; recalled by her son, 300; her treatment of Marie Louise, 301, 302, 307; her policy, 308, 309; dies, 312

Marie Louise of France, marries Philip, son of Philip V, 374

Marie Louise of Orleans, marries Charles II of Spain, 300-301; her conduct, 302, 307; conspiracy against, 303; death of, *ib.*, 307

Marie Louise of Savoy, marries Philip V, 321; her government, 323; rouses Andalucia to arms, 326; overcomes Louis XIV's opposition, 331; dies, 347

Marignano, battle of, 8, 45, 47, 64

Marlborough, Duke of, on the Rhine, 325; conquers Cologne, 328; wins Schellenberg and Blenheim, 329; wins Ramillies, 333; in the Netherlands, 337; wins Oudenarde, 338; takes Bruges, Ghent, and Lille, *ib.*; wins Malplaquet, 339; takes Bouchain, 344; recalled, *ib.*

Marseilles, its value to France, 52; attacked by Charles, 53

Marsin, Marshal, ambassador at Madrid, 320, 323, 333

Martin, Commodore, 378

Martinique, taken by England, 395

Mary, Queen of Hungary, sister of Charles I, Regent of the Netherlands, 66; concludes a truce with France in 1537, 71

Mary de' Medici, Queen Regent of France, adheres to Spain, 216; effects a double marriage with the Spanish house, *ib.*; overthrown, 229

Mary Tudor, schemes of marriage for, 48; Charles I's attitude towards, 75; marries Philip II, 94, 98, 115; enters London, 115; childless, 116; parts from Philip, 117; declares war on France, 121; dies, 123

Mary Stuart, Queen of Scots, Dauphiness, 125; Philip II's attitude towards, *ib.* 173; Queen of France, 132; proposed as a wife for Don Carlos, 148; marries Darnley, *ib.*; imprisoned, 158; Don Juan proposes to marry, 163; throws herself into Philip's hands, 174; disinherits James and makes Philip her heir, 179; implicated in Babington's plot, *ib.*

Mary Stuart, daughter of James II, marries Orange, 293

Mary Anne of Neuburg, marries Charles II of Spain, 308; secures Oropesa's fall, 309; greed of, 310; her policy, 312-314; struggles with Diaz and the Inquisition, 315, 316; sent to Toledo, 319; to Bayonne, 336

Masaniello (Tommaso Aniello), 273, 274

Mascarenhas, Leonor de, educates Philip II, 102

Massa, Prince of, 274

Matilla, Father, 309, 313, 314

Matthews, Admiral, 379

Maurice of Nassau, joined by the Protestant princes, 203; besieges Nieuport and defeats Archduke Albert, *ib.*; takes Sluys, 206; concludes the 12 years' truce with Spain, 207, 208

Maurice of Saxony, makes a treaty with Henry II, 92; drives Charles I from Innsbrück, *ib.*

Maximilian I, Emperor, 7, 8; proposed as regent of Castile, 32; his hostility to France, 45

Maximilian II, Emperor, resents Charles I's settlement of the succession, 94; marries his daughter Maria, 108; Charles guarantees his succession, *ib.*; co-regent of Spain, 111

Mayenne, Duc de, heads the League, 187; proclaims the Cardinal de Bourbon, *ib.*; defeated by Henry IV, 188; quarrels with Farnese, *ib.*; hates the Spaniards, 189; opposes the marriage of Guise and Isabel of Spain, 190; proxy for Louis XIII, 216

Mazarin, Cardinal, abandons Guise in Naples, 274; Peace of Münster a blow to, 275; struggles with the Parliament of Paris, *ib.*; treats with Spain, 277

Medici, Alessandro de', marries Margaret, daughter of Charles I, 63; restored to Florence by Charles I, *ib.*, 64; murdered, 96
— Cardinal, *see* Clement VII
— Catherine de', *see* Catherine
— Cosimo de', Duke of Florence, 71, 96; forces the French in Siena to capitulate, 97
— Mary de', *see* Mary

Medina del Campo, burnt, 36; mart of the woollen trade, 83

Medina Celi, Viceroy of Sicily, 137; commands the expedition to Tripoli, *ib.*; flees, 138

Medina Celi, Duke of, prime minister of Spain, 302, 304, 305, 307; remonstrates against French influence, 333; in power, 340; dies in prison, 341

Medina Sidonia, Duke of, commands the Armada, 180-183
— — Gaspar, Duke of, plots against Philip IV, 255

Meilleraie, Marshal, 262

Melgar, Count de, a traitor to Philip V, 325

Melilla, 5, 403

Mello, Don Francisco de, Governor of Flanders, wins Honnecourt, 267; defeated at Rocroy, 268

Mendoza, Bernardino de, Philip's ambassador at Paris, 178, 179
— Diego de, Viceroy of Valencia, 43; leads the Spanish bishops at Trent, 94
— Inquisitor-General, 317, 322
— Juan de (Marquis de Guadelete), occupies Cleves and Westphalia, 203

Mercœur, Duc de, opposes Henry IV in Brittany, 189

Mers-el-Kebir, besieged by the Turks, 138

Messina, taken by the Austrians, 354, 355; siege of, 372

Mesta, the, 84

Metz, taken by Henry II, 92; besieged by Charles I, *ib.*

Mexico, conquest of, 90, 91; attacked by Cromwell, 277

Miguel of Portugal, heir to Spain and Portugal, 9; dies, *ib.*

Milan, Duchy of, occupied by Louis XII, 7-9; held by Francis I, 46; hatred of the French in, 46, 50; Parma and Piacenza detached from, 49, 50; occupied by Francis I, 53; joins the Italian league, 56; Francesco Sforza besieged by Charles' troops in, 58; he is invested by Charles, 64; reverts to Charles on his death, 70, 71; Charles' proposals regarding, 72, 75; conferred on Philip II, 72, 97, 118; lost to Philip V, 336; retained by Austria at Rastadt, 344; captured by Don Philip, 380

Millan, Don Francisco, 234

Millions (tax), 135, 179, 245, 271, 351, 381, 388, 409

Mina, Marquis de la, commands in Italy, 383

Minas, Marquis de las, 329, 335, 337

Minorca, overrun by the Turks, 137; ceded to England, 344;

448 *Index.*

taken by Richelieu, 390; offered to Ferdinand VI, *ib.*; ceded to England, 395; captured by Spain, 497
Mirandola, French protectorate of, 71; anti-Spanish intrigues in, 74
Mississippi, the, Soto's expedition to, 90, 91
Mobile, capture of, 406
Modena, held by the Duke of Ferrara, 62; helps Philip IV against Richelieu, 232
Mollwitz, battle of, 377
Moluccas, the, spice trade with, 88; sold to Portugal, *ib.*, 89
Moncada, Hugo de, 10; envoy at Rome, 59; surprises the Vatican, *ib.*; Viceroy of Naples, 60; fights the Genoese, 61; his death, *ib.*; attacks Algiers, 68
Mondejar, Marquis of, governor of Granada, protests against the persecution of the Moors, 153; defeats the rebels, *ib.*; complaints of his moderation, 154
Monjuich, Fort, 260, 332
Mons, taken by Louis XIV, 308; restored at Ryswick, 311; taken by the allies, 339
Montalto, Duke of, 317, 331
Montalvan, Fort of, 330
Montellano, Count, 327
Montemar, Duke de, 375; invades Italy, 377; retires before Charles Emmanuel, 378
Monterey, Count, 313, 331
Montesclaros, battle of, 282
Montferrat, overrun by France, 232; recovered, *ib.*; seized by Charles Emmanuel of Savoy, 217; assigned to Savoy, 328
Montgon, Abbé, 367
Montigny, Florence de Montmorenci, lord of, sent to Madrid by the Flemings, 147, 158
Montmédy, capture of, 278
Montmorenci, House of, jealous of the Guises, 132
— Constable de, defeated and taken prisoner at St Quentin, 122; represents Henry II at Cateau Cambresis, 123
Montmorenci, Florence de, *see* Montigny
— Marshal, 237
Monzon, Philip II at, 103; seized by the French, 263; recaptured by Philip IV, 269
Moors, in Spain and Africa, 3, 4; expelled from Andalucia, 155, 213; from Aragon, Murcia, Catalonia, Castile, La Mancha, and Estremadura, 213
— of Granada, religious liberty guaranteed to, 17; enforced conversion of, *ib.*; buy exemption from the Inquisition, 77; expelled, 154
— of Valencia, defend the nobles, 44; their enforced conversion, *ib.*, 46, 77; they rebel and are crushed, 78; their thrift and industry, 152, 210; Espinosa's persecution of, 153; revolt, 153, 154; intrigue with Elizabeth and the Swiss, 211; persecuted by Ribera, *ib.*; expelled from Spain, 211-213
Mora, Cristobal de, 169, 197
Morone, Secretary, intrigues against Charles I in Italy, 57
Mortara, General, captures Tortosa and Barcelona, 279
Motte, Count de la, invades Catalonia, 261; captures a Spanish force, 262; defeats Leganes, 263
Mountjoy, Lord, Viceroy of Ireland, defeats Tyrone and the Spaniards, 204
Mühlberg, battle of, 92, 93
Muley Hassan, driven from Tunis, and restored, 68-70
Muniain, General, 398
Münster, Peace of, 275
Murcia, Moors expelled from, 213
Murray, General, defends St Philip, Minorca, 407
Musquiz, 398

Namur, taken by William III, 311; offered to Holland, 340

Naples, taken by Alfonso of Aragon, 4; claimed by the House of Anjou, 6; taken by Charles VIII, *ib.*; divided by Ferdinand and Louis XII, *ib.*; Ferdinand obtains the whole of, *ib.*, 45; heavy taxation of, 27; Charles I holds, 46; Pescara proposed as king of, 57; the French besiege, 62; conferred on Philip II, 118; dreads the Inquisition, 139; extortion and chronic revolt in, 171; revolts, 273; Guise claims the Crown of, 274; recovered by Don Juan, *ib.*; revolts against Philip V, 322, 324; accepts Charles VI, 336; retained by Austria at Rastadt, 344; Charles III king of, 372; Ferdinand king of, 392, 410

Navarre, 2, 7, 45; French invasion of, 49-52; proposed settlement of, 72; supports Philip V, 335, 336

Navarro, Pedro, 28, 29

Navy, Spanish, strengthened by Olivares, 243; re-created by Ensenada, 385, 390, 391; under Charles III, 403

Neerwinden, battle of, 311

Nemours, treaty of, 186

Netherlands, relations with France, 45; power of England over, 47; attacked by Robert de la Marck and the Duke of Guelders, 49; Margaret Regent of, 63; truce with England, *ib.*; Mary, Queen of Hungary, Regent of, 66; truce with France, *ib.*, 71; proposed union with Franche Comté, 72; their treatment at Crespy, 75, 109; relations with England, 97, 98, 107, 115; attached to the Spanish Crown, 108; Charles' plans regarding, 109; conferred on Philip II, 118; Charles takes leave of, *ib.*; Philip's ecclesiastical measures in, 126; petition for the withdrawal of the Spanish troops, *ib.*; the Duchess of Parma Regent of, 126; hate Granvelle, 127, 143; troops withdrawn from, 143; religious troubles in, 144; emigration to England from, 145; the Iconoclasts in, 146; peace restored in, *ib.*; Philip determines to visit, 147; Alba in, 158; Alba's tyranny in, 159; resist the *Alcabala*, *ib.*; Alba recalled from, 160; Don Juan sent to, 164; 'Spanish Fury,' *ib.*; Don Juan breaks with, 165; Farnese sent to conquer, *ib.*; Alençon crowned sovereign of, 171; left by Philip to the Archdukes Albert and Isabel, 194; Maurice in, 203; the 12 years' truce of 1609, 208
— *see* Flanders and United Provinces

Nevers, Duc de, claims Mantua, 236; receives it at the Peace of Casale, 237

Newfoundland, ceded to England, 344; fishing in, 395

Nice, truce of, 71

Nicosia, captured by the Turks, 161

Nieuport, besieged by Maurice of Nassau, 203; offered to Holland, 340

Nimeguen, peace of, 294

Nithard, Father, 283-288, 285; forced to leave Spain, 289, 295

Nivernais, Duke de, 395

Noailles, François de, 121
— Marshal (Duc de), in Catalonia, 292, 309, 311; attacks Barcelona, 334; in Roussillon, 341; takes Gerona, 343

Nobles, Spanish, their position and influence, 13, 14, 15, 20, 22, 31, 32, 35, 38, 41, 61, 79, 80, 82, 134, 135

Nordlingen, battle of, 238

Norfolk, Duke of, plots to marry Mary Stuart, 158

Norris, Sir John, 185

North, Lord, 406

Northumberland, Duke of, 115

Noyon, treaty of, 45

Nuremberg, Compromise of, 66

O'Donnell, rebels in Ireland, 204; dies in Spain, 205
Olavide, Count de, 403
Oleron, fortress of, 236
Olivares, Count de, Spanish ambassador at Rome, 177; negotiates for financial aid from Sixtus V, 178
— Gaspar de Guzman, Count de, plots against Lerma, 220; declines the Roman embassy, 224; attempts to murder, *ib.*; controls Philip IV, 225; obtains Lerma's dismissal, *ib.*; made a duke, 226; his measures, 227, 228; and the marriage of Charles Stuart, 230; quarrels with Buckingham, 231; projects of, 232; overawes the Valencian Cortes, 235; treats with England, 236; and the navy, 243; his economic measures, 245; his method of government, 249; his Portuguese policy, 251, 252; suspects Braganza, 252; tries to have him murdered, 255; causes Lucena's death, 256; his policy in Catalonia, 257, 259; relieves Tarragona, 261; opposes Philip's taking the field, 262; intrigues with Cinq Mars, 263; dismissed, *ib.*; his policy, 264
Oñoa, Fort, 406
Oñate, Viceroy of Naples, 274
Oran, 10, 67, 337, 370, 406
Orange, Henry Frederic, Prince of, allied with Richelieu, 239; besieges Breda, 240
— Philibert, Prince of, one of Charles I's generals, 60; forces the French to capitulate at Aversa, 62; requests Charles to come to Italy, 64
— William I, Prince of, with Charles at Brussels, 118; represents Philip at Cateau Cambresis, 123; petitions for the withdrawal of the Spanish troops in the Netherlands, 126; remonstrates against Granvelle's conduct, 144; begs the Regent to summon the States-General, 144; Philip tries to win, 146; embraces Protestantism and sides with the rebels, *ib.*; raises troops in Germany, *ib.*; escapes Alba's trap, 158; defeated at Heiliger Lee, 159; joined by the Catholic Flemings, 164, 165
Orange, William III, Prince of, *see* William III of England
Orders, Military, Ferdinand made Grandmaster of, 14; Council of, 24; their revenues farmed by the Fuggers, 87
O'Reilly, Count, in Portugal, 394; invades Algiers, 403; defeated, 404
Orendain, Don Juan, 360, 366, 367
Orleans, Gaston, Duke of, wins Courtrai, 270
— Philip, Duke of, defeated at Turin, 333; regent for Louis XV, 350; rejects Alberoni's overtures, 353; declares war on Spain, 355; delays to surrender Fuenterrabia, 357; dies, 359
Ormond, Duke of, 325, 344, 375
Oropesa, Count de, his reforms, 307; falls, 309; recalled, 312; supports the claims of Joseph of Bavaria, 314; exiled, 315
Orry, Jean, reorganises Spanish finance, 321, 328; dismissed, 330; reinstated, 331; supreme, 348; driven from Spain, 350
Osnabrück, negotiations at, 275
Osorio, Doña Isabel de, her connection with Philip II, 113, 115
Ostend, negotiations at, 180; sieges of, 205, 206, 333
— Company of the Indies, 365, 367, 368
Osuna, P. T. de Giron, Duke of, Viceroy of Naples, 218; falls and dies, 225
— Duke of, invades Portugal, 281
Oudenarde, capture of, 278; battle of, 338
Oviedo, Mateo de, 203

Pace, Richard, 54

Padilla, Juan de, insurgent leader, 35, 36, 40, 41; defeated at Villalar, 42
— Don Martin, 202
Palermo, revolt of, 273
Palisse, Jacques de la, 47
Pamplona, 341, 342
Panama, 374
Papacy, the, its relations with Spain, 15, 16, 38, 61, 65, 93, 120, 128, 389
Paraguay, R., 404
Parana, R., 404
Pardo, convention of the, 374
Pardo, Governor of Habana, 395
Paris, besieged by Henry III, 187; besieged by Henry IV, 188; relieved by Farnese, *ib.*; entered by Henry IV, 190
— treaty of (1783), 407
Parma, added to the Papal States by Charles I, 49, 50; held by the French, 96; occupied by Philip II, 120; joins Philip IV against France, 232; opposes Philip V, 348; accepts Charles III, 368; annexed to Milan, 372; Don Philip Duke of, 384
— Alexander Farnese, Duke of, *see* Farnese
— Antonio Farnese, Duke of, marries his heiress to Philip V, 348; his policy, 355, 358; dies, 368
— Margaret, Duchess of, daughter of Charles I, and Regent of the Netherlands, 126; marries Ottavio Farnese, 126; summons the Knights of the Golden Fleece, 144; her rule, 144, 145; urges gentle measures, 146; enters Antwerp in state, *ib.*; retires, 147; *see also* Margaret
— Philip, Duke of, 384, 386, 390
Parsons, Father, 175, 205
Partition Treaties, 314–316
Pastrana, Duke of, 216
Patiño, Don José, 354, 366, 367; advocates peace, 368; proposes the conquest of Naples and Sicily, 371; dies, 376; his naval and colonial policy, *ib.*
Paul III, 67, 69, 71, 92, 93, 95, 96, 104
Paul IV (Caraffa), 92, 120, 121, 137
Pavia, occupied by the Imperialists, 53, 54; taken by Lautrec, 60
— Peace of, 217; repudiated by Osuna and Toledo, 218
Pedernales, Juan Martinez, alias Siliceo, tutor to Philip II, 103
Pedro II of Portugal, joins the league against Philip V, 327
Penn, William, 277
Pennington, Admiral, 243
Peñon, attacked by Algiers, 67; taken by Barbarossa, 68; captured by Don Garcia, 139
Perennot, A. de, *see* Granvelle, Cardinal
Perez, Antonio, on Don Carlos' death, 150; hates Alba, 160; principal secretary to Philip, 163; proposes the mission of Escobedo, *ib.*; leads the peace party, 164; breaks with Don Juan, *ib.*; has Escobedo murdered, 166, 190, 191; discovered by Philip II, 191; imprisoned and tortured, *ib.*; flees to Aragon, 192; imprisoned and escapes *ib.*; dies, *ib.*
— Gonzalo, Secretary under Charles I, 82
Perpignan, besieged by Henry II, 74, 103; repels the French, 262
Perquisidores, 24
Persia aids Philip III against Turkey, 210
Peru, trade with, 88; conquest of, 90; Charles vindicates his authority in, 91; anarchy in, 407
Pescara, Marquis of, as a general, 47, 50; quarrels with Bourbon, 53; relieves Pavia, 54; refuses the crown of Naples, 57; betrays Morone, *ib.*
Peterborough, Earl of, lands in Portugal, 331; in Valencia, *ib.*; takes Barcelona, 332

Philip I, claims Castile, 7, 31; marries Juana, 9; intrigues with Castilian nobles, 31; lands in Spain, *ib.*; keeps Juana in close confinement and rules alone, 31, 32
Philip II, frequently calls the Cortes, 21; his birth, 60, 101; Charles I's plans for, 76, 94, 110; Regent of Spain, 93, 105, 108; marries Mary Tudor, 94, 98; receives Siena and the Vicariate in Italy, 97, 108; Cortes of Castile swears allegiance to, 102; his ancestry, *ib.*; his education, 102, 103; accompanies Alba to Perpignan, *ib.*; plan for his marriage to Jeanne d'Albret, 72, 105; marries Maria of Portugal, 104, 106; Charles' instructions to, 105, 106; financial straits of, 106; loses his wife, *ib.*; wins the affection of the Spaniards, *ib.*; his views on the Imperial succession, 110; at the Cortes of Valladolid in 1548, *ib.*; his reforms, 111; leaves Valladolid, 112; with Charles in the Netherlands, 113; negotiates for a Portuguese bride, *ib.*; his morganatic connection with Isabel de Osorio, *ib.*, 115; attends the Diet of Augsburg, *ib.*; summons Cortes, 114; proposed as Mary Tudor's husband, 115; lands at Southampton, 116; his policy in England, *ib.*; keeps persecution in check, 117; leaves England, *ib.*; King of Naples and Sicily and Duke of Milan, sovereign of the Netherlands and King of Spain, 118; his character and political position, 119; his view of the Papacy, 120; excommunicated by Paul IV, *ib.*; his position in Italy, *ib.*; sends Alba thither, 121; makes peace with the Pope, *ib.*; visits England, *ib.*; gains her support against France, *ib.*; returns to Brussels, 122; forbids Savoy to march on Paris, *ib.*; obtains an English fleet, 123; his financial straits, *ib.*; his marriage negotiations with Elizabeth, 124; signs the Peace of Cateau Cambresis, *ib.*; his policy of alliance with England, *ib.*; betroths Don Carlos to Elizabeth of France, 125; his attitude towards Elizabeth Tudor, 125, 173; his treatment of Mary Stuart, 125, 158; marries Elizabeth Valois, 126, 131; his Flemish policy, 126, 127; and the Castilian Cortes, 128, 157; his religious policy, 128; supports the Inquisition, 129, 130, 141, 142, 161; his system of government, 134–137, 169; tries to recover Tripoli, 137, 138; lays siege to Malta, 139; quarrels with Pius IV, 142; and the Council of Trent, 143; withdraws his troops from the Netherlands, *ib.*; recalls Granvelle, 145; allows the suppression of the Inquisition and forgives the confederates, 146; withdraws the permission, *ib.*; sends Alba to the Netherlands, 147; imprisons Don Carlos, 149; loses his third wife, 150; sends Don Juan to Granada, 154; his financial straits, 155–158; expels the English ambassador, 156; recalls Alba, 160; aids Venice against the Turks, 161; and Pius V, *ib.*; wins Lepanto, 162; orders Don Juan to dismantle Tunis, 163; sends Escobedo to him, *ib.*; orders him to the Netherlands, 164; suspects him, *ib.*, 191; orders Escobedo's murder, 165, 190, 191; sends Farnese to Flanders, 165; aids the Irish rebels, 166, 173; intrigues with the Guises, 166, 173; claims the Portuguese Crown, 167; loses his fourth wife, 168; accepted by the Portuguese Cortes, *ib.*; builds the Escorial, *ib.*; his 'Council of Night,' 169; his court, 170; his quarrel with the Papacy, 172; expels the Nuncio, 173; plans the invasion of England, 174–

177; aided by Sixtus V, 178;
intends Isabel to be Queen, *ib.*;
made heir by Mary Stuart, 179;
levies *millions, ib.*; hears the fate
of the Armada, 184; his policy
in France, 186, 188; claims the
Crown for Isabel, *ib.*; proposes
her marriage with Guise, 190;
evacuates France, *ib.*; imprisons
and tortures Perez, 191; punishes
the Aragonese rebels, 192; his
last illness and death, 194; leaves
the Netherlands to Isabel, *ib.*

Philip III, born, 168; his accession
and character, 197, 223; under
Lerma's influence, 198; marries
Margaret of Austria, *ib.*; asks
the Cortes for money, 199; his
extravagance, *ib.*, 214; pardons
the rebels of Aragon, 199;
lavishes titles and offices, *ib.*; his
poverty, 201, 208; tries to invade England, 202; sends Aguila
to Ireland, 204; makes terms
with the English Catholics, 205;
makes peace with James I, 206;
makes a twelve years' truce with
the Dutch, 207, 208; his superstition, 208; expels the Moors,
212; at war with Savoy, 217;
recalls Osuna, 218; aids Ferdinand II in the Thirty Years' War,
219; visits Portugal, 222; dies,
220, 222

Philip IV, born, 216; betrothed to
Elizabeth of Bourbon, *ib.*; married, 217; becomes king, 225;
ruled by Olivares, *ib.*; cuts down
his expenses, 227; at war with
Holland, 228, 233; signs the
treaty for the English match, 231;
at war with France, 232, 233;
crushes the Valencian Cortes, 234;
quarrels with the Catalonian
Cortes, 235; makes peace with
England, 236; at war with
France, 237; makes his brother
Ferdinand governor of Flanders,
238; his pleasures, 248; loses
Portugal, 254; quarters troops on
Catalonia, 258; takes the field
himself, 262; dismisses Olivares,
ib.; recaptures Monzon, 269;
loses his wife and son, *ib.*;
his licentiousness, *ib.*; marries
Mariana of Austria, 270; accepts
the Peace of Münster, 275; supports the Fronde, 276; friendly
to Cromwell, 277; signs the
Treaty of the Pyrenees, 279;
attempts to reconquer Portugal,
281; hears of Montesclaros, 282;
his character, *ib.*; dies, 283

Philip V, claims the Crown, 314;
appointed heir by Charles II,
317, 318; proclaimed, 319; his
reception in Spain, 319-321;
marries, 321; in Italy, 323, 324;
agrees to cede Flanders to Louis,
324; his melancholy, *ib.*, 359;
his reforms, 327; reorganises the
army, *ib.*; invades Portugal, 329;
invokes Louis XIV's aid, 334;
flees from Barcelona, 335; re-
enters Madrid, *ib.*; abolishes
the privileges of Aragon, 337;
dismisses French officials, 339;
protests against the proposals of
Gertruydenberg, 341; defeated at
Almansa and Almenara, 342;
master of Spain, 343; accepts the
treaties of Rastadt and Utrecht,
344; conquers Catalonia, 346;
loses his wife, 347; introduces
the Salic law, *ib.*; marries Elizabeth Farnese, 348; makes a commercial treaty with England, 352;
at war with the Empire, 353;
takes Sardinia and Sicily, *ib.*,
354; expels Alberoni, 356;
makes peace, ceding Sardinia to
Savoy, 357; relieves Ceuta, *ib.*;
aids the Pretender, 359; resigns,
360; resumes the Crown, 362;
makes the treaty of Venice, 364;
at war with England, 366; makes
the treaty of Seville, 367; makes
the treaty of Vienna, 1731, 368;
allied with France, 371; aids
Charles III in Italy, *ib.*; makes

the treaty of Vienna, 1736, 373; an art collector, *ib.*; claims the Empire, 377; invades Italy, 378; makes the treaty of Fontainebleau, 379; dies, 381; his rule, 381–383
Philip, Don, son of Philip V, marries Marie Louise of France, 374; projected kingdom for, 377, 379; invades Italy and retreats, 379; joins Gages and defeats Charles Emmanuel, 380; Duke of Parma, Piacenza, and Guastalla, 384; makes a treaty with Maria Theresa, 386; plots for the Spanish Crown, 390
Philippine Islands, 5
Piacenza, added to the Papal States, 49, 50; occupied by Gonzaga, 96; held by Philip II, 120; Don Philip, Duke of, 384
Piali Pasha, 137, 139
Piedmont, the French occupy, 70; war in, 71; the French in, 120; war in, 217
Pirates, Moorish, 43, 73, 202, 208, 233, 408
Pitt, William, Earl of Chatham, 390
Pius IV (Medici), his relations with Philip II, 139, 142
Pius V, threatens Philip with excommunication, 129; summons him to fight the Turk, 161; accepts his conditions, *ib.*
Pizarro, Francisco, conquers Peru, 90; his house crushed by Charles, 91
Plate, River, exploration of, 11; navigation of, 404
Pocock, Admiral, 395
Poland, disputed succession to, 371; offered to Ferdinand for Don Philip, 390
Pole, Cardinal, 116
Pombal, Marquis of, 404
Pomerania, assigned to Sweden at Münster, 275
Pontevedra, battle of, 355
Population of Spain, in 1559, 136; in 1600 and 1619, 221; under Charles III, 410

Portalegre, Fortress of, 330
Porter, Endymion, envoy to Spain, 230, 236
Porto Bello, blockaded by Hozier, 366; sacked by Vernon, 374
Portocarrero, Cardinal, heads the French party in Spain, 312–317; his reforms, 319; truckles to France, 320; refuses to call a new Cortes, *ib.*; retires, 327; dies, 340
Portugal, her relations with Castile, 2; her discoveries, 3; matrimonial alliances with Spain, 9; supports Isabella of Castile's rival, 11; buys the Moluccas, 89; disputed succession in, 167; invaded by Alba, 168; Philip King of, *ib.*; Don Antonio's party in, 171, 184; invaded by England, 184; Philip II's policy in, 250; Olivares' taxation of, 251; revolt in, 251–254; Braganza, King of, 253, 254; invaded by Haro, Don Juan, and Osuna, 280, 281; aided by England, 281; civil strife in, 283; her independence recognised, 285; invaded by Philip V, 329; negotiates for the exchange of Tuy and Sacramento, 387; invaded by Charles III, 394; attacks Buenos Ayres, 404; cedes Sacramento to Spain, *ib.*
Prague, battle of, 219
Prices, rise of, 86, 89, 136
Provence, invasion of, 52, 53; promised to Bourbon, 52; Charles I invades, 71; invaded by Charles Emmanuel, 383
Prussia acquires Guelders, 344
Puerto Rico, Dutch expelled from, 233; demanded by England, 406
Pyrenees, Treaty of the, 278–280.

Quesnay, capture of, 276
Quevedo, Francisco de, 248
Quiñones, Francisco, General of the Franciscans, 60
Quintin, Madame, 302

Rábago, Father, 386
Ramillies, battle of, 333
Ramirez, Francisco, 28
Rastadt, treaty of, 344
Ratisbon, treaty of, 306
Ravenna, 8, 45, 47, 62, 64
Regidores, 18, 19
Renard, Simon, Imperial ambassador to Mary Tudor, 115, 116, 117
Requesens y Zuniga, Don Luis de, sent to the Netherlands, 160; calms the Southern provinces, *ib.*; dies, *ib.*, 163
Revenues, Crown, their sources, 25-27; alienated by Philip I, 32; under Philip II, 135; under Charles II, 286; under Philip V, 382; under Charles III, 410
Rhé, Fortress of, 286
Rhodes, captured by the Turks, 68; the Hospitallers expelled from, *ib.*
Ribera, Archbishop of Valencia, 211
Richelieu, Cardinal, forms an anti-Spanish league, 232; invades the Valtellina, *ib.*; gains over England, *ib.*; takes Rochelle, 236; forms a second anti-Spanish league, 237; makes the treaty of Casale, *ib.*; aided by Gustavus Adolphus, 238; subsidises the Dutch, 239; declares war on Spain and the Empire, *ib.*; his successes, 240; twice attempts to invade Spain, 241, 242; aids the Catalans, 259-263; dies, 263
— Armand, Duke of, 274
— Louis, Duke of, 390
Ricla, Spanish general, 394
Ridolfi's plot, 158
Rimini, 62
Rincon, murder of, 74
Ripperdá, Baron, 352; revives the Spanish cloth trade, 364; negotiates the treaty of Vienna, *ib.*; falls, 365; prime minister of Morocco, 366, 370
Robinet, Father, 348
Rochelle, siege of, 235; fall of, 236

Rochford, Lord, 396
Rocroy, battle of, 267; taken by Condé, 276
Rodney, Admiral, relieves Gibraltar, 406; saves Jamaica, 407
Rome, sacked by Bourbon's troops, 59, 61, 101
Ronquillos, the, 307, 313, 340, 347
Rooke, Sir George, 325, 329, 330
Rosas, Bay of, 112
Rouen, siege of, 189
Roussillon, Catalan character of, 2; mortgaged to Louis XI, *ib.*; final union with France under Louis XIV, *ib.* 262, 280; ceded to Spain by Charles VIII, 6, 45; overrun by Henry II, 103
Rudolph, Emperor, claims Cleves, 216
Ruggio, 62
Russia, and Poland, 371; joins in the 'armed neutrality,' 406
Ruthven, Raid of, 175
Ruyter, De, Admiral, 292
Ryswick, treaty of, 311

Sacramento, proposed cession of, 387; taken by Spain, 404; ceded to her, *ib.*
Ste Aldegonde, Philip de, 145
St André, Marshal, 123
St Honoré, 240
St Kitt's, 344
St Marguerite, 240
St Omer, siege of, 241
St Philip, Castle of, 407
Saint-Pol, Count of, defeated by Leyva, 62
St Quentin, battle of, 122
St Vincent, taken by England, 395
Salcés, siege of, 242
Salic Law, introduced by Philip V, 347
San Domingo, 88, 277
San George, Duke of, 260
San Guillain, capture of, 276
San Juan, Prior of, 40, 41
San Pol, 260
Sande, Alvaro de, defends Los Gelves, 138

Santa Catalina, 404
Santa Coloma, Viceroy of Catalonia, 257, 258
Santa Cruz, Alvaro de Bazan, Marquis of, shares in the attack on Algiers, 73; his conduct at Lepanto, 162; beats Don Antonio's fleet under Strozzi, 171, 176; wishes to invade England, 176; estimates the cost of invasion, 177; dies, 179
— Marquis of, 210, 237, 276, 335
Santa Junta, the, at Avila, 36; petitions Charles I, 37, 38; dissolved, 39, 40
Santa Lucia, taken by England, 395
Santiago (Spain), 34
Santiago, Order of, 14
Santiago de Cuba, 376
Sardinia, conquered by Aragon, 4; captured by Lake, 337; retained by Austria at Rastadt, 344; taken by Spain, 353; surrendered to Savoy, 357
Sarmiento, captured by Spain, 395
Sauvage, Chancellor, 33, 34
Savoy, French leanings of, 70; in French hands, *ib.*, 237; acquires Sicily, 344; acquires Sardinia, 357
— Carlo Emmanuele, Duke of, marries Philip's daughter Catherine, 178; enters Marseilles, 189; receives Saluzzo at the Peace of Lyons, 215; seizes Mantua and Montferrat and invades Lombardy, 217; makes peace at Pavia, *ib.*; joins Richelieu against Spain, 232; joins Spain, 236; dies, 237
— Charles III, Duke of, marries Beatrice of Portugal, 68, 70; receives Asti from Charles I, 65; refuses the French passage through Savoy, 70; at Nice, 74
— Christine, Duchess of, Regent for her son, 250
— Emmanuel Philibert, Duke of, wins St Quentin, 122; a candidate for Elizabeth Tudor's hand, 124; a claimant to the Crown of Portugal, 167
Savoy, Prince Thomas of, defeated at Avenne, 239; in Italy, 241, 250
— Victor Amadeus, Duke of, 311; joins the allies, 328; acquires Sicily as King, 344, 354; exchanges it for Sardinia, 357
Saxe, Marshal, 384
Saxony, Frederic, Elector of, captured at Mühlberg, 92
Schellenberg, battle of, 329
Schomberg, Cardinal, 48
— Marshal, before Rochelle, 236; in Spain, 262, 292; in Portugal, 281, 282
Schulemburg, Count of, 384
Scotland, detached from the French alliance, 8; Spanish intrigues with, 174–176, 193
Scotti, Marquis, 357
Sebastian, Don, King of Portugal, his birth and parentage, 127; killed at Alcazar, 167
Secretary of State, origin and functions of, 82, 134
Segovia, revolt of, 35, 36; a manufacturing town, 83
Selim, Sultan, attacks Cyprus, 161; takes Nicosia, *ib.*; negotiates with Venice, *ib.*; defeated at Lepanto, 162
Semple, Colonel, 205
Seron, battle of, 155
Servicio, the, 21, 27
Sessa, Duke of, Ambassador at Rome, 51, 52, 59; his death, 60
— Don Carlos de, 130
Seville, the centre of Judaism and the Inquisition, 17; factions in, 20; *Audience* of, 23; forms a 'loyal union' with Cordoba, 39; manufactures of, 84, 88, 409
— treaty of, 367
Seymour, Lord Henry, 182
Sforza, Francesco, Duke of Milan, 46, 50, 56–58, 64, 70
— Maximilian, Duke of Milan, established by Swiss arms, 8

Index. 457

Sheep-farming, 84, 85
Shovell, Sir Cloudesley, 330
Sicily, its relation to Africa, 3; an Aragonese possession, 4; taxation of, 37; revolt in, 46; conferred on Philip II, 118; ravaged by the Turks, 137; revolt in, 292; ceded to Savoy, 344; taken by Spain, 354; part of Charles III's kingdom, 372
Siena, admits the French, 96; the French capitulate, 97
Sigismund, Archduke, replaces Don Juan, 279
Siguenza, 35
Silesia, occupied by Frederic II, 377
Siliceo, *see* Pedernales.
Silk manufacture, among the Moors, 83, 210; in Seville and Toledo, 84; encouraged by Ensenada, 389
Silva, Felipe de, 269
Simancas, 40
Sinan the Jew, 74
Sisa, 80, 81, 135
Sixtus IV, his contest with the Spanish Crown, 15
Sixtus V, and the Scotch Catholics, 177; promises money for the Armada, 178; excommunicates Henry IV, 186
Slave trade with America, England secures the monopoly of, 344, 367, 374
Sluys, taken by Maurice of Nassau, 206
Soissons, Congress of, 367
Solyman, Sultan, 120
Soria, envoy at Genoa, 61
Soto, Fernando, his expedition to the Mississippi, 90, 91
— Pedro de, 93
South Sea Company, 374, 384
Spain, consolidation of, 1, 2; foreign relations of, 3, 5; under Ferdinand and Isabella, 30; military position and power, 46, 47; under Charles I, 76, 80, 81; agriculture in, 84, 5; sheep farming in, *ib.*; economic difficulties of, 85-7, 89,

90, 195; colonial trade of, 88; financial problems of, 89, 90, 195; the people of, 107; friendship with England necessary to, *ib.*, 109, 115; ruined by the Netherlands, 109; economic condition of in 1548, 112; in 1559, 133 *seq.*; in 1559, 136; in 1600 and 1619, 221; morals of, 170; poverty of, *ib.*, 195, 240, 271, 297; Moors expelled from, 213; state of in 1621, 226; destruction of industry in, 244, 271; luxury in, 246; the drama in, *ib.*, 247; literature in, *ib.*; state of under Charles II, 285, 297, 303, 305, 310; revenues of, 286; state of, under Philip V, 351, 380-382; progress under Ferdinand, 388-391; under Charles III, 402, 409, 410; after his death, 411
'Spanish Fury, the,' 164
Spes, De, 136
Speyer, Diet of, 74
Spinola, Marquis of, besieges Ostend, 206; crosses the Rhine, *ib.*; reduces the Lower Palatinate, 232; recovers the French conquests, 233; takes Breda, *ib.*; dies, 237
Squillachi, Marquis of, 393; his reforms, 397; dies, 398
Stafford, Thomas, 121
Stanhope, William, Earl of Harrington, ambassador at Madrid, 312, 316, 342, 343, 357, 358, 366
Stanislaus, King of Poland, 371; Lorraine assigned to, 372
Staremberg, Count de, 338, 342, 343
Strasburg, taken by Louis XIV, 305, 306
Strozzi, Filippo, 71, 96, 171
Subsidio, the, or clerical tenth, 27
Sully, Duc de, minister to Henry IV, 215; dismissed, 216
Sweden, receives Pomerania at Münster, 275; intervenes between Louis XIV and Spain, 287; joins the League of Augsburg, 307
Swiss, the, 8, 46, 49

458 *Index.*

Syracuse, battle of, 354; siege of, 372

Talavera, Archb. of Granada, 17
Tallard, Marshal, 328, 329
Tamarit, 261
Tangier, acquired by England, 281
Tarragona, occupied by d'Epernon, 260; Colonna besieged in, 261; held by the Spaniards, 270
Tavara, Archbishop of Toledo, 105
Taverna, Bishop of Lodi, Nuncio in Spain, 172; expelled, 173
Taxation, 15, 21, 26, 27, 80, 87, 89, 90, 135, 136, 157, 179, 210, 228, 245, 271, 381, 382, 388, 409
Ter, battle of, 306
Terranova, Duchess of, 301
Tessé, Marshal, 330, 331, 334, 337, 362, 363
Thionville, taken by Condé, 268
Thirlby, Dr, Bishop of Ely, 123
Thirty Years' War, begins, 218; ends, 275
Tilly, John, Count de, 233, 235, 238
Tlemcen, Moorish kingdom of, 10, 67
Tobago, taken by England, 395
Toledo, 33, 35, 42, 49, 83, 84
— Don Fadrique de, 233
— Don Garcia de, captures Peñon, 139; Viceroy of Sicily, *ib.*; relieves Malta, 140; governor to Don Carlos, 148
— Don Pedro de, Viceroy of Naples, 95
— Don Pedro de, Constable of Castile, 217, 218
Tordesillas, 36, 40
Torrecusa, C. Carraciolo, Marquis of, repulsed from Barcelona, 261; at Rosas, 263
Torres, Count de las, 366
Tortosa, 343
Toul, taken by Henry II, 92
Toulouse, seized by the Spanish, 189
— Count de, 330, 334
Towns, Castilian, their origin, and constitution, 18—20; revolt against Charles I, 35; rise of the lesser gentry in, 80, 81; municipal life destroyed, 133
Trapani, 372
Traun, General, 378
Tremouille, Louis de la, 47
Trent, Council of, meets, 91; alarms Paul III, 92; Charles I's policy at, 94; transferred to Bologna, *ib.*; reassembles in 1562, 142; its discussions, 142, 143; its resolutions published in Spain, 143
Triple Alliance, the, 288, 290, 357
Tripoli, acquired by Spain, 10; Hospitallers settled in, 68; captured by the Turks, 137; Philip II's expedition to, *ib.*
Tromp, Admiral Van, 242
Tunis, Muley Hassan driven from, 68; occupied by Barbarossa, 69; invaded by Charles I, *ib.*; Muley Hassan restored, 70; captured by Don John, 160; recovered by the Turks, *ib.*
Turenne, Marshal, joins the Spaniards, 275; returns to France, 276; his Flemish campaigns, *ib.*
Turin, taken by the French, 70; battle of, 333
Turks, the allies of Francis I, 47, 70—74; threaten the Empire and Catholicism, 63; advance on Vienna, 66; retreat, *ib.*; gain the suzerainty of Algiers, 67; the fleet attacks Nice, 74; make a truce with Ferdinand, 91; overrun Minorca and capture Tripoli, 137; defeat Philip's fleet, 138; besiege Mers-el-Kebir, *ib.*; besiege Malta, 139, 140; attack Venice, 161; capture Cyprus, *ib.*; defeated at Lepanto, 162; recover Tunis and Goletta, 163; Philip III and Persia attack, 210; struggle with the Empire, 283, 307, 311, 352
Tuscany, assigned to the Dukes of Lorraine, 372
— Duke of, 359
Tuttlinghen, battle of, 268

Tuy, Province of, proposed exchange of, 387
Tyrone, Hugh O'Neil, Earl of, intrigues with Spain, 203; aided by del Aguila, 204; defeated by Mountjoy, *ib.*
— John killed at Barcelona, 260

Uceda, Duke of, son of Lerma, plots against his father, 220; falls and dies, 225
Ulm, 329
United Provinces, join Richelieu against Spain, 232; harry Spanish commerce, 233; subsidised by Richelieu, 239; prosperity of, 240; Spain recognises the independence of, 275; trade of the Indies opened to, *ib.*; intervene between Louis XIV and Spain, 287; attacked by Louis, 291; allied with England, 293; make peace, *ib.*; united with England under William III, 308; formally recognise Philip V, 322; form a league with William, 325; acquire the 'frontier towns,' 344; join the alliance against Alberoni, 355; treat for peace, 357
Urbino, Duke of, 58, 62, 65
Urgel, 309, 355
Urraca, 313
Ursinos, Princess of, adviser of Marie Louise, 322, 323; outwits Louis XIV, 327; forced to retire, 330; recalled, 331; revolt against, 339; rules Philip after his wife's death, 347; arranges his second marriage, 348; banished by Elizabeth, 349
Ustariz, Jerome, encourages industry, 380
Utrecht, peace of, 344

Valdés, Alfonso and Juan, defend Charles I, 61
— Don Pedro de, 182
Valencia, resists the Inquisition, 18; does not recognise Charles I, 34; rising in, 42, 44; Moorish rebellion in, 77, 78; manufactures of, 84; Moors expelled from, 210-213; the Cortes crushed by Philip IV, 235; proclaims Charles VI (III), 331
Valenciennes, 144
Valenzuela, Don Juan, his rise, 295, 296; arrest and death of, 298
Valladolid, 23, 77, 83, 200
Valparaiso, Count de, 387
Valtellina, the, disputed by France and Spain, 229, 231; overrun by the French, 232, 233; recovered by Feria, 233; settlement of, *ib.*
Vargas, Alonso de, 192
— Juan de, Philip's ambassador at the Council of Trent, 142
Vasconcellos, Secretary, 252-254
Vasquez, Mateo, 169, 190, 191
Vauban, Marshal, 291, 306
Vaucelles, treaty of, 119-121
Veedores, 24
Vega, Lope de, 247
Velasco, Constable of Castile, 206
— Don Francisco de, 311; surrenders Barcelona, 332
Velez, Marquis de los, slaughters the Moorish rebels, 154
— Marquis de los, sent to crush the Catalans, 259; makes terms with d'Epernon, 260; viceroy of Sicily, 273
Venables, Robert, 277
Vendôme, House of, jealous of the Guises, 132
— Marshal, takes Barcelona, 311; in Italy, 324, 333; in the Netherlands, 337; defeated at Oudenarde, 338; wins Brihuega and Villa-Viciosa, 343; dies, 348
Venezuela, colonisation of, 88
Venice, 9, 50, 56, 58, 61, 62, 64, 73, 121, 161, 217, 218, 237, 335
— League of, 6, 9
— treaty of, 364
Vera Cruz, trade with, 85, 374
Verdun, taken by Henry II, 92
Vernon, Admiral, sacks Porto Bello, 374; attacks Cartagena and Santiago de Cuba, 376

Viana, battle of, 168
Vicariate of Italy, the, conferred by Charles I on Philip, 97, 108
Victor Amadeus, Duke of Savoy, King of Sicily and Sardinia, *see* Savoy
Vienna, treaties of, 1725, 364, 365; 1731, 368; 1736, 373
Vigevano, ceded to Sardinia, 379
Vigo, 326, 355
Villadarias, Marquis de, 330, 342
Villa-hermosa, Duke of, 292
Villalar, battle of, 41, 42, 76, 78, 80
Villamediana, Count de, 205
Villa Mediana, Count de, 249
Villarias, Marquis of, 383, 385
Villars, Marshal, 328, 337, 339, 341, 344
Villars, De, ambassador at Madrid, 300, 305
— Madame de, 297, 300, 301
Villa-Viciosa, battle of, 343
Villeroy, Marshal, 324, 333

Wager, Sir Charles, 368
Waldeck, Prince of, 308
Wall, Richard, Spanish ambassador in London, 386; recalled and restored, 387; minister of State, *ib.*, 393; exposes Ensenada, 388; his peace policy, 389; retires, 395
Wallenstein, Duke of, defeats Mansfeld, 235; defeated at Lützen, 238; murdered, *ib.*
Walpole, Sir Robert, opposes war with Spain, 374, 376

Weimar, Duke of, 241
Welser, House of, 88
Wentworth, General, 375
— Lord, loses Calais, 122
William III of England, defends Holland, 291, 292; makes peace with Louis, 293; marries Mary of York, *ib.*; becomes King of England, 308; his policy, *ib.*; defeats James II, *ib.*; defeated at Neerwinden, 311; takes Namur, *ib.*; recognised by Louis at Ryswick, *ib.*; makes the Partition Treaties, 314, 316; resents Louis' recognition of the Pretender, 322; forms a league with Holland, Denmark, and the Empire, 325; dies, *ib.*
Wimbledon, Lord, 232
Winwood, Sir Ralph, 215, 229
Wolsey, Cardinal, 52, 55, 75
Worms, Diet of, 49
— treaty of, 379
Wotton, Dr, 123
Würtemberg, Duke of, 65

Ximenes, Cardinal, *see* Jiménez

Yorktown, 407
Yuste, Charles I retires to, 118

Zamora, 20, 35, 81
Zaragoza, 18, 336, 337, 342
Zeeland, 145, 159, 160
Zumel, Dr, 33, 40

CAMBRIDGE HISTORICAL SERIES

Edited by G. W. PROTHERO, Litt.D., LL.D, Honorary Fellow of King's College, Cambridge, Editor of the "Quarterly Review," and formerly Professor of History in the University of Edinburgh.

The Volumes already published are indicated by an asterisk, those not so marked are in hand, for which the orders are registered, and others will be added from time to time.

*1. **The French Monarchy, 1483—1789.** By A. J. GRANT, M.A., Professor of History in the Yorkshire College, Leeds. With 4 Maps. In 2 vols.

2. **Germany and the Empire, 1493—1792.** By A. F. POLLARD, M.A., late sub-editor of the "Dictionary of National Biography," and author of "England under Protector Somerset."

3. **Italy in disunion, 1494—1792.** By Mrs H. M. VERNON (K. Dorothea Ewart), late scholar of Somerville College, and author of "Cosimo de' Medici."

*4. **Spain; its greatness and decay, 1479—1788.** By MARTIN A. S. HUME, author of "Philip II," "The Courtships of Elizabeth," &c. With an Introduction by EDWARD ARMSTRONG, M.A., Fellow of Queen's College. Oxford, author of "Elizabeth Farnese," "Lorenzo de' Medici," &c. With 2 Maps. Second Edition, revised and corrected.

5. **Eastern Europe, 1453—1792.**

*6. **The Revolutionary and Napoleonic Era, 1789—1815.** By J. HOLLAND ROSE, Litt.D., author of "Life of Napoleon I." With 6 Maps and Plans. Fourth Impression. Rs. 2-14.

7. **Modern France, 1815—1900.** By W. A. J. ARCHBOLD, M.A., author of "The Somerset Religious Houses"; and late sub-editor of the "Dictionary of National Biography."

8. **Modern Germany, 1815—1889.** By J. W. HEADLAM, M.A., author of "Bismarck and the Foundation of the German Empire," &c. In 2 vols.

*9. **The Union of Italy, 1815—1895.** By W. J. STILLMAN, L.H.D., formerly "Times" correspondent in Rome, and author of "The Life of Crispi," &c. With 4 Maps. Second Edition.

10. **Modern Spain, 1815—1898.** By H. BUTLER CLARKE, M.A., author of "The Cid Campeador," "Spanish Literature," &c.

Cambridge Historical Series.

*11. The Expansion of Russia, 1815—1900. By F. H. SKRINE, F.S.S., formerly I.C.S., author of "The Life of Sir W. W. Hunter," "An Indian Journalist," and (with Prof. E. D. Ross) of "The Heart of Asia," &c. With 3 Maps.

12. The Levant, 1815—1900. By D. G. HOGARTH, M.A., author of "The Nearer East," "A Wandering Scholar in the Levant," "Philip and Alexander of Macedon"; editor of "Authority and Archaeology" (Essays), &c.

13. The Netherlands since 1477. By Rev. G. EDMUNDSON, M.A., author of "Milton and Vondel," &c.

14. Switzerland since 1499. By Rev. W. A. B. COOLIDGE, M.A., author of "Swiss Travel and Swiss Guidebooks"; editor of Rev. Aubrey Moore's "Lectures and Papers on the History of the Reformation," J. D. Forbes' "Travels through the Alps," &c.

15. Denmark and Scandinavia since 1513. By R. NISBET BAIN, author of "Gustavus III and his Contemporaries," "Charles XII and the Collapse of the Swedish Empire," "The Daughter of Peter the Great," "The Pupils of Peter the Great," &c.

16. History of Scotland. By P. HUME BROWN, M.A., LL.D., Fraser Professor of Ancient (Scottish) History and Palaeography in the University of Edinburgh, author of "John Knox," "George Buchanan," &c. In 3 vols.

*Vol. I. To the Accession of Mary Stewart. With 7 Maps. Second Impression.

*Vol. II. From the Accession of Mary Stewart to the Revolution of 1689. With 4 Maps and Plan.

Vol. III. From the Revolution of 1689 to the Disruption of 1843.

*17. Ireland, 1494—1868. With Two Introductory Chapters. By WILLIAM O'CONNOR MORRIS, late County Court Judge of the United Counties of Roscommon and Sligo, author of "Ireland, 1798—1898," "The Campaign of 1815," &c. With Map. Second Edition.

*18. The United States of America, 1765—1865. By EDWARD CHANNING, Ph.D., Assistant Professor of History in Harvard University, and author of "Student's History of the United States," &c. With 3 Maps.

*19. Canada under British Rule, 1760—1900. By Sir J. G. BOURINOT, K.C.M.G., Litt.D., LL.D., author of "Parliamentary Procedure and Practice in the Dominion of Canada," "Manual of the Constitutional History of Canada," &c. With 8 Maps.

20. European Colonies in South America. By E. J. PAYNE, M.A., author of "History of European Colonies," "History of the New World called America," &c.

21. British India, 1603—1858. By G. W. FORREST, M.A., author of "The Administration of Warren Hastings," "Selections from Indian State Papers," &c.

*22. Europe and the Far East. By Sir R. K. DOUGLAS, Professor of Chinese in King's College, London, and Keeper of Oriental Printed Books and MSS. in the British Museum. Author of "Language and Literature of China," "A Chinese Manual," &c.

*23. A History of the Colonization of Africa by Alien Races. By Sir HARRY H. JOHNSTON, K.C.B., late Commissioner in Uganda, author of "British Central Africa," "The River Congo," &c. With 8 Maps. Second Edition.

Cambridge Historical Series.

*24. The History of the Australasian Colonies,
from their foundation to the year 1893. By EDWARD JENKS, M.A., Reader in English Law in the University of Oxford, author of "Law and Politics in the Middle Ages," "The Government of Victoria, Australia," &c. With 2 Maps. Second Edition.

*25. Outlines of English Industrial History. By
W. CUNNINGHAM, D.D., Fellow of Trinity College, Cambridge, and Vicar of Great St Mary's, author of "Growth of English Industry and Commerce," &c., and ELLEN A. MCARTHUR, Lecturer at Girton College. Crown 8vo. Second Edition.

*26. An Essay on Western Civilization in its Economic Aspects. By W. CUNNINGHAM, D.D. Crown 8vo. Vol. I. Ancient Times. With 5 Maps. Vol. II. Mediaeval and Modern Times. With 3 Maps.

Extracts from the Reviews.

Prof. Hume Brown's "History of Scotland."

The Athenaeum.—"The promise of Prof. Hume Brown's first volume is more than fulfilled in the second. The author's thorough knowledge of the sources, his gift of lucid condensation, and fine sense of proportion have made this comparatively short work the most complete and satisfactory history of Scotland which we possess. His pages are not overcrowded with details, and the reader's interest is secured from beginning to end by the admirable way in which he is led to find, in the conflict of political and social forces, the gradual evolution of the national destiny."

The Times.—"Mr Hume Brown's learning and accuracy are as great as ever and his conclusions are clear and definite. Every page of the book shows that Mr Brown is a careful and patient investigator. He is always scientific alike in manner and in method, and he can condense the results of weeks of patient work into fine, clear and lucid lines. He can resist all temptations to wander from the path which he has marked out for himself; his book is invariably consistent in treatment, and its divisions show a due sense of proportion. He has produced a work which will render immeasurably easier the attempt to understand the difficult and involved story of seventeenth century Scotland."

Manchester Guardian.—"Bids fair to be by far and away the best extant compendium of Scottish history. Here we have a calm and judicious verdict on all, based on a thorough examination of a vast mass of evidence. A thoroughly good piece of work, which we can heartily recommend as singularly trustworthy, and eminently readable."

Prof. Grant's " French Monarchy."

The Spectator.—"This is a clear, thoughtful, readable, and most useful history of the Monarchy in France, from the consolidation of its power under Louis XI to the many causes of its downfall with Louis XVI."

The Pilot.—"The series to which these volumes are contributed belongs to the utilitarian school of history. It is not designed for the entertainment of those who merely desire, with the story-teller's audience, to know 'what happened,' but is intended rather to assist those more serious persons 'who are anxious to understand the nature of existing political conditions.' Such readers will find much to interest them in these clear, impartial pages."

[*Turn over*

Cambridge Historical Series.

Major Hume's "Spain."

The Speaker.—"Major Hume's volume is in all respects worthy of the great reputation which he has won as an expert in the domain of Spanish history....Major Hume's knowledge is as complete as possible, and to a perfect mastery of his material he adds an impartiality and luminous insight which are exceedingly rare....His wide and deep acquaintance with the immense literature of his subject, his singular grasp of detail, and his cold lucidity have enabled him to present us with an historical handbook, convincing, brilliant and final in its kind. This is no dry chronicle, but a vivid and picturesque transcript of events."

Dr Stillman's "Union of Italy."

The Times.—"Few men are better qualified by personal knowledge, by political sympathies, or by direct contact with events than Mr W. J. Stillman to write a history of modern Italy....His volume is, especially in its later chapters, a history largely written from sources of knowledge not yet fully accessible to the outside world."

Sir J. G. Bourinot's "Canada."

Daily Chronicle.—"It would scarcely be possible to find a man in the Dominion better suited to play the part of its historian than the author of this volume....As a textbook of Canadian history Sir John Bourinot's work is admirable."

Sir H. H. Johnston's "Africa."

The Times.—"Sir Harry Johnston has devoted both industry and ability to its performance, and deserves the thanks of future students for the result. This history...presents within handy compass an extremely valuable expanded index of African history as a whole....As a textbook of African study his book supplies a want which has been generally felt, and should be in proportion warmly welcomed."

Dr Cunningham's "Western Civilization," &c.

The Athenæum.—"One of the most important portions of the equipment of the student of economics. They are not merely storehouses of trustworthy and wide-ranging fact, of lucid and stimulating generalization, they are a trenchant blow struck in the long strife over the method of economics....The sweep and scope of the work are immense."

The Guardian.—"Dr Cunningham's book is the outcome of unusually wide and various learning. The references in his footnotes are numerous enough to form a bibliography of economic history. Nor is his overwhelming material unskilfully put together. On the contrary, he is clear and connected, and succeeds in holding the reader's attention throughout."

English Historical Review.—"It may be doubted whether any book of equal educational value for its size has appeared for many years past."

London: C. J. CLAY AND SONS,
CAMBRIDGE UNIVERSITY PRESS WAREHOUSE,
Ave Maria Lane.

Glasgow: 50, WELLINGTON STREET.

www.ingramcontent.com/pod-product-compliance
Lightning Source LLC
Chambersburg PA
CBHW051850300426
44117CB00006B/338